Nicaragua: The Sandinista People's Revolution

NICARAGUA: THE SANDINISTA PEOPLE'S REVOLUTION

Speeches by Sandinista Leaders

PATHFINDER
New York   London   Montreal   Sydney

Edited by Bruce Marcus

Copyright © 1985 by Pathfinder Press
All rights reserved

ISBN 978-0-87348-653-8
Library of Congress Catalog Card Number 85-061096
Manufactured in the United States of America

First edition, 1985
Seventh printing, 2019

Cover photo: Michael Baumann

Pathfinder
www.pathfinderpress.com
pathfinder@pathfinderpress.com

Contents

Preface   11

Chronology   17

U.S. working people can stop intervention
in Central America
Sergio Ramírez (March 4, 1982)   25

We demand an end to the policy of aggression
Daniel Ortega (March 25, 1982)   36

Without solidarity it is difficult to talk about revolution
Carlos Fernando Chamorro (March 31, 1982)   44

Defense can be assured only by increasing production
Lucío Jiménez (April 24, 1982)   49

This revolution was made to create a new society
Tomás Borge (May 1, 1982)   54

Without the people, saving Lake Managua
will not be possible
Tomás Borge (June 5, 1982)   79

Women and the Nicaraguan revolution
Tomás Borge (September 29, 1982)   89

Letter to leaders of the Sandinista
Defense Committees
Bayardo Arce (October 7, 1982) 111

Large-scale aggression is being prepared
Tomás Borge (December 12, 1982) 114

The new education in the new Nicaragua
Tomás Borge (February 4, 1983) 122

It is imperialism that is in crisis
Jaime Wheelock (February 5, 1983) 140

Problems of the Atlantic Coast
Ray Hooker (February 23, 1983) 144

Improvement in the situation of workers
is the task of the workers themselves
Víctor Tirado (February 26, 1983) 157

Karl Marx: The international
workers' movement's greatest
fighter and thinker
Víctor Tirado (March 14, 1983) 166

The FSLN and the Nicaraguan revolution
Tomás Borge (May 20, 1983) 174

The great challenge
Jaime Wheelock (May 1983) 202

This is a revolution of working people
Tomás Borge (June 1983) 274

Our promises were made to the poorest
of our country
Sergio Ramírez (July 14, 1983) — 290

We are a very small country confronting
a truly colossal force
Daniel Ortega (July 18, 1983) — 304

The Sandinista people's revolution
is an irreversible political reality
Daniel Ortega (July 19, 1983) — 316

U.S. destabilization in Nicaragua
Sergio Ramírez (August 13, 1983) — 335

Nicaragua has won its right to be free
Daniel Ortega (September 27, 1983) — 352

Nicaragua's proposals for peace in Central America
(December 11, 1983) — 370

We speak to you from a country at war
Tomás Borge (December 1983) — 379

We women learned what we were capable of doing
Magda Enríquez (February 29, 1984) — 395

Justice in Nicaragua is no longer the same
Tomás Borge (April 12, 1984) — 405

The Sandinista Front is the organization
of the working people
Jaime Wheelock (May 1, 1984) — 416

A dirty war is being carried out against Nicaragua
Daniel Ortega (May 4, 1984)   444

The people are going to defeat and annihilate
the mercenary forces
Humberto Ortega (June 5, 1984)   458

The Sandinista Front is the fire of popular justice
Daniel Ortega (July 17, 1984)   472

Plan of struggle
Sandinista National Liberation Front   478

The unity of the FSLN cannot be challenged
Tomás Borge (July 17, 1984)   499

The relevance of Sandino's thought
Sergio Ramírez (July 1984)   505

Economic production is the rear guard
of the battle front
(September 1984)   516

We had difficulty in grasping the ethnic character
of the Miskito problem
Tomás Borge (September 1984)   527

The U.S. is escalating its military and economic
aggression against Nicaragua
Daniel Ortega (October 2, 1984)   533

The producers of this country support
our revolutionary government
Daniel Núñez (October 5, 1984)   544

If the peasantry did not trust the revolution,
we would be through
Daniel Núñez (October 9, 1984) 556

The organized people are the backbone
of the Sandinista Police
Tomás Borge (October 17, 1984) 568

Is it possible for Nicaragua to defeat
the war of Yankee imperialism?
Luis Carrión (November 1984) 577

Today we speak naturally of Atlantic Coast autonomy
William Ramírez (December 8, 1984) 591

Appendix: Political manifesto
Augusto César Sandino (July 1, 1927) 599

Glossary 605

Index 613

Preface

On July 19, 1979, a massive popular insurrection, led by the Sandinista National Liberation Front (FSLN), overthrew the forty-six-year-long U.S.-backed dictatorship of the Somoza family in Nicaragua. A revolutionary government came to power, a government of workers and peasants. It pushed forward the struggle championed earlier in the century by Augusto César Sandino, the "General of Free Men and Women," for Nicaragua's national independence from imperialist domination. It brought democracy to the country and began to carry out policies to advance and defend the interests of the exploited urban and rural producers.

From the very start, the United States government opposed the Nicaraguan revolution. It backed the dictatorship of Anastasio Somoza almost to the bitter end. Even when it became clear that this murderous regime could not be saved, the administration of Democrat James Carter maneuvered in an attempt to deny power to the Sandinista-led workers and peasants in any new government. Up until the last moment, Washington sought to secure a place in post-Somoza Nicaragua for the hated National Guard, which was the main prop of the landlord-capitalist power and prerogatives defended by the dictatorship.

The speeches by Sandinista leaders and documents of the Nicaraguan revolution collected in this volume come from the period of early 1982 through the end of 1984. The opening selections thus coincide with the massive escalation of the bipartisan U.S. war against Nicaragua conducted by

CIA-organized counterrevolutionaries, or *contras* as they are known.

The war and the resulting national mobilization to defend the revolution have become the dominant factors in Nicaraguan politics throughout this period. The death and destruction caused by the *contras*, and the need to allocate growing human and material resources to defense, provide the framework in which the Sandinista-led government has worked to rebuild Nicaraguan society.

Land has been distributed to tens of thousands of agricultural laborers and peasant families, strengthening the alliance between the workers and peasants. The extensive holdings of the Somoza family were confiscated immediately after the July victory, and since then nationalizations of banks, insurance companies, and other selected enterprises have added to a growing state-owned, People's Property Sector. Measures have been implemented to protect the living conditions of working people as much as possible from the effects of the war on an economy still dominated by capitalist production and distribution.

In the first phase of a national literacy campaign launched in 1980, more than 400,000 people learned to read and write. Construction of new hospitals and clinics throughout the country began almost immediately. Since 1982, however, the massive expenditures for defense have set the limit on any major new expansion of social programs in education, health care, and housing.

FSLN-led union organizing drives have raised union membership to over 260,000. Laws have been passed abolishing capital punishment and guaranteeing freedom of speech and association, the right to join unions, freedom of religion, equal rights for women, and the rights of Blacks and Indians to their own languages, traditions, and cultures.

As a result of the policies pursued by the Sandinistas throughout this period and since July 1979, the revolutionary government has broadened its base of support among the workers and peasants, expanded the involvement of working people in the revolution, and deepened their political consciousness and commitment to the revolution.

This, in broad strokes, paints the political background to the documents in this collection. In their own words, the Sandinista leaders answer Washington's lies. They explain that Nicaragua, for the first time, is independent and free, that it now has a government that represents the vast majority of its people, and that it is taking the first steps toward building a new society, without exploiters or exploited.

Many of the accomplishments from the revolution's first five and a half years are explained in the speeches published in this collection. To appreciate the scope of these accomplishments, it is useful to keep in mind the conditions facing the Nicaraguan people in 1979.

The Somoza family had ruled Nicaragua ever since it was installed in power by U.S. Marines in the 1930s—over Sandino's murdered corpse. The Somoza dictatorship protected the investments of U.S. corporations and ensured an uninterrupted flow of profits. The price paid by the Nicaraguan people was landlessness, poverty, widespread disease, tyranny, and exploitation.

Take, for example, social conditions in the early 1970s. Infant mortality was ten times that in the United States; the illiteracy rate ran at more than 50 percent; life expectancy was less than fifty years. Nine-tenths of the population of Managua, the capital and largest city, lacked some combination of running water, electricity, or paved roads. Unemployment ranged up to 50 percent, and the National Guard saw to it that less than 6 percent of the country's workers were unionized.

Conditions were particularly intolerable in rural areas. A handful of wealthy landholding families owned half the land, while the poorest one half of peasant families held less than 4 percent. In the early 1970s, the average income in rural areas was about thirty-five dollars a year.

These oppressive conditions resulted in constant struggles to get rid of the dictatorship. These struggles met with fierce repression by the National Guard. Trained by Washington, the guard murdered, raped, and tortured indiscriminately, earning the undying enmity of the Nicaraguan people. Today these ex-Somoza National Guardsmen are the backbone of the *contra* forces. It is no wonder that the *contras* have been unable to win a base of popular support inside Nicaragua.

After a protracted struggle, through which the FSLN won the leadership of the revolutionary workers and peasants, the tyranny was finally overthrown in 1979. The revolutionary government immediately set about trying to overcome the legacy of decades of Somoza rule. Much to Washington's dismay, the government's priority was meeting the needs of Nicaragua's workers and peasants. Education, land reform, health care, unionization, women's rights—these became the government's central tasks.

While these steps are popular with the vast majority, not everyone has been pleased. Many ex-National Guardsmen and former cronies of the old regime, guilty of crimes on an immense scale, fled to Miami or to other Central American countries right after the 1979 victory. Some wealthy landholders and businessmen, who had opposed the Somoza dictatorship and initially supported the new government, turned against it as they became convinced that the Sandinistas were firmly committed to preserving the political power of the exploited workers and peasants.

Moreover, both the U.S. government and its client dictatorships in Central and South America opposed the revolution, fearful of the mighty force of its example.

And so, beginning just before the first speeches in this book were given, Washington launched an invasion of Nicaragua. Acting through the CIA-organized *contra* armies, the

U.S. war against Nicaragua has steadily escalated. It is a war *now in progress*.

Recorded in the speeches and documents published here are the Sandinistas' answers to the propaganda campaign orchestrated by Washington, as well as their recounting of the struggle to defend the revolution. A brief chronology that emphasizes the time period of this book and a glossary of selected individuals and organizations have been supplied by the editor.

Getting out the story of this revolution and its accomplishments is one of the most important tasks of its supporters as they work to mount the broadest possible opposition to Washington's war. Learning the truth and telling it to others—that is the first step to help defend the people of Nicaragua and support their right to national sovereignty. Visiting Nicaragua or joining an internationalist brigade to help with construction or harvesting, as growing numbers of people have been doing, is one good way to arm yourself with the facts. We hope that this volume will provide another political tool in this effort.

※

This is the third collection of Nicaraguan revolutionary materials published by Pathfinder Press. *The Nicaraguan Revolution* was published shortly after the July 1979 triumph. It was replaced in 1981 by *Sandinistas Speak,* which is still available from Pathfinder Press. That volume contains important documents, such as the 1969 "Historic Program of the FSLN" and Carlos Fonseca's "Nicaragua: Zero Hour." The present Pathfinder collection takes up where *Sandinistas Speak* left off, and brings us up to date. The speeches and documents published here have been edited for stylistic consistency and length.

Several sources are available for those interested in regularly following developments in Nicaragua. *Barricada Inter-*

national, published weekly in English and Spanish by the FSLN, can be obtained by writing to Apartado 576, Managua, Nicaragua.

In addition, the U.S. publications the *Militant* and *Intercontinental Press* were the source of most of the English-language translations of the items in this collection. These publications, together with the biweekly *Perspectiva Mundial,* maintain a permanent reporting bureau in Managua. Subscription information for them can be obtained by writing them at 410 West Street, New York, NY 10014. The assistance of the Managua bureau of these publications in assembling this collection is gratefully acknowledged.

Bruce Marcus
MARCH 1985

Selected chronology of events

1979

June 17 – Junta of Government of National Reconstruction established in exile; composed of Daniel Ortega, Sergio Ramírez, Moisés Hassan, Alfonso Robelo, and Violeta Barrios de Chamorro; plans for a Council of State to serve as a provisional legislature and to draft a constitution are announced

July 19 – FSLN-led mass insurrection overthrows Somoza dictatorship; revolutionary junta becomes government; National Guard disbanded

July 30 – Agrarian reform and expropriation of *somocistas'* land announced

September – The nine members of the FSLN National Directorate (Daniel Ortega, Humberto Ortega, Víctor Tirado, Luis Carrión, Carlos Núñez, Jaime Wheelock, Bayardo Arce, Tomás Borge, Henry Ruiz) are named "Commanders of the Revolution"

October 22 – Government postpones convening of Council of State and announces council will be restructured to broaden representation of workers and peasants

November 7 – 100,000 rally in Managua to commemorate death of FSLN founding leader Carlos Fonseca; Borge announces nationalization of foreign-owned mines

December 19 – Government announces 50 percent cut in most rents

December 20 – First national congress of Association of Rural Workers (ATC)

1980

February 16 – First national congress of Sandinista Workers Federation (CST)
March 2 – Decree Number 329 bans decapitalization of enterprises
March 16 – Government junta member and businessman Alfonso Robelo relaunches bourgeois Nicaraguan Democratic Movement after visit to Washington
March 30 – National Crusade for Literacy and Adult Education launched
April 21 – Government announces that worker and peasant representatives will hold majority in Council of State
April 22 – Alfonso Robelo resigns from junta, announcing that Violeta Barrios de Chamorro's resignation from junta shortly before was also act of political opposition
May 1 – 300,000 rally in Managua to celebrate May Day
May 4 – Council of State convenes
May 18 – Arturo Cruz and Rafael Córdova Rivas added to government junta
June 11 – Council of State enacts law raising wages for 300,000 lowest-paid workers
July 19 – 500,000 celebrate first anniversary of revolution at Managua rally; Daniel Ortega announces plans to confiscate idle lands
August 23 – 350,000 rally to celebrate completion of first stage of literacy drive
November 12 – Representatives of Supreme Council of Private Enterprise and bourgeois parties stage walk-out from Council of State
December 20 – Banana production, largely in hands of foreign-owned corporations, is nationalized

1981

March 4 – Junta reorganized; Cruz becomes ambassador to U.S.

July 17 – First land titles distributed to peasants under land reform

July 19 – 500,000 celebrate second anniversary at Managua rally; revolutionary government announces second stage of agrarian reform, confiscating large under-utilized landholdings

December – CIA-backed *contras* invade Northern Zelaya in "Red Christmas" operation

December 11 – Revolutionary government distributes 22,000 acres to peasants under land reform

December 12 – Bomb explodes in Aeronica plane in Mexico City

December 27 – U.S. press reports on public opening of Florida training camp for *somocista* counterrevolutionaries

1982

January 8 – 15 *contra* commandos captured trying to blow up Nicaraguan oil refinery and chemical plant

February – Government relocates Miskitos living along Coco River, by now a major combat area, to new settlement of Tasba Pri; action is criticized by Nicaraguan council of bishops

February 20 – *Contra* bomb at Sandino Airport kills 3 on eve of visit by Mexican President José López Portillo

March 10 – *Washington Post* reveals $19 million in U.S. aid to *contras*

March 15 – CIA-backed *contras* blow up two major bridges in north; revolutionary government declares state of emergency

March 25 – Daniel Ortega addresses special session of United Nations Security Council

April 6 – U.S. naval maneuvers begin in region, involving 39 ships and 200 planes

April 15 – Well-known Sandinista figure Edén Pastora breaks with revolution at news conference in Costa Rica, announcing plans for armed struggle against revolutionary government

May 1 – May Day rallies sponsored by Sandinista union federation with theme "Defend the revolution, for the construction of socialism" draw 170,000

May – Torrential rains cause flooding that destroys 60 per cent of harvest of basic food grains, damages roads and bridges; losses total $250 million

– 170,000 acres of idle or abandoned land confiscated under land reform; new announcements of distributions to peasants under agrarian reform made weekly in May and June

September 30 – Revolutionary government cancels $8 million bank debts owed by small, medium, and large farmers

October 19 – Over U.S. opposition, Nicaragua wins seat on UN Security Council; thousands celebrate in Managua

October 26 – U.S. Standard Fruit cancels five-year contract to market Nicaraguan bananas; Nicaragua finds replacement marketer

November – 800 counterrevolutionary troops from Nicaraguan Democratic Force (FDN) suffer sharp defeat in attempt to seize territory after invading from bases in Honduras

November 4 – Northern border area with Honduras declared "zone of military emergency"

November 8 – *Newsweek* magazine cover story "America's Secret War—Target Nicaragua" reveals scope of war

1983

February – 2,000 CIA-backed *contras* invade across Honduran border; 1,600 U.S. and 5,000 Honduran troops begin "Big Pine" military maneuvers

March 4 – Pope John Paul II visits Nicaragua, refuses to condemn *contra* terror

March – End of month—2,000 *contras* infiltrate from Honduras

April – Revolutionary Democratic Alliance (ARDE) *contras* led by Pastora and Robelo begin attacks along southern border from bases in Costa Rica

April 27 – Reagan speech to Congress threatens open, large-scale military action against Nicaragua

April 28 – Armed demonstration of 150,000 in Managua answers Reagan threat

April 30 – 1,200 CIA-backed *contras* invade Nueva Segovia province

May 9 – U.S. announces 90 percent cut in Nicaraguan sugar quota

June 6 – Nicaragua expels 3 CIA agents operating out of U.S. embassy for plotting murder of Sandinista leaders and for organizing economic sabotage; Washington responds by closing 6 Nicaraguan consulates in U.S.

June 29 – U.S. vetoes $2.2 million road-building loan from Inter-American Development Bank

July 19 – 150,000 in León celebrate fourth anniversary of revolution under slogan "All arms to the people! Everyone to defense!"

July 22 – U.S. press reports Reagan approves plan for possible limited military blockade of Nicaragua

July 26 – 20,000 rally in Managua to greet first three battalions of Territorial Militia

August 29 – Nicaraguan Catholic bishops announce opposition to Patriotic Military Service (military conscription)

September 8 – Aerial bombardment of Sandino Airport; Pastora group later takes responsibility

September 9 – Aerial bombardment of port city of Corinto

October 2 – *New York Times* admits CIA using Salvadoran air force to drop military supplies to *contras*

October 10 – CIA sea-borne commandos set fire to Corinto oil storage tanks, 1.6 million gallons destroyed

October 21 – U.S. formally rejects new Nicaraguan peace proposals

October 25 – U.S. invades island of Grenada, begins military occupation

November 1 – Tens of thousands demonstrate in Managua in support of Patriotic Military Service

November 17 – U.S. Congress votes additional $24 million for *contras*

December 4 – Council of State adopts decree on amnesty, permitting virtually all rank-and-file *contra* troops to return upon agreement to lay down arms against revolution

December – End of month—2–3,000 *contras* infiltrate from Honduras

1984

February – U.S. conducts "Big Pine II" military maneuvers

February 24 – U.S. mines port of El Bluff

March – U.S. mines port of Corinto

March 15 – Council of State adopts election law, sets elections for November 4

March 28 – CIA-backed *contras* attack Corinto

April – U.S. refuses to accept credentials of Nicaraguan ambassador-designate Nora Astorga

April 1 – U.S. begins "Granadero I" military maneuvers in Honduras

April 17 – Sandinista People's Army drives *contras* from area of San Juan del Norte after 11-day battle with Pastora forces

April 20 – U.S. "Ocean Venture '84" naval maneuvers begin, involving 30,000 troops and 350 ships

April 22 – Nicaraguan bishops' Easter message criticizes revolutionary government and calls for opening talks with *contra* terrorists

April 24 – International Trade Union Conference for Peace in Managua draws 300 delegates from 50 countries

May 5 – Daniel Ortega announces emergency wartime economic measures

May 10 – World Court unanimously orders U.S. to stop mining Nicaraguan ports

May 30 – Bomb explodes at Pastora press conference on Honduran border following his dispute with CIA over joining up with FDN forces

June – Nicaraguan "Operation Sovereignty" destroys major ARDE concentration near Costa Rican border and FDN base in north

June 1 – Attack on northern town of Ocotal repelled, with *contras* suffering heavy losses in battles with militia and army; lumber mill, grain stores, and radio station severely damaged

– Council of State adopts law formalizing emergency wartime economic measures; authorizes government control of distribution of basic products

June 20 – Catholic priest Luis Amado Peña caught red-handed, involved in terrorism

July – 12,000 more peasant families receive land titles totaling 720,000 acres under agrarian reform

July 14 – AMNLAE demonstration celebrates first contingent of women participating in Patriotic Military Service

July 17 – Newspapers in U.S. reveal right-wing sources funneled at least $17 million to contras

July 19 – More than 200,000 rally to celebrate fifth anniversary of revolution

July 22 – MISATAN (Organization of the Miskitos of Nicaragua) founded as prorevolution group

September – *Contra* groups FDN, based in Honduras, and ARDE, based in Costa Rica, announce plans to fuse

September 1 – Two U.S.-citizen CIA mercenaries killed when their helicopter is shot down during air raid on Santa Clara

September 5 – Ray Hooker and two others kidnapped by *contras* while campaigning for FSLN slate; are held in *contra* camp of Brooklyn Rivera

September 21 – Nicaraguan government announces intention to sign Contadora peace accord; U.S. refuses to sign

October 21 – Miskito leader Brooklyn Rivera returns to Nicaragua under amnesty decree for talks with government

October 30 – Ray Hooker and others kidnapped in September freed by captors

October 31 – U.S. SR-71 spy planes overfly Managua, causing repeated sonic booms

November 4 – FSLN candidates win 67 percent of vote for National Assembly; Daniel Ortega and Sergio Ramírez elected president and vice-president

November 5 – FSLN leader Enrique Schmidt killed in battle with *contras*

November 6 – U.S. falsely charges that Soviet freighter is bringing MiGs to Nicaragua; threatens open military action

November 10 – 20,000 high school and college students who had volunteered to pick coffee choose instead to begin militia training in Managua

November 12 – National military state of alert declared

December 5 – National commission established to draft statute on Atlantic Coast autonomy; members include Luis Carrión, Ray Hooker, and Hazel Lau

U.S. working people can stop intervention in Central America
by Sergio Ramírez*

The following speech was given to a March 4, 1982, meeting of the Standing Committee of Intellectuals for the Sovereignty of the Peoples of Our America held in Managua. The committee was founded at a September 1981 congress in Havana. The Managua meeting was attended by intellectuals from throughout Latin America, including figures such as Colombian writer Gabriel García Márquez and Cuban Minister of Culture Armando Hart. The closing declaration of the Managua meeting called on U.S. intellectuals to "remember for a moment the tremendous lesson of Vietnam" and to "make yourselves heard by your own people in time to prevent a repetition of that suicidal madness in Central America." This translation was originally published in the March 28, 1982, issue of the English-language Cuban periodical, *Granma Weekly Review*.

On behalf of the Government of National Reconstruction I would like to greet you all, both the members of the Stand-

---

* See Glossary for information on individuals and organizations.

ing Committee of Intellectuals for the Sovereignty of the Peoples of Our America and the other writers and artists who have been invited by our revolution to participate in this meeting. To all, a warm welcome to our liberated land.

The committee of which you are members is a committee of intellectuals formed for the purpose of defending and promoting the sovereignty of our peoples; and today I want to say to you that we have before us an urgent case, very close to home. The sovereignty of Central America, the sovereignty of the Caribbean, the sovereignty of Nicaragua are threatened as never before by the arrogance and the imperialist pretensions of those who are trying to revive the past history of aggression. Both in the shadows and in the glare of the public eye, a web of aggressive actions and threats against Nicaragua is being woven, and we are sure that many underground and official mechanisms have been put in motion to prepare the way for this aggression.

Once again, we have heard how the U.S. government justifies its assumption of imperial rights over our country, speaking of its "fourth frontier" under the pretext that its national security interests and the safety of its maritime trade routes come before the sovereignty of our country. Like an echo from the past we are hearing again of the "American continent" in terms that see the whole hemisphere as [James] Monroe saw it in the nineteenth century—as a Yankee hunting reserve. We are hearing the same old voices proclaiming "manifest destiny," we are hearing [William] Howard Taft again trumpeting "gunboat diplomacy" and Theodore Roosevelt announcing sending his imperial forces out over the Caribbean. And we are also hearing [former CIA Director] Allen Dulles again plotting diabolical machinations against Central America as he did in Guatemala in 1954, and we are hearing how they are hastily preparing to land on our soil, as happened in 1912 and 1926, and in the Dominican Republic in 1965.

Here we have a very long experience of Yankee intervention. We learned to defend our sovereignty not through theoretical rumination, but on the most heroic battlefield of practice. Our nation, our nationality, our sovereignty, our territorial integrity, our autonomy as a nation, as General Sandino called it—we have constantly defended them, we have consolidated them with arms and with the decision to use those arms whenever necessary.

In recent months we have watched the growth of maneuvers and threats against our country and our revolution. What is being used against Nicaragua is not merely imperialist rhetoric; they are using terrorism, military plans, intimidation of neighboring countries, and the most aggressive weapons of diplomacy, such as blackmail and covert operations. Just from the immediate past we can make the following list of acts that are evidence of this forbidding picture:

The establishment of the so-called democratic community formed by Honduras, El Salvador, and Costa Rica is a U.S. ploy to legitimate the use of an intervention force linked to the implementation of the Inter-American Treaty of Mutual Assistance in Central America. This "community" has subsequently been joined by the United States and Colombia, the latter having authorized the setting up of U.S. military bases, and still more recently by Guatemala. The intention is obviously to surround Nicaragua by a political—and doubtless military—cordon.

U.S. military bases are being set up, such as those presently being established on the island of Amapala, in the Gulf of Fonseca and on the Caribbean island of San Andrés, on Nicaragua's continental shelf. What is envisaged here are naval and air bases whose presence is intended to ensnare Nicaragua between her two oceans.

U.S. warships carrying highly sophisticated communications equipment are present in the Gulf of Fonseca with the admitted authorization of the president of the Salvadoran junta. [José] Napoleón Duarte.

Money, training, and arms are being supplied to groups of former National Guardsmen operating from inside Honduras as part of a covert operation handled by the Central Intelligence Agency (CIA). The existence of this operation was admitted by the assistant secretary of state for Latin American affairs, Mr. Thomas Enders, to the Joint Intelligence Committee of the U.S. Congress, in a secret session held in December 1981.

President Reagan's roving ambassador, retired general Vernon Walters, has undertaken the job of carrying out preparations in the area, and Néstor Sánchez, a long-time CIA agent and assistant to the secretary of defense for Latin American affairs, has been placed in charge of the operation.

The National Security Council of the United States has approved a budget of $19 million to finance a campaign of military, political, and economic destabilization against Nicaragua. It has also approved an eight-point action plan for this destabilization which includes using military officers from countries of the Southern Cone, principally Argentina, training *somocista* groups, and infiltrating them into Nicaraguan territory as mercenaries.

One of the ringleaders in a plot to blow up our national cement factory confessed that they had received $50,000 from members of the Argentine high command and that an Argentine special commando was to have been located in Tegucigalpa to direct sabotage operations against Nicaragua.

Encouraged by all this fabric of terrorist activity, the *somocista* groups of former National Guardsmen, in league with one Steadman Fagoth, one of Somoza's former security agents, began to organize, for the months of December 1981 and January 1982, an operation code-named Red Christmas. Their intention was to ravage the indigenous communities along the Coco River and thus establish a beachhead in Nicaraguan territory. Before the revolutionary government took total control of the zone, Operation Red Christmas had already been responsible for the deaths of about sixty Nicaraguan border guards, members of the armed forces and state security, and civilians. Red Christmas forced considerable numbers of indigenous people to leave their communities for Honduras. *Somocistas* tortured and raped inhabitants of the communities and medical personnel.

The revolutionary government considered it necessary to move the inhabitants of the riverside communities to safer places within Nicaragua, where our Miskito brothers and sisters would for the first time have access to regular health care, education, decent housing, electricity, and land to grow their crops. Their relocation has sparked off one of the most vicious campaigns of calumny the CIA and the State Department have ever mounted against our revolution.

The state security bodies of the Ministry of the Interior uncovered a conspiracy in Costa Rica, Honduras, and the United States whose object was to blow up our national cement factory and our oil refinery, and for which purpose large quantities of explosives were brought into the country.

A passenger plane belonging to the national airline Aeronica was blown up in Mexico City airport. The real intention was to destroy the aircraft in midair and kill its 100 passengers.

A suitcase containing explosives blew up in the Sandino Airport terminal in Managua, killing three baggage porters. It had been put on board a plane in Tegucigalpa. The aim of this terrorist action was to prevent the visit of the president of Mexico, José López Portillo. It was only by chance that the explosion did not kill many more people among the passengers waiting to collect their baggage.

It is obvious that the whole arsenal of terrorism, aggression, and flagrant international propagandizing is being used against us. Bands of *somocistas* drawn from the National Guard that murdered and massacred so many of our people are being used, are being armed and trained not only in the United States itself but in Honduras and Guatemala as well. Steadman Fagoth was used blatantly to appear in Washington before Congress and before human rights organizations, so that State Department spokesmen could immediately repeat the lies he told. Freedom House and the Religion and Freedom Institute, which are CIA agencies, are being used, as are *Figaro* magazine and the September 15 radio station which broadcasts from Honduras; and all these lies and falsehoods are being fed to newspapers and radio stations in Central America and throughout the continent.

To this mounting aggression, to the imminent danger of a rapid escalation of the aggression, our revolution has responded with maturity and calmness. We are a firm and determined people; we will not retreat before any threat; but we have indicated, and will continue to indicate, that we desire and seek a global understanding in favor of peace in Central America, an understanding that will make our region safe and stable. We stated this position at the last meeting of the Permanent Conference of Latin American Political Parties held recently in Managua and I want to reiterate it now, so that you can convey it and disseminate it and so that the world will understand that we are a worthy, free country with a clearly defined international policy:

1. Our nation reiterates its policy of nonalignment. This is a fundamental policy of ours and one that represents our genuine line of practice at the international level. We wish to maintain relations with all countries of the world without exception; this is a right our people have won through struggle.

2. We are ready to sign nonaggression and reciprocal security agreements with our neighboring countries based on the principle of nonintervention and mutual respect.

3. The Reagan administration has repeatedly accused Nicaragua of supplying and transporting arms to El Sal-

vador. We have challenged U.S. representatives to prove these assertions and they have never been able to do so. Today we call once more for a delimitation of military borders and the establishment of joint systems of patrolling our border with Honduras—for we do not border on El Salvador—and also joint border patrols with Costa Rica. This would give a measure of territorial security and would help to counter the activities of disaffected elements from any of our three countries.

4. Once again we repeat our willingness to maintain steady, friendly relations with the government of the United States. We are ready to begin talks at any time, on any topic concerning us both, toward reaching a negotiated solution of any conflict and developing economic cooperation in the region.

No project for economic development in the region, no overall economic plan embracing Central America, can be implemented without the participation of Nicaragua. It is absurd to try to envisage Central America without Nicaragua. Nicaragua cannot be excluded from any regional economic strategy.

5. Our only requirement is absolute, unconditional respect for our sovereignty, no intervention in our internal affairs, no support or cover-up for counterrevolutionary activities, and no aggression or blockade.

We vehemently deny that the problems of Central America are the result of an East-West confrontation. Such a notion ignores the long history of poverty and injustice, of exploitation and plunder, that has led our peoples to rebel. Such poverty and injustice have been caused by ruthless exploitation by national oligarchies and plunder by the imperialists; but they are also due to the appalling inequality in the terms of trade, which is also a form of exploitation. Low prices and restricted markets, the price we have to pay for exporting our products, the burden of foreign debt, are all factors which it is up to the powerful countries to change, not to perpetuate.

We vehemently deny that our revolutions and the establishment of truly democratic regimes pose a threat to United States territorial security. But we also refuse to accept that our territories be used to guarantee the United States that security.

The false propaganda circulated against our revolution never mentions the efforts we have been making for nearly three years to consolidate a political system that has room for pluralism and a mixed economy. We are always accused of what we might try to do in the future, of totalitarianism in the future, of the abolition of political parties in the future, of the suppression of the freedom of the press in the future, of the total expropriation of private property in the future. The Sandinista process is a process which has the assent of the vast majority of our people and is validated by our dead, our heroes, our martyrs. It is a true revolution, it is a revolution deeply rooted in the people, a revolution that reaffirms its political pluralism and has demonstrated it. Our intention to hold national elections no later than 1985 is a decision of the Sandinista National Liberation Front and in no sense a concession.

Aggression against any one of the peoples of the Caribbean or Central America, an intervention in El Salvador, an attack on Nicaragua, could change the history of Latin America. Not long ago President José López Portillo said here in Managua that such a step on the part of the United States would be a huge historical error. The peoples of Latin America, in their search for a true democracy and a true system of social justice, have viewed the Nicaraguan revolution as a beacon of hope, and we are sure they will be ready to defend that hope with fervent solidarity, mobilizing to prevent any aggression against our nation.

I want to speak also about the people of the United States.

A few days ago I read in a cable statements from [U.S. ambassador to the UN Jeane] Kirkpatrick claiming that we have refused to change a line in our national anthem which calls the Yankees "enemies of humanity." In fact, this line is not in our national anthem but in the anthem of the FSLN, and we certainly have no intention of changing it. The "Yankee" to whom the Sandinista anthem refers is that Yankee who has intervened in our country twice this century; he is the Yankee who drove our country into poverty, plundering our forests and mines; he is the filibuster; he is the phalanx of adventurers who tried to take possession of Nicaragua in the nineteenth century. He is the Yankee who wanted to prevent Somoza's dictatorship from being overthrown, and he is the same Yankee who propped up that dictatorship for fifty years. He is the Yankee who today cannot accept the reality of our victorious revolution and is arming, training, and funding the *somocista* ex-guardsmen, the counterrevolutionary bands; who is supplying explosives to blow up our factories, to kill our simple working people.

When we speak of that Yankee we do not mean the working people of the United States, so often manipulated and cheated. We do not mean the humiliated and discriminated-against Black people, the thousands of Spanish-speaking immigrants; we do not mean the ordinary U.S. citizens, their academic communities, their students, their honest intellectuals, their trade union organizations which understand Latin America. Neither do we mean the members of religious orders, the priests and nuns who have shed their blood in Guatemala, in El Salvador, in the factories, in the countryside, in the universities. These are the people who can stop a Yankee intervention in Central America. It was that people who, together with the Vietnamese people, defeated the Yankee aggression in Vietnam. And now we are sure that that people will not forget the lessons of history; that they remember Vietnam and that they will oppose, with all their strength, a new imperial incursion into Central America. It is time for that people to decide whether there will be another Vietnam in its history or whether that second Vietnam can be avoided.

Plans are under way to hold a meeting in Mexico of Central and North American intellectuals for sovereignty this coming September. It will be an excellent opportunity to decide on positions together, with a view to establishing real unity between the people of the United States and our own. But we think September may be too late; our intellectuals should make contact with U.S. writers, scientists, artists, and academics at once and urge them to protest against any kind of intervention in Central America or the Caribbean.

In 1927 a father in the United States, a man of the people, wrote to President Calvin Coolidge after his son, a marine, had died in the mountains of Las Segovias in Nicaragua fighting against the Army for the Defense of National Sovereignty, whose general was Sandino. In that letter he wrote that his son's death in Nicaragua was an injustice, that he had died fighting unjustly against a people who had never done the United States any harm at all, and—what was worse—fighting to defend interests which were not his own, but were those of Yankee bankers, hegemonic ambitions which were far removed from the interests of the U.S. people. And in January 1928 General Sandino said to the journalist Carleton Beals:

"If the people of the United States had not had their sense of justice and elementary human rights dulled, they would not so easily be able to forget their own past, when a handful of ragged soldiers marched through the snow, leaving bloody footprints behind them, to win their freedom and their independence. If their consciences had not been hardened by material riches, the Americans would not forget so easily that sooner or later, no matter how weak it may be, a nation obtains its freedom, and that every abuse of power hastens the downfall of those who wield it."

We know that the U.S. people's sense of justice has not been dulled, and that they cannot so easily forget their past. We are confident that they will stand beside the peoples of Latin America and the world, that they will form a bastion to hold back intervention in Central America.

Free homeland or death!

We demand an end to the policy of aggression
by Daniel Ortega

The following excerpts are from a speech given March 25, 1982, to the Security Council of the United Nations. Nicaragua had requested the special UN session because of the escalating U.S.-inspired and directed aggression against Nicaragua that Ortega outlines. The English-language translation was released by Nicaragua's permanent mission to the UN.

When our revolution triumphed, we felt that it was necessary to normalize relations with the United States within a new framework of respect and cooperation, despite the historical fickleness of U.S. policy. In this spirit I met in Washington in September 1980 with President Carter, and we must acknowledge that an effective dialogue then became possible. This mutual disposition to readjust and improve relations between Nicaragua and the United States was brusquely affected in January 1981 when the new administration assumed the presidency of the United States.

The new U.S. administration had to face the reality of a

triumphant revolution in Nicaragua and the determination of oppressed peoples in El Salvador and Guatemala fighting for far-reaching changes. The new administration had proclaimed in its electoral platform action aimed among other things at destroying the revolutionary process in Nicaragua and at halting, at all costs, the process of change in the Central American region.

We can affirm at this time that the policy of the current U.S. administration and the threats against the region contained in the administration's election platform were not mere campaign rhetoric, but have become an increasingly dreadful reality.

The consummation of covert actions against our revolution has now reached the point of deepening the crisis. The imminence of an intervention in Central America has forced us to request a meeting of this Security Council of the United Nations.

I come to appeal to this body of the United Nations because we cannot accept being left with the sole option of dying in the defense of our homeland, since we would never allow ourselves to be subjugated by force.

We want you to know of the existence of training camps for *somocista* counterrevolutionaries in the state of Florida, in United States territory, and of the paltry legalistic reasons offered by the U.S. authorities when we have demanded the dismantling of these camps, which violate the Neutrality Act that is part of United States law.

We want you to know of the existence of camps of *somocista* counterrevolutionaries in the Republic of Honduras, near the Nicaraguan border, where some 2,000 counterrevolutionaries are gathered, trained, supplied, and armed by officials of the Operations section of the Division of Hemispheric Affairs of the Central Intelligence Agency.

You should know that the United States has made the decision to construct in Honduran territory both air and naval bases, the first of them on Amapala Island, and in coming days a treaty is supposed to be signed legalizing the U.S. military presence in Honduran territory.

The U.S. Navy destroyer *Caron*, equipped with sophisticated electronic espionage technology, has been stationed off Nicaragua's Pacific Coast facing the Gulf of Fonseca, carrying out surveillance tasks, as the United States government has publicly acknowledged.

When U.S. media publish reports that the U.S. National Security Council has approved a budget of $19 million to promote destabilizing and covert actions, not a single spokesperson or authority of the United States government has denied such reports. After these disclosures were made, we began to feel the concrete effect of terrorist actions: bombs aboard our passenger airlines and in civilian airports, [causing] deaths and injuries; destruction of bridges; and the resurgence of actions by the counterrevolutionary bands, such as the so-called Red Christmas operation along the Coco River, which took the lives of sixty compatriots who were murdered.

We want you to know that from June 1981 until March 11 of this year, we have been the victims of forty violations of our airspace by RC-135 aircraft of the United States Air Force.

All these flights have been over the Pacific Coast of Nicaragua and along our borders with Honduras and Costa Rica. It seems highly significant that ten of them took place in October and ten others in November 1981, precisely when President Reagan and Mr. Haig were voicing the possibility of decisive and immediate military actions against Nicaragua.

On the basis of what norms of international law does the United States government give itself the right to conduct espionage against our country and violate our airspace?

Our military resources are the most modest in the region. We have no air force and yet it is Nicaragua that is being encircled with military bases and it is against Nicaragua that a permanent and hostile, bellicose attitude is being directed, with spy planes and vessels and naval maneuvers. We are the only state in Central America over which hangs the permanent threat of the world military might of the United States.

The only true military superiority for the defense of our homeland resides in our entire people's formidable combative and organizational disposition, given that we are the only government in Central America that can, in all confidence, distribute arms to the people.

These are the basic elements that forced us, beginning March 15, to adopt exceptional measures for the defense of the integrity and sovereignty of our homeland, by decreeing a state of national emergency.

But at the same time as the aggressive U.S. actions have been implemented, it is only fair to acknowledge and support the efforts made over the past few months by the governments of Mexico and France in search of a political solution to the crisis of the Central American area.

In addition to these efforts, there is the consistent proposal for global negotiations in pursuit of peace in the Central American and Caribbean region made resolutely and in a Latin American spirit by Mexican President José López Portillo on February 21 in Managua, the capital of Nicaragua.

This global proposal considers as indispensable parties [to such negotiations] the United States, the warring sides in El Salvador, Cuba, and Nicaragua. It has been welcomed by the Cuban revolutionary government, by the revolutionaries of the Farabundo Martí National Liberation Front and the Revolutionary Democratic Front of El Salvador, and by the Government of National Reconstruction of Nicaragua.

Since then, the U.S. government has entered into a period of meetings with representatives of the Mexican government. After a round of meetings with the Mexican foreign minister, Don Jorge Castañeda, Mr. Alexander Haig made public a five-point proposal aimed at initiating conversations with Nicaragua following the elections scheduled for March 28 in El Salvador.

The mere fact that the United States makes public a willingness to negotiate with Nicaragua on the basis of these points could be considered an encouraging element. But it turns out to be contradictory because, as I have been demonstrating, the aggressive and destabilizing actions against Nicaragua by the U.S. administration have been dramatically on the rise.

We must affirm that while the United States makes public its willingness to negotiate, it has been developing the alternative of aggression all along.

The five points announced by Mr. Haig fail to take into account the fact that the fundamental cause of the Central American crisis is not the allegation that arms are reaching the Salvadoran revolutionaries via Nicaragua. This charge has never been proven.

On the contrary, the causes of the Central American crisis lie in the injustice that reigns in El Salvador. Moreover, the United States is supplying arms, airplanes, helicopters, advisers, technical support, and rapid military training to the Salvadoran army.

It is inconceivable that the country that is carrying out the greatest arms buildup and spending the most on weaponry in the history of humanity, seeks to demand that we not fulfill the minimum requirements for the defense of our nation. Nicaragua rejects the attempt by the United States to impose humiliating restrictions on our inescapable rights with respect to national defense. We are certain that no sovereign nation in the world would accept such a thing.

This stance is even more unjustified since Nicaragua, as a revolutionary country, has proclaimed in categorical fashion that it will never use its arms against any brother in Latin America and the Caribbean.

We feel that we are all obliged to find a solution to the problems facing the region through negotiated political means, and to never consider the possibility of negotiations to have been exhausted.

The peoples of the region demand a negotiated political solution; U.S. public opinion demands a negotiated political solution; the peoples of Latin America and the worthy governments demand a negotiated political solution; the peoples and governments of the world are expecting a negotiated political solution.

We do not wish to see ourselves forced to resist and struggle to prevail over foreign intervention with the same vigor which enabled the Americans to win their independence in 1776.

We have not come to accuse, but to demand an end, once and for all, to the policy of aggressions, threats, interventions, covert operations, invasions against our homeland and the region. And to make it clear that the unfairly distributed resources of humanity on this planet do not give the powerful a right to act against weak and small peoples.

Finally, I would like to sum up this presentation with concrete points:

1. Neither Nicaragua nor any of the countries of the Central American and Caribbean region can be considered as a geopolitical reserve of the United States, or as part of its so-called strategic frontier, a concept that restricts the exercise of our sovereignty and independence.

2. Therefore, Nicaragua can in no way represent a threat to the security of the United States. We are a small country, a dignified and poor country, that follows a policy of international nonalignment.

The national interests of the people and nation of the United States should not be confused with the particular policy of the present administration, which is trying to make its own point of view prevail, even at the cost of the peace and security, of its own citizens and an entire conglomerate of countries, which like ours have a right to determine their own destiny.

3. We are willing to improve the climate of relations with the United States on the basis of mutual respect and unconditional recognition of our right to self-determination.

4. We are willing to immediately begin direct and frank conversations with the government of the United States, even in a mutually agreeable third country, with the objective of reaching concrete results through such negotiations.

5. The Salvadoran patriots of the FMLN-FDR have authorized us to transmit their willingness to begin immediate negotiations, without preconditions.

6. The revolutionary government of Cuba has authorized me to communicate to this Security Council its willingness as well to begin negotiations without delay.

7. The Government of National Reconstruction of Nicaragua, the government of Cuba, and the Salvadoran patriots of the FMLN-FDR back the initiative for negotiations taken by the president of Mexico, José López Portillo, on February 21 in Managua.

8. Nicaragua is willing to immediately sign nonaggression pacts with all bordering countries of the Central American area in order to ensure peace and internal stability in the zone.

9. Nicaragua is obliged to reject the attempt by the United States to impose humiliating restrictions on its inescapable and sovereign rights regarding national defense.

We demand, on the other hand, that the government of the United States immediately:

- Put a stop to the use of Honduran territory as a base for armed aggressions and terrorist operations against our homeland.

- Put a stop to the existence of counterrevolutionary military training camps in U.S. territory, mainly in Florida.
- Put a stop to the traffic in arms and counterrevolutionaries between the territory of the United States and Honduras.
- Put a stop to the participation of the United States intelligence community in the financing, training, and organizing of forces and clandestine plans against our homeland.
- Put a stop to the presence of U.S. warships in waters of Central America and off Nicaragua's coasts.
- Put a stop to the flights of spy planes that violate Nicaragua's airspace.

The United States must, in an official and explicit manner, voice its commitment not to attack Nicaragua, nor to initiate or promote any direct, indirect, or covert intervention in Central America.

Nicaragua calls on the Security Council of the United Nations to issue an explicit pronouncement in line with the charter of the organization, regarding the obligation to search for a peaceful means of resolving the problems of the Central American and Caribbean region; rejection of acts of force and threats; and repudiation of any direct, indirect, or covert intervention in Central America.

In memory of the millions of people killed in wars throughout history; in memory of the millions tortured and murdered in the Nazi concentration camps in the Second World War; in memory of the thousands of patriots who fell in the struggles for liberation against colonialism, racism, and all kinds of oppression; in memory of the Central American patriots who have fallen fighting for independence, justice, and peace, for the right of the peoples to be free, sovereign, and independent, for the right of humanity to want peace and demand peace:

Let there be peace in Central America.

Without solidarity it is difficult to talk about revolution

by Carlos Fernando Chamorro

The following speech was given March 31, 1982, in Toronto, Canada. The meeting, attended by 250, was sponsored by the Ontario Federation of Labour, the Ontario New Democratic Party, and several church and solidarity organizations. Chamorro's remarks were originally published in the April 19, 1982, issue of *Intercontinental Press*.

A few days ago a continental women's conference was held in Managua. At that conference, one of our leaders spoke about the concept of solidarity. He said that we put such a high value on this aspect of our revolutionary struggle that one could say that without solidarity it is difficult to talk about revolution.

We have learned through our experience that the struggle against U.S. imperialism is carried out on all fronts. Solidarity has a fundamental role to play in isolating the enemy, neutralizing other enemies, encouraging other forces, and directly supporting the struggles of the people.

The present situation in Central America poses a real challenge for people who are conscious, who are responsible, and above all, for revolutionary people.

We believe that in solidarity with the struggles of the people of Central America there must be the unification of the broadest range of forces because there are common causes which unite us, there are common points we can work on together.

Within the Central American region right now we are struggling basically for peace. The people of Central America are confronting more than empty threats. The transition has already been made from rhetoric to aggression. In addition to backward oligarchies opposed to any kind of change in the region, the people of Central America are also confronted with the government of the United States.

There are people who have asked me here in Canada if we really believe there could be an intervention in Nicaragua, in El Salvador, or in Central America. We don't see intervention as a future possibility, but as a process that has already begun in Nicaragua and in El Salvador. There are destabilization plans which are actually under way in Nicaragua today.

There are acts of terrorism we have had to face. There are some 2,000 *somocista* ex-National Guardsmen on the Honduran border who have killed 141 Nicaraguans during the past eighteen months. There are other very dangerous military groups in Central America linked with the Southern Command in Panama.

The U.S. has officially admitted that it is spying on us from the air and from ships at sea. When Mr. Reagan has been asked whether or not he has approved a plan of aggression against Nicaragua he answers that he is not free to comment. We believe his replies are very indicative and that we cannot sit back with our arms folded.

It is the responsibility of Nicaraguan revolutionaries to

defend the future of our people. And that is why we were forced to declare a state of emergency within our country. This was not done to repress our population, but to prepare ourselves to face the aggression that is coming. That is why the Nicaraguan people are prepared to defend our territory. In an atmosphere of calm and normalcy you have Nicaraguan men, women, and children—the poor people of Nicaragua—defending the bridges, the factories, the strategic points.

We do not want war but we have to prepare ourselves. That is why Nicaragua went to the Security Council of the United Nations to warn the world about the dangers of a regional conflict, a conflict that could bring all of Central America into danger.

We were able to supply absolutely clear evidence of the actual plans that are under way to organize aggression against us. In addition, we also made peace proposals because we feel war is not what our people need. We need peace in order to rebuild our country.

That is why we proposed direct and unconditional negotiations with the United States. This is an act of responsibility and revolutionary maturity.

We have also told our neighbors that we are ready to sign military nonaggression pacts so that they don't go on saying Nicaragua is a threat to the whole region. And we have also proposed to them that we carry on joint patrols of the borders so that they don't go on saying we are sending arms to El Salvador, a country with which we do not even share a border.

All that we are asking from the United States is that it allow us to rebuild our country in peace. At the same time, we are supporting the revolutionaries who are struggling in El Salvador so that they might reach a negotiated settlement of the conflict there. Together with the Cubans and the Salvadoran revolutionaries, we have supported the peace proposals made by the president of Mexico. We are still waiting for a serious and responsible reply to these proposals from the American government.

We have begun to build a new society in Nicaragua in which our people have begun to have access to education, to health care. The peasants are beginning to have access to land, the workers are organized in unions and participate in decisions about production and political questions.

Perhaps our people have not yet reached the standard of living we would like to have, but at least we feel that we are in charge of our own destiny. We feel that we are a sovereign nation. One of the best signs of this is that our whole people are ready to defend the Sandinista revolution.

There are also those who say that Nicaragua is a totalitarian country. Yet I don't see how anything could be more democratic than our own country, where you find an entire people ready to give its life to defend its revolution. In neighboring countries the rulers would not likely give arms to their people as is the case in Nicaragua.

The imperialists have made up a bunch of lies about the Sandinista revolution in order to try to prevent its example from inspiring other people. In fact, the Sandinista revolution represents an alternative, a hope for the peoples of the Third World.

This is something the imperialists don't like, so they have tried to paint us as if we are against democracy and claim that we are exporting revolution, implying that the Salvadoran revolutionaries are not capable of doing it themselves. Or as if revolutions could be exported the way you export other products. What you do export is your example and that is the power and moral authority which the Sandinista revolution has.

We are worried about the days that lie ahead. For the first time, some representatives of the U.S. government have said a few words about dialogue and negotiations. Nevertheless, even as they utter such words they are continuing their aggressive preparations and military acts against Nicaragua.

We are confident that our people are ready to respond to any situation. We know perfectly well that the people of the United States, the U.S. Congress, and religious and popular forces in the United States do not want another Vietnam in Central America.

We also know that we can count on the support of the Canadian people. Yet this support has to increase significantly. It has to be organized and have clear objectives. The main focus should be against intervention.

You have a great challenge to mobilize people against intervention. You must organize so as to have some impact on the position of your government. We also count on the direct solidarity you show with the struggles in Central America.

You can be sure that the Nicaraguan people are an organized people and that we are doing everything possible to avoid a war. Because we know very well what war means. We have lived it. And we want to avoid it because we need peace in order to rebuild our country.

We are living through critical days. We hope that the solidarity work done here might also become a source of strength for us. We hope it can be united with the efforts of the people of the United States in order to build a very powerful anti-interventionist movement.

We are counting on our own strength. We have denounced internationally the aggression that is occurring. And we also believe that we can count on your solidarity.

If these three elements are not enough to stop the aggression, you may be sure that we will struggle for our sovereignty.

We ask you to become a militia of solidarity with the people of Nicaragua, a militia for peace.

Defense can be assured only by increasing production
Interview with Lucío Jiménez

The following interview was printed on the first page of the April 24, 1982, issue of *Barricada,* the Managua daily published by the FSLN. In April, the national emergency that had been declared the previous month was extended, as U.S. aggression against Nicaragua continued to mount. In that context, wide-ranging discussions were held across the country in preparation for the 1982 May Day celebration. Those discussions were concretized in the slogan adopted by the Sandinista trade unions for the May Day march and rally—"Defend the revolution; for the building of socialism." In *Barricada* the interview was titled "We want to move on to socialism." This translation originally appeared in the May 10, 1982, issue of *Intercontinental Press.*

QUESTION: During the second month of the national emergency, what will be the central axis of the mass mobilization on May Day?

LUCÍO JIMÉNEZ: From the point of view of propaganda, workers will be discussing in mass meetings the objectives for which we are fighting and making sacrifices. Because the objectives we are defending are the revolution and its conquests—in short, socialism. In the days leading up to May Day this year, workers are grappling with and discussing the ideas of scientific socialism.

We have to take into account that in this period of emergency, many workers have had to be mobilized and many sectors of production have been affected. Our orientation from the beginning to compensate for the personnel who have been mobilized has been to make greater efforts to assure production with the remaining personnel. But even maintaining the same levels of production is not enough. We have to attain higher levels, for defense can be assured only by increasing production, so as to meet the most urgent necessities of the population and create the material conditions for carrying through the plans for defense of the revolution.

The great conquest of this May Day is that both of these aspects are the subject of broad discussion. The ideas of socialism are being widely publicized, and conscious efforts are being made to regain and advance production levels in the various sectors, particularly those affected by the national emergency.

QUESTION: The mobilization of thousands of reserves—can you tell us how and to what extent it has affected production?

JIMÉNEZ: It is difficult to give an answer in percentages. We can say that the effect has been minimized by the fact that we understood beforehand that greater efforts would have to be made so as to produce at the same capacity with fewer workers.

The exact percentages we have fallen behind will have to be established by governmental institutions; then we can begin the task of catching up as far as possible.

QUESTION: In some enterprises, however, it is clear that

the level of production has fallen. What do you think the Sandinista Workers Federation [CST] should do to regain this ground?

JIMÉNEZ: The CST has supported and will soon issue, along with the rest of the labor organizations, a statement declaring that this May Day we are setting concrete goals aimed at reaching optimal labor efficiency over the next few months.

Our orientation is to reach a level of 100 percent attendance at work. That is, we intend to make great efforts to increase labor discipline, not only now but permanently, something that is quite in keeping with the situation of national emergency. Consequently, the unions will be meeting to discuss not only the establishment of labor discipline, but also how to meet production and productivity goals.

QUESTION: When will the statement you referred to be released?

JIMÉNEZ: Well, the orientation has already been made clear that the unions are to hold meetings, that they are to set their goals democratically. We have also reached an understanding that this is not something that will come and go with May Day, but that instead May Day is the framework for setting goals and dedicating ourselves to fulfilling them in the months that follow.

Specifically, two fundamental aspects are involved. First we are proposing specific, realizable goals for certain aspects of production in a given enterprise. We must reach a 100 percent level in attendance and punctuality at work. We produce for defense of the country, which, it should be added, also requires 100 percent attendance at militia training, something that has slipped a little lately. The unions, therefore, will have to establish in a democratic fashion that the workers who have signed up actually attend the training.

On the other hand, the unions have to reach a maximum level of organization to carry out these tasks. In this framework we have set an orientation that the payment of dues be kept up to date, something that can only be accomplished if the unions refine their organizational methods, provide orientation for the actions of their members, and in general function in a correct manner.

QUESTION: What can you tell us about the central slogan for May Day, "Defend the revolution, for the building of socialism"?

JIMÉNEZ: We, the toilers, workers, peasants, and most progressive sectors of society, under the leadership of our vanguard the Sandinista National Liberation Front, have taken power in order to make substantial changes and radically transform the country's economic and social structure. For we are convinced that only a transformation of this type will enable us to fulfill the most deeply felt needs of the workers, which can be summed up as social progress, a sense of well-being among the people, and the attainment of a just, dignified, and durable peace.

This is the way we defend the conquests the revolution has already made. We are not prepared to return the land, the factories, and the banks, nor are we prepared to see the agrarian reform law disappear. We are fighting to hold onto these things, but also for a future in which exploitation of man by man will be done away with forever, a future in which the workers and the entire people will be the rightful owners of the product of their labor and sweat. In other words, we are fighting for a socialist future.

For the workers, the triumph of the Sandinista people's revolution is the starting point for a slow but sure advance, led by our vanguard, our national leadership, to this strategic objective.

QUESTION: The Ministry of Industry pointed out recently that in Nicaragua the creation of an economic base for the revolution will be no easy matter. What strategy is the CST proposing for helping to attain this necessity?

JIMÉNEZ: We have for some time been encouraging the appropriate government agencies to strengthen ties with the socialist countries so as to diversify our markets, a step that will objectively enable us to break our economic dependence on the United States and other capitalist countries.

In general, however, the strategy of the CST to reach a new stage of production is to build a strong union organization that continually links its activity to the problems of production, that makes its central concern such questions as labor discipline; fulfillment of production goals; effective operation of the institutions that administer the national economy and the budgets of local enterprises; and the fight against bureaucratism, against administrative inefficiency, and for a new consciousness toward work.

We also want to see the unions make it their special concern to promote a fundamental savings—that of imported resources that we do not produce, such as energy, fuel, and paper, as well as of raw materials, which are in many cases wasted.

This in general is the long-term line of action of our unions. Only in this way can we play a dynamic, active role in building a society that breaks with dependency.

This revolution was made to create a new society

by Tomás Borge

The following are major excerpts from a May 1, 1982, speech by Tomás Borge. The speech was delivered to a crowd of 100,000 in Managua's Carlos Fonseca Plaza of the Revolution as part of May Day celebrations held across the country. The celebrations also drew crowds that totaled more than 70,000 in cities outside Managua. This translation by Elizabeth Reimann originally appeared in the May 31, 1982, issue of *Intercontinental Press*.

When we came from the Plaza of the Nonaligned to the Carlos Fonseca Plaza of the Revolution, we marched for a good part of the way in the midst of the workers, and on the way we thought back a bit about our past. And we thought a bit about the symbolism involved in our coming over in the midst of our workers. We did not come at the head of the workers, we came in the midst of the workers, with the working class at the front of the march, heading north, but not toward the brutal and stormy north, but rather toward the north of the revolution.

But we were thinking of something else. The crowd was so compressed, the mass of workers was so compact and so combative that if Daniel [Ortega] and I had wanted to turn back—something that will never happen—this mass of workers would never have allowed us to take a step backward. [*Applause*]

This is not a May Day like any other. It is a May Day where there have been important qualitative leaps within the Nicaraguan revolutionary process. We have assembled not merely to speak of the struggle of Nicaraguan workers, but to draw lessons from this struggle. We have assembled to specify more exactly the role of the working class within the revolution.

The struggle of the working class has been long, complex, full of sacrifice and martyrdom. You, the workers, know very well the enormous difficulties that the working class has suffered, all the workers in general, all our people, in order to achieve their liberation. The struggle of the working class has been as long as its own history.

At what moment does the working class appear in the history of humanity? Because the working class has not existed always. When man appeared upon the earth, the scarcity of material resources, cultural poverty, the extraordinary limitations of that historical moment, forced man to live in a state of community, but one that was completely primitive; they produced no wealth for the sake of which some men would fight other men. When work tools were developed and men began to produce some wealth in excess of the bare needs of survival, some men enslaved other men, and for very many years there were masters and slaves. The slaves rebelled against the masters, and when slavery, in its fundamental form, disappeared, a new society emerged: the society of the great landowners. The society of kings, of barons, the lords who wielded power over life and death. This was called feudal society, just as the previous society had been called slave society.

Little by little, within this feudal society, manufacturing production, mercantile production developed, and the foundations of what later would become great industry began to be built up. In order to enrich themselves, the owners of this new system of production, the owners of the factories, began to exploit the labor force capable of producing this wealth. This labor force was composed of the factory workers, that is to say, what is called the working class. There were great movements in Europe and the French Revolution is the climax of the revolution of the owners of these factories, the revolution of the bourgeoisie; and it is within bourgeois society, therefore, that the working class emerges, the most revolutionary class in history.

The bourgeoisie then gave rise to a society full of illusions and beautiful phrases. It spoke of liberty and fraternity. It gave rise to a bureaucracy, a police, and an army, which were presented as instruments serving society as a whole. But these illusions of all kinds—including the legal, moral, and political illusions forged by the bourgeoisie—collapsed when confronted by the reality and by the essence of bourgeois exploitation. When in a bourgeois society, for instance, the workers ask for an improvement in their wages, when the peasants lay claim to the land, the police and the army of the bourgeoisie turn into instruments of repression.

You, workers of Nicaragua, saw it in daily practice during the bourgeois regime of *somocismo*. When the workers rose up in strikes and marched in the streets demanding better living conditions, when the peasants energetically claimed the land, the National Guard, an instrument of the bourgeoisie, did not stop to ask whether the industrialist or the landowner affected by the workers' struggle was a Liberal or a Conservative, pro-Somoza or anti-Somoza, whether or not they belonged to the so-called opposition bourgeoisie. In order to defend the interests of the rich, the National Guard repressed the rural workers, the workers in the cities, and the peasants, even though these forces sometimes mistakenly tried to defend themselves against repression by declaring themselves to be Liberals and even *somocistas*.

What does this prove? That the National Guard had a chief, Somoza, but that its job was to defend certain social classes, regardless of their political coloration or their religious beliefs; that is to say, it was at the service of the industrialists and the landowners.

What happens now? What is the difference between yesterday and today? Who are the ones who complain about the Sandinista People's Army (EPS), the Sandinista Police, the organs of State Security—apart from some justified complaints against isolated cases of abuse which, though less each day, unfortunately are still committed? Who are the ones who complain? Do you complain against our glorious EPS [*Shouts of "No!"*], against our ever more efficient Sandinista Police ["*No!*"], against our self-sacrificing comrades from State Security? ["*No!*"] Who are the ones who are complaining? [*Shouts of "The bourgeoisie!"*]

Is it the peasants and the workers? No. Those who complain are the ones who in the past had an unrestricted instrument for repressing workers and peasants; those who complain are the great landowners and the big industrialists and the tiny groups that still allow themselves to be confused by counterrevolutionary preaching. [*Applause*] And the reason is very simple. While yesterday the industrialists and the landowners had an army and a police like the National Guard and an office of security serving their interests, today the workers and the peasants, all the working people, the ordinary people of Nicaragua, have at their wholehearted service the Sandinista People's Army, the Sandinista Police, and the organs of State Security. [*Applause and chants of "One single army!"*]

One would really have to be an idiot or a victim of delusion, or both things at once, to ask for the support of the people in order to give back the lands that were taken away from the landowners, or to return the holdings that were confiscated from the *somocistas*.

One would really have to be an idiot or an evil person, or both things at once, not to realize that our people have gained awareness of their real history, that our workers have gained awareness of the class they belong to.

Because the proletariat does not gain class consciousness spontaneously. The proletariat is, without a doubt, the most revolutionary class in history. But it gains this awareness only when it comes into intimate contact with revolutionary theory and practice. At certain stages, the working class may be confused by the illusions sown by bourgeois propaganda. The false bourgeois saying, the false bourgeois principle that all men are equal before bourgeois law, can be refuted only when it comes into conflict with practice and through the knowledge of revolutionary theory.

The working class, during its lengthy struggle, has learned and continues learning from its mistakes and its failures. During the development of its struggles it discovered new forms of political combat, forms that go much further than the just demands for more humane working hours, better wages, and better social conditions. Nevertheless, many times the working class has been guilty of economist errors, meaning that it has raised, as a final goal, the achievement of economic demands. In a society of exploitation, it is absolutely justified that the workers should struggle for economic demands; but it can never be correct that the workers should forget their political struggles and their political goals, even under a regime of exploitation.

In a society where, as in Nicaragua, the power of imperialism and of the bourgeoisie has been decapitated, it is correct that the workers should continue putting forward their economic demands. But to struggle for economic demands, and leave in a secondary place the consolidation of their political power as a social class, would mean going against common sense and against history.

This means that, at the present moment of our history, when the rule of bourgeois and imperialist exploitation has been eliminated forever in Nicaragua, the fundamental duty is and should be the consolidation of the workers' power within the revolution.

A revolutionary process is made up of various phases. During the first phase of national liberation, which in Nicaragua was the war against the National Guard and the domination of the *somocista* bourgeoisie, the working class and the vanguard that represented its historical interests drew together other sectors and strata of society. At that moment it was correct to form a broad national unity to achieve a goal that was common to all our society: to get rid of a regime that was both criminal and ready to deliver our riches to foreign interests. And this regime was, at the same time, a gigantic obstacle to the historical development of our country.

With the victory of the revolution, a new phase begins. It is still necessary to unite the widest possible strata of Nicaraguan society to confront the common enemy of all Nicaraguans, which is U.S. imperialism. This means that this new phase, after victory, puts the main emphasis on the defense of the nation, on the struggle to have our national sovereignty respected, on the right of self-determination, and on the need to unite all Nicaraguan patriots to confront a huge and cruel enemy.

But in this new phase, serious internal contradictions begin to come to the surface, when the revolution is forced—by its own dynamic and to remain in harmony with the political, economic, and social principles that were its reason for being—to determine which social sectors shall be given priority within the revolutionary process. Our people already know who the privileged ones were yesterday, and our people already know which classes have priority today, for whom this revolution was made.

Nevertheless, it is necessary to maintain national unity with wide sectors of our society, including those sectors of the bourgeoisie who are ready to work in a common cause with the workers, in production and in the defense of the sovereignty of our homeland.

This new phase, however, is extraordinarily complex, because on one side we have the interests of the workers and peasants, the backbone of the revolution. And on the other side there are those capitalist sectors that the revolution wants to keep on its side, even giving them economic incentives. But at the same time these sectors are torn apart by the dashing of their political hopes, and because the umbilical cord that ties them to imperialism, due to their antipatriotic traditions, refuses to disappear.

But is it possible that some industrial or capitalist sectors linked to agricultural production might be able to cut that umbilical cord? Is it possible that these social sectors might be capable of understanding that the guiding axis of the new society is the workers? Does the possibility exist that they might give up their political expectations and utilize their experience and capabilities to work for the benefit of production linked to development of the country as a whole?

Experience tells us that on one hand, a certain number of elements belonging to these social groups cannot resign themselves to the new reality, and that even within the revolution, there are those who believed that ultimately the dreams of the workers and peasants would end in a nightmare and the dreams of the bosses as a class would end in paradise.

Experience has also shown that there are capitalist sectors who are ready to work with the revolution, and that broad middle strata and the majority of small and medium agricultural producers have incorporated themselves into the revolutionary process.

Within the first group, there are those who had illusions about the nature of the revolution, but who eventually realized that the revolution was not made in order to satisfy their hunger for power, their poor and sad aspirations for power. Among them there are also those who were incapable of realizing that the real stars are not those sewn on uniforms but those that shine in the heavens.

There have been many great deeds in the grand and glorious history of our homeland. In all these great deeds, the protagonist was the Nicaraguan people, and, of course, we shall not forget our heroes because that would not be right. But heroes are nothing more than the instrument of the masses to make history.

I would rather not even mention, because he may be present here, that young man who defied imperialism on its own soil.* But I should like to hear one single witness who ever heard him boasting of his feat. He has simply accepted it as part of his revolutionary duty and because he is aware that there are tens of thousands of young Nicaraguans who, like himself, are capable of adopting the same attitude when confronted with imperialism. [*Applause*]

Is there not even greater heroism in work? Heroes are the workers, who labor selflessly to increase production; heroes are the peasants, who under our pitiless sun now work not only for themselves but to satisfy the needs of the country. Heroes are the comrades who work until late at night; while the brightly lit windows of their offices fall like a weight

---

* Orlando Tardencilla, a nineteen-year-old Nicaraguan captured fighting alongside the guerrillas in El Salvador, was brought to Washington to testify that Nicaraguans and Cubans were intervening in El Salvador. But at the State Department's March 12, 1982, press conference to air the charges, Tardencilla, risking return to El Salvador and certain death there, refuted Reagan's lies before the assembled press corps.

upon their eyes. Prevailing against sleep and fatigue, they continue working to complete their jobs. Heroines are our women, who are not only exemplary in their self-sacrifice at work, besides taking care of all the tasks of the home, but have also known how to be part of the vanguard when it is time to defend the homeland. A heroine is a woman over there, the mother of our frontier guards who carried in her body the hero who gave his life for his country. [*Applause*]

Heroes are our people; a poor people, hounded by their economic limitations, bent under the weight of the inheritance from the past, yet who every day confront with incomparable valor that powerful, boastful, and criminal country whose imperialist government tries to make them knuckle under. And there is no possibility that this people, which is truly heroic, will ever surrender or sell out.

This revolution was made, not to reaffirm the old society, but to create a new society. [*Applause*]

Well now, this struggle, which is fundamentally a task of the working class, has special characteristics stemming from the economic, historical, and cultural conditions of Nicaragua.

When imperialism emerged as the highest stage of capitalism, a struggle for world markets was initiated by the large capitalist countries, and during that first division of the world, Nicaragua, together with other Latin American countries, suffered the terrible fate of falling into the hands of the U.S. imperialists. Our economy, therefore, developed as a dependent economy. This forced our people to struggle for their national liberation, and this struggle took on a specific form, which is nationalism.

This also explains why our country, ferociously subjected to the United States, never produced a true national bourgeoisie. The dominant force in our country was never the local bourgeoisie: it was imperialism, through its brutal local instruments. The development of Nicaragua took place through investments and loans administered by an overseer named Anastasio Somoza, as in the past there had been, to mention only a couple of examples, Chamorro and Moncada.

When Sandino's army of peasants and workers kicked the Yankee invaders out of our homeland, the astute invaders established a docile army which had the characteristics of an army of occupation, and which was the foundation not only of the Somoza dynasty but of the power of the oligarchy as a whole. That is why the struggle of our people took the form of a struggle against the *somocista* dictatorship, which was, in its essence, a struggle against imperialism. And through this dialectical link between national liberation and the anti-Somoza struggle victory was reached, a victory that took the *form* of the overthrow of the *somocista* tyranny, but whose *content* was a victory of national liberation.

Who was capable of deciphering this historical synthesis?

It was the Sandinista National Liberation Front, it was *sandinismo* that knew how to apply the theory of revolution to the concrete reality of Nicaragua.

Therefore, the Sandinista front was the living instrument for the conquest of power by the workers, and the living instrument for the consolidation of the power of the workers.

What does this mean? Just like the human body needs vitamins and protein to nourish itself and develop, the Sandinista front needs to draw its sustenance from the working class. The vitamins and protein of the Sandinista front are the Nicaraguan workers and peasants. The intellectuals, professionals, and other sectors of society who want to identify with the Sandinista people's revolution, must identify with the interests of the workers and peasants. And the capitalists, regardless of their ideological conceptions of the Nicaraguan workers and peasants, have to identify with the patriotism of the peasants and workers if they are to remain in Nicaragua.

The Sandinista front is the vanguard of the revolution.

The Sandinista front is the vanguard of all Nicaraguan patriots.

The Sandinista front is the vanguard of national liberation.

The Sandinista front is the vanguard of the workers and peasants, and is the vanguard of these social sectors; the Sandinista front is the living instrument of the revolutionary classes, the guide leading toward a new society. [*Applause*]

It had the wisdom and the courage to find the essence of the antagonistic contradictions between Nicaragua and U.S. imperialism. It knew, and it will know, the role of the revolutionary classes in the process of the political and economic transformations of Nicaragua. It knows the point when it is necessary to have qualitative changes, while always keeping its feet firmly on the ground, simultaneously bearing in mind our most beautiful dreams and reality—which is sometimes challenging, difficult, and terrible.

That is why the Sandinista front is the vanguard of our people; that is why the Sandinista front is the irreplaceable vanguard of the unity of the nation, a unity that must be based on the interests of the workers and on national patriotism.

But revolutionary power is only an instrument for accomplishing the achievements of the people. What are the achievements we have won so far, and what objective obstacles, for the time being, hold back the accomplishment of new achievements?

Before speaking of some concrete accomplishments of the revolution during the brief historical period since the workers have begun their participation as the moving force of this process, we must refer with all frankness to the economic situation of our country. It can be said that our economy has been recovering, little by little, both from the destruction caused by the war and the *somocista* destruction and pillage, as well as from the decapitalization and pillage carried out by certain capitalist sectors after our victory. Nevertheless, this recovery has run head-on into a drop in the prices for our products, our agricultural exports, and this has meant a reduction of the receipts of hard currency, that is to say, of dollars, for Nicaragua.

Why do the products that we sell abroad continually bring lower prices? Our workers must understand this problem clearly. There is a crisis in the world capitalist economy, and the Nicaraguan economy that we inherited from the past is still fundamentally oriented toward the capitalist markets. The logic of capitalism is cold and cruel. They buy from us at cheap prices, and the raw materials they buy from our poor countries are transformed through advanced technology and sold back to us at extremely high prices. There are other products, such as oil, whose prices have been raised excessively, and unfortunately our production, the electrical energy that we use, is intimately linked to oil.

But it isn't only oil. There are all our export products. Sugar, for instance, is down one-third from its price only a year ago. The price of cotton has dropped 20 percent, the price of beef is down, the price of gold is down, and the same has happened with the prices of other articles we normally export. This has meant, for Nicaragua, a drop in its income, this year alone, of $110 million. We can add to that the antipatriotic decapitalization of many business enterprises; we can also add the denial of numerous credits, such as the criminal cutoff of the AID [Agency for International Development] credits for wheat purchases.

When we speak of hard currency, fundamentally we mean dollars. In other words, we have been seriously affected in our commercial trade with the capitalist countries and, above all, with the United States. We therefore have less hard currency at our disposal. And hard currency is required for medicines, many essential consumer goods, and the products that in technical terminology are called inputs—such as fertilizer—which are used in the production of food, or in the production of clothing and shoes. All this means that to satisfy the demands of health and food and clothing a certain amount of hard currency is needed, and therefore the revolution is forced to give priority to the use of this hard currency for the benefit of the basic requirements of the people.

But however great our efforts to establish priorities, hard currency is still scarce, which opens up the possibility that we may have to stop importing some raw materials used in producing consumer goods that are not essential. This can have some consequences for workers. The workers will have to face this problem with wisdom and efficiency, as they must also face the limitations and injustices that are committed against them, the arrogance and misuse of power on the part of some government administrators, the corruption that prevails in some enterprises, the administrative disorder, excessive expense accounts, unjustified firings, the inconceivable fact that when some members of the militia come back from the border and return to work, they find a letter telling them they have lost their job. This even happened in some state-owned enterprises, as if there were not a law against this, as well as a moral obligation of elementary justice.

To face these problems—abuse of power, bureaucracy, the limited participation of workers in the enterprises—there is only one road: the unity of the working class.

There are some workers who believe that the main enemy of the working class is the bourgeoisie. But the bourgeoisie as a class has been mortally wounded in this country, and the dying have never been dangerous enemies. The main enemy of the working class is the division of the working class. However, the dying still have enough breath left to say, in a shaky voice, in the midst of their historical death agony, that the workers have the right to "trade union freedom."

And what does this mean, "trade union freedom"? "Trade union freedom" means the division of the working class. I have often said that the bourgeoisie is united, and at this stage it is inconceivable that the united summits of the bourgeoisie should be calling for trade union freedom. What interest can the bourgeoisie have in trade union freedom? When have they ever cared about the workers? But what is still more inconceivable is that some small sectors of the working class, although they are a minority, should still lend an ear to these siren songs of the bourgeoisie.

True freedom for the unions means the freedom to defend the interests of the working class. True freedom for the unions is expressed in the undeniable fact that after the victory, many more unions have formed than in all the previous history of our country. Freedom of unions to defend the interests of the bosses? [*Shouts of "No!"*] Freedom of unions to join the chorus of those who want to sell out our country? ["*No!*"] Freedom of unions in the waiting rooms of the Yankee embassy? ["*No!*"]

No. True union freedom to consolidate the role of the working class in the revolutionary process; true union freedom to defend, in the trenches of the homeland, the sovereignty of our country; true union freedom for defense against misuse of power, against bureaucracy, and against the injustices that still persist; true union freedom so that the workers participate in the process of production, which is the best school for the working class to understand the laws of economy and be able to control them.

True union freedom to defend the true interests of the nation, because the defense of this nation is fundamentally a task of the working class.

And as for the economic situation that our country faces, what can the workers do?

With every bit of hard currency we save, with every dollar we save, we shall be defending the job of a comrade, of a brother worker, of a class brother.

This way, taking care of the machinery, saving materials, monitoring the quality of production and also acquiring new technical skills, the workers will raise productivity, which means that they will produce more per workday. And the more we produce, the more we will be able to raise the standard of living to which men in a revolution are entitled.

Confronting the problem of prices also requires the initiative of the workers. The state has expended great efforts to keep the prices of essential products low, for instance subsidizing basic food items. But government efforts would be wasted if they were not supported by the vigilance of the workers in the fight against speculators, those who hoard goods and cause shortages in order to sell products at a higher price later. There are other ways to hold down price increases, and one way is the initiative of reusing containers to make costs cheaper. We are sure that the problems we are facing will, as always, stimulate the creativity of the masses, who will always find new initiatives to solve them.

Therefore, in spite of the enormous difficulties, we have advanced. Although we too are victims of the economic crisis of the world capitalist system, our conditions are infinitely better than those of other neighboring countries or other Latin American countries. Inflation, sharply rising unemployment, elimination of social programs have been the characteristics marking many countries, almost all Latin American countries, and even the United States, where arms spending, as we have said on other occasions, means the incredible amount of *$1.5 trillion*. This has caused an inflationary process and a process of economic recession that has forced the U.S. government to make grave cuts in the programs benefiting children, invalids, and the poor in general.

We, on the contrary, have pressed forward with social programs. And even more important than the social programs the revolution has carried out so far are the vast projects that, in a planned manner, will be changing the structure of the Nicaraguan economy.

Our workers must educate themselves in the idea that our revolution would be mean and petty, and would stop being a revolution, if it did not think in terms of solidarity with other fraternal peoples of the world. And that, even though we still have not left our backwardness and poverty completely behind, we must have, always present, an internationalist consciousness. We must be prepared to share our own poverty if necessary, whenever other hungry and ill-clothed peoples should need us. We, the Nicaraguan workers, will be the brothers of every worker on earth.

Just as we have now received thousands of doctors and teachers from Cuba and other countries, some of whom are also poor like us, so we have to be ready to give away, not whatever we have too much of, because that would be no sacrifice, but whatever is necessary to other peoples that may need it. [*Applause*]

People of Nicaragua, a people of solidarity by definition, by history, and by conscience. People of Nicaragua, a people of solidarity because they have learned to assimilate the teachings of their great heroes. People of Nicaragua, a people of solidarity with the struggle of the Salvadorans. People of Nicaragua, a people who have known and know how to maintain, in spite of everything, their unconditional solidarity with Argentina in its confrontation with a colonial power, with the people of Argentina who were today attacked by British aircraft at Port Stanley in the Malvinas Islands.* [*Applause*] A people of solidarity who know how

---

* On April 2, 1982, several thousand Argentine troops took possession of the Malvinas Islands (referred to as the Falkland Islands in the imperialist media), located 250 miles off the coast of Argentina. The

to distinguish their friends from their enemies. A people of solidarity who know that today imperialism took off its mask, because instead of standing by Argentina, it stood by the side of the colonial power.

We, a small and poor country, do not stand by the side of the powerful. We stand by the side of our fraternal people of Latin America. [*Applause*] And this shows once more the need for the peoples of Latin America to unite to oppose those who, every day more obviously, are the enemies of our peoples.

[U.S. Secretary of State Alexander] Haig's declarations against Argentina are not Haig's declarations against Argentina. They are Haig's declarations against Latin America and against this Nicaraguan people which will demonstrate solidarity to the utmost, whatever the consequences. [*Applause*] A people that is in solidarity with other peoples, but that is also in solidarity with the future generations. Workers and peasants who voice solidarity internationally and solidarity at home. Every worker is the brother of every other worker. All workers are brothers of every worker, and all Nicaraguan workers are brothers of all of the workers of the world.

---

islands had been seized by the British Empire in 1833. Argentina had been negotiating for their return for several decades and in 1971 an agreement was reached providing for their eventual reintegration into Argentina. Subsequent negotiations, however, had led to no progress. All the major imperialist powers, including the U.S., which was supposedly treaty-bound to aid Argentina, sided with Britain in the dispute. Virtually all the Latin American countries, including Nicaragua, supported Argentina's claim to sovereignty, as did opponents of imperialism throughout the world.

A British task force of thirty ships, four nuclear submarines, and 3,000 troops sailed for the Malvinas on April 5. Attacks against Argentine positions on the islands began on April 25. On May 2 an Argentine cruiser was sunk, with a loss of several hundred dead. On May 21 the British invaded, and by June 14 the Argentine troops had surrendered and British control had been reestablished.

Therefore, this workers' revolution has projected not only programs for economic development, but ambitious and realistic social programs as well.

Within these programs, education and health have priority. The successes of the revolution in our educational system are already well known. It is enough to mention one example: in preschool education, enrollment jumped from 9,000 children before the triumph of the revolution to 41,215 in 1982. And this after Nicaragua had been one of the countries most indifferent to primary, and therefore to secondary and higher education. Beginning July 19 [1979], the numbers have grown; education in agricultural and cattle-raising technology has been intensified; so have industrial technical education, teacher training, commercial education, and special education. And all this without taking into account military and police technical training, which brings the total of those in our country who have received education to more than 1 million.

But the great fundamental educational undertakings in Nicaragua, such as the National Crusade for Literacy and Adult Education, have an importance that has not always been sufficiently stressed: that is, their success is due fundamentally to the participation of the people, to the support of the workers, a support both dynamic and full of historical vision.

Within a true revolution, this is to be expected. The strategic goals of education are a part of the strategic goals of the Sandinista people's revolution, and their aim is to create a new society. The aim of education is to draw out the abilities, the energy, the best values of the people, so that they will gain awareness of their historical value, so that they will gain confidence in their endless capacity for transforming nature and for transforming society.

Our education aims to encourage collective participation, human solidarity, and the organizational capacity of the people. It is an education that proposes to carry to the highest levels the extraordinary intelligence of our people, so that they acquire the awareness and knowledge needed for the transformation of the productive structure, so that they become capable of forceful leaps ahead in economic development—and I am not going to refer to this, because our people already know all about it. I am only going to mention two things.

The first great battle we must fight during the next years, and in which the participation of our people is vital, is the battle for the fourth grade. Every child, without a single exception, must as a minimum complete the fourth grade as a first step, so that during the whole of the next decade all Nicaraguans complete at the very least nine years of general basic education. The battle for the fourth grade is extraordinarily important for the revolution. If we do not win it, it means we have lost the battle against illiteracy.

When we say we shall fight the battle for the fourth grade, we are saying that all our people are going to make a joint effort and that we shall design a strategy to win it.

We must not permit our children to drop out of school. We must achieve this goal to avoid the return of the terrible evil of illiteracy. We are struggling for the future of the homeland, and not to do so would be to go against the very essence of our revolution. And in the meantime, it is essential to eliminate, from the roots up, the remnants of illiteracy, and to consolidate popular adult education.

Within the area of education, logically the revolution gives priority, and will have to give even more priority in the future, to technical careers and to careers related to agriculture and cattle-raising, but there is one school that requires more attention immediately, and that is the school of medicine.

During the months of January and February alone, forty-two doctors deserted, and besides these forty-two, another forty-eight have left the public clinics. This means that in two months, practically three doctors have left every two days. But maybe it is better that those health merchants should leave. [*Applause*] Those who write prescriptions to make money and not to cure the sick, those who were never disciples of Hippocrates, the father of medicine, but rather were hypocrites who simulated a social service they were never ready to render.

Nevertheless, we must add that those who have stayed, many of them magnificent doctors, not only identify with the interests of the people in the hospitals and clinics, but have gone to suffer hardship in the wildest and most undeveloped areas of our country. Last night our comrade Lea [Guido, minister of health,] was telling us that four medical brigades, composed of doctors and nurses, had gone to the Atlantic Coast to work in that area, traditionally our country's most backward and abandoned region.

Since July 19 [1979], 224 doctors and 1,862 paramedical personnel, all educated in a new mentality, have graduated. At this moment, 2,024 young people are studying medicine. These figures, though not to be scoffed at, are still insufficient for the enormous needs facing our country.

To sum up, all our efforts are directed toward destroying the negative habits that are a part of the *somocista* inheritance so that those habits enter a crisis simultaneously with the breakdown of imperialist domination in Central America. This domination started to break down when the Sandinista people's revolution triumphed, and the process was speeded up with the development of revolutionary struggle in Central America.

Within this imperialist crisis, the U.S. government has frequently resorted to threatening words against Nicaragua. The imperialist expectations in El Salvador failed; in the Salvador voting process, victory did not go to those right-wing sectors best suited to the interests of the Reagan administra-

tion, which sought to exhibit to the world the electoral triumph of a political tendency under the guise of democracy.*
Victory went, as was to be expected given the intensification of the internal contradictions in that brother country, to the extreme right, headed by the murderer of Monsignor [Archbishop Oscar] Romero, Roberto D'Aubuisson, who is much harder to defend before international public opinion. This made it very difficult for imperialism to implement a scenario of intervention to defend its odious counterpart, although deep down this is what imperialism wanted.

The European allies of the U.S. government would not look kindly upon a more open armed support for the most notorious chief of the murder gangs in El Salvador. The Guatemalan coup and the Honduran elections, regardless of their nature, did not help the openly interventionist policy of the United States.

Equally, the Malvinas problem and the confrontation between a Latin American country and a colonialist power put the U.S. government in a difficult position, which will certainly have repercussions in the use of such instruments as the Rio Treaty, whose original goal was to implement the aggressive policies of imperialism against Latin America.

Exceptionally important was the audacious and determined mobilization of the Nicaraguan people in defense of our homeland. But does all this mean that the defeat, at the conjuncture of imperialism's desire to carry out direct aggression against Central America, and against Nicaragua in particular, does this defeat mean it will abstain from ag-

---

* At the urging of the U.S. government, the Salvadoran regime staged elections on March 28, 1982. Washington had hoped that President José Napoleón Duarte's Christian Democrats would gain a large majority, thus putting a more acceptable face on the reactionary regime. Instead, Duarte's party won only twenty-four of the sixty seats in the new Constituent Assembly, with the majority of seats going to two extreme right-wing parties.

gression against our countries?

We reiterate our policy of peace toward the United States and our proposals to Honduras. This policy and these proposals reject the offensive and arrogant language that scarcely deigns to hide its aim of blocking any understanding.

But it is this arrogance I refer to. Nicaragua, they say, has become a threat to peace in Central America. This is a situation, they say, that they don't want and will not tolerate. What do they mean by that? That they neither want nor will tolerate . . . What are they going to do to us? More than they have done to us already? We are ready to receive not only their insolent blustering, we are ready to meet with them too, so they will know what we are going to do. [*Applause*]

But what is perhaps more important than that, because it is a truth already known by heart, is that this way of speaking to us is a concrete obstacle to our efforts for conciliation and peace between Central America and the United States. Between Nicaragua and the United States. We continue to be in favor of peace and negotiations. And it seems that for the time being the prospect of a direct U.S. intervention has been defeated by our people.

We initiated a diplomatic and political campaign in the world, which culminated in the speech of our brother Daniel [Ortega] to the Security Council of the United Nations. [*Applause*] Of course, we are still in favor of peace, but peace must begin with mutual respect, and not with insolent messages that injure our dignity. Although we have told you that apparently that prospect has been defeated, does this mean that imperialism has given up all ideas of direct aggression against Central America and Nicaragua? It does not mean this. It means that they have given up, for the moment, perhaps, on direct aggression. But we would be naïve dreamers, we would be stupid if we believed that imperialism had already given up on wiping out our revolution. Maybe for the time being—and I repeat, for the time being—imperialism considers direct aggression impossible, but it has not renounced aggression. What new forms is it using and will it use in the immediate future to attack us?

It is trying to develop even further the tactics of destabilization used against our revolution. Internal corrosion within the vanguard is one objective. It wants to sow mistrust and internal violence inside Nicaragua. To give priority to the technical capacity and firepower of the counterrevolutionary bands, especially in the northern areas of the country. They propose to increase sabotage, assassination attempts, and other forms of terrorism. They will try to disorient the people, encouraging ideological confusion, manipulating the religious feelings of the Nicaraguan people, and exploiting the consequences of our economic difficulties. They will try to bring together all the representatives of counterrevolution and all elements who, in one way or another, have come into conflict with the working class and the revolutionary process.

All this explains why imperialism has used delaying tactics in negotiating with Nicaragua.

It is a kind of invasion using another type of soldier—the soldier of disorientation, the soldier of slander, the soldier of ideological confusion—with weapons as dangerous, and maybe more dangerous, than the members of the counterrevolutionary bands. It has been said in counterrevolutionary circles and in circles of the right-wing parties, many of whose supporters have left the country, that a government junta-in-exile will be set up, which, if it turns out to be true, would no doubt be a junta of betrayal. We shall announce the names of the members of this proposed junta, knowing well that some of them may not even have been consulted but will surely have to define their position on this matter.

The proposed junta, approved by imperialism and called the "Supreme Directorate," would be made up of the following: Alfonso Robelo, Edén Pastora, Monseñor Miguel Obando, Steadman Fagoth, Enrique Bolaños, Adolfo Calero Portocarrero, Col. Guillermo Mendieta, Col. Enrique Bermúdez, José Francisco Cardenal, Fernando Agüero, and Fernando Chamorro Rapaccioli. [*Hoots*] It is said that very soon this Supreme Directorate will announce its existence publicly, once the *somocista* bands have occupied at least a small portion of our national territory, and that it will replace the present government junta and the National Directorate of the Sandinista front. [*Chants of "They shall not pass!"*]

I believe that those who have conceived this plan are going to live and die deceived. I think that those who have conceived this plan have not been able to understand that our people, that our workers, have gained complete awareness of their historical destiny. Here, during the Spanish conquest, they deceived the Indians with little glass marbles and mirrors. Those who dream of overthrowing the revolutionary government and its political leadership have not yet realized that the time of the conquistadors has gone, and that here the only thing we will conquer will be the establishment of a new and higher society. [*Applause*] They do not know what direction we are going in. [*Chants of "Socialism! Socialism!"*] But our working people know what direction we are going in, and that is why I ask the workers and peasants of our country, what are we moving toward? [*Chants of "Socialism! Socialism!"*]

And here, near the tomb of Carlos Fonseca, we should like to speak a little with our brother and tell him . . . Carlos, listen to how your bones, your forceful and beautiful bones, march ahead under the fullness of the sun, stepping over the ruins of the old and putrefied society, knocked down by the stone fists of these men and women.

Carlos . . . the anger, the tenderness, the burning coals, the hopes belong to you. Maker of flint stones, brother, tamer of wild horses. Carlos . . . your dreams have come true! Here is your working class, our working class [*Prolonged applause*] with its calloused hands and its shining eyes. Here is your working class, standing at attention, which will be faithful to you until victory, until blood, until death. [*Prolonged applause*]

Here is your working class—comrade postman, street seller of candies and of splendors. We are the gatherers of your resurrection. We are not frightened by phantoms, we are not frightened by mummies, we are not frightened by imperialism, nor are we afraid of the Cains.

We, Carlos, beloved brother, are your thirst and we are the riverbed through which runs the mighty stream of our working class. Once we said to you, brother, "Free homeland or death!" But today we say to you, we are moving toward a new society, we are moving toward development and the consolidation of a revolutionary party, the Sandinista National Liberation Front, as the party of the workers and peasants, of the intellectuals and the Nicaraguan patriots, we are moving toward the total elimination of the exploitation of man by man, and we say to you, regarding the belief and the thoughts of our people:

Free homeland or death!

[*Ovation. Chants of "People's power! People's power!"*]

Without the people, saving Lake Managua will not be possible
by Tomás Borge

The following speech was given at the First Seminar for Saving Lake Xolotlán (Lake Managua). It was originally published in the June 5, 1982, issue of *Ventana*, a cultural supplement to *Barricada*. The translation for this volume is by Michael Taber.

Indeed, if capitalism is not interested in men themselves, how could it be interested in nature?

Capitalism sees men only as a source of labor and sees nature only as a raw material to produce merchandise; the capitalist conception of the world is that of an immense market. And all activity of this market has but one goal: accumulating profits in the capitalist's pockets. What could converting a forest into a desert matter to a timber company, provided the sale of the wood is profitable? What could poisoning a river matter to a producer of chemical products, provided the products sell well on the market? What could poisoning the rivers with cyanide matter to a mining company?

Our conception of nature is completely different. Man as

a physical being does not end where his organic body does. Without nature man is nothing; equally, nature would be worth nothing without man. Man is made for nature and, above all, nature is made for man; it is his inorganic body which completes his organic body.

Man not only lives in nature physically, he also lives with it spiritually. What is art if not nature that man appropriates under the form of beauty? What is science if not nature which man appropriates with thought?

But initially nature is not man's nature. In order for nature to be his inorganic body, man must transform it; he must humanize it. And this is a process that has lasted for centuries, for all of human history. In this respect, the characteristic of capitalism is that it utilizes humanity's discoveries to dehumanize nature, and even to make it inhuman.

How could man feel himself part of nature while breathing smog in the great urban centers?

How could man feel himself completed by a nature that is converted into biochemical weapons and neutron bombs?

There are those who orient their philosophy, their science, their political will, and their practice to destroying nature, even to destroying man, and they become violently ill when men decide to save nature and man.

For us, all this work of capitalist destruction of nature is summed up in the current state of Lake Managua. The importance of this lake strikes you at once: on the one hand, we have its indisputable strategic situation: a zone where, if I'm not mistaken, almost 24 percent of the country's total population and some 40 percent of the urban population is situated; a region where the largest productive investments, the greatest amount of infrastructure, and the country's highest-quality soil are found.

On the other hand, nature could not have been more generous in bestowing on us the immense beneficial potential which our lakes represent, and in particular what Lake Managua provides us: drinkable water, fish, irrigation for this soil which we've recognized as the country's best, energy for a population which has the country's greatest demand for it, and finally, recreation, tourism, and beauty.

What did *somocismo* do with this lake? That is to say, what did imperialism and its local agents do during the forty-some years that the *somocista* dictatorship functioned as the instrument of its domination in Nicaragua?

Obviously, natural problems do exist. These are essentially the process of salinization and the lack of significant drainage that aggravates this process. The creation of drainage, which would permit us to take advantage of the energy and irrigation potential of Lake Xolotlán [Lake Managua], is the most arduous task raised for us by nature.

Of course, this problem did not exist for *somocismo*, for imperialism and its lackeys. What interests them are easy and fast profits, and for the local, second-rate capitalism these fast profits became an urgency—the urgency of the overseer of the crumbs and leftovers of the satisfied boss. How then could *somocismo* be interested in a long-term plan in which collective interest came before private interest?

That then, is the natural problem. But this problem becomes an artificial, man-made problem when we take into account the effects that capitalist activity in the lake's basin had on the problem. You, as engineers, agronomists, geologists, and specialists in the various branches of production and science, have already examined in detail the diverse elements of the problem. We will limit ourselves to focusing on the more general aspects, pointing out the revolutionary approach to it.

In the first place, we should focus on the effects on the strip of land surrounding the lake, brought about by the type of agriculture imposed on us by the imperialist requirements of the world market. The intensification of the cultivation of coffee, sugar, and above all cotton, signified the progressive loss of the natural soil layer, especially beginning with the 1950s. We should not forget that coffee, sugar, and cotton are imported crops, foreign to our soil, so that capitalist intensification of these crops simply develops a process of destroying our natural ecological system that drags it further back. The consequence of this is the running off of sediments into the lake.

But, in addition, technological dependency imposed on the country the importation of costly products, of pesticide substances that don't decompose for a long time and which drain off into the lake with the sediments.

Later, during the 1960s, when an attempt was made to carry out the program of substituting imports, those factories appeared which, in accord with capitalist logic, began to fill the lake with untreated toxic industrial wastes.

And to complement capitalist anarchy of production—that egoistic anarchy for which no collective interest existed—we found ourselves with a state in power that gaily resolved the problem of polluted water, which drained off into the lake an enormous volume of organic matter, whose decomposition absorbs oxygen, in addition to entailing bacteriological contamination. A state that, finally, showed "its interest" in public welfare by converting the beaches of our people's lake into a beautiful garbage dump.

The general result is that the natural problem of saving the lake, a problem projected more or less as a long-term one, becomes an immediate, urgent problem for us.

What happens to collective wealth doesn't matter very much to the capitalist, who amassed his profits from the sweat of the collectivity in his factories and cotton plantations. It doesn't matter very much to the capitalist that 250 fishing families live from the contaminated fish of Lake Xolotlán. It doesn't matter very much to the capitalist—who could go enjoy the wealth resulting from this ecocide on the beaches of Miami—that the poor people of Managua are deprived of the recreation and beauty that nature bestowed on them with Xolotlán. It's interesting to note, in passing, how at the same time that the rich fled toward the highway to Masaya and south, the Managua poor clung to the coasts of this filthy lake as to debris from a shipwreck.

To our third-rate capitalists, not only did this not matter to them in the slightest, but they even came to actively oppose the possibility of halting this process of destroying our lake. Some conscious intellectuals raised the need for biological control, which would substitute for the agricultural use of pesticide contaminants of the lake. Then, the representatives of the firms producing these pesticides, together with the *somocista* agricultural minister, united in a holy crusade which, of course, had to be crowned with the trophy of an increasingly sick ecosystem.

But imperialism did not have time to complete here that ecocide which other parts of the world can brag about. Capitalism in Europe, its cradle, has had sufficient time to completely contaminate the Rhine, the Danube, the great rivers that the poets, musicians, and ancient chronicles accustomed us to admire.

In the United States, where to a greater extent than anywhere else, *"time is money,"* capitalism has carried out in a few years the job of ecocide for which the Europeans needed centuries; for example with Lake Erie. In other places, capitalism has even had time to complement ecocide with genocide. No one is unaware, for example of the cases of those manufacturing companies of lye and chlorine, who contaminated seas in Japan and Sweden, provoking the poisoning and death of populations that consumed fish from its waters.

In the discussions you've had, you will have recalled the case of one of those multinational companies, Penwalt, whose lye and chlorine factory in a span of some ten years dumped a quantity of mercury into our lake calculated at some forty tons. But all these tons of industrial waste, all that sedimentation contained in pesticides, all the polluted water that *somocismo* dumped for more than forty years (significantly, the conversion of our lake into a sewer is Somoza's work), all the filtrations that are derived from the garbage piled up on the beach, all this did not achieve the destruction of our lake, although clearly, Somoza wanted to convert the lake—and all Nicaragua—into a sewer. And Nicaragua, as well as the lake, is ill from that heritage.

We inherit a sick lake, but not mortally sick. This makes the task of saving it less arduous. But at the same time, the ecological destructive work of imperialism and its local partners contributed enormously to aggravating the natural problem of salinization and lack of drainage.

These are the general terms of the problem. The terms that should be taken into account in being able to raise it correctly, that is to say, to be able to resolve it. Let us now examine the plans, the steps for the solution, which you have been discussing in this seminar.

Before everything, it's evident that the first step has been taken with the revolution itself. Our general problem is the problem of underdevelopment, and in acquiring political power we have conquered the possibility of resolving it, a possibility that was completely cut off under the conditions of imperialist domination. In particular, with this political power we have similarly conquered the possibility of saving our lake.

Whichever plan is definitively chosen to save the lake must be rooted in the perspective of the wealth of the collective interests. It must be a profitable plan economically, although not economist. It must look at all the beneficial potentials: to fish, energy, irrigation, without leaving anything behind. It must finally look at recreation, at our people's aesthetic enjoyment, without falling into aestheticism, without being antieconomical. Finally, it must look at the limited resources we have at our disposal, as well as the possible methods of financing from abroad.

The second step for solving this problem is that which our government has begun to take together with you in organizing and holding this seminar. This step looks toward creating consciousness of the problem, toward the discussion and investigation that should be devoted to the plan which most meets and coordinates the previously mentioned requirements. It looks toward proposing the most suitable methods and instruments to carry them out.

In the first place, it's evident that in the short term we must proceed to the tasks of halting the contamination process. We must proceed to reforestation; we must modify the system of polluted water, preventing it from winding up in the lake. We must push forward biological pest control that *somocismo* boycotted in its time. We must legislatively regulate the treatment of industrial wastes (the engineer Rappaccioli has promised to present this legislation preventing the dumping of industrial wastes into the lake when the Momotombo geothermic plant begins to function). Finally, we must regulate the system of agricultural exploitation in the river's basin.

Secondly, in the medium-term level, it's indisputable that the definitive plan must consider the renewal of the lake with massive amounts of water from elsewhere. The plan most structured in this respect is that of developing a system of transferring the water of Cocibolca to Lake Xolotlán (whether through floodgates, which would imply expenditures of energy through pumping, or through the method of moving vessels that utilize the force of gravity). However, the possibility also exists of bringing this massive amount of water from another area, for example Matagalpa River, as one of the participants here has maintained. The indisputable thing in any case, is to bring the water. In addition, whatever system is chosen must permit the multiple use of the water, and must not break up any ecological system.

Thirdly, this imposes the need to create an interinstitutional committee which jointly represents the interests of the different institutions: irrigation, energy, fish, recreation; a committee which is given responsibility for coordinating all the efforts related to the lakes, including actions of investigation, planning, formulating plans, carrying them out, and administering them. A committee with sufficient authority to undertake the immediate task of halting the contamination, given the responsibility of stabilizing the dumping of the sediments, of legislating the use of land, of industrial treatment, of investigating the appropriate technology and preventing foreign dependence; a committee which is responsible for leading the efforts which concern each particular institution, for example, the treatment of polluted water; a committee that brings pressure to bear on these institutions to formulate concrete plans before international bodies that are in a position to give aid.

Now then, none of these steps—like all those that our revolution is taking, like the enormous step that our very revolution signifies—can be taken firmly without the foundation of the people's participation. I think that you all agree with this. The Sandinista people's revolution is no more than our people in action, and without the people's participation, all our efforts run the risk of losing the social content that makes these efforts truly revolutionary.

Therefore, all the plans and schemes must be translated into the language of the people, explained to the people. The people must understand that it is their interests that are in jeopardy, and that satisfying these interests is not going to fall from the sky, but rather must be an effort in which they figure as the principal protagonist. Without the people as the principal protagonist, our revolution would not have been possible, and without this role of the people, saving the lake will also not be possible.

This means that the people, besides listening to the explanations of the technicians, must at the same time add their own experiences. We must make the plans come alive, bringing those involved into the discussion. We must submit these plans, for example, to the criticism of the 250 fishing families, who make up the small village of San Francisco del Carnicero and other communities. Above all, we must submit these plans for discussion by the people of Managua themselves.

It's evident that the CDSs [Sandinista Defense Committees] and other people's organizations have a decisive role to fulfill as broadcasters of the problem and as transmitters of the concerns from the grass roots to the higher levels. It's also their role to think of other mechanisms, for example, referenda that stimulate and speed up this participation by the people, without which it will be impossible to carry out the revolutionary plan.

Compañeros: our revolution was nurtured in the mountains; that was our first ally in the struggle against *somocismo*. The nature that imperialism destroyed in the city is the same nature that got its revenge in the mountains by hiding us revolutionaries, by erasing our tracks, by resisting the felling of trees and the fires, and by becoming impenetrable to the enemy's bombardment. In the mountains the children of Sandino contracted a pact with nature. Now we want to fulfill our part.

The dictatorship that imperialism imposed on us was not sufficient to break the ties that exist between us and nature. It didn't have time to form those great urban centers, where nature can barely be recognized in some sickly trees, or that grows in the parks like animals in a zoo. But it was in the mountains where we learned that imperialism, destroyer of human lives, finds its necessary complement in imperialism, destroyer of nature.

The imperialists will ask once more how it is possible during this time of emergency for us to be able to hold seminars such as this. They will also have asked how in the mountains, between battles, and how in the jails, between tortures, we could have found time to write poems and songs to our fallen compañeros, to our mothers, our children, our women. They cannot understand any of this. None of this fits within the logic of the merchants.

For us, it's enough to understand ourselves; we know where we come from. We come from the dreams of all who loved humanity because they loved nature, and who loved nature because they loved humanity. We come from the dreams of Sandino and Carlos Fonseca. And we know where we are going. We are going toward that society where, like St. Francis, we will be able to call the sun "brother sun," to call the moon "brother moon," to call the star "brother star," and to call man "brother man."

We are going toward the society where Lake Xolotlán will not be that legend of silver, as the song says, but a transparent reality, where the blue sky will be reflected in the green of the most beautiful orchard of Central America, and above whose banks full of the laughter of our children, Momotombo will raise its vigilant head of "father of fire and stone."

Somocismo murdered tens of thousands of Nicaraguans; it wanted to murder Lake Xolotlán. But Somoza could not kill the people as he could not kill the lake.

We Nicaraguan revolutionaries would be irresponsible and clumsy if we permitted our lake to be converted into a dead lake; even more, I believe we would cease being revolutionaries if we did not save the lake. Saving the lake and converting it into an agent of production, irrigation, energy, and beauty.

Women and the Nicaraguan revolution
by Tomás Borge

The following speech was given September 29, 1982, at a rally in León commemorating the fifth anniversary of the Nicaraguan women's movement. More than 2,000 women and men attended the rally, and thousands more who were unable to enter stood outside. As the first major speech by a leader of the Nicaraguan revolutionary government specifically on the question of the status of women, it was broadcast live on national radio and printed in *Barricada*. This translation originally appeared in the November 1, 1982, issue of *Intercontinental Press*.

TOMÁS BORGE: How do you feel? Is it too hot in here?

AMNLAE WOMEN AND GENERAL PUBLIC: No!

BORGE: You're not bothered by the crowded room and by the heat?

AMNLAE WOMEN: No! National Directorate, we await your order!

BORGE: With all the heat and revolutionary enthusiasm of Nicaraguan women, it's imperialism that should be worried.

[*Applause and slogans*] Because in the hearts of Nicaraguan women there's more than heat—there's fire! [*Applause and slogans*] I believe that first we should greet the invited compañeras—the compañera representing Venezuela, Minister of Women's Affairs Mercedes Pulido; the compañera representing Cuba, the general secretary of the Federation of Cuban Women, Dora Carcaño; a group of women representing Chile, Guatemala, and the Dominican Republic; and the ambassador of our sister republic of Bulgaria. [*Applause and slogans*]

Dear compañeras, in the world today, profound changes are taking place. New offspring of history are being born in the midst of grief, anguish, and heroic splendor. Social revolution is the order of the day in Africa, Asia, and Latin America. Central America is being rocked with social earthquakes. Poor people of all latitudes are demanding—each time more vigorously—profound transformations in the old and rotting structures of class exploitation and imperialist domination.

And in Nicaragua, land of volcanoes and wildcats, we are winning national liberation through the Sandinista revolution.

Therefore it's normal, absolutely logical that we now speak of a new revolution—that is, a revolution of women [*Applause*], a revolution that will complete the process of national liberation.

Many of those women who participate in this revolution live far away from here. Thousands of compañeras couldn't get into this room.

We don't want to make a criticism of anyone, but it seems there was an underestimation of the capacity for struggle and the revolutionary enthusiasm of the masses.

The revolutionary masses have fresh enthusiasm. We couldn't program the presence of 2,000 women here, because something like that cannot be decreed. In fact, thousands of women came who unfortunately could not enter this room.

Let this experience teach us to have more confidence in the masses! [*Applause*] And above all to understand that our sisters are full of revolutionary spirit and patriotic enthusiasm. [*Applause*]

We would like to extend a special greeting to the compañera representing the fraternal people of El Salvador, compañera Ana María.

[*AMNLAE women shout: "Revolution or death, El Salvador will win!"*]

At the head of our revolution, I think it would be correct to say, are the mothers of our martyrs, these dear old women who we have here in front of our eyes. [*Applause*]

Inside the revolution, we must understand what should be the position in the social organism of women who forged with their blood the Nicaraguan people. Now it's a question of bringing together the mechanisms that will unleash all the energies and capacities of women so that they become full members of the new society with full rights.

The woman question is nothing more than an aspect of social reality in its totality. The definitive answer to the liberation of women can emerge only with the total resolution of the class contradictions, of the social diseases that originate in a society like ours—politically liberated but with the rope of economic dependence still around our neck.

Nevertheless, we must have patience to deal with the woman question in an independent and concrete manner.

We have to talk about what the position of women was before and after the revolutionary victory, and what the position of women will be in the beautiful future we are going to build. We must also—however briefly—talk about women in the context of the historical development of humanity.

If we read ancient books, we come to know how great the painful discrimination of women has been. In slave society, as in feudal and capitalist society, the working classes were exploited and oppressed.

Women—all women in general—were oppressed, but working women were oppressed as workers and as women.

The workers became fully conscious that they were victims of exploitation. Women, too, became conscious of their exploitation as workers but it was a much slower, more complicated process that led them to realize their degree of oppression as women.

Woman was the first enslaved human being on earth. Even before the state of slavery existed, women were slaves.

As you know, dependence and social oppression is based on the economic dependency of the oppressed with respect to the oppressor. Woman was economically dependent on man even before class exploitation arose.

Given this reality, some muddleheaded ideologues have advanced the philistine sexual philosophy that woman is a dependent being by nature. These ideologues resemble—as two drops of water resemble each other—those who hold the thesis that the difference between rich and poor always existed and always will because it falls in the natural order of things.

Experience, however, demonstrated that relations between the sexes are transformed, like relations between classes, in the process of transforming the means of production and the means of distribution of that which is produced.

Naturally—and this confirms the relationship between sex and the economy in the context of social development, which we don't have time to elaborate on right now—there were epochs when the woman fulfilled the principal role inside the family, under what was called the matriarchy.

But what's important here and what we want to emphasize is that what has predominated is the dominance and the oppression of man over woman.

In ancient times, women completely lacked rights, and today in many places lack rights, and still in Nicaragua women have not won—not even remotely—all their rights. Women were bought for their property just as you buy an object.

Other things were imposed on women, such as strict chastity and a barbaric prohibition of sexual pleasure, while men had the right to live in the same house with several women.

If on their wedding night the man believed or simply suspected that the woman had previously lost her virginity, he had the right not only to repudiate her, but also to kill her. In the past—this was in the past. I should add, although it seems ridiculous, that there still are those who think they have the right to repudiate a woman for these reasons—today, in the present epoch.

According to the fifth book of Moses in the Bible, a man had the right to repudiate a woman he had recently married even if it was just because she caused him displeasure.

In some societies women were destined to take on the heaviest tasks, treated virtually like draft animals—sometimes with less consideration than a house pet.

Within the family, the birth of a girl was considered a reason for mourning while the birth of a boy was cause for rejoicing and celebrating.

In the Middle Ages there was a certain fashion of romanticism and chivalry toward women, riddled with discrimination as brutal as the use of a chastity belt. Wandering gentlemen left their women in chastity belts and put them in convents for reasons of family honor and many times for economic reasons.

Capitalist society came, under the banner of "equality and brotherhood," to reinforce discrimination against women, fundamentally in the economic arena. The possibility opened, in this stage of development, for women's participation in productive work. The bourgeoisie was interested in enlarging the labor market, so as to have a larger army of unemployed and less pressure for higher wages.

This explains the presence of women in the textile centers, where they began to be exploited as workers and as cheaper manual labor than men.

In modern capitalist society, even when women participate or are allowed to participate in production, there are still strong reminders of the brutal discrimination women suffered in former societies.

Doesn't it really amount to selling a woman, when she marries a rich man without feelings playing any role? What is the act of a landowner or a bourgeois capitalist when he takes a woman worker who is under his domination, under circumstances of nothing more than self-centered and brutal impulse to possess her, followed immediately by repudiation and repugnance? Isn't a fruit of this inheritance also the masculine pretension that still remains in our underdeveloped countries—countries that have inherited the values of feudal Spain—for the insistence on a woman's virginity at the time of marriage?

The very existence of prostitution—a fact that covers the great cities of the capitalist world—is a direct result of economic discrimination against women, who, to survive and feed their children, are forced to sell their bodies as if they were merchandise.

Today, in the hypocritical world of the bourgeoisie, where the cruel and insulting luxury of the rich exists side by side with the misery, hunger, and nakedness of the dispossessed, women don't just occupy, as I said, a totally secondary place; they are also the object of the most offensive and humiliating exhibitions. They are placed in shop windows so the client can choose which one pleases him the most, as if they were suits of clothes, bottles of whiskey, or slices of ham.

In capitalist society, therefore, bourgeois man gives thanks to the gods, just as the Greek philosopher Plato did, for not having been born a woman, although he also surely thanks

God for his ability to insult, sell, exploit, or buy women.

Our people suffered colonial and semicolonial slavery. Slavery gave rise to heroic campaigns of combat in which women not only shared the general suffering of the people and their struggles, but also had to take on the difficult tasks of family reproduction and the constant anguish of knowing that the lives of their children were threatened under the terror of tyranny.

Before the revolutionary triumph, the incorporation of women in productive work was minimal. The great majority of women were condemned to slavery in the home. When women could sell their labor power, in addition to fulfilling their obligations on the job, they had to fulfill their duties in the home to assure the upbringing of their children. All of this in a regime of political oppression and misery imposed by a dependent capitalist society. And subjected, on the other hand, to exploitation by man—the males of the species—who placed on the woman's shoulders the fundamental weight of household chores, thereby endlessly prolonging her working day.

Did this end with the triumph of the Sandinista people's revolution, we ask ourselves?

The triumph of the Sandinista people's revolution eliminated the terror and opened the way for the process of national liberation, initiating at the same time economic and social transformations that represented a qualitative advance in the conquest of freedom and development.

It can't be said, therefore, that the situation of women in Nicaragua has in no way changed.

The entire society seized its future and women gained the right, taking into account their varied and even spectacular participation in the revolutionary struggle, to participate in an active manner in the process of national transformation.

Nevertheless, all of us have to honestly admit that we haven't confronted the struggle for women's liberation with the same courage and decisiveness.

Independently of the fact that women, in this stage, continue to bear the main responsibility for reproduction and the care of children, the burden of housework and discrimination still relentlessly weighs down upon them.

From the point of view of daily exertion, women remain fundamentally in the same conditions as in the past.

Of course, behind this objective reality is an economic basis. Workers' living conditions continue to be difficult and incompatible with the political will of the revolution. For reasons that are well-known to you and because barely three years have passed [since the revolution], it has not been possible to meet the legitimate expectations for improvement in workers' general living conditions.

This explains why many times women are still compelled to do work that pays no wages, that is not taken account of anywhere, that is not credited toward social security.

Independently of the fact that women often receive the help of men, the truth is that the customs and level of development of our society impose this superexploitation on women. And it is in this sense that women are not only exploited—they're superexploited. They are exploited in their workplaces, if they work. They are exploited by lower wages and exploited in the home. That is, they are triply exploited.

What can be done to eliminate this dramatic plight of women?

There is no other alternative except to change the basic economic structure of society. There is no alternative but to develop an economy that guarantees the satisfaction of the fundamental needs of our people. There is no alternative but to create a productive apparatus whose rationale is not individual profit, but rather satisfaction of the demands of the entire society, the demands of the workers—whose rationale is to reaffirm and emphasize the potential of man and woman to live together socially as human beings.

This process of change, compañeras, is complicated, difficult, and will take place over time. But are we going to wait until economic development and social transformation have reached their culmination before we begin to think out the woman question? This would certainly be an inconsistency.

But how can we begin to conceive of women's liberation right now with all the existing limitations?

We took, as we said, the first step, which was national liberation. Now we must take concrete steps to legally guarantee in daily practice full equality between the sexes. [*Applause*]

Men and women had the right and the duty to fight—to participate in the revolutionary struggle. Women played an outstanding role in the guerrilla struggle, in the clandestine struggle, in self-denial, in sacrifice, and in dedication.

It's no accident that here in León the leaders of the military detachments were women [*Applause*]—among this constellation of women leaders, Dora María Téllez, Vicky Herrera, María Lourdes Jirón, and Ana Isabel Morales are distinguished, among others.

In other parts of the country there were compañeras whose work stood out, even above that of many men—like Mónica Baltodano, Doris Tijerino, Gladys Báez, Olga Avilés, and Eleonora Rocha. [*Applause*] Women who have certainly continued to distinguish themselves in revolutionary activity.

Right here, on the very soil of León, Luisa Amanda Espinoza shed her blood, and the last guerrilla song of Arlen Siu was heard.

In addition, it was right here that the internationalism of the Mexican compañera Aracelly Pérez ended with the sacrifice of her life alongside the Nicaraguan Idania Fernández. [*Applause*]

Somewhere in the mountains was stilled the heart of Claudia Chamorro, who had yearned for a child up until the final moment. And today the revolution has made her dreams a reality in the Claudia Chamorro Child Development Center. Claudia Chamorro now has 150 children there—many times more than the child she was not able to bear. [*Applause*]

Women, because of their courage and consciousness, have reclaimed and continue to reclaim their role in Nicaraguan history. Women make up 22 percent of the FSLN. Of all the positions of political leadership in the FSLN, in the regions and provinces, women hold 37 percent. In intermediary leadership positions and the supporting apparatuses, the figure is 24.6 percent. In the Ministry of the Interior, nearly 21 percent of those who work with us are women. [*Applause*]

At the governmental leadership level, there are a range of compañeras with high level responsibilities, like Commander Mónica Baltodano and [Minister of Health] Lea Guido. Four compañeras are vice-ministers. Women are also represented in the Supreme Court and in the Council of State.

However, of the fifty-one representatives in the Council of State only seven are women, and women have more right to be represented in the Council of State than simply by the seven they have there. [*Applause*] This situation is perhaps a reflection of an insufficient participation in the mass organizations present in that body, represented in the Council of State.

On the level of political leadership, there can be no doubt about the creative participation of compañeras like Dora María Téllez, Vicky Herrera, and Gladys Monterrey [AMNLAE's general secretary], among others.

Today, you learned through the newspapers of the naming of compañera Lea Guido as president of the Pan-American Health Organization. Compañera Lea is the first woman to be named president of this institution in its eighty years of existence. We understand that this was done by acclamation, which is an acknowledgment of the important participation of women in our revolutionary process.

In spite of all this—in spite of all the cases mentioned, right now women are not yet massively incorporated into the governmental and political tasks of the revolution.

Let us take a look at a few facts concerning Nicaraguan women. Women workers constitute 40.5 percent of the work force in the country. This means that 183,448 women work outside the home. At first glance, this seems like a very high proportion and could bring us to the conclusion that women's participation in production is very significant. Yet, if we analyze the type of work women carry out, we see that a high percentage of these women are really underemployed, and that another large layer is employed in domestic service—work that is not productive and that will have to be regulated and limited in the future.

What reflects the difficult situation of women is that 83 percent of women who work also carry on their shoulders the weight of economically maintaining their household, raising the children, and doing the household chores. Eighty-three percent—that's barbaric! [*Applause*]

This indicates to us—in a certain sense—a high degree of family instability and the carefree attitude of irresponsibility many men assume toward a couple's relationship, to say nothing of toward the children. We are all, men and women alike, obliged to be responsible in our love relationships and to be responsible in our family obligations.

The law Glenda [Monterrey] referred to, the Law on Nurture,* states that men who father children have to pay

---

* The draft of a law, under discussion in the mass organizations at the time, stipulating parental (including divorced, separated, and unmarried fathers) responsibility toward children, as well as children's responsibility toward their parents. Nurture, a social concept in the draft law, includes not just food but also education, shelter, and clothing. The law was adopted by the Council of State but never approved by the government junta.

their children's upkeep. This is what the Law on Nurture is about! [*Applause*] As we once said to the women—referring, however, to the men—he who wants to go to heaven will have to pay for it! [*Shouts, laughter, applause*]

As for those men who do not comply with the Law on Nurture—the Sandinista front and the National Directorate will respond in full force, and the Ministry of the Interior is right here to take the necessary measures. [*Applause*]

I see that the men aren't applauding with much enthusiasm [*Laughter*] and some aren't even applauding [*More laughter*] and over there I see some who look downright worried. [*The audience shouts, "National Directorate, we await your order!"*] And concerning this there will be no exceptions, no matter who is involved. [*Ovation*]

How can we fail to seriously consider the equality of women if we are to be elementally just to their struggle, their sacrifice, and their heroism? How can we not guarantee their participation in social life, in work, and in the political leadership of the country? How can we not guarantee that a woman can be both a mother and a worker, both a mother and a student, both a mother and an artist, both a mother and a political leader, both fulfill all tasks the revolution demands of her and at the same time fulfill the beautiful work of a self-sacrificing, capable, and loving mother?

A concrete answer to these questions will be possible only to the extent that the individual tasks of women are socialized. It is society that has to provide the necessary day-care centers, laundries, people's restaurants, and other services that will, in effect, free women from household work. This is not easy.

So far, the revolution has only been able to build twenty child-care centers—obviously an insufficient number. The problem is that the cost of construction, equipment, and maintenance is very high. With all the economic difficulties that are holding our country back, it's impossible for us to move forward to the massive creation of these centers. And yet we must do it—not only to enable women to dedicate themselves to productive, social, and cultural tasks, but also to assure that the overall education of our children is as rich as possible.

How can we do it? How can we overcome this contradiction between the possible and the necessary?

We must look for audacious answers, I believe—answers based not so much on purely budgetary considerations but on the initiative, organization, and strength of the masses. Here AMNLAE should be the leading force and catalyst of these initiatives, fundamentally in coordination with the CDSs. [*Applause and slogans*]

This is possible in a revolutionary society. There is no task that wouldn't be possible for the revolutionary masses and there is no task that wouldn't be possible for Nicaraguan women. [*Applause*]

However difficult a task may be, the challenges that are being put forward now can hardly be compared with what Nicaraguan women faced and conquered in the past when they were capable of participating in the trenches with rifles in hand.

On the other hand, the revolution must guarantee equal pay for men and women and at the same time open the doors of production to women's participation in new fields of development—in industry as well as in agriculture.

We have already taken the first steps to guarantee this equal participation. To assure the effectiveness of the principle, "equal pay for equal work," we enacted decrees 573 and 583 for the rural sector. These decrees for the first time establish norms governing agricultural labor in coffee and cotton, and provided that everyone above fourteen years of age, man or woman, will be paid directly. Because before the victory, only the head of the household received the wages for the family—the young ones and women were not treated as real workers.

But the important thing is that we watch over the execution of laws the revolution has created to guarantee equality between men and women.

That's why we are going to enthusiastically support AMNLAE's creation of a legal-aid office. We were talking with Doris [Tijerino] a moment ago about the possibility of giving them a lawyer who is a very important cadre in the Ministry of the Interior. If the AMNLAE compañeras accept him, we will gladly offer him to head up this office.

Many women will have to come to this office to lay out their problems, above all after the Law on Nurture takes effect. [*Applause*]

We are going to redouble our efforts, but to achieve all these objectives, it's essential to involve the entire society. And it's good to emphasize that this struggle will mainly benefit—who? Who will benefit the most?

[*AMNLAE women shout: "The women!"*]

The women. The men, too, but men are full of prejudice and bad habits from the past. Don't pay much attention to us! [*Applause. The women shout, "At all costs, we will fulfill our duty to the country!"*]

At whatever cost we will also fulfill our obligation to women! [*Ovation*]

Just as workers gained consciousness of the exploitation they suffered and of their vanguard role in the revolution, women must also gain full consciousness of the discrimination they are still subjected to and of their role in the revolutionary struggle. We said that women were triply exploited, which means that women should be revolutionary in three different dimensions, seeking a single objective—the total liberation of our society.

It is good to remember, however, that economic development by itself will not accomplish the liberation of women, nor will simply the organization of women be sufficient.

We have to struggle against the habits, customs, and prejudices of men and women. We have to embark upon a difficult and prolonged ideological struggle—a struggle that equally benefits men and women.

Men must overcome a multitude of prejudices. We know compañeros who are revolutionaries in the street, in their workplaces, in their militia battalions—everywhere—but they're feudal *señores*, feudal lords in the home. [*Applause. Borge points to a group of men*] Those men over there say that's exactly right. We've already started something!

These compañeros and all of us inside our homes must— we must—convert ourselves into compañeros of the women, into teachers and students of women—sharing political education with them, sharing in whatever means possible the housework [*Applause*], love and care of the children, and love and defense of the revolution. [*Applause*]

Equality between men and women shouldn't go in the direction of diminishing respect toward women. Courtesy isn't an attribute of the exploiting classes. Chivalry isn't the private property of the bourgeoisie. We should create a new courtesy and a new revolutionary chivalry—Sandinista courtesy and chivalry of man unto woman. [*Applause*]

Woman is physically weaker than man, but is as intelligent as man [*Applause*], and from the moral viewpoint—in my personal opinion—is better than man. [*Applause*] And just as it's the woman who helps us in the difficult hours, we too should offer our support and share not only the happy moments but the difficult ones as well—searching for answers at the time of the most intimate contradictions.

Nor does equality mean lack of gallantry. We have to create Sandinista gallantry [*Applause*], full of good taste, tenderness, and respect toward women; recognizing as well their undeniable merits, their courage in every test, their tenacity and heroism that was demonstrated and continues to be demonstrated in defense of the country.

How could we not raise as a symbol for new generations of Nicaraguan women the possessor of that famous smile, Brenda Rocha? [*Applause*]

The constitution of AMNLAE, which was born out of AMPRONAC [Association of Women Confronting the National Problem], is a conquest of women that could have been produced only in a revolution. It's important to remember that the Luisa Amanda Espinoza Association of Nicaraguan Women emerged from AMPRONAC in the final stage of the revolutionary armed struggle. Before this, other groups were formed that didn't succeed, for reasons connected with the development of the revolutionary movement, in attracting a great number of women.

Right now, if we consider the path traveled by AMNLAE from the moment of its founding, it's evident that the self-sacrificing activity of the compañeras has achieved quantitative advances, and in some aspects qualitative advances. With respect to the present tasks, and above all regarding the state of emergency, women's participation has noticeably increased. The work of the Committees of Mothers of Heroes and Martyrs in denouncing the enemy's crimes and plans of aggression against Nicaragua has been outstanding.

However, in the militias, for example, the presence of women varies geographically. In Managua, women are 14 percent of the militia members, but in places like León, their participation is very low. León ranks twelfth in the incorporation of women into the militia, after having been first in the revolutionary struggle in combat against the dictatorship. It's a contradiction that perhaps they will explain to me later.

The participation of women has been important in the people's health campaigns. In relation to organizational tasks, we can see a greater stability in leadership cadres, a greater coordination among the various mass organizations, and an advance in the consolidation of the provincial executive committees—and therefore in overseeing the carrying out of tasks in the provinces.

In the field of propaganda, work has advanced to the point of achieving a better definition in the propaganda directed at the rank and file—resulting in better organization.

The planning of campaigns has been more effective—for example around the Continental Meeting of Women* and the third anniversary [of the revolution]. The publication of a bulletin was a decisive step toward enriching consciousness about the woman question.

In the field of international relations, it's correct to single out AMNLAE's participation in the Continental Meeting of Women as marking a considerable advance in establishing relations with different political and women's groups worldwide.

It would be an error, however, if we considered these accomplishments satisfactory. The revolution demands that we confront with dedication the deficiencies that limit the development of AMNLAE. The links between the leadership of the association and the ranks are not sufficient. At times general lines of action are put forward without being followed by specific concrete tasks. Adequate forms and mechanisms to assure the active participation of women in the work of the association do not exist.

All this results at times in improvisation and amateurish work habits.

Of course this is not just AMNLAE's problem but a problem of all the mass organizations and forms a part of the process of development of our revolution.

But our revolutionary society has to begin from a fundamental premise—the active, conscious, and permanent

---

* An international peace conference of women leaders from sixty-seven countries, held in Managua March 24–26, 1982.

participation of each man and woman not only in aspects solely concerned with daily life but also in determining the course of our revolution.

If the masses participate in their workplaces, in their neighborhoods, in their schools, and in their organizations, then this revolution will advance toward a revolutionary society where the dignity of man will be counterposed to the alienation of man.

AMNLAE, for example, should promote the massive participation of women. Events such as the discussion in the Council of State over patria potestas [family code] legislation should serve as a source of greater discussion for women in each workplace and neighborhood. This is not to say that men should not discuss this as well, but here we are stressing that AMNLAE should, through massive campaigns, using every available means of communication, promote a discussion among women.

Are women discussing the Law on Nurture?

[*AMNLAE leader: "Yes."*]

Have you already discussed the Law on Nurture?

[*Some AMNLAE women: "Yes."*]

All of you?

[*The majority of AMNLAE women: "No!"*]

No, no—not all women. All women must discuss the Law on Nurture and laws dealing with women.

And we must take into account that analyzing this concrete problem means not only gaining knowledge of one particular aspect, such as legislation, but advancing the process of women's politicization as a whole.

If we don't do this our men and women will not be able to carry the process of liberation to its completion.

Right now AMNLAE should be more a great movement than an organization—a great movement that encourages the participation of women in the various mass organizations, in the CDSs, in the Sandinista Youth, in the ATC

[Rural Workers Association], in the CST—and that at the same time groups women together in their common bond, which is their status as women.

The central task of AMNLAE should be the integration of all women into the revolution, without distinction. It should be a broad and democratic movement that mobilizes women from the various social sectors, so as to provide a channel for their political, social, economic, and cultural demands and to integrate them as a supporting force in the tasks of the Sandinista people's revolution.

AMNLAE should become a broad propagandistic, educational, and agitational movement that encourages women to play an active role in the economic, political, and social transformations of the country.

The peasant woman, for example, is a peasant and as such has specific demands. But she is also a woman—just like the woman worker, the woman militia member, the woman who is a housewife, the woman student, the professional woman, and so forth.

Being clear on this dual role is key to the development of AMNLAE.

Another immediate task of AMNLAE, we believe, is to deepen the analysis of the status of the Nicaraguan woman, to fight to massively incorporate women in productive work, to reclaim women's right to participate more fully in production, to participate more fully in leading the government, the mass organizations, and the Sandinista National Liberation Front. [*Applause*] And to make sure that in scholarship awards, a considerable number are given to women, which in large measure is already happening.

The task of organized women should be—in our opinion—massive involvement, in many different ways, in defense of the revolution. This includes daily defense of the revolution against provocateurs who frequently spread their counterrevolutionary filth in buses, in the supermarkets, and in the streets without getting what they deserve—a dignified and energetic response. We think that women should head up this fight against provocateurs in buses, in supermarkets, and everywhere else. [*Applause*]

When we see that humble children of our people are continuing to die in defense of the country we know it can't be done any other way.

Barely two days ago in the community of Musawás, fourteen kilometers from Bonanza, there was a new confrontation in which counterrevolutionaries killed four and wounded several others.

From our side, compañero Jaime Sanders, a Sumo Indian from the Atlantic coast and a member of State Security, fell, in addition to compañeros Jesús Isidro González, Noel Cruz, and Nery Noé García Ruiz—all of whom were from Battalion 80-15 of Masaya and Monimbó.

However, we know how to defend ourselves. Since May we've dealt heavy blows to the enemy, wiping out several counterrevolutionary bands whose only reason for existence was assassination, sabotage, and terrorism.

- In Río Blanco and Bocana de Paiwás, 100 counterrevolutionaries were killed.
- In the Seven Benk region, ninety counterrevolutionaries were killed.
- In Tasbapauni, Bluefields, six were killed.
- In Punta Gorda, another six counterrevolutionaries.
- A group of four involved in the attack on San Francisco del Norte were killed.
- In Moradón, Quilalí, three counterrevolutionaries.
- In El Limón valley, four counterrevolutionaries from Honduras were killed.

And while we've been talking here, we received a message informing us that near where our four comrades were murdered, twenty more counterrevolutionaries were killed. [*Ovation and slogans*]

In this same time period, from May to September, we've captured seventy-six members of the counterrevolutionary bands, which in addition to the number killed gives us a total of 337, plus twenty—a total of 357.

Arms of various types have also been recovered, as well as radio transmitters, plastic explosives, freeze-dried food rations—items surely not bought in a supermarket in Tegucigalpa, but delivered by special agencies of the U.S. CIA. We also captured seven pounds of marijuana—which gives us an indication that these people not only carry the arms that imperialism gives them, but also its vices and defects.

Compañeras: We in the Ministry of the Interior have suffered tragic losses for accidental reasons, as you all know. We have decided to bring in a man from the west—and besides being from the west he's from Nicaragua, as he is one of the most distinguished guerrilla commanders, one of the bravest combatants we had during the six or seven years in the mountains: Guerrilla Commander David Blanco, as head of the Ministry of the Interior for this region. [*Applause. Women shout: "One single army!"*]

Compañeras: Our National Directorate salutes Nicaraguan women with profound respect and affection. We can assure you we are not going to consider anyone a revolutionary who is not ready to fight the oppression of women. [*Applause*] We would not be Sandinistas if in the new society we did not make women an essential pillar of this new society. [*Applause*] If we are revolutionaries, even if we are men, we should be with AMNLAE. [*Ovation*]

From Conchita Alday and Blanca Aráuz to Luisa Amanda Espinoza, women have blazed a path of fire and tenderness that has given life and color to this revolution. Nicaraguan women have not only given the country the fruit of their bellies but also their enthusiasm and courage—selflessly, without limitations.

A revolution with these women is a revolution that will

not be defeated by anyone—that will march invincibly into new dawns. [*Applause*]

It's important that the imperialists know, that the National Guard murderers know, that the nation's traitors know, that in Nicaragua they will be confronted not only by men but by the women as well. [*Applause*] And these women! Women that leave the fragrance of flowers for the fragrance of gunpowder—women who are as fertile in their wombs as they are in revolutionary consciousness.

Imperialists and members of the bourgeoisie: you will have to confront this sweet rampart of granite. [*Applause*]

Bourgeoisie and traitors: Here are our women, sisters of Arlen and Claudia and Luisa Amanda, [*Applause and slogans*] here are the sisters of Luisa Amanda standing up in tenderness and heroism, with their hands caressing the delicate skin of their children, with their eyes open and watching, with their fingers on the triggers of their guns and on their lips the war cry of the men and women of this land. Let the Yankee imperialists hear this cry in all its magnitude—this cry that the bourgeoisie should listen to as well—the cry of "Free homeland . . ."

[*The people shout: ". . . or death!"*]
[*Ovation and slogans*]

Letter to leaders of the Sandinista Defense Committees

by Bayardo Arce

The following is an October 7, 1982, letter from the National Directorate of the FSLN to the municipal, village, neighborhood, and block committees of the Sandinista Defense Committees (CDS). Following the revolution, these committees, which grew out of neighborhood military and defense squads formed during the struggle against Somoza, took on new responsibilities. By the time this letter was written they had grown to nearly half a million members.

The biggest mass organizations in Nicaragua, the CDSs include both Sandinistas and non-Sandinistas, and involve community members in making decisions on a local level. They help enforce regulations against profiteering and hoarding, assist with health care campaigns, and aid in food distribution. During the period of this letter the CDSs had begun to organize regular night watch to warn and protect against counterrevolutionary sabotage. This translation originally appeared in the December 27, 1982, issue of *Intercontinental Press*.

The FSLN National Directorate sends greetings to the 459,750 CDS members throughout the country, who on a daily basis are strengthening the defense and preserving the gains of our people by carrying out their tasks. That is precisely why we want to repeat to you the concepts outlined by your national coordinator, Commander Leticia Herrera, and by Sergio Ramírez, at the commemoration of the CDS's fourth anniversary.

We affirm that the entire CDS membership, fully involved in their tasks and continually working to become more responsible, contribute decisively to the way in which the Sandinista people's revolution confronts the difficulties inherited from the past. The same holds true in regard to the problems brought in by the war policies that have sought to strangle our aspirations to be respected, sovereign, and independent.

We firmly believe that the CDS leadership and membership must express qualities that can be measured by:
- participation in defense activities;
- respect for the revolution's laws;
- discipline and respect in carrying out the directions of their immediate superiors; and
- Willingness to be the best servants of the people, avoiding and combating opportunism, bureaucratism, favoritism, and bossism.

In this framework, a concern has arisen that troubles the National Directorate. We consider it an unavoidable duty to present it to you. There are signs that many coordinators have not accurately understood the line of the revolutionary directives. Based on its persuasive character, this policy has the aim of attracting the sympathy of sectors that, because of their situation, ought to be in favor of defending the revolution.

We refer to arbitrary attitudes and actions that have effects that are contrary to Sandinista principle. For example:
- Authorization of arbitrary land or building seizures, despite the fact that all legal efforts are being made to give a plot of land to all who need and deserve it.

- Withholding the sugar distribution card from someone who has still not come to understand the revolution, instead of using the revolution's achievements to raise his or her consciousness. We know that this method is used at times to pressure people into doing CDS tasks, which are supposed to be voluntary.
- Harassment by words and deeds of citizens who profess another ideology, religious or political, or who work with persons or institutions not identified with the revolution.
- Arrogant and haughty attitudes, taking on a kind of authority that only discredits the organization; creating small elite groups; and fostering divisiveness and intrigues among neighbors in a community.
- Misusing one's position in order to transform personal problems into problems of the organization, or promoting destructive campaigns to discredit persons with whom one has conflicts.
- Falling into an abuse of authority and using a responsible post in the organization as a way to enjoy personal or family privileges. A concrete case, for example, would be to award lots to close relatives, bypassing the directives of the revolutionary state. This only encourages and puts into practice notions left over from *somocismo*.
- To tolerate or lead in abusing revolutionary vigilance [voluntary night-watch duty], especially through taking repressive measures against those who still have not joined in this task. (In some cases this has gone so far as the breaking of someone's door, or the casting of doubt on them, forgetting the fact that all CDS tasks are voluntary.)

It is absolutely necessary that we review our positions and make corrections. We have been thinking that we ought to meet in the near future to discuss these matters internally. Today, more than ever, national unity is the determining factor in defense. That is why we have put forward these ideas, upon which you will surely reflect.

Large-scale aggression is being prepared
Interview with Tomás Borge

The following interview was conducted by Peruvian journalist Ricardo Gadea, and published in the December 12, 1982, issue of the Lima daily *La República*. This translation originally appeared in the February 28, 1983, issue of *Intercontinental Press*.

RICARDO GADEA: Could the upcoming maneuvers by Honduras and the United States mark the beginning of a war against Nicaragua?

TOMÁS BORGE: For some reason they have given the maneuvers a name in the Miskito language that means "Big Pine" [*Ahuas Tara*]. They want to base the operations among the Miskito population of Northern Zelaya. People there are backward and confused, tending to take positions contrary to the revolution.

GADEA: How serious is the Miskito problem?

BORGE: We have never hidden the truth about this. Despite the efforts we have made, part of the population of Northern Zelaya remains confused. This can be explained by the backwardness of this population, their unmet expectations, the campaigns of the "September 15" radio station that broadcasts from Honduras, and the attitude of many Moravian clergymen who have turned religious questions into elements of separatist ideology.

The revolution is struggling to provide concrete responses to the problems of the Atlantic Coast. We have finished the highway that runs from the Pacific to the Atlantic. Telephone lines are being installed through tremendous sacrifices by the compañeros of Telecommunications. We are planning to bring television, health centers, and schools to the region. We also intend to expand the agrarian program between Waslala and Siuna in order to distribute thousands of hectares of land among the peasants. This will necessarily affect the largest landlords of the zone.

With such new measures we have succeeded in substantially raising the living standards of the Miskito population. But there is still much to be done.

GADEA: What factors point to the imminence of direct aggression against Nicaragua?

BORGE: All along our northern border an army of several thousand *somocista* ex–National Guardsmen is camped, trained and armed by the imperialists. They continually attack our territory with the complicity of the Honduran armed forces.

We must also note the activities of the Honduran army and the accelerating increase in its firepower, as well as its joint maneuvers with the United States, the construction of three military air bases very close to the border, the aggressive language of Honduran military leaders, and the ridiculous excuses that country's government gives for refusing to speak with Nicaraguan government leaders.

Using official figures, I can affirm that between August and October, Nicaragua suffered fifty-eight violations of its air space, thirty-seven attacks on border posts, five ambushes, four acts of sabotage, three attacks on patrols, fourteen infiltrations, and nineteen incursions. As a result of these acts of aggression originating in Honduran territory, we have suffered nearly 120 casualties, counting dead, wounded, and kidnapped.

To this escalation of foreign aggression must be added the campaign launched by the United States against Nicaragua, using religion as a pretext; the systematic aggression; the sabotaging of credits for Nicaragua; and the open U.S. fight to prevent our country's election as a member of the United Nations Security Council. In our view, all this indicates that a large-scale military aggression is being prepared.

GADEA: What form would that aggression take if it were to actually come about?

BORGE: A direct aggression is indeed being prepared, but its form remains to be seen. Perhaps the entry of all the guardsmen at one time, in a military thrust, along with the utilization of the Honduran army to provoke conflicts at other points along the border.

Perhaps they will not dare to put the Honduran army deep into our territory. That would be a stupidity.

But, all right, it is very likely that the CIA, which is frequently affected by subjectivity, has convinced itself that the Nicaraguan people are against the revolution. They could be such imbeciles as to believe that.

They are making a mistake, because here there is gut hatred against the National Guard murderers. Any foreign army that invades this country will cause the entire Nicaraguan people to rise up in struggle to defend their homeland and their revolution!

GADEA: How will the Nicaraguan people respond if the North Americans intervene directly in an invasion?

BORGE: The Yankees came here in 1926, in 1912, and in 1856. Each time they have attacked us, our people have risen up in arms. We defeated William Walker in 1856, and

Zeledón heroically confronted the U.S. Marines [in 1912]. Sandino's story is widely known: for six years he fought and defeated them. A small army, ragged and barefoot, defeated the Yankee marines!

If the U.S. Army attacks us directly, it's possible that we won't be able to beat them militarily, because their power is very great. But they will never conquer our will to resist any aggression. What would happen? They would have to kill every single Nicaraguan and rule over a cemetery!

It could be that the Yankees won't come directly—that they will try to send the armies of their Central American friends to the front lines. It seems to me that this would be a serious error. In trying to devour one dish they consider tasty they could lose the whole Central American buffet. That is what could happen!

The imperialists should think twice because we are not going to simply resign ourselves to being invaded. The peoples of Central America are not going to resign themselves to a new aggression. It's sufficient to remember what happened in Guatemala, what happened in Chile, what happened during fifty years in our own Nicaragua.

GADEA: How would an aggression affect the radicalization of the process and private enterprise?

BORGE: I don't know exactly. We think, however, that the original plans for a mixed economy and political pluralism should remain intact. If there are problems with the businessmen right now it is because they have become disoriented with respect to history.

Mixed economies in other countries that have not had revolutions are not the same as the one in Nicaragua. There are more private enterprises here, relatively speaking, than in Venezuela, for example, but here political power is not in the hands of the businessmen. The revolution wants to cooperate with them in production and economic planning.

In Nicaragua there does exist a truly mixed economy,

within the revolution. We provide the businessmen many concessions, credits, facilities, but many of them remain discontented. They will not resign themselves to losing political power!

We honestly do want them to participate in running the economy; it is a promise that we have repeated publicly many times and we insist on it again.

If a war breaks out here, the businessmen will continue to enjoy the same consideration, except for those who conspire and participate in the aggression against Nicaragua. Those who do conspire will fall under the weight of the revolutionary laws.

GADEA: What kind of new society is being built in Nicaragua? What is the dominant ideology?

BORGE: Here there is a democracy that has a popular, anti-imperialist, and internationalist character. I make this last point because I think we seek to look outward, with open arms to other countries.

We have similarities with other revolutions, and also some differences with them. In Nicaragua the predominant ideology is not one of those that are already well-known—socialist, social democratic, or social Christian. What is our ideology? We have said many times that we are Sandinistas.

What is *sandinismo*? It is the thought of Carlos Fonseca and Augusto Sandino, applied together with worldwide revolutionary experience and the concrete realities of Nicaragua.

At some point we are going to lay out our own characterizations. For now we are trying to find, through world experience and through our own experience, the best road, the one most appropriate for Nicaraguans, taking into account the interests of Central America and of Latin America as a whole.

GADEA: How does political pluralism function under these conditions?

BORGE: The FSLN and the Revolutionary Patriotic Front (FPR) are currently holding discussions with a body known as the Democratic Coordinating Committee, in which various opposition political parties are represented.

I believe that we have to have discussions on a realistic basis: the reconstruction of Nicaragua, the defense of the country, and the plans for general elections in 1985. We agree on the first two points. And we agree that there have to be elections in 1985.

The discussions with the opposition parties are taking place because we understand that it is one thing to belong to a party that is an adversary of the revolution from the ideological and political standpoint, but another thing to conspire against the revolutionary state.

Some believe or claim that we persecute the church. That is completely false. We have never persecuted the church or opposition political parties. We have persecuted conspirators who at times disguise themselves as Christians or as political activists.

GADEA: Does the state of emergency limit democratic freedoms and pluralism?

BORGE: A state of emergency does in fact exist. It has been indispensable for the revolution to have legal instruments to defend itself against the continual attacks.

It is clear that within Nicaragua the forces opposed to the process are insignificant. For this reason there is no repression here of the kind that exists in many other Latin American countries. Under no circumstances do the people suffer any repression. The Nicaraguan people have never enjoyed more democratic freedoms and rights than they do now.

This is a revolution that has never used tear gas, a revolution without executions or torture, where the police don't use clubs. Thus there will never come a moment when the people suffer the weight of repression, for a simple reason: because it is the people themselves that control it. The people are not going to repress themselves.

Now, clearly, the people in the streets, the militias, the voluntary police, the armed people in the streets, may instill terror. In whom? In the enemies of the people, those who are opposed to the changes and the transformations that favor the majority.

GADEA: How are norms for political activity and the news media to be set in order to guarantee the institutionalization of the process?

BORGE: The FSLN used to be a kind of outlawed political-military organization, and we were always suspicious of political parties—to the point of being opposed to them. For many years we were preoccupied with how to defeat Somoza and how to carry out the war. Since then, we have had to turn our attention to raising the country up from the ruins and laying the initial foundations of a revolutionary state.

Today, as political leaders of this nation, we have had to draw up regulations that establish norms for political parties and a law on the communications media. These are questions that are being discussed within the National Directorate.

We are studying the laws of other countries to help serve as points of reference and to help us find the most appropriate measures for Nicaragua. We seek to guarantee complete political pluralism and authentic freedom of expression. Obviously, not the kind peddled by the Inter-American Press Association.

GADEA: Would the FSLN be willing to hand over power to an adversary if it were to lose the 1985 elections?

BORGE: A little while ago I talked with Günter Grass, a very renowned German writer, and I told him that we could not even conceive that as a possibility. If the Nicaraguan people were to choose as their ruler a Fernando Agüero or a [Alfonso] Robelo or some such figure, I would at that moment cease to believe in history. I would become the most skeptical man in the world, to the point of ceasing to believe in humanity.

How could a people that has recovered its freedom, that did away with tyranny, want to retreat and return to the past? That is contrary to common sense!

So I can't answer that question because it is not going to happen. If Agüero or Robelo or any other figure of that ilk were to come back to Nicaragua they would be met with rocks instead of votes. We would have to give them an army for protection.

GADEA: Nevertheless, in the early period of the revolution the FSLN maintained good relations with Robelo.

BORGE: Well, it's just that some of us thought that Robelo would be able to evolve to the point of becoming a human being. Unfortunately, he is one of those who does not evolve, either ideologically or mentally.

GADEA: What about the spirit of the Nicaraguan people in the face of the threats and difficulties?

BORGE: Under the worst conditions, even if a war were to come about, the Nicaraguan, born to be happy, will be joking, laughing with joy. They are not going to see terror on the faces of our people. They are going to see happiness and love for the future.

GADEA: A message for the Peruvian people?

BORGE: I am very fond of the Peruvian people. I lived there for several months during Velasco's time. I encountered enormous affection on the part of Peruvians whom I had the privilege and the good fortune to know. I have good friends in Peru, individuals from among the people, including journalists. Some political and religious leaders I could speak of are excellent personal friends, among them Father Gustavo Gutiérrez and others whom I'm not going to mention. Peru has a special place in my heart.

The new education in the new Nicaragua
by Tomás Borge

The following speech was given February 4, 1983, in Managua, before an audience of 2,000 at the congress of the National Association of Nicaraguan Educators (ANDEN), the country's main teachers' union. The speech was broadcast on television, published in the February 7, 1983, *Barricada*, and issued as a pamphlet by ANDEN. This translation originally appeared in the March 14, 1983, issue of *Intercontinental Press*.

Since ANDEN's founding congress February 3–4, 1979, much water, blood, and sweat has flowed—a long drama, the unfurling of many triumphant flags for our people. That kind of teachers' congress and this enthusiastic celebration take place in two qualitatively different times.

In February 1979 we were just about to see the Monimbó insurrection take place. The first anniversary of the fall of compañero Camilo Ortega had just passed. Our people were entering, with cleansing violence, a brilliant place in modern history. That congress was held in the midst of repression so fierce that it seemed a hallucination, repression in which the Nicaraguan people's capacity for struggle and ability to determine their own future were put to the test.

This meeting of commemoration is taking place at a time when people's power is being consolidated, in the midst of a revolutionary situation that grips Central America and is spreading to the rest of the continent.

It is not at all unusual that teachers who yesterday fought the *somocista* dictatorship today defend the revolution they helped make, that they do not stand apart from the heroic struggle of the peoples of Central America. In February 1979 Nicaraguan teachers did not struggle, could not struggle, for a new system of education. They had to fight to create the conditions of struggle for a new education.

Right now that struggle is the order of the day. A new philosophy, a new structure, a new strategy of education constitute the most important task of this revolutionary process, a task that belongs to the entire society but whose fundamental responsibility lies with the teachers.

Of course, when we speak of the new education, we are not only referring to academic programs or to the social priorities of this great challenge. We are referring to the quest for the new man, to the transformation of man through education. We are referring to the unpostponable task of converting our people into a nation of students and teachers—that is, a country where the students learn to be teachers and the teachers learn to be students.

One of the most important challenges is to create in teachers the consciousness that they too must be students. To be capable of teaching others, the teacher must learn to be his own instructor as well.

In this universe of education, in the field of teaching, the teachers in the countryside are the ones who confront the most serious problems. Many times the rural educators do not have an adequate place to give classes or, worse, no place at all. Generally they lack housing as well. They are often separated from their families and have serious difficulties in obtaining school texts, not only for their students but also for their own pedagogical guidance. In addition to earning low wages, they have to travel some distance just to pick up their checks.

The country's economic limitations have not made it possible to undertake a special housing program for teachers. However, in our opinion, ANDEN should put forward the demand that homes be constructed beside each school, with community participation.

There is receptivity in the Ministry of Housing for such a program. It not only makes sense socially but also makes headway in a practical sense as well, given that teachers contend, and with some justification, that they can't live in the rural communities with their families because homes are lacking.

A house for rural teachers means not only an increase in their real wages, but also makes it possible for them to live as part of the community that is the object of their attention as teachers. Right now the fact is that a great number of rural teachers give classes only three or four days a week, a situation they blame on the housing shortage.

ANDEN's demand for priority to wage increases for rural teachers was just, as was the response it received in the Ministry of Education. In addition to benefiting from the general pay raise, beginning last year teachers received a bonus depending on where they are located.

This morning the National Directorate, in discussing the conditions of rural teachers in the country's most remote areas—the Atlantic Coast, north and central Zelaya provinces, and other similar regions—agreed to propose to the Junta of the Government of National Reconstruction that it study, as quickly as possible, forms of material incentives for this entire layer of teachers.

Naturally, the rural teachers also have the obligation to respond to this notable effort with more dedication and commitment to their work.

An aspect of singular importance is the need to confront teachers' empiricism, the need to seek new mechanisms to assure the continuity of their studies. Teachers should identify with the content of the new education, becoming part of a system that enables them to advance in the fields of teaching, culture, science, and particularly in the field of political education. All of this is extremely difficult and complex.

But how can teachers raise the cultural level of their students if they haven't mastered new teaching techniques; if they lack culture adequate to the level that should be imparted in their teaching? How can teachers form patriotic and revolutionary consciousness in their students if they lack the basic elements for projecting this capacity as architects or sculptors of consciousness?

How can teachers explain the politics of the revolution to their students if they have no basis on which to form an opinion, if they themselves don't know what the revolution is? How can teachers explain to their students the essence of exploitation, exploitation that has stripped part of their own hides, if they don't know how to explain exploitation conceptually? How can they create profoundly anti-imperialist consciousness if they are ignorant of the essence of imperialism?

How can they speak to their students of the perspectives of the new society if they don't know what pillars the new society must be built on? How can they involve their students in conceiving a strategy of education if they don't have the remotest idea of what the new education is?

To answer all these problems we must understand their roots. Before speaking about what the new education means, it's essential that we understand what the role of education has been in the social process. It's necessary for us to define education in the full sense in order to later place it in the context of the revolutionary process.

Education is the process through which society reproduces the ideas, values, moral and ethical principles, and behavioral habits of the successive generations. All social organization is a function of the class interests that hold state power. Education is a process of forming individuals in ideology, in a complex system of values and ideas that justifies the interests of the class that wields state power.

In primitive society there were no special educational institutions, not even a special layer of teachers. Children learned through everyday practice. Guided by adults, they assimilated customs and ethical norms inside their own primitive communities, where prizes, taboos, and imitation played a role.

In primitive society, where social classes didn't exist, there was no objective interest in ideologically ensuring the reproduction of a system where some men exploited others. The productive forces, obviously very rudimentary (arrows, stone axes, etc.), were barely able to produce what was necessary for subsistence. There they couldn't form groups based on different social classes.

But this society had its own dynamic. It began to change with the development of the means of production. This development made necessary the first great division between intellectual and manual labor. This division made possible the appearance of a ruling minority that monopolized man's incipient knowledge and a ruled majority of laborers who, in the course of a long process, were converted into slaves.

The minority not only monopolized knowledge but also the apparatus of coercion, that is, arms. A complex process of development gave rise to private property—monopoly over the means of production, land, and the most important instruments of labor.

Along with the means of material production, the ruling

class also appropriated the means of spiritual production. In other words, education was converted into a monopoly of the exploiters. The schools that arose projected the philosophical ideas of the time. Science began to take its first steps and art began to develop—all to assure the dominance of the masters over the slaves.

The slaveowners' philosophy was designed to legally and morally justify slavery. Art and culture were intended to satisfy refinement, man's natural appetite for beauty, but always with the slaveholders' interests in mind.

Courses in history usually take note of Athenian democracy, philosophical dialogues, beautiful oratory, the creation of beautiful sculpture, broad discussions of the political problems of the times, and the development of sport in the famous Olympics. Rarely, however, is it pointed out that all this was the exclusive property of the nobles.

When currents arose that contradicted the Athenian aristocracy's interests—such as the sophists, who did not recognize the existence of the gods and who attacked the basis of that aristocratic democracy—they were persecuted! Their books were burned in the agora, or public plaza.

Of course slaves, peasants, artisans, plebeians, helots, and the exploited were exiled from education. At that time, the development of the means of production didn't require workers to be specially trained, and the ruling social classes' only interest was to make use of men's physical capacity for work. Unlike what has occurred in other epochs of social development, they had no interest whatsoever in developing, for the sake of exploitation, the intellectual capacity of the exploited.

By feudal times there was growing interest on the part of the landowners in ideologically influencing the serfs under their rule. A double coercion, physical and spiritual, was exercised against workers. The use of physical force as a coercive means was accompanied by the use of the church's ideological influence to keep the peasant serfs subjected to feudal society.

Of course, the church was the educational vehicle of the times. It trained the aristocracy in the art of administering its domains. It transmitted scientific knowledge to kings and emperors, and it transmitted to the great masses of serfs the ideology of resignation, dressed up in prayers, solemn rites, and a constant pounding away at docility and promises of a better life after death.

The medieval church promised the poor a paradise after death, while helping to build them an inferno on earth. Of course, it justified the paradise of the rich in this life, while selling them, with endless indulgences, paradise after death as well.

In general, education in feudal times was monopolized by the church. It exercised control over philosophic wisdom and dominated a certain kind of science, which was really more of a fraud than anything else. To block the development of true science, already incubating in the minds of some men, the power of the Inquisition was used.

Everybody is familiar with the story of Giordano Bruno, a pioneer of science near the end of feudal times. Everyone is familiar with the practice of burning people at the stake. The scientists of the time were condemned to death, accused of being heretics or witches. The feudal epoch was a struggle of the ruling classes against scientific development and for the imposition, at all costs, of the most primitive concepts from the point of view of philosophy.

The liberal revolution, or the bourgeois revolution, gave education a new content. It pushed science and technology to levels heretofore unknown.

The industrial revolution gave birth to an important leap in the development of productive forces. Machinery became complex. Technology in the service of production became complex. Moreover, the bourgeoisie not only required the exploitation of physical labor, which acquired brutal forms during this period, but also demanded that broad layers of workers acquire skill and knowledge in the technology linked to production. So the bourgeoisie gave an important push to education, stimulating to some extent the need for workers to learn to read and write.

In the early part of the bourgeois revolution, in order to confront the tremendous backwardness imposed by feudalism, the bourgeoisie fought religion, ignorance, and superstition. In its struggle against the dogmatism of feudal ideology, it raised the banner of science. That is, economic requirements and political necessity compelled it to give general education a certain development, but always within limits that would not endanger its class interests.

But science and critical thinking have a tendency to spread, preventing the bourgeoisie from being able to control their overall scope. This enables workers to accumulate knowledge and experience that facilitate new forms of organization. When the working class acquires class consciousness and initiates its struggles to confront exploitation, the bourgeoisie acquires a reactionary character, not only in content but in form as well.

The bourgeoisie tries to manipulate science in its favor; organizing higher education in such a manner that it remains far out of workers' reach. With time, the bourgeoisie seeks to utilize religion, which had been cast aside during the struggle against feudalism, as an instrument of ideological domination.

At one and the same time it uses physical repression as well as a new level of spiritual repression, creating an ideological apparatus far more refined but hardly less brutal than that of the feudal epoch. Just like the feudal lords, the bourgeoisie uses religion as an instrument to preach conformity, resignation, and the conciliation of classes.

It is interesting to note how the bourgeoisie returns desperately to the church when its world is at the point of collapse or has collapsed, when it looks around and sees with terror and fright that the "natural order" it invented in its consciousness was only an illusion. It is interesting to see how irritated the bourgeoisie get with Jesus Christ dressed in rags, demanding that he return to wearing the shining sequins that adorned his old altars.

It is inside capitalist society that the sector of educators is developed. It is inside capitalism that they are going to acquire consciousness of their condition as wage workers and, in many cases, consciousness of being utilized as a tool of ideological domination in the educational programs of the capitalist regime.

In Nicaragua, at the time it was incorporated into the capitalist world market, at the end of the last century when massive coffee production began, the oligarchy's vehicle of ideological domination was fundamentally the church. The great masses of urban and rural workers, the so-called marginal sectors, and the great mass of the peasantry were denied access to education at any level.

This paved the way for an almost bloodcurdling illiteracy in our country. It was the rich coffee growers and landlords, the political sectors that controlled the government, and the rich merchants who sent their sons to the national and foreign universities.

There were no teachers colleges. It wasn't until 1938 that the first teachers college was founded. This explains why in 1929, of the 745 primary grade teachers, barely 107 had teaching degrees. That first teachers college, significantly, bore the name of a U.S. president, Franklin D. Roosevelt, and produced teachers with an eyedropper.

In 1950, according to Miguel de Castilla's data, a little more than 68,000 students were enrolled in primary school, a figure that grew to a little more than 164,000 in 1960. In the same epoch, the number of students enrolled in higher education rose to 1,441.

This was logical. Cotton production demanded that the bourgeoisie not only proletarianize the peasants, but also that it develop a certain number of trained personnel to administer technology and accounting in capitalist cotton production. For the same reason efforts were made to create an ideological educational apparatus and, at the initiative of the U.S. government, the Cooperative Inter-American Public Education Service was formed.

Between 1952 and 1961 more than 2,000 teachers were trained as unconscious instruments of imperialism and the local bourgeoisie's ideological plans. After that the Nicaraguan-American Organization of Technical Cooperation was founded, along with the so-called First National Education Development Plan. In operation from 1972 to 1980, it was developed by staff members from the Southwest Alliance for Latin America, who were sent by the Agency for International Development.

Teachers began in 1947 to confront this entire plan of ideological domination through education. In that year they founded their first embryonic organization—the Nicaraguan Teachers Trade Union Federation—which logically enough emerged bearing characteristics of its origin as a vehicle for economic demands.

From that point on, collective activity and political consciousness began to grow among teachers. This was reflected in a teachers' struggle in 1967, coinciding with the FSLN's armed struggle in Pancasán. Teachers began to identify with the views and program of the Sandinista National Liberation Front.

In 1970–71 the teachers' struggle drew *somocista* repression. It seemed during these years that the teachers had been overwhelmed by the tyranny, which tried to turn them into ideological repressors of the population.

But in 1977 there was a renewal of organized struggle among Nicaraguan teachers. This culminated in the founding congress of ANDEN exactly four years ago. At that congress ANDEN became part of the United People's Movement and entered a determined and decisive struggle against the dictatorship.

A great number of teachers began to participate in the clandestine and armed struggle, as well as in the ideological struggle, laying the basis for the formidable strength that today's teachers represent. The teachers helped liquidate the material means of coercion of *somocista* rule. These means were liquidated forever. But the enemies of our people, the reactionaries and those nostalgic for imperialism, did not give up their spiritual means of coercion, nor their ability to manipulate consciousness back to darkness and ignorance.

The enemies of our people still hold onto some weapons—the most dangerous weapons—weapons that can kill consciousness.

After victory in the war of liberation against all the material means of domination, all our people and you teachers in particular opened up a second battle, just as important, in the field of ideological liberation. I am referring to the National Literacy Crusade.

However, other battles remain to be opened, perhaps some of the most difficult battles and confrontations, battles in the sphere of ideological formation. And you, teachers, you who can carry in your knapsacks the reproduction of ideology, science, and culture should be part of the vanguard in this battle for the new education and the formation of the new man.

This battle is going to complete the liberation of Nicaragua. It will open the way for the formation of a society where man can unleash all his physical, spiritual, scientific, and artistic faculties, that is, a society that develops man's freedom to create, construct, and fabricate beauty and culture, to master science.

A society where a new morality will be born, a society of

abundance of man's material and spiritual needs. A society that ends ignorance, a society that halts the degradation of man, a society that ends competition between individuals, a society that does not put aside social interests for individual interests, a society without robots and mental slaves.

A society where education is not an obligation but rather a vital necessity. We are going to create a new education so that men will be masters of machinery instead of machines mastering men—a new education to establish the reign of freedom, a paradise on earth.

Workers must take over the productive forces and means of production to create this new society, so that one day, relatively soon, the resources our people need to construct this paradise will burst forth like water from an uncontainable spring.

Economic development alone will not be enough. It is the basis, but the infrastructure will not develop spontaneously. It's necessary to construct it in a conscious manner. Man's realization as an individual cannot be simply a mechanical product of economic determinism; it must be developed in a concrete manner, and in the ideological arena as well.

You teachers are the main workers in the ideological construction of our people. You ideological workers are directly responsible for the creative capacity, the critical spirit, the banishment of selfishness, the political strength, and the audacity of our new generations.

But to educate new generations you have to begin by educating yourselves. You have to blow away the clouds of ideological and political confusion. You have to confront the ideas of the past that contaminate the beautiful ideas of the present. You have to confront negative habits, the totality of soiled ideological remnants that imperialism and the exploiting classes imposed on us and whose presence still has not been entirely eliminated in the realm of ideas.

You have to use the weapon of criticism to confront the old world, the old altars, the dogmas that are directly responsible for obscuring man's consciousness. You teachers must raise the banner of science, so that science can become the property of the entire people.

You teachers must be bearers of people's participation in education itself, as well as in the various aspects of government and administration. You should be examples of participation and should teach participation. You must be bearers of collectivist ideas and enemies of bureaucracy.

As was indicated in the document "Aims and Objectives of the New Education," you should teach all those who enter your area of influence to be patriots, revolutionaries, exemplars of solidarity, dedicated to the interests of the workers and peasants and of all the toiling masses. You should teach them to be anti-imperialist, to fight discrimination and oppression, and encourage love for justice, liberty, and defense of the homeland.

You should help create a new man who is responsible, disciplined, creative, cooperative, an efficient worker, with high moral, civic, and spiritual principles, endowed with a critical and self-critical capacity, and with a scientific view of the world and society.

Teachers should help to create a new man who will know how to appreciate beauty and who will recognize and value the dignity of sweat and daily labor, to create a new man who is profoundly humanitarian, reliable, and selfless, a man ready to fight in the quest for the great joining together of individual and collective interests.

And what does it mean to be honest, selfless, truthful, humanitarian, and objective? It means being prepared to defend the new society, which is being attacked with knives, threats, and menace.

The qualities cited in the document "Aims and Objectives of the New Education" are linked to the forging of a patriotic and anti-imperialist spirit. They are linked to forming men who love creative work, to forging workers who fully possess discipline and love for labor.

These principles are linked to the necessity to form specific values in the new generations, not abstract or general values but rather the values of the Sandinista people's revolution, the values of a new democracy—not of democracy in the abstract but workers' democracy. These principles are destined to forge a new man in the likeness of the great men of humanity, of Latin America, and of our own Nicaragua.

The lines of action proposed for the expansion of educational services to the entire population, even if they develop gradually, should give preference above all to workers and peasants. The courses of those who receive education should have a revolutionary content.

And within this framework it is necessary to encourage, with more than just verbal declarations, a continuing recognition of the moral, social, economic, and professional value of teaching, and it should be made clear how these values are to be recognized. We cannot remain at the level of just talking about an increase in educational, scientific, and technological research. What is required is the immediate creation of serious centers of research.

We must go much farther than good wishes for the development of sports and physical education. This is the only way to do away with anatomical underdevelopment, physical weakness, and get out of last place in sports competitions.

Our youth should participate in sports not as spectators but rather as players. We should fight the tendency to create sports fetishes and promote instead a policy of creating sports championships on a mass level. We're not interested in being world champions in commercial extravaganzas. We're not interested in being champions so we can return as millionaires and enemies of our homeland. We aren't interested in our people producing champions to give glory to Nicaragua.

We are in absolute agreement with the creation of all necessary mechanisms to assure ongoing coordination between all state institutions and the mass organizations. That is, we cannot conceive of education without the organized participation of the masses. Education cannot be created systematically if the working masses are only objects of education and are not leading in creating it.

At this point the importance of the links between education and work is perhaps all too obvious. One time we put it this way: We should create a society where all students work and all workers study.

In Nicaragua there are new social classes in power. These new social classes are responsible for ideological reproduction in the new Nicaragua—not only for interpreting social phenomena but also for instilling values, opinions, and morals in these new social classes, the workers and peasants.

This obliges the revolution to create a new methodology in the organization and structure of the educational system. This obliges the revolution to forge in teachers the ideological point of view of the workers and farmers. Educational institutions play a most important role in the struggle to raise the level of consciousness of our people.

On what, if not the new education, depends the attainment of the necessary link between theoretical and practical knowledge, on the one hand, and economic necessity and the general development of the country, on the other?

Transforming an educational system is a long, difficult, complex, and contradictory task. It is precisely for this reason that we cannot continue to postpone for even one more day this transformation that has so much to do with the very destiny of the revolution.

We must confront with audacity, decisiveness, courage, and strength the remnants of the old teaching system, elements that remain bearers of reaction and imperialism. From now on we must fight teaching deformations that turn students into machines that repeat lessons learned by rote, instead of beings with a critical spirit, endowed with imaginative and creative ways of thinking.

We must develop scientific and technical knowledge in general, and political science in particular, without letting ourselves be pressured by prejudices and influences that come from the centers of imperialist domination. Through education we must promote revolutionary strength, hatred of man's exploitation by man, loyalty to the revolutionary principles that sustain our vanguard, the FSLN, and open the floodgates of science so that man's beliefs in fantasies and superstitions, accumulated over centuries, can be washed away.

Whose responsibility is this? This responsibility is the exclusive property of the revolution. It is up to the revolutionary state to organize and direct the new education without a single concession, to determine its aims, its objectives, and all its future plans.

It isn't possible to conceive of an education that can go in two separate directions. There must be one single process for the entire country. We cannot limit our education to scientific and technical teachings. It must also be the prime factor in the search for answers to the scientific and social problems posed by the new revolutionary development.

All this means it's necessary to elaborate and execute a plan of action to increase the pedagogical and political-ideological capacity of the teachers, to make this task a priority in the teachers colleges. This means it is necessary to develop new texts and educational programs that are guided by revolutionary principles, and to create adequate means of control to assure that the educational programs of the revolution are not slighted or deformed in the private high schools.

To create a new education we must create a new teacher. What should this new teacher be like? The teacher should:

1. Be revolutionary—that is, master of the new morality, archetype of the new man.

2. Have a high degree of commitment.

3. Identify with the interests of the workers.

4. Be a bearer of critical and self-critical attitudes.

5. Be capable of teaching and capable of learning.

6. Give each student the same love as would be given to his or her own children.

7. Be responsible and disciplined.

8. Be a teacher in the classroom and in the community.

9. Participate in defense of the homeland.

10. Participate in and bring participation from the community into all decision making.

These are principles that cannot be negotiated. Sovereignty of the homeland cannot be negotiated. The arms that defend this sovereignty are not negotiable.

And what are these arms? The cannons, the tanks, the rifles. We don't ever want to use them, and it is to be hoped that we won't have to. The violent fire of these arms will be used only to defend ourselves. We are sure that one day, when the ferocious fangs of imperialism have been pulled, we are not going to need these arms any more.

But there are other arms, ideological arms, that also defend the sovereignty of our homeland. The main ideological arm our people possess is the new education. This is an arm that cannot be laid down. The imperialists can shout all they want. Even if they shout their heads off we will hold tight to our ideological arms with the same tenacity that we hang on to our rifles.

There are those who seek to go back to the times of Torquemada. There are those who want to return to the Inquisition. There are those who want to condemn Galileo all over again, and burn Giordano Bruno at the stake. There are some who want to return our educational system to the feudal epoch. There are those who are building gallows and sharpening their knives to kill the dreams turned reality of education of the people, by the people, for the people.

We are not going to retreat an inch in the decision to forge a new people's education, a democratic and anti-imperialist education, a scientific education. We will confront without vacillation those who would like to return to the Inquisition.

You teachers, who have a calling for the rifle and the trenches, are pledging here to clench the powerful arm of revolutionary ideology, so that you will fire without pity on ideas that stink of the decaying carcass of a past that will never return.

Teachers, we would like to extend public recognition, an elemental expression of gratitude—because people who aren't grateful cease to be revolutionary—to all the internationalists who are setting an extraordinary example of solidarity and who have shared the heroic effort of bringing the illuminating energy of education to our people, especially to the internationalist teachers of the unyielding, strong, and combative sister republic of Cuba.

Teachers, march with new fire in the conquest of the new man, to defend the homeland in the units of military combat, and to defend the homeland in the ideological battalions. Teachers, we have deep confidence in and respect for all of you.

Teachers, march with Ricardo Morales, who had windows in his eyes and violent and sweet rivers in his fists. March with Ricardo Morales Avilés at the head of this invincible army of new educators of the new Nicaragua.

Long live the National Association of Nicaraguan Educators!

Long live the new education!

Let the immortal heroes of the homeland live forever!

Free homeland or death!

It is imperialism that is in crisis
by Jaime Wheelock

The following is an excerpt from a speech given February 5, 1983, to 11,000 volunteer coffee pickers in Matagalpa. In December 1982 and January 1983, Nicaragua successfully mobilized 15,000 volunteers to harvest a record 70,000 tons of coffee, despite unfavorable weather and repeated attacks by counterrevolutionary bands. The speech was published in the February 10, 1983, issue of *Barricada*. This translation originally appeared in the April 18, 1983, issue of *Intercontinental Press*.

It is true that we have our problems. This can be seen. But it is not we who are in crisis. It is imperialism that is in crisis. It is the way they've organized the exploitation and their lives that puts them in crisis. And, enmeshed in this crisis, they want to violently detain the advance of other peoples. They want to resolve their profound political contradictions, and their now even more profound economic contradictions, not only at the cost of our people's blood, but also through the ruination of the poor in their own countries.

Unemployment in [the seven major capitalist] countries has gone from 21 million in 1980 to 32 million today who cannot find any work whatsoever. And how do those governments want to resolve their economic problems? They have assembled a monstrous apparatus of organized plunder, so as to drain our countries' flow of wealth to benefit their economies in crisis.

The multinational corporations are ripping off billions of dollars through unequal trade arrangements. For example, they buy coffee cheaply from us and sell us equipment, machinery, and inputs at high prices—robbing us of much of our income. They raise interest rates to such an extent that while they were lending to us at 6 percent, now they lend to us at 20 percent and sometimes as high as 30 or 35 percent.

Latin America registered a trade deficit of $13 billion in 1973. That figure rose to $35 billion in 1981. The region's overall debt rose from $34 billion to $268 billion in 1981. It jumped to $350 billion in 1982.

Brazil owes $87 billion. Just to pay the interest it will have to use all its exports and it will still come out 26 percent behind. Mexico owes $80 billion. Using all its exports for payment, it will be left owing 24 percent. Argentina owes $43 billion and must pay back $18 billion next year—which it cannot do even if it were to use all its exports.

Where are the imperialists taking us? To economic ruin, to a debacle, to economic destruction. This is the contradiction that today's world suffers from, a contradiction that will be difficult to resolve because there are factors weighing down on our economies that will not be resolved easily.

To give you an example, if we could sell today's coffee harvest at 1979 prices, we would get $280 million. However, selling the harvest at today's prices we are barely going to get $150 million; that is to say, only about half the price.

In Nicaragua, we're not doing so bad, but there are other

countries that are. Costa Rica's gross domestic product is going to drop 5.6 percent; El Salvador's 10 percent; Guatemala's 2.5 percent; and Nicaragua's between 2.5 percent and 3 percent. But if we hadn't had flood damage and the drought, it's likely that Nicaragua's economy, for the second time since the triumph of the revolution, would have been the only economy in Latin America to have grown.

Our exports, compañeros, have not been declining. Coffee production rose from 50,000 tons in 1979 to 70,000 tons today. In 1981 our meat exports totaled $21 million; this year, $31 million. Sugar climbed from 245,000 tons to 265,000 tons in 1982. In spite of the floods, we will have more cotton in Nicaragua. So the basic exports of the Nicaraguan economy—coffee, sugar, meat, and cotton—have grown this year. But their prices are much lower.

If the imperialists were to pay us the 1979 prices, Nicaragua would be exporting $740 million. But how much will we actually export this year? We won't reach $500 million—we'll export about $460 million.

Who took the difference of almost $300 million? Ask Reagan's government and his political economy.

We should also note that in basic foodstuffs—compared to what there was under Somoza—we've grown 10 percent more corn, 45 percent more beans, 89 percent more sorghum, and 100 percent more rice. In other words we're growing in a sustained manner in a way that responds to our needs.

There are some interesting indicators of this.

- In 1977, the best year of the Somoza regime, 384,000 gallons of cooking oil was produced. We produced 756,000 gallons in 1982.
- Under Somoza, 35,000 dozen eggs were produced daily; today we produce 88,000 dozen eggs daily.
- Fish production was 300,000 pounds a year then; today it is 2.5 million pounds.
- Before the revolution, 14 million pounds of pork were

produced; now we produce 22 million pounds.
- Twelve million pounds of chicken were produced then; now we are producing 23 million pounds.

Is this a crisis? Is this decline? No, it's sustained growth based fundamentally on the strength of the revolution and the fact that the revolution has a formidable base among the labor of the workers, peasants, and humble people led by their vanguard, the Sandinista National Liberation Front.

Problems of the Atlantic Coast
Interview with Ray Hooker

The following are major excerpts from a February 23, 1983, interview conducted by a group of North Americans visiting Bluefields, on Nicaragua's Atlantic Coast. The transcript, provided by the group, was not edited by the participants.

RAY HOOKER: The Pacific region of Nicaragua, as you have probably been told, was conquered by the Spaniards. But the Spaniards were never able to conquer the Atlantic region, for lots of reasons. Geographically, we're speaking about a distinct region. In the Atlantic region, we have lots of rainfall during the entire year—it rains from January to December. On the Pacific Coast, rainfall is not as abundant.

The native tribes of the Pacific were basically exterminated. But here on the Atlantic Coast they were not. It was very difficult for the European powers to really take over the Atlantic Coast. It's very difficult, for example, to build highways on the Atlantic Coast. Communication is still a tremendous problem. Besides, many of the native tribes lived in very inaccessible regions.

The objective of British foreign policy in the sixteenth, seventeenth, and eighteenth centuries was basically to try to diminish the strength of the Spanish Empire. This was Britain's objective. So in order to try to weaken Spain, Britain tried to establish footholds in different parts of the Caribbean. Jamaica was conquered, and after the conquest of Jamaica other areas in the Caribbean were taken over.

In 1631 the British began their contact with the Atlantic Coast of Nicaragua. From the Island of Providence, British traders began to establish contact with Indians living along the shores of the Atlantic Coast. When you read the records, you'll find the owners of the Providence Company telling its traders, its ship captains, to be very careful in their treatment of the Indians. Do your best to gain their support; do your best to win their friendship. Don't mistreat the Indians. It wasn't because of any altruistic feelings on the part of Britain. But it was a sound policy at that time because the support of the native Indians on the Atlantic Coast diminished the expenses and costs of British conflict with the Spanish. When we read, for example, about Nelson, when Nelson attacked in San Juan, many of the soldiers who fought with him were Miskito Indians. Many of their attacks were carried out with the help of natives, Indians from the Atlantic Coast, fighting along with them. It was not an altruistic policy, as I said. It's not that Britain loved the Indians more than the Spaniards did, because in the United States the British practically wiped out the original population. The basic attitude of the British toward the Indians was the same as that of the Spanish, but in this particular context it served British interest to gain the support of the natives living here.

It was Central America's geographical position which really interested Britain, because the idea of building an interoceanic canal to a certain extent became an obsession to Europe, building a canal connecting the Atlantic and Pacific oceans.

Obviously it was through Central America where this had to be done. So as Spain had already attained control over what is the Pacific Coast of Central America, Britain tried to acquire control over the Atlantic Coast of the region.

Now you had this situation existing until about 1860. Remember that the Central American states got their independence in about 1821, more or less. In the 1860s Britain and the United States came to an agreement wherein either Britain or the United States would build an interoceanic canal. If Britain built the canal, U.S. ships were to have equal rights in traveling across it. If the United States were to build the canal, then British ships were to have the same types of rights as American ships in traversing it. Through the Clayton-Bulwer Treaty between the United States and Britain, they came to this agreement. After that, Britain began losing interest in the Atlantic Coast of Nicaragua.

Before this Britain was claiming that the native tribes of the Atlantic Coast had developed a really refined culture, and traditionally had been absolutely independent of Spain, independent of Nicaragua. The British fomented hatred of the Spaniards. That is, the British taught the native population to hate the Spaniards. Now the Spaniards on the Pacific Coast also taught the people there to hate the natives of the Atlantic Coast region. So we had two European powers teaching the local populations to hate one another.

Anyhow, the Atlantic Coast continued as a British protectorate until 1860. After 1860, the British abandoned their protectorate. In 1894, what was the Atlantic Coast became incorporated into Nicaragua—officially, a part of Nicaragua—with the help of U.S. troops. U.S. warships were out at El Bluff helping Nicaragua, helping the Pacific Coast, to take over the Atlantic Coast.

After the Nicaraguans incorporated the Atlantic Coast, the natural resources of the Atlantic Coast were systematically exterminated. You had, for example, the forestry resources, which were wiped out, practically exterminated. If you go to the north of the country, near the border with Honduras, you'll find basically all the pine forests have been systematically exterminated. The mineral resources of the region were also systematically finished. And if you go to many of the Miskito villages now, you'll find a number of families sick with tuberculosis, which they acquired while working in the gold mines.

When you study the records of gold production, you'll find that during the 1940s and 1950s, there was a time when Nicaragua was among the ten greatest producers of gold in the world. Now this is quite a bit for such a small country as Nicaragua. And most of this gold was taken out of the Atlantic region of the country. But if you go to the mining region now, what do you find? You don't find anything. That is, you'll find equipment that is obsolete, you'll find shantytowns—ghost towns to a great extent—and you'll find lots of people sick with tuberculosis, sick with silicosis.

Since the triumph of our new government, more than 1,200 miners, miners who lost their jobs in some cases twenty years ago, in some cases twelve to thirteen years ago, are now receiving a monthly pension from the revolutionary government. It's not as much as they deserve but it's as much as we can afford. We can't even afford it but it's being done. In most cases they get between 1,200 and 1,500 córdobas a month, in some cases as much as 4,000 córdobas in monthly compensation, as a pension. These are people who became sick with tuberculosis and silicosis under the previous administration. This government had no obligation to these workers, but even so they're being taken care of.

Basically, on the Atlantic Coast the Somoza government practically controlled everything in the region. The fishing companies were basically Somoza's companies or companies Somoza was in partnership with. The mining companies were foreign companies in which Somoza was in a certain type of partnership. You have the lumber companies—basically foreign companies also. They exterminated our natural resources and abandoned the country once the natural resources were exterminated.

This was the situation, one in which practically no schools existed, practically no roads were built, practically no hospitals existed. Contact with the outside world was extremely, extremely difficult. Very, very difficult. Now, what Somoza used to do was, he kept the Atlantic Coast isolated from the Pacific Coast. Maintain the mutual isolation; divide and conquer.

The fishing companies were established basically to export shrimp and lobster to the North American market. Notice where the fishing companies were established—two in Corn Island, one at the Bluff, one at Schooner Key, and the smallest in Bluefields. If you are going to establish a company dedicated to bettering the diet of your population, you would try to select a site where communication with the different parts of the region and the country would be easiest. But basically the idea was to export shrimp and lobster to the North American market. So what happened? When you fish for shrimp, for example, you use these huge nets that are dragged behind the fishing boat. Generally when they catch one pound of shrimp, for example, they also catch about fifty pounds of other species of fish. Now, you don't get a very good price for fish, or you don't get as good a price for fish in the United States as you get for shrimp. So the fishing boats dumped back into the sea the other fish that were caught. So because of the establishment of these fishing industries, what really happened was that the diet of the population of the Atlantic Coast became systematically impoverished. That is, shrimp, lobster, turtle—the type of seafood which was a traditional part of the diet of the people of the Atlantic Coast—was not available any more. When we were kids growing up in this area you had people practically giving away shrimp, giving away turtle. Now the people can't get shrimp, they can't get lobster, they can't get turtle. It's very, very difficult, because the companies were established for export purposes, not to better the diet of the population.

After the triumph in July 1979, what happened? First you found the people from the Pacific Coast, who knew very little about the people from the Atlantic Coast. And the people from the Atlantic knew very little about the people from the Pacific, because people from the Atlantic Coast belonged to different cultures. You have the Miskitos, you have the Sumos, you have the Ramas, you have the Caribs, you have the English-speaking population, but on the Pacific you have basically the Spanish-speaking population. Two populations, people who knew very little about one another.

The English-speaking population did not understand the Spanish-speaking population, and the Spanish-speaking population did not understand the English-speaking population. And this was the situation which existed, which still exists; but an attempt is being made to try to correct these difficulties. But it's not easy. You see, revolution is a very difficult thing. To change human beings, to really bring about a genuine change in human beings is one of the most difficult tasks which any government, which any society, has ever attempted.

QUESTION: Could you go into more of the specific responsibilities of the government. I understand that roads have been paved since the triumph, that a new hospital is being built. Do you have supervision over that project? What kinds of responsibilities does the local government have?

HOOKER: Construction costs here are about three times the cost on the Pacific Coast. That is, for the money we need to build one hospital here, you can build three hospitals on the Pacific. The same amount of money we need to build one mile of highway here will build three miles of highway on the Pacific. And there's another thing about the Atlantic

Coast. The type of soil we have is very good for the growing of things such as coconuts, rubber, African palm—permanent crops. Our soil is very good for this. But it's not very good for the growing of beans, rice, corn—annual crops. It's not good for that type of thing.

Now coconut is a wonderful product. Once it begins to bear, to produce, it will produce for seventy-five, eighty years or more, consecutively. But the big problem you have is that once you plant a coconut it takes between five and six years for it to begin to produce. So the initial investment which you need to get this crop into production is huge. The initial investment you need to get, let's say, five acres of coconut into production is huge in comparison to the amount of money you would need to plant five acres of wheat, beans, or rice. And you're not going to get any return on your investment until about five years, six years afterwards. Once these things begin to produce, then you have it made. But to get them to begin to produce, that's where the difficulty lies. Now because traditionally most of the people on the Atlantic Coast have been poor, they did not have this initial capital that is required to get this type of crop into production.

What I'm trying to get at is that infrastructure on the Atlantic Coast is tremendously expensive. Maintenance of infrastructure is also tremendously expensive, much more expensive than it is on the Pacific. But even though it is damned expensive, what the revolution has done in three years' time is also really impressive. For example, the area of health and education on the Atlantic Coast is where we have been most successful. Before the revolution, the hospital here in Bluefields functioned for approximately four to five hours per day. After the revolution an attempt was immediately made to get the hospital functioning twenty-four hours a day. Most of our local doctors were opposed to this. Three or four or five of the doctors who were here have left the country. But with the help of doctors from other countries the hospital is now functioning twenty-four hours per day, with resident doctors during the entire twenty-four hours, offering services. This is not only in Bluefields. Go to the smallest communities and you'll find health services where no doctors previously reached. The amount of consultations have increased by more than 400 percent since July 19, 1979.

QUESTION: How do the different levels of government work?

HOOKER: After the revolution an attempt was made to establish neighborhood committees. These neighborhood committees are CDSs, as they are called. Basically they are committees established to try to find solutions to the problems of specific communities. That is, what are the main problems of the neighborhood? Supposedly the people from a neighborhood should understand their neighborhood better than anyone else, because they have lived in that neighborhood over a long period of time, they are well-acquainted with one another, so they should have more understanding of the situation existing in a neighborhood than, let's say, a judge, a police officer. So they should try to solve their neighborhood problems right in their own communities.

Now what we're finding is that some of the things that work on the Pacific Coast won't work on the Atlantic Coast. We're coming to the conclusion that we must identify spontaneous situations in the different communities which are of interest to most members of the community, and work with the people to try to find solutions to the problems of their communities. But if we go to the communities and try to impose patterns which are alien to them, then we don't get any results. So what we try to do is work in that way. Identify the situations which are, for many people of the neighborhood, important, and work with the people from that neighborhood to try to find solutions to these problems.

We have, for example, problems here with foodstuffs.

Not all foodstuffs, but there are scarcities of certain things here, such as flour. There's scarcity, for example, of toilet paper. A scarcity for a while of sugar. In December there was a scarcity of rice. Now these are problems which practically all the members of a community are worried about. So we work with the members of a neighborhood to try to find solutions to them. Now the solution is not only getting Managua to send more rice or sugar, for example. We'll work with a community to try to get them to plant more rice, to plant more beans, to get the community to stop relying so much on refined sugar.

When I was a kid during the 1940s—it was the Second World War and the years immediately following—there were tremendous scarcities in all Nicaragua. There were scarcities of flour, of sugar. We had our people planting more rice, more beans, eating cassava instead of depending on imported wheat for the making of bread. These are some of the things we're trying to get our people to begin to do again. Because you see what has happened with the type of semi-industrial development that was established, getting people to work in the fishing companies or to abandon the country. You have our people not producing what they used to produce. We used to produce all the rice we consumed on the Atlantic Coast.

QUESTION: Could you give us a general overview of the short-, medium-, and long-term planning for the Southern Zelaya region?

HOOKER: Okay. Short-term planning: we're trying to satisfy the basic needs of the people. That's our short-term objective. That there is sufficient food for the people, not plentiful—sufficient, not expensive food, nourishing food. See that adequate clothing is available to the people, not elegant clothing but adequate clothing. Try to satisfy the housing needs of the people. See that every individual has an educational opportunity here in the region. See that the health needs of the people are met. In other words, satisfy the basic needs of the people. And the other thing is to try to produce, for example, enough rice, enough beans in each region to satisfy the needs of that region. Not to go into any big rice plantation. This area is not good for the planting of rice. But when you take into consideration transportation costs and other costs, then if you can produce a certain limited amount for local consumption, it makes sense. So that's what we're trying to do.

In terms of medium range: we're trying to get qualified, well-trained people, which we need. Most of our qualified people—lots of them have left the country. We're on a crash program to try to get new people trained. Now this is not an easy thing. Because to train, let's say, a qualified economist, if it's university training, he's going to need about five years.

We want to establish a transportation system, which is a very difficult and costly thing. In the long run we've already begun planting 5,000 manzanas of coconut.* We've already brought some hybrid coconut seeds from West Africa, which are being planted right now and we have the money already to plant this amount of coconut. We've already begun planting about 27,000 manzanas of African palm for the first time here on the Atlantic Coast. But the African palm takes six to eight years to come into production. So there is quite a bit of waiting ahead for us.

We're trying to transform the Bluff in Bluefields into the most important port in Nicaragua. If we do this, then our products don't have to go through the Panama Canal. Most of our trading is done with countries in the Atlantic. So the goods could come directly to the Bluff. From the Bluff they could be distributed to different parts of the country. A port

---

* 1 manzana = 1.73 acres

like this makes a tremendous amount of economic sense. In terms of transportation, for example, it takes a ship about seven additional days to go from the Bluff down to Panama and then up to Corinto. So we're saving lots of money in terms of the cost of transportation.

A highway system is being built from Managua directly to Puerto Cabezas. One is being built from Managua directly to Bluefields also. But this is going to take some time. And then we're going to have Puerto Cabezas, Bluefields, and Managua connected by highway. We're trying to modernize our fishing industry so that it will not only bring us dollars for our exportation but also will contribute to a better diet for our people.

If you're going to make this land productive, the coconuts are going to take eight years. To really change the fishing industry, these things take time. When you go immediately after the triumph promising your people all these things tomorrow, you're creating expectations which you cannot fulfill. And you not only create expectations which you cannot fulfill, but you're laying the groundwork for future antagonisms. And these have been some of the difficult situations through which this revolution has gone. Compounded with the lack of knowledge by some leaders of the revolution regarding some cultures of the Atlantic Coast, this compounded the situation.

I would say that we're not doing so badly really—that's what I would say. We're not systematically killing our people. We're definitely not doing this. We're not forcing people to remain in our country. If you want to leave, you can leave. When you go and find that things are not paradise on the other side and you want to come back, you can come back. This is basically what we're telling people. Now this is very costly to us.

I would say, look, we're not doing so terribly well but we're chugging along. The more difficult the situation becomes, the more we are going to be forced to use our creative capacities. The more we use our creative capacities the better human beings we are going to become. And we're going to develop a tremendous amount of self-confidence, self-reliance, pride in our country, in ourselves. And with this, it's going to be unstoppable.

QUESTION: What about the CST here, its development?

HOOKER: The CST basically works in the fishing industry. That's the major industry here. They've been able to do quite a bit of organizing. Before you had practically no unions allowed in the area. For example, when the miners tried to organize the union, the National Guard came in. It squashed all attempts at organization. Right now the attempts that have been made have been quite successful in the field of organization. But the CST has difficult problems.

We're on a crash program to get every person in the country to reach more or less a sixth-grade level of education by 1986 or 1987. So one of the top priorities is adult education classes in all the different work centers.

QUESTION: What progress has been made in getting people to participate in the militia?

HOOKER: We have people in the reserve battalions. We have our own battalions which have been trained and are being trained; battalions which are made up of our own people. It's not as difficult as we thought to take up the work of defense once people really acquire the understanding, the meaning, of these different programs. In that respect, we've done quite well I would say.

QUESTION: What about the effort to establish bilingual education?

HOOKER: That's the goal but we haven't been able to put it into practice. It's a law, but we haven't been able to put it into effect. The law says that we're going to teach children in their native language during their first four years of elementary education. Simultaneously, they'll be receiving two hours of Spanish as a second language. Supposedly by the fifth grade they should be able to receive most of their education in Spanish and continue to receive their native language, the way you receive French or Spanish in American schools.

But what are the problems?

For example, the only books translated into Miskito are some of the books of the Bible. [*Someone says "Humberto Ortega's book."*] But it's a lousy translation. Very few books are translated into Miskito. Into Sumo—the New Testament, a few daily texts of the Moravian church, the Book of Psalms, basically. I think Exodus, maybe Genesis.

Our problem is we have to train people to speak Miskito. Then translate from Spanish to Miskito. Then train those people who can translate from Spanish to Miskito to make textbooks. Then you have to train them to make textbooks in biology, social studies, mathematics, natural sciences plus all the works of literature which you have to use in any worthwhile institution. So the job is tremendous. And we haven't been able to do much with the program so far.

Improvement in the situation of workers is the task of the workers themselves

by Víctor Tirado

The following speech was given February 26, 1983, in Managua to 300 delegates attending the National Constituent Assembly of the Sandinista Workers Federation (CST). This translation originally appeared in the April 18, 1983, issue of *Intercontinental Press*.

We come to this National Constituent Assembly of the Sandinista Workers Federation in a period of difficult and complex conditions in the international arena.

We come here at a time of an unrestrained arms race, directed by reactionary groups in the United States government. They are providing arms and creating conflicts in many parts of the planet. The Nicaraguan working class has the duty to struggle to prevent a nuclear war. Total and general disarmament is the banner of the world working class, as is the struggle for the destruction of all nuclear arms.

We come here at a time when the 100th anniversary of the death of Karl Marx is being commemorated. Nicaragua, the Sandinista people's revolution, and the CST in particular, will pay homage to the genius of proletarian revolution.

Today, February 26, we are also commemorating the fall in combat of the Apostle of Sandinista Unity, Commander Camilo Ortega, and are initiating a new course of military instruction for the Sandinista People's Militias, ready for the defense of the revolution.

The CST, the Nicaraguan working class, takes all the traditions and experiences of the revolutionary movement of our country and people as its own.

Working compañeros:

The National Directorate of the FSLN is very grateful and pleased to address the organized workers of the new Nicaragua's productive centers, gathered for the National Constituent Assembly of the CST.

The CST represents the distillation of the great and difficult battles fought by the workers' movement for its demands throughout this century, as well as the struggles of the Nicaraguan people against foreign intervention, against imperialist domination in our country, and against oligarchies and dictatorship.

All over the world the working class was born in struggle. Nicaragua was no exception. At the beginning of this century, when the Nicaraguan working class was barely beginning to emerge, the newspaper *Obrerismo Organizado* began to circulate. It published the first anti-imperialist manifestos of the urban workers' associations calling for the abolition of antipopular and antinational laws and decrees issued by the Yankee invaders. Workers from the banana companies, lumber mills, and mines carried out powerful actions against intervention.

But, as everyone knows, the most important and decisive combat came from the Army for the Defense of National Sovereignty, with Sandino at its head, an army made up of poor peasants and rural and urban workers.

The epic struggle of the General of Free Men raised the

anti-imperialist consciousness of the working masses and strengthened the class and popular character of the struggle. Proof of this is that the father of the democratic, people's, anti-imperialist revolution put forward the need to establish a government of workers and farmers, such as the one that now exists in Nicaragua.

Later, during the *somocista* regime, the working class never stopped struggling in spite of the harshness of the repression.

Since its foundation, the FSLN has worked tirelessly to organize and lead the working-class forces of Nicaragua. Its presence was felt in the land takeovers of Tonalá, Ranchería, and Sirama, and in the great strikes of teachers, hospital workers, and construction workers, as the FSLN sought to give these strikes a revolutionary content.

In the severest conditions of repression and clandestinity, the committees established to fight for trade union rights and a union movement of working people played an outstanding role in the organization of the working class, in the development of revolutionary consciousness among the workers, in changing the traditional methods of struggle, and in the very preparation of the insurrection that culminated in the triumph of 1979. Those three organizations [ANDEN (the teachers' union), FETSALUD (the health workers' union), SCAAS (the construction workers' union)] are the result of earlier union struggles, and those who led those struggles now lead the CST.

Thus, the roots of the CST go way back. Its formation is the consequence, the outcome of a series of economic, political, social, and military struggles.

All major demands of the workers were put into the labor code in the 1940s but were not satisfied until after July 19 [1979]. It was necessary to make a revolution to be able to apply basic precepts that already reigned in capitalist countries not ruled by tyrannical governments.

During the three and a half years of the Sandinista revolution, the situation of the workers has changed radically. From the political point of view, they have moved ahead because the new government is fundamentally at their service—at your service—and at the service of the peasants.

Socially and economically, your situation has improved in spite of the difficult conditions in which the economy must develop—the aggressions at the border, the constant threats of invasion that force us to invest economic and human resources in defense, to the detriment of reconstruction of the country. All this puts us in the situation of not being able to show all the advantages that this revolution could give to its people if we could dedicate ourselves entirely to the economic and social rehabilitation and reconstruction of Nicaragua.

Although on a small scale, wages have increased. Here, we are speaking of the wage that is paid directly—the economic wage, let us say. However, what we know as the social wage has grown considerably, through increased and improved educational, health, and social security services; subsidies on basic foodstuffs and transportation; and enactment—in the very near future—of the Law on Housing.

At the present moment, the working class has great responsibilities to face and serious problems to confront. In our judgment there are two basic tasks before the working class and its trade union organizations at the present time: raising production and productivity; and military defense of the country.

Neither is less important than the other. The two have the same weight at the present time. Both go hand in hand and share the same tremendous importance. There cannot be defense without production nor production without defense.

In the field of production we have overcome, fortunately, in large part—not totally—labor indiscipline and disorder, the unnecessary confrontations—at times bordering on anarchy—with government representatives, administrators, technicians, and professionals.

Labor discipline has been strengthened but we still cannot sing out "victory"—we still cannot rest on our laurels. We must continue to strive to get all workers to come to work on time, to make maximum use of the workday, to increase production with the required quality, to raise productivity, conserve raw materials, fuel, electricity, water, and to give adequate maintenance to the equipment and machinery.

At the same time, we have to encourage the innovators movement in order for production not to stop.* This work is the CST's and the CST must create a strategy for it. We must avoid company and factory closings, and offer solutions to problems resulting from lack of resources or hard currency.

We are convinced that improvement in the situation of workers must be the task of the workers themselves in the new Nicaragua, where a government at the service of workers and farmers has been formed. This means that the economic, political, and social demands that you formulate are demands made to your government, or really to yourselves. Therefore, the standard of living is now going to depend on your own disciplined work, on the degree to which you improve production and productivity.

If you raise production, there will be more schools, more health centers and hospitals, more and better transportation, more homes, more jobs, and better salaries.

Compañeros, there is no other way to resolve the prob-

---

* To reduce stoppages of production caused by lack of hard currency to import spare parts and raw materials, an intensive campaign was initiated in mid-1982 to manufacture needed parts and adapt production processes to the use of domestically available materials.

lems of backwardness and poverty that we still have not overcome, that are going to take several years to overcome, and for which enormous sacrifices on your part will be required. And these sacrifices will be greater if the invasion the Yankee government threatens us with becomes a reality and if the financial blockade in the international multilateral organizations and private credit institutions continues as it has up till now.

From this also comes the necessity of joining the defense efforts, the necessity of enlisting in the militias, in the reserve battalions.

I don't believe I need to argue this point. You know what is happening on the northern border.

You know the historic and irresponsible threats made against Nicaragua by President Reagan, who says he will not permit revolutions to triumph and be consolidated in Central America, who reiterates that in the region there is no room for the Sandinista revolution because, according to him, this space was reserved—it seems—for genocide, traitors, and oligarchies.

On the other hand, the sensible governments of Latin America and Europe are pushing for a nonexclusionary negotiated solution to the conflicts, without U.S. predominance.

It seems that the hour is drawing near in which it must be decided how to resolve the crisis of Central America. In a matter of weeks or months it seems that we will be faced with this. And we must be prepared to confront whatever eventuality: a military solution or a political solution.

And here the workers will play an enormous role. They must—no matter what—guarantee production and defense of the country. And this is not just a phrase provoked by enthusiasm. It is a task that can and must be accomplished.

The Nicaraguan working class has demonstrated that it has the vigor, the energy, the intelligence, and the courage necessary to conquer adversity.

In this assembly you are going to examine various documents—the declaration of principles, the tasks of the CST, and your statutes. These materials were already analyzed by the ranks during assemblies that took place in all the work centers of the country. More than 50,000 workers participated in the discussions, an indication of the level democracy has reached in the CST. Everyone who wished to express himself has done so freely.

We have to make some adjustments in these documents. We have to make it clear what the CST is, what its structure will be, and we have to outline a flexible plan of action. We have to reformulate the tasks of the unions more specifically. But this we will see take place in the commissions and plenary assemblies, with greater thoroughness.

Finally, I want to direct my remarks to a subject that has been present in workers' discussions and on the minds of many compañeros. This is the question of socialism.

The Nicaraguan working class—we believe its big majority—sees socialism as the radical long-term solution (and some see it as the short-term solution) to its problems. Ideas about what socialism will be or should be in Nicaragua are still diffuse, not very clear, and it is natural that it be that way.

At the right moment we will embark on the road to socialism, but before traveling this path it is essential, necessary, indispensable to have a very clear idea of the steps that we are going to take.

It is necessary to take into account that socialism is going to be constructed in a backward country, without large-scale industry, and in a country whose economy basically revolves around agriculture and the processing of agricultural products. In a country that has few trained cadres to organize, administer, and direct industrial, agricultural, and service enterprises. That has a cultural backwardness that has been overcome, but not completely, and that is struggling to provide all workers at least a fourth-grade education. A country that has a very small accumulation of capital, and for that reason only a distant perspective for the creation of large-scale industry.

In a nutshell, socialism will not be constructed starting from great abundance, as would be ideal, but rather from the little that we have.

These are objective facts that we should not lose sight of; otherwise we might think it is enough to proclaim socialism and then by magic the problems will be resolved.

The socialism that we are going to create in these conditions requires from the working class and the peasants great sacrifices, labor discipline, an increase in their cultural and technical level, and above all a lot of work, as well as unselfish international aid.

Socialism—in the particular condition of Nicaragua—demands a lot of work. In a first stage it does not mean shortening the workday, but rather maintaining and perhaps increasing it.

Socialism requires titanic efforts because—let us repeat—we are not beginning from a society of abundance.

If we had the level of development of the United States, of Japan, of Germany, or of France, things would be different. It would also be different if our level of development was on a par with Mexico, Brazil, or Argentina.

We do not say this out of desire to create discouragement, but rather to show the complexity, the magnitude of the task we will be embarking on at the time we decide to take the socialist road, to make clear that it is a venture more difficult and intricate than the struggle to overthrow *somocismo*, or the fight against the bands that are attacking us on the northern border, or than any other of the efforts or tasks we have embarked on up to this point.

It's very gratifying that the Nicaraguan working class has come to look to socialism in its search for radical and concrete solutions. We salute your stance and say to you: Onward! We will push on in that direction, but without creating illusions, and with a very clear idea of what we want and what we can really achieve.

Karl Marx: The international workers' movement's greatest fighter and thinker

by Víctor Tirado

The 100th anniversary of Karl Marx's death was commemorated in Nicaragua with several weeks of educational presentations and discussions on the life and work of the founder of scientific socialism. The closing ceremony was held March 14, 1983, in Managua's Rubén Darío National Theater. The 2,000 invited guests included representatives of four political parties that were supporters of the revolution at that time (the Sandinista National Liberation Front, Nicaraguan Socialist Party, Independent Liberal Party, and People's Social Christian Party); workers selected by their unions; leaders of mass organizations; and representatives from workers' states and national liberation organizations.

The following was the main speech of the evening. It was published in the March 16, 1983, issue of *Barricada*. This translation originally appeared in the May 16, 1983, issue of *Intercontinental Press*.

One hundred years ago today Karl Marx ceased to exist. "He went to sleep forever in his armchair—softly and without regrets," according to what his biographer Franz Mehring wrote. He had applied the materialist conception of history to the study of philosophy, economy, and politics—enabling him to discover the laws of capitalist production.

On that day, the international workers' movement lost its greatest fighter and thinker—its most notable scholar and teacher. But he and Engels left a solidly based theoretical and practical work that served as a guide for future generations of revolutionaries the world over.

With his profound scientific analysis of capitalism, he demonstrated that this social system had within it elements, contradictions, and great antagonisms that would destroy it.

Capitalism will be replaced by a new regime in which there will be no more exploitation of man by man, he concluded, after having examined with great thoroughness and in great detail the economic, social, historical, and philosophical basis for the structure of the regime he called wage slavery.

Differing with other thinkers—contemporaries or those who came before him—he did not see the advent of a society without exploiters as a utopia; as an ideal that humanity had to make happen independently of classes and levels of economic, political, and social development.

He foresaw the arrival of socialism and communism because it is a historical necessity. Because social forces interested in attaining this ideal exist. Because it is the radical and definitive solution to the great and serious structural problems capitalism brings with it. It is the way out of poverty; economic crisis; national, regional, world, and social imbalances. It is the response to the arms race and to war.

He left behind a great intellectual heritage and a powerful workers' movement in a historic offensive—an offensive that he helped build and guide in its incipient stages. This workers' movement housed various tendencies, but at the time of Marx's death the majority of these tendencies had grown weaker or disappeared because they couldn't stand up to the tests of life. Marxism stood out as the predominant current among the organized proletariat from that time on.

When Marx died the International of which he was one of the founders and principal leaders had already ceased to exist, but it left a seed that flourished. It had left workers' organizations a sense of class consciousness, an internationalist consciousness, that no one could contain or destroy. It left the most advanced proletariat a clear conception that they must be the first to rise up in struggle against capital and that in this battle they must unite around them all workers and exploited peoples.

When Marx died, there were already workers' parties in Belgium, Denmark, Germany, England, France, Holland, Italy, Norway, Austria, Sweden, Switzerland, Spain, Hungary, and the United States. In Russia, Marxist groups and proletarian organizations existed that were the precursors of the Russian Social Democratic Labor Party. In Latin America, the revolutionary workers' movement took its first steps. Parties or socialist currents existed in Argentina, Mexico, Chile, and in other nations.

One hundred years ago, the center of gravity of the revolutionary struggle was in Europe. And the responsibility for this battle fell almost exclusively on the shoulders of the industrial workers.

One century later, the situation has changed completely. Eastern Europe now lives under a socialist regime and, in the western part of that continent, capitalism still dominates. The impetus of the working classes in Western Europe has been weakened, but it has not been extinguished nor eliminated. It can reappear at any moment, because the last word has not been said. The workers of these countries will also arrive at socialism, as Marx promised, by roads that differ perhaps from those that others have followed up to this time and in much better circumstances. This will be a big help for us, the countries of what is called the Third World.

Peoples have risen up on the world political scene who 100 years ago were considered inferior by the ruling classes of the metropolitan centers. They were colonized or about to be colonized. Now, the great emancipating movement is continuing in Asia, Africa, the Near and Middle East, Latin America, and the Caribbean.

We are reviewing 100 years of Marxism, and in this period capitalism ceased to be able to monopolize and dominate the entire world. Next to it, a socialist system arose in Europe, Asia, Africa, and in the lands of America—a vast and powerful anti-imperialist movement and national liberator.

One hundred years later in Central America, the peoples of the region do not want to be banana republics, nor imperialism's backyard. They want to forge their own destiny. They have said "Enough!" and have begun marching in this direction, come what may—military threats, diplomatic threats, or blockades.

Capitalism has been weakened. Undoubtedly it is less powerful than it was 100 years ago or than it was fifty or thirty years ago.

As revolutions triumph and the anti-imperialist movement grows stronger, capitalism withers away—it wears out.

What hasn't changed is its aggressive nature. It has not ceased to be the source of armed conflicts. All wars that have broken out—since Marx's death up to the present time—have been provoked by imperialism, be they world, regional, or local wars.

But in the course of a century, the conditions in which these wars can take place have changed. Imperialism can provoke wars of varying scale. But forces exist in the world that are capable of putting the brakes on imperialism and avoiding war.

If up until now regional warfare has not broken out in Central America, it's because U.S. imperialism has very little support for the undertaking—inside its own country as well as abroad.

Besides this, another factor has appeared in the last twenty-five or thirty years. The United States is no longer the great power that emerged victorious from World War II. It has been weakened as an economic and political power. In its own camp, the capitalist camp, it no longer exercises absolute hegemony. The decision-making centers of capitalism have been subdivided.

Washington's orders—which until recently were respected—have encountered opposition on various occasions in Western Europe and Japan, and also by medium-size powers such as Brazil, Argentina, Venezuela, and Mexico.

Reagan has overestimated the United States. For him, time hasn't passed by or taken its toll. The dream has not faded in his eyes. He firmly believes his country still maintains the strength and supremacy it had in the cold war years, when it pulled its allies into all the adventures it carried out.

The policies of the current president of the United States are outside of reality. That's why he hasn't been successful. However, he is not conscious of this situation and therefore insists on seeking forceful solutions, which have little chance of succeeding.

However, so long as they continue, his persistent efforts are dangerous. We cannot rule out that in his stubbornness, despite world public opinion and that of his own country, he may unleash an armed conflict of incalculable consequences.

We listened with amazement and concern to the speech the U.S. president delivered last week. Besides the aggressive tone that is his custom, we found that he justifies his intervention in the area with the shameless thesis that U.S. national security is in danger because Central America is the fourth border of the United States.

Perhaps, in the past—100 or fifty years ago—imperialism

drew our borders. Today, however, the situation is different. It is the peoples of Central America who define them, who draw their own borders with a firm and powerful hand.

We are fighting for the strengthening of independence, sovereignty, and self-determination because this helps construct the basis for socialism. We want to change our relationship with the United States. We are not—nor do we wish to be—a border or a link to imperialism. We want to have normal relations, on an equal footing, with the United States.

However, Reagan won't give up the old framework and, consistent with this view, has taken a dangerous step in El Salvador. He is asking Congress for $110 million to reinforce the armed forces of that country and $20 million to prop up his allies in the region.

Millions of dollars so that the massacre in El Salvador will not be stopped—so that counterrevolutionaries can continue killing on the northern border of Nicaragua. Millions of dollars so that the problems of our economies can be aggravated, so that democratic development and a solution to the problems of our peoples can be delayed, so that the possibility of a negotiated way out of the crisis of the isthmus becomes further removed.

Right now, given the new military escalation of the White House in El Salvador, who can take it seriously when Reagan says he's in favor of a political solution?

And, if the war—which is hardly a secret—continues against us, how can he ask us to lower our guard? How can he ask us to disarm? Not to strengthen the army, militias, and reserve battalions?

Under such circumstances, the state of economic, national, and military emergency must continue because the dangers and threats surrounding us remain serious and ever-growing.

And we must reinforce our defense.

A hundred years after Marx's death, we are turning our eyes toward the past, the present, and the future. It becomes clear that history has followed the course the author of *Capital* foresaw. It didn't come, as we have said on another occasion, in a straight line, but rather in a zigzag. At times the march has been accelerated and on other occasions it has been slow. There are retrogressions and rapid progress. In one day, as Marx said, twenty years can be condensed.

As Marx demonstrated scientifically, socialism is the future of humanity because, in spite of its errors and imperfections, it is the best answer to the big problems facing humanity today. It is the best solution to the sharp conflicts that capitalism poses.

We live in an era of transition from capitalism to socialism that began in 1917 with the triumph of the October revolution. We don't know when this era will come to a close. However, what we are sure of is that all peoples will arrive at socialism—at different moments, with a different rhythm, each in their own way—using more original resources that right now we can't even begin to imagine.

In these days of homage to Marx we have said, and we want to repeat, at the risk of becoming boring, that Marxism for the Sandinistas was a complete revelation—the discovery of a new world. And the first thing we learned from it was to know ourselves, to look inside our country, into our people's revolutionary heritage—toward Sandino. Through Marxism, we came to know Sandino, our history, and our roots. This is, among other things, the great teaching we received from Marx—reading him, as Fonseca said, with Nicaraguan eyes.

From Marx, we have much to learn. We never intend to apply—nor will we in the future—his doctrine as a dogma. It was he who said that this is not a sacred scripture, nor is it the key to open all doors.

We value his writings as we do Lenin's, as a guide for

action, as a creative instrument that must be continually recreated. We have worked in this direction and so have revolutionaries the world over. That is the first and great requirement of Marxism.

The FSLN and the Nicaraguan revolution
by Tomás Borge

The following speech was presented at the "Commander Iván Montenegro Báez" Second National Seminar of Political Education in Nicaragua, May 20, 1983. It was printed in the August 1983 issue of *Cuadernos del Tercer Mundo*, published in Mexico. This translation originally appeared in *New International* number 3.

We have agreed to make some comments on the history of the Sandinista front. They will at least serve as a basis for us to reflect more seriously and finally to make some notes toward a modest contribution to the glorious history of our organization.

Those who killed Sandino believed they had killed the revolution. They believed they had killed even the possibility of a revolution. Such superstition is akin to fetishism, which affects everybody in some way. It has something to do with the way individuals tend to be presented either as standing outside of history or as the exclusive architects of history.

The other side of this coin involves denying, in a rather

scholastic way, the role of individuals in history. Nonetheless, history (which is not just "noise," as [the eighteenth-century French Enlightenment philosopher] Montesquieu asserted) takes place under certain conditions, and it is regulated by laws that operate independently of the will of individuals. So, in this concrete case, those who sought to wipe out the memory of the man who became even more than the architect of the Nicaraguan people were mistaken once again. The material conditions that had led Sandino to point out the road of popular struggle remained in force after his death as a result of the economic and political domination of Nicaragua by the United States. The commonplace egoism of the domestic exploiting classes remained, as did, of course, the existence of an instrument of coercion—the so-called national army. Hence the bullets that killed Sandino did not mark the end but rather the prologue to a new principle, to a leap forward with a will to persist, to the future founding of the Sandinista National Liberation Front. Meanwhile, the objective strength of the National Guard, the instrument of Yankee domination, provided life insurance for the superexploitation of the Nicaraguan people.

Due to the death of Sandino and domination by a brutal instrument of repression, the period from 1934 to 1956 was to be a dark and sad interlude. The practical expression of this—as we have said on other occasions although perhaps in different ways—was a downturn in the revolutionary movement. The people went on struggling stubbornly, but they were weak and undernourished in terms of ideology and organization.

What was lacking in that period was undoubtedly a revolutionary leadership. Throughout that period, the opposition bourgeoisie dominated the struggle against *somocismo*. They went through a lengthy process of bargaining in which the astute and cruel godfather of the Somoza dynasty always came out ahead.

The objective conditions—and all of us have already become familiar with this notion—were dramatic and evident: hunger, poverty, malnutrition, social insecurity, and a ridiculous culture, sugary and imported like Adams Chiclets. But the subjective conditions of organization and consciousness were invisible at that time, which is to say virtually nonexistent. This contradiction between the objective and subjective conditions eventually served to shed enough light on the situation so that the people could discover that without a vanguard it was impossible to defeat the *somocista* dictatorship.

The cultivation of cotton in Nicaragua dates from the 1950s. With cotton came the dust storms as well as the imported pesticide toxins that were added to the meager, indigenous fare of our agricultural workers. Capitalist development was thereby concretized historically in Nicaragua in accord with the narrow pattern of single-export agriculture, with its productive structure bound up with demand on the world capitalist market.

Cotton was the determining factor in the agro-export character of the Nicaraguan economy. It was a key symptom of the development of capitalist relations of production in agriculture. The surpluses accumulated were applied either to expansion of the area allotted to cotton cultivation; to the construction, in bad taste, of some new residential areas such as you can see in León and other Nicaraguan cities; to periodic visits by the cotton growers to the Louvre museum in Paris; or to the formation of one part of the private financial system.

This process contributed to the consolidation of the state and to the development of certain industrial and commercial activities having to do with the dazzling but unstable market for cotton. The necessary result—which couldn't be added up the same way cotton bales were at the Banco de América—was a greater class polarization within the framework of a historical reality (a reality that is generally denied from the pulpits and banquet tables of the bourgeoisie). A polarization between the exploiting and exploited classes placed at one extreme in our country the agro-exporting bourgeoisie and the commercial and industrial groups, and at the other extreme the agricultural workers. This represented the deepening of a process that had begun with the cultivation of coffee at the end of the nineteenth century and had led to a greater concentration of landed property and finally to the technological development of cotton production. Reflected through the *somocista* government and its laws, this process had as its consequence the sharpening of the class struggle between exploiters and exploited.

The 1956 economic crisis began, of course, on the world capitalist markets. It subjected the Nicaraguan economy to the effects of a cyclical fluctuation in external demand (a fall in prices for coffee and cotton and a drop in the volume of exports). This crisis of the agro-export model dealt blows to profit rates, and it increased popular discontent. But the agricultural proletariat and semiproletariat that had been born along with the cotton seeds, as well as the incipient urban proletariat, were not yet able to respond collectively to the repression and poverty.

That explains why there was no political organization with the strategic clarity necessary to overcome the silence, stagnation, and inactivity. The bringing to justice of Somoza García took place in this framework.

On September 21, 1956, Rigoberto López Pérez marked the beginning of the end of the dictatorship. To do so was the hero's express aim, as lucidly explained by Carlos Fonseca and further discussed by José Benito Escobar.

Twenty different armed movements took place one after the other following Rigoberto's action. This crisis put an end to the dark interlude.

At the beginning of the 1960s, the plan for Central American economic integration began to take shape. This plan, a product of the developmentalist strategy, was presented with a smile far broader than the resources allotted to it. Its aim was to slow the wave of popular uprisings. In that regard, however, the errors committed by enthusiastic Latin American revolutionaries who had mechanical conceptions about the victory of the Cuban revolution proved more effective.

The Alliance for Progress was part of a new period of expansion in U.S. foreign investment, now primarily directed at the industrial sector. The idea of the Central American Common Market originated from the United Nations Economic Commission for Latin America, which held developmentalist notions of how to overcome economic backwardness. The initial plans called for a gradual process of import-substitutions and balanced industrial development. This abstract project was soon distorted by the conditions imposed by those who financed it. The Central American Common Market served as the institutional and political framework for the transfer of local and foreign capital into the industrial sector, with the aim of consolidating the basis for capital accumulation. But the effort was distorted, since land reform and income redistribution—preconditions for industrial development—were not contemplated in this integrationist strategy.

Rigoberto's action, as has been said many times, was not a terrorist act. But we cannot resign ourselves to saying that and nothing more. It is necessary to say also that it corresponded to the conditions of underdevelopment and economic and cultural backwardness that prevailed at the time. Under such conditions, there is a tendency to individualize social conflicts. The dramatic individual phenomenon of Somoza found its parallel at that moment in a response of similar character. This also helps explain why a personal military dictatorship was an adequate instrument for guaranteeing foreign and oligarchic domination.

Rigoberto's action showed that the dictator was not physically invulnerable. This constituted the first step in making the people conscious of the social forces that were hidden behind Somoza's apparently personal power. Rigoberto's action was the first in a cascade of popular actions and armed movements through which our people answered the thoughtless and cannibalistic leaders of the bourgeois opposition. It marked a new beginning for the popular movement—the first stirrings around Sandino's enormous sepulcher before his resurrection.

The Cuban revolution, as Carlos Fonseca observed, had an impact on Nicaragua even before its victorious culmination. As we pointed out in the pamphlet, *Carlos, el amanecer ya no es una tentación* [Carlos, the dawn is no longer a temptation], "The victory of the armed struggle in Cuba, more than a joy, was the drawing back of innumerable curtains, a powder flash that shed light from afar on the naive and tiresome dogmas of the moment. The Cuban revolution certainly sent a shiver of terror through the ruling classes of Latin America. It was also a violent assault on the suddenly forlorn relics with which we had first adorned our altars. Fidel was for us the resurrection of Sandino, the answer to our reservations, the justification of the dreams and heresies of some hours before."

The repressive actions of the dictatorship were only the political expression of one of the sides of the contradiction. The popular classes sought political expression through the Patriotic Youth, the teachers' and workers' strikes, student demonstrations, land seizures, and the creation of trade unions and labor and peasant federations.

This popular agitation involved sectors that had never before demonstrated openly against the *somocista* regime. The ferment pointed up the congenital helplessness of the Nicaraguan bourgeoisie, or, more precisely, the absence of a national bourgeoisie able to assume leadership of the anti-*somocista* movement.

The armed opposition movements repeatedly covered Nicaraguan territory with blood, but at no time did they manage to involve the entire people in the armed struggle. We can seek the explanation for this in the diversity of social composition, ideologies, and political programs of those guerrilla groups. At that time, there was still no theory that could make it possible to determine the character of the social forces in conflict, and to guide their strategic and tactical priorities.

All the spontaneous actions with which the masses illuminated this opening phase of revolutionary ascent serve to show us the revolutionary potential of the Nicaraguan people. They also highlight the lack of a revolutionary organization and leadership. Without a vanguard, this revolutionary potential could not be converted into a powerful popular fist capable of bringing down the *somocista* dictatorship.

Such a vanguard is necessary to give organized expression to the sweat, rage, and intuition of the people. I repeat that in this phase of ascent the economic conditions for the emergence of a revolutionary vanguard did exist. On the basis of these objective conditions, certain subjective conditions had also been forged. But these forces still lacked an ideology or a theory that could put them in order and give them coherence.

The Sandinista National Liberation Front was founded in July 1961. This historic event signified the people's alternative, as opposed to the bourgeois reformist alternative, in the struggle against *somocismo*.

We cannot speak of a vanguard without a vanguard theory. In referring to the creation of the vanguard, we must emphasize the way Carlos Fonseca rehabilitated Sandino and his revolutionary ideas. Carlos saw in Sandino and his ideas not an ethereal symbol, not an abstraction, but rather a guide for understanding Nicaraguan reality and transforming it in a revolutionary way.

We could say that Sandino's thought can be summed up in two great ideas retrieved by Carlos Fonseca:

Only the workers and peasants are capable of struggling to the end against imperialism and its local political representatives. With this notion, Sandino's intuition grasped above all the class character of the revolutionary movement, the class struggle as the motor of history.

Besides pointing to the workers and peasants as the fundamental subjects of this struggle, Sandino also grasped the form the popular revolutionary movement in Nicaragua had to take. In the economic, social, and political conditions of Nicaragua, the armed struggle was the only road that could lead to the revolutionary transformation of society. Stated from our current perspective this seems like all too obvious a notion. But at the time, when contradictory notions were playing a role, it was very important to retrieve this essential idea of Sandino: "Freedom is not conquered with flowers but with bullets," the general said. This became for us a beautiful saying, an axiom in the formation of a people's army, a guerrilla army to begin with, for the conquest of national liberation.

This was the sufficient foundation, from the standpoint of consciousness, for the defense of national sovereignty. In these two great ideas is summed up the strategy that led us to victory—the combination of guerrilla struggle with the mass movement, through a dialectic in which the guerrillas became the people and the people became an army.

These inexorable ideas were rooted in Nicaraguan soil. They were brought together with the revolutionary theory that synthesizes the experiences of all revolutions. And it was the application of this notion, without dogmatism, that led a handful of revolutionaries to found the Sandinista National Liberation Front in 1961.

The founding of the Sandinista front confirmed the truth of Sandino's words: "We will go toward the sun of liberty or toward death, and if we die it doesn't matter, our cause will go on living, others will follow us."

Sandino's cause had indeed gone on living, and the Sandinista front did no more than take it up again under different material conditions and with the guidance of a revolutionary theory. Sandino's cause defied dangers and betrayals and turned the vacillators into pillars of salt. Sandino's cause lives and will go on living.

The armed struggle was initiated with the Coco River and Bocay guerrilla front in 1963. This was the first armed action prepared by a revolutionary group that was more or less homogeneous from the military and political-ideological standpoint. That is, the inevitable contradictions that arise in any revolutionary movement were not ones of principle in this case. The men involved were united first of all by ideological conceptions; later by the terrible privations they underwent in the bitter moments of the first armed actions; and, finally, by the bouts of pessimism that often harden men at difficult moments and by the basic initial optimism that our brother Carlos knew how to instill.

It must be taken into account that at that time in Latin America a schematic interpretation of the Cuban revolution had been propagated, one that isolated the guerrilla warfare from the mass movement. We have already referred to the different basis on which the Sandinista front had begun. (This question ought to be studied someday, in order to analyze further the struggle of the peoples of Latin America, their difficulties, failures, and achievements.)

Nonetheless, unity between theory and practice is not something that is established once and for all at the outset. Rather, it is something that must be achieved in the course of the struggle itself. The vanguard itself needed to grasp this principle at that first moment, in that initial armed experience.

Around the Coco River and Bocay a minimal infrastructure at the level of the masses had been prepared to support the guerrillas, but not within the zone where the guerrilla struggle was initiated. The efforts that had been made there had broken down owing to the persistence of certain mechanical conceptions, even though some of us had managed to grasp the need for adequate conditions before initiating the guerrilla movement in the areas along the Coco River. One such effort had indeed been made in the area around Wiwilí. It was not possible to take advantage of that because of other factors, so the guerrillas began operating in an area that had not been previously explored, where no political work had been done with the local population. This tactical error became for us a makeshift and difficult source of lessons that both reaffirmed the correctness of our overall conception and revealed from the outset the importance of work among and with the masses.

The Coco River and Bocay experience constituted a defeat—not precisely from the military standpoint, since the main problems did not arise from armed engagements but rather from the absence of the minimal conditions on the ground necessary for the guerrillas' survival. There were no supply lines. Even food, clothing, and weapons were lacking. This led to a decision to return to the original base.

The vanguard turned the military defeat of 1963 into a source of lessons. The correction of its errors had allowed it to survive and put together a clandestine apparatus in the cities. It managed to carry out certain armed propaganda actions, economic blows, and the distribution of Sandinista materials. These were always beautiful—some of them were ingenuous, but they never lacked that special profundity that Carlos Fonseca knew how to impart. Small training schools were set up.

The experiences of the Coco River (or Wankí, as the Miskitos call it) and Bocay constituted a defeat that coincided with the temporary decline of the anti-*somocista* movement.

Nonetheless, between 1963 and 1966 the FSLN managed to establish certain contacts with the masses in the barrios, workplaces, student milieus, and rural unions. This work among the masses was carried out not only by the intermediate organizations of the FSLN, such as the People's Civic Committees and the well-known Revolutionary Student Front [FER], but also through temporary alliances with the Republican Mobilization Party (which ceased to exist a little while later) and with the Nicaraguan Socialist Party (which still exists).

The military defeat of 1963 coincided with, and contributed to, a temporary downturn in the anti-*somocista* movement. A period of economic upswing was under way (*somocismo's* best period in that sense). The most dynamic sectors of the bourgeoisie took full advantage of this. They were able to combine their agro-export and commercial interests with the new phase of industrialization spurred by the government's economic policy.

Imperialism's new development strategy for Latin America, the so-called Alliance for Progress, which some of you may not even recall, was Kennedy's political response to the Cuban revolution. This famous alliance received a great deal of publicity, and it had an effect in altering the facade of many Latin American countries. In Nicaragua, it gave a certain cover to the *somocista* dictatorship.

As a variant of the dictatorship's form of political domination there arose the cosmetic civilian regime of René Schick. More than anything else, his period in office made possible the reorganization of bourgeois politics in the framework of a strictly electoral struggle. This engendered a certain pessimism regarding the possibility of continuing with the armed struggle.

But the FSLN was already in existence. It had the will to struggle and had organized in a way that went beyond guerrilla characteristics. This made it different from other,

Left, Gen. Augusto César Sandino. Right, Carlos Fonseca.

U.S. Marines parade in Managua after 1927 invasion.

Left, in final days of insurrection, dictator Anastasio Somoza (right) ordered massive destruction of Managua barrios.

Jubilant Sandinistas ride into Managua's central plaza on July 19, 1979, as insurrection topples Somoza and destroys National Guard.

Top, Tomás Borge, Luis Carrión, Víctor Tirado. Bottom, Humberto Ortega, Bayardo Arce, Jaime Wheelock.

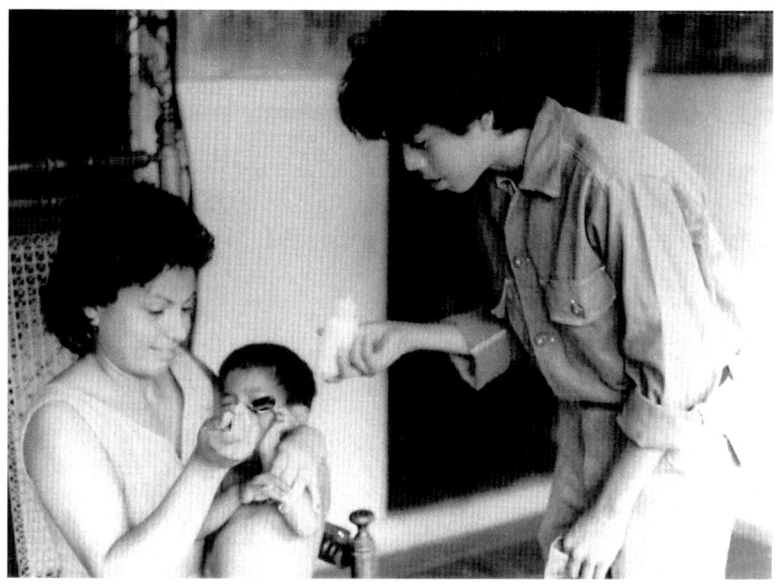

Top, militia member distributes antimalaria drug in door-to-door campaign in Ciudad Sandino, November 1981. Bottom, in first phase of national literacy crusade, volunteers taught more than 400,000 people to read and write.

Top, formerly landless peasants display land titles distributed June 13, 1982, in Carazo under agrarian reform. Bottom, December 11, 1983, land-reform celebration in Santo Tomás.

Top, Maurice Bishop (left) and Daniel Ortega in Grenada at March 13, 1980, celebration of first anniversary of Grenada revolution. Bottom, June 25, 1982, Managua demonstration protests Israeli invasion of Lebanon.

Top, September 28, 1984, demonstration celebrates seventh anniversary of Nicaraguan women's movement. Bottom, trade union contingent in 1984 May Day demonstration.

exclusively guerrilla, organizations that had disappeared completely once guerrilla warfare came to an end. We expanded beyond a guerrilla conception. We overcame that limitation, and when the guerrilla movement temporarily disappeared, the Sandinista National Liberation Front continued to exist.

The civic maneuvers could not succeed, given the economic process they were supposed to structure politically. In fact, the growing decomposition of the system and the revolutionary ascent that had begun with the 1956 assassination of Anastasio Somoza García had as their consequence the failure of these maneuvers ten years later. The dictatorship then opted for the military alternative, with Anastasio Somoza Debayle himself at the head. This process, whereby the repressive character of the *somocista* dictatorship was thoroughly unmasked, culminated in the massacre of January 22, 1967—the year that Don Fernando Agüero went around passing out smiles and false promises.

The bourgeois opposition led the people into a massacre on January 22. That opened the final chapter in the bourgeoisie's hegemony as the social sector guiding the anti-*somocista* struggle in our country. Along with the peasants who died that day, the possibility that the Nicaraguan bourgeoisie would lead the anti-*somocista* struggle was also buried. Not only because of what occurred there, but also because after that massacre of hundreds of Nicaraguans, the bourgeois opposition withdrew comfortably and made a pact with the regime—the so-called Kupia Kumi Pact that Fernando Agüero signed with Somoza in 1971. Its fundamental proposition was not the restoration of peace in Nicaragua, which from the bourgeoisie's standpoint was not endangered anyway, but rather the smashing of the Nicaraguan revolutionary movement. From 1967 on, the FSLN established direct contact with the people, making use for this purpose of its own basic clandestine apparatus, out of which an open apparatus arose.

In the course of the year 1967, the FSLN also went about preparing the Pancasán front. A communiqué signed by leaders of the FSLN was issued; among the signers was Compañera Doris Tijerino, who used the pseudonym Conchita Alday. The guerrilla movement now managed for the first time to rid itself of its earlier preference for invasions from outside Nicaragua. At Pancasán the armed actions were organized not from Honduras but rather in the mountains in the central part of our own country. The work of preparing the guerrilla campaign was centered at Pancasán and Fila Grande, with the support of the peasants of the area. Compañeros such as Oscar Turcios and Rigoberto Cruz began to stand out in this work; Cruz had already been involved in the armed incursion of 1963.

In the Pancasán campaign the vanguard suffered a military defeat that Ricardo Morales would later analyze quite correctly. When we begin to study this history more carefully we will have to take into account the whole bibliography that has arisen on those events.

Despite the military defeat, Pancasán had immense significance for the revolutionary movement. The armed struggle was reaffirmed, while the impossibility of overthrowing the military dictatorship through peaceful methods was demonstrated. When I say this, I mean that the Nicaraguan people became conscious that only armed struggle was capable of defeating the *somocista* dictatorship. This involved a total discrediting of the so-called civic methods of struggle. Despite everything, such methods became famous later in the pulpits of our Catholic churches, from which certain members of the hierarchy always insisted on the need for civic struggle, right down to the last moments of the *somocista* dictatorship. Such a position was nonetheless discredited in the consciousness of the people. The need for armed struggle became powerfully felt.

Despite the military defeat at Pancasán and Fila Grande, that struggle had immense significance for the Sandinista front, because it managed to consolidate the FSLN's influence among the Nicaraguan people. It convinced the people that ours was the only organization truly able to represent the people's interests, the only force capable of seriously confronting the *somocista* dictatorship. This elevated the moral authority and the political standing of the Sandinista National Liberation Front.

By then the Sandinista front had managed to create a vanguard detachment that survived despite the serious blows we suffered. You will recall that near Pancasán they massacred a group of compañeros, among them Silvio Mayorga. There were no survivors from that guerrilla column Silvio led; it included a series of extraordinarily valuable cadres—Rigoberto Cruz, Chelito Moreno, and so many others. We already had a clandestine apparatus in the cities, which allowed us to carry out certain armed propaganda actions and actions to secure funds, which helped us overcome our great scarcity of resources.

There were days when the clandestine fighters didn't even have their daily bread. We lacked tortillas. We had no transportation to get supplies to the mountains. There were no resources to maintain the guerrillas. The extraordinary spirit of sacrifice certain compañeros showed at that time, as in 1963, is worthy of being recalled in the pages of the history of our organization.

Sandinista propaganda by then had reached a certain level of circulation. We had set up a few tiny training schools. We had already put to the test the incipient mechanisms of contact with the masses through what we began to call around that time, I believe, the intermediate organizations: the People's Civic Committees and the Revolutionary Student Front, which played an extraordinarily important role.

In 1967 we drew up the outline of a program and some

statutes, as well as notes on the strategic line of the Sandinista front. These later served as the basis for further development of the program and statutes. By then we were also involved in internationalist activity; it was around that time that Compañero Patricio Argüello died heroically in defense of the interests of the Palestinian people. Another expression of internationalism was that Compañero Víctor Tirado had joined our ranks.

We had already made a critical analysis of the notion of the guerrilla foco. The foco had aroused great enthusiasm among fighters for national liberation in Latin America, but Carlos Fonseca and all the rest of us viewed it with something more than distrust. Our critical analysis of this notion was of great value in finding an adequate strategic road.

After Pancasán the Sandinista front again took up the guerrilla struggle by establishing a front in the mountains of Matagalpa and Zelaya. While there was a certain reassessment in our ranks, the idea of guerrilla combat was not abandoned. We began to prepare the conditions in the mountains.

Within this framework, we also managed to set up some tactical combat units in the cities. Moreover, supply lines to those guerrilla columns and their very survival called for close ties to the barrios and the trade unions. The Sandinista front thus began to make efforts to penetrate certain cities of the country, especially León but also Managua, Masaya, Matagalpa, and Chinandega.

The immediate aim of this work was to organize the barrios to struggle for better living conditions, raising immediate demands such as potable water, electricity, medical services, and so on, but without falling into making these demands ends in themselves. We differed from other groups that made immediate demands their final aims. For us, they were instead a means for seeking out the best individuals among the people and instilling in them the notion that they must organize for the taking of power.

This is very important. From the beginning, we had always had a nose for power, and we went on developing that instinct and transmitting it to our cadres even when we recruited them through struggles around immediate demands.

In sum, the key question was achieving a close link between the work in the barrios and the work in the mountains. The latter received the most attention at that time.

Our link to the masses was maintained through intermediate organizations like the FER and through mass mobilizations for the release of political prisoners. In the struggle to free the prisoners, we made contact with the most conscious and combative groups of Christians in the student movement.

We were well aware that the banners of the Sandinista front had to be upheld, and it was in that spirit that the character of the struggle was taking shape. This was expressed throughout our history in extraordinarily heroic acts, such as that of Julio Buitrago.

Julio Buitrago was not just an anecdote, not an isolated instance. Julio Buitrago was the product of an entire philosophy and an entire attitude toward life. Julio Buitrago did not do what he did solely out of personal courage—which of course he had—but rather because he was the expression of an entire conception, an overall attitude toward the revolutionary struggle. Just as those who went on hunger strikes did not yield to the temptation of eating, those who were putting up resistance to the enemy also did not yield in face of danger. Like Julio, they were capable of giving their lives without the slightest vacillation. A style was being forged that was finally transmitted to the entire people.

Those mobilizations I referred to were the product of broad mass work the vanguard carried out between 1970 and 1975. They made it possible to save the lives of many compañeros who had been taken prisoner. In that period the vanguard functioned in such a way as to deliberately avoid combat with the *somocista* troops. Tactically, we evaded combat. This corresponded to the military strategy we adopted in those years, which consisted in accumulating forces but not appearing publicly, and engaging in combat openly when this was unavoidable. It was a question of fighting not when the enemy wanted to, but when the vanguard considered it appropriate. That period is today generally referred to as the "silent accumulation of forces."

This silent accumulation of forces was ended on December 27, 1974, by the Juan José Quezada Command, led by Commander Eduardo Contreras, a member of the National Directorate. This action dealt a severe blow to the *somocista* military dictatorship.* I emphasize the role of Commander Eduardo Contreras, because I have seen it written in several places that this action was led by both Germán Pomares and Eduardo Contreras. We ought to be faithful to historical truth—Germán Pomares has merit enough without receiving credit for actions for which he was not responsible. Germán Pomares was a thousand times a hero, but it was Commander Eduardo Contreras who had the merit of having led that action. We ought to have the decency to rise above any sectarian hangovers, such as giving to others the honor of having led an action that they did not lead. I say this because it is something that could be repeated in other cases.

In leading that action, Eduardo Contreras had a particular virtue—he did not take off his mask. He remained anonymous until the enemy discovered through its own resources

---

* On December 27, 1974, a squad of Sandinistas seized the house of top Somoza crony José María Castillo during a reception being held there for the U.S. ambassador. The ambassador had left, but more than thirty top cabinet ministers and Somoza cronies were taken hostage. After a three-day standoff, Somoza was forced to back down and grant a series of FSLN demands.

who he was. This was different from certain others who—as soon as they could, as soon as they had the slightest opportunity—pulled off their mask, so that everyone could see them as the great heroes of the movie.*

By taking over the house of a *somocista* on December 27, 1974, the vanguard broke through the stage of accumulation of forces. This action accelerated the decomposition of the regime and the development of the Sandinista front. In fact, it brought to light the fragility of the dictatorship, which was forced to free the prisoners and broadcast a revolutionary statement on radio and television and even publish it in the newspapers. The regime also had to hand over a million dollars and provide a plane to take the victorious command and the released prisoners to Cuba.

These achievements by the FSLN attest that our organization was the only vanguard force our people had. They were also important because they had big international repercussions, contributing in a certain way to the isolation of the dictatorship and also helping to make the FSLN known worldwide and to enhance its prestige. Men like [Panamanian leader Omar] Torrijos began to pay more attention to us and lend us some assistance. Even our strategic allies began to take us more seriously.

From 1975 on, despite the *somocista* repression, the popular struggle not only continued but became more and more intense. The repression did not permit the launching of large-scale military actions by the vanguard, however. It was an unfortunate period for us, in that extremely valuable militants of the Sandinista front fell in action, among them no less than Carlos Fonseca. Eduardo Contreras fell the day after Fonseca. Later, we also lost that great fighter named

---

* A reference to publicity stunts by FSLN traitor Edén Pastora, who took off his mask and posed for photographs after leading the August 1978 seizure of the National Palace in Managua.

Carlos Agüero; the peasant Jacinto Hernández; Pedro Aráuz, Carlos Roberto Huembes, Filemón Rivera, Mauricio Duarte, René Tejada; the young compañera Arlen Siu; Edgard Munguía, Crecencio Rosales, Augusto César Salinas, Bonifacio Montoya, and many others.

The death of Carlos, of course, was interpreted as a victory by the reaction and the dictatorship. They assumed his death would effectively put a stop to the Sandinista struggle. The phenomenon was repeated once again: when Sandino died, they thought it was all over for Nicaragua, that Nicaragua was going to be the perpetual colony of the United States. When Carlos Fonseca died, they thought that now the Sandinista front would be liquidated once and for all.

I remember how triumphantly they came to tell me when I was in jail—they thought we were crazy, because we insisted that victory would still be ours. When we said in jail, "Carlos Fonseca is among the dead who never die," we meant that the revolutionary classes never die, the workers and peasants are as immortal as their historic tasks. That is what we meant. Carlos could not die because he represented a synthesis, an idea that was not only comprehensible but ready to be put into practice. Carlos died, but he did not die—that is what our enemies did not understand. Carlos did not die because it is the peoples who make revolutions. Revolutions are nothing but the resurrection of the heroes.

At first sight, nonetheless, the results of the repression justified the illusions held by the National Guard and the reactionaries. The exigencies of an organized struggle had given rise to a sort of division of labor in the FSLN, in which militants were distributed among complementary activities in the mountains, in the cities, and in tasks related to mass work. The blows of the dictatorship turned this division of labor into the isolation of the various elements one from the other. Various perceptions of reality emerged, based on different experiences, conditioned by this division of labor and their isolation. This led, along with other factors, to the formation of three tendencies inside the Sandinista National Liberation Front.

As I understand it, no one today wants to mention these tendencies. It's as if they had been a mortal sin. But I think that this forms part of our history, and we must make the effort to analyze it. I have seen some of our documents where the history of our organization is analyzed, and it would seem from those documents that there never were internal tendencies in the Sandinista front.

And of course there were! Besides, everyone knows it.

It is necessary to analyze this experience. We think that isolation is one of the factors that contributed to the formation of those tendencies. The existence of tendencies does not harm the image of the revolution. The great thing about this revolution is that we have been able to unite despite the tendencies. We have provided the peoples of Latin America with the example of what maturity means among Nicaraguan revolutionaries. That is the great thing, the important thing, about our experiences. To emphasize that greatness, we have to say that we were divided at a certain point in our history, but that we were mature enough to unite.

Only those who are ignorant of the fact that the movement of history unfolds through contradictions, only those who do not grasp the fact that a political organization is nothing more than an instrument in the class struggle, could have concluded that as a result of the tendencies the front would dissolve into factions and would disperse the popular struggles in isolated actions without any major impact on the dictatorship. In fact, the three tendencies continued to uphold the name of the Sandinista front. The people always recognized but a single Sandinista front, and all the compañeros know that fighters from the three tendencies all shouted "Free homeland or death!" They fought in the same trenches and shed their blood together. So why should it be strange that we united?

Unity on a higher level was required in order to synthesize the different experiences. The first stone was laid toward this end with the continuation of the popular movement. In the cities, hunger strikes continued for the political prisoners. Labor conflicts became more acute owing to the stepped-up selling off of our economy and the voracity of foreign capital. Protest movements demanding human rights continued. Land seizures were carried out in Tonalá, Sirama, and San José de Obraje, in response to the massive expropriation of the western peasants. Sandinista militants carried out literacy campaigns, neighborhood improvement projects, youth and cultural movements.

Our aim in all this work was to project ourselves into the various sectors of society. Committees of solidarity with the Nicaraguan people were set up in a number of countries at the initiative of members of the vanguard. In response to the popular upsurge, reaction and imperialism activated the Central American Defense Council (CONDECA). In Somoza's time military advisers from Brazil, Colombia, Central America, and Vietnam (from the reactionary Vietnam of those days), and of course Yankees from the United States as well, came to Nicaragua to smash the armed struggle of the people.

The relative downturn that affected the vanguard on the military level after 1974 was brought to an end in October 1977 with a Sandinista offensive that began with the seizure of the San Carlos barracks and continued with the taking of the village of Mozonte, the attack on the main barracks in Masaya, and the seizure of the San Fernando barracks.

October 1977 was the result of a shift to an offensive mode of operations in the armed struggle at a moment when the crisis of *somocismo* was becoming acute. This crisis began after the 1972 earthquake and deepened after 1974.

The Somozas' corruption, while it had its worst effects

on the masses, also harmed the interests of the small and middle bourgeoisie. This led to broadening the base of opposition to the dictatorship. To this must be added the fact that the big-business sectors themselves began to lose confidence in Somoza's abilities. Somoza came to be an obstacle to capitalist development, and even to the preservation of the bourgeois order in Nicaragua.

More and more, the regime was being called into question internationally for its stupid and repressive policies. In the particular conditions of our country, the Somoza family and its cronies had a tremendous appetite for wealth and power and began to utilize the state apparatus to satisfy their own needs.

The growth of the *somocista* dictatorship and all its ramifications began to harm a broad sector of the bourgeoisie. Somoza refused to share the wealth of the country equally among the bourgeoisie as a whole. The use of exemptions from taxation, easy bank credit, loans, and even smuggling to benefit a minority provoked conflicts between the *somocistas* and a sector of the bourgeoisie. That sector, in turn, tended to modernize in order to offset its lack of opportunities.

This economic contradiction was later expressed in political terms. We wrote a letter from jail saying, "A party of the bourgeoisie is about to appear." But it was already too late for that. Somewhat later such a party did arise, known as the MDN [Nicaraguan Democratic Movement], but it was too late.

The bourgeoisie really did not have a party of their own. The Liberal Party belonged to the Somozas and upheld the interests of an oligarchy that was highly centralized around a single family. The Conservative Party was the party of the landowners, a rather anachronistic party. No modern party of the bourgeoisie had appeared in this country. The MDN was born at the moment when the bourgeois regime was in total agony—it did not even manage to be a premature infant. In the end it could only survive artificially through the umbilical cord that tied it to imperialism.

The bourgeoisie was thus trapped by the voracity of imperialism, which under the circumstances of crisis was reducing the bourgeoisie's rate of profit; by the loss of economic activities to groups of Somoza's cronies (construction, insurance, urban development, banks, finance corporations, and so on); and by the rise of the popular movement. It had no other alternative than to desperately change its clothing and try to gain the leadership of the anti-*somocista* struggle.

But what could a premature infant do at such a moment? The Robelos and the other gentlemen of the COSEP [Supreme Council of Private Enterprise] were obliged by the course of events to function within the framework of the developing popular movement, which for them was a sort of straitjacket. While the dictatorship was losing ground both nationally and internationally, the guerrillas were carrying out a tenacious struggle with the aim of regaining the military initiative we had lost to the *somocistas* at the end of 1975. Guerrilla activity was combined with the FSLN's day-to-day work. At the national level, the enemy's plans aimed at liquidating the vanguard had failed.

Faced with the acute crisis of the Somoza dictatorship, imperialism and reaction maneuvered to provide the regime with a way out. With this end in view, they sought to make certain adjustments in the *somocista* system without touching in any way the system's fundamental bases: its economic might and the National Guard. Somoza was forced to lift the state of siege and martial law and to call municipal elections. With these measures, the regime sought to improve its discredited image before public opinion and play along with the imperialists' maneuvers.

Of course, these maneuvers were carried out at a time when the imperialist enemy and the local enemy both assumed that they had managed to reduce the FSLN's capacity for struggle, if not to liquidate it. They thought we had been very hard hit.

So, when we decided to go on the offensive in October 1977, our aim was to cause these maneuvers by the enemy to fail. After we regained the initiative in October, we were not to lose it again.

October was a historic achievement, because it disrupted the enemy's plans, strengthened the vanguard's hegemony among the masses, and fortified the masses' self-confidence. All this led the *somocistas* to commit one of their gravest errors: they murdered Pedro Joaquín Chamorro [on January 10, 1978]. Chamorro had become the leader of the incipient national bourgeoisie. Through journalistic activity over many years, he had also managed to gain the sympathy of broad sectors in our country. The crime caused the masses to take to the streets—you saw this better than I did, since I was still a prisoner. They expressed their repudiation with revolutionary violence. In those demonstrations the masses openly identified with the Sandinista National Liberation Front. The people reiterated that the Sandinista front was the only possibility for confronting the Somoza dictatorship.

The October actions, as well as the armed actions the vanguard launched in February 1978 (at Granada and Rivas, and the taking of the counterinsurgency base at Santa Clara, Nueva Segovia), had the aim of keeping alive the people's spirit of struggle. This was achieved; the masses' willingness to fight multiplied like manna in the desert.

The overall impact of these actions had its highest expression in the Monimbó insurrection. While the Monimbó events were not planned by the vanguard, they were a response to the encouragement the FSLN had provided by taking over several towns a few days earlier. Still, the FSLN managed to put itself at the head of the Monimbó insurrection. This spurred the morale and the efforts of the people as a whole. They were encouraged by the mounting activities of FSLN combat units in the cities and countryside. Everything was ready for the insurrection.

Another significant event that helped to raise the fighting spirit of the people and that demonstrated the Somoza regime's inability to halt the advance of the popular struggle was the taking of the National Palace on August 22, 1978, by the Rigoberto López Pérez Sandinista Command. This operation was entitled "Commander Carlos Fonseca Amador—Death to *somocismo*." It was led by Edén Pastora, the traitor. As Humberto Ortega has pointed out in his interesting and thorough analysis of Pastora's activities, Germán Pomares was originally designated to lead the action at the palace. But for health reasons Pomares couldn't take on that responsibility.

The seizure of the palace had a great impact, not only among the people but also on international public opinion. But something happened there that is not too well known or that has not been sufficiently explained; Pastora revealed his lack of political and ideological consistency at that moment.

When we arrived from the Tipitapa jail, we found him and realized that there were a number of our compañeros who were not included on the lists of freed prisoners—not because they were deliberately omitted, but as a result of certain slip-ups. We told Pastora that having the hostages there meant we had the real possibility of getting those other compañeros out of jail as well. He refused; we insisted. Afterwards, it was said that we had had our first falling out. That is true, we had quite a serious discussion. We insisted that the freedom of those compañeros omitted from the list be demanded as well. But he had already achieved his objective—becoming what Reagan would now call "a paladin."

The rest of the story you already know—he's still there under the bright lights filming the movie he dreamed of acting in as the leading man, allied with imperialism and locked in a fraternal, tight, and amorous embrace with the murderous *somocista* guardsmen. He had already achieved his aims.

There is a sharp contrast between what Pastora did, smilingly posed on the stairs of the airplane, and what Eduardo Contreras did, or what all the other compañeros who participated in the taking of the palace did—Hugo Torres, Walter Ferreti, and Dora María Téllez. They all kept their masks on. The error was not his alone; rather, it was our fault for not having had the instinct, the foresight we sometimes lack for detecting traitors that skulk inside our shirts like scorpions. We ought to have enough sense to realize who they are. I don't think anyone should be startled when I say this—only those with something to hide could think I was alluding to them.

The dictator Somoza—with his image tarnished and feeling pressure for change from an obscure human-rights policy that U.S. President Carter was trying to impose—found it necessary to utilize more and more brute force against the people. This led to events like those of September 1978, which opened the road to victory. There were insurrections in Estelí, Masaya, León, and Chinandega, and popular uprisings in certain barrios of Managua. Through these struggles, the people began to lose their fear of the National Guard. So the people began to move forward and take the offensive. While September did not bring the overthrow of the dictatorship, it was, in a certain way, a strategic victory for us. It was a historic achievement, because the vanguard emerged from it fortified. Our ability to recruit was extended to the entire people; we gained in weaponry and, more importantly, in decisiveness and confidence.

The rising struggle was headed by a revolutionary organization, and imperialism and the reaction began to view this with fear. They saw that their interests were in danger. So they cooked up the "mediation" scheme, which involved removing the dictator and leaving in place *somocismo* without Somoza. Somoza, being arrogant, would not accept this. He proposed holding a plebiscite that never took place. Mediation was to reconcile, through shady deals, the interests of the corrupt party of Somoza, the genocidal National Guard, the bourgeois opposition political parties, and private capital. It sought to unite all the oppressive and exploitative forces that were dispersed or in opposition to Somoza. In this way, they sought to isolate and destroy the popular revolutionary movement.

These mediation maneuvers were shattered by the unity of the vanguard; by the political alliance of the revolutionary parties and organizations of the country in the FSLN-led United People's Movement (MPU); and by the broad alliance of the MPU with the anti-imperialist and antidictatorial parties and organizations that made up the National Patriotic Front (FPN). The mediation scheme ran up against the unity of the entire nation that was taking shape around the FSLN, which kept on fighting with arms in hand down to the end. Whatever vacillations arose were neutralized by the FSLN's will to carry the fight to a higher level.

Plans for insurrection were drawn up on the basis of the people's experience in struggle; military actions by armed detachments were combined with popular uprisings and the general strike, which played a complementary and very important role. The final insurrection began in May 1979. The general strike called by the FSLN combined with the uprising of the masses to give to the people the historically inevitable victory that rightly belonged to them. All the factors had been brought together exactly at the opportune moment and in the opportune places.

The July 19, 1979, victory was possible because of the years-long struggle our people had carried out against the *somocista* military dictatorship. It was possible owing to the emergence of a revolutionary vanguard, whose founder,

Carlos Fonseca, has been quite justly placed where only the saints, heroes, and immortals belong.

July 19 was possible because at a crucial moment of historical maturity we set aside the search for personal power in the spirit of revolutionary unity, putting the interests of the nation above all. July 19 was only the beginning. Great dangers still await us along the road. The powerful imperialists are trying to invent a machine to turn back the course of history and, meanwhile, scratching and biting us with the ferocity of a tiger.

We have confidence in the toilers, in this people that was born to make history and is expert at forging new victories.

Free homeland or death!

The great challenge
Interview with Jaime Wheelock

The following interview was conducted by exiled Chilean journalist Marta Harnecker. It was first published in the May–June–July 1983 issue of the Mexican magazine *Punto Final,* and later reprinted in Nicaragua as a book, *El Gran Desafío* (The great challenge). This translation originally appeared in the November 14, November 28, and December 12, 1983, issues of *Intercontinental Press*.

1. THE FSLN NATIONAL DIRECTORATE

"Our being nine members equal in rank has its advantages. It multiplies the possibilities for carrying out international missions, for internal propaganda tasks, and for being at the front of different areas of national life."

MARTA HARNECKER: You have an experience in revolutionary leadership that is unique in the world. In the sense that there is no leader, at least up to now, who stands out above the other members of the National Directorate and who, at the same time, is recognized by the people as their top leader. To what circumstances do you attribute the existence of this phenomenon? If Carlos Fonseca were alive, would the situation be different?

JAIME WHEELOCK: I think there are several factors behind this, some of a historical character related to our process of formation, others of a practical type having to do with the predominant mode of struggle that developed in Nicaragua. I think it has also been influenced by the way the National Directorate of the Sandinista front was put together in the last stages of the struggle.

There are also antecedents from the point of view of *sandinismo*. The Sandinistas called each other brother, and practiced a life based on respect and equality. Sandino was loved, not feared.

Carlos Fonseca also helped to forge a certain sentiment of *anticaudillismo*, of equality among us. Carlos was the founder of the Sandinista front, its real creator. His authority was transmitted to the organization in such depth and profundity that from the beginning the members felt this authority as an organic substance, something not linked to individuals. Carlos lived obsessed with the continuity of the FSLN, of the struggle. I think he saw the danger of its possible disappearance, and that of course had its impact.

The leadership role that Carlos assumed early on was the result of the leadership qualities he displayed from the beginning, combined with his irreproachable conduct and his tireless attitude toward work.

At its foundation and in its early period, the FSLN did not really have a one-man leadership. It arose and was formed on the basis of democratic concepts of collective leadership that rejected *caudillismo*, that is, that rejected the traditional political style of the oligarchic and *somocista* parties.

On the other hand there are also elements of a practical sort that led to this situation. The struggle the FSLN carried out was an armed and clandestine struggle. The members didn't live long, and lines of formal leadership were very unstable. Over time most of the founding members and leaders of the FSLN were killed. Quite often the actual leadership of the Sandinista front was made up of those cadres still alive in the country. At times, to preserve the continuity of the struggle and assimilate the experience of the organization, the leadership had to leave the country for a period. When this happened intermediary cadres still inside the country prepared conditions for returning to the offensive and, in practice, assumed the leadership.

In addition, we had a command structure that was very much our own creation. We didn't have supreme chiefs but rather a political leadership that generally included new cadres. This should not be taken to mean that in this situation the FSLN had a leadership structure that functioned perfectly and completely. The very conditions of harshness of the struggle meant that not all the leadership cadres could enter the country, and that for lengthy periods contact would be lost between the leadership and the cadres in charge of operations.

The internal life of the Sandinista front was very collective. From 1969 to 1975, committees functioned inside the country. For example, a political committee in the city, a political committee in the mountains. Each committee had three members, who, together, made up the leadership inside the country. There was of course one individual with major responsibility in each of the committees, but they did not assume the function of supreme chief.

It should also be pointed out that the death of Carlos Fonseca and the death of the main leaders of the Sandinista front meant that at the moment the FSLN reunified there was no single leader who stood out above the others. Remember that in 1975 there was an internal discussion of a political-military character that for a period kept some structures of the front separated, practically acting as factions, although the general idea of the FSLN as an organization was always maintained. We were all members of the Sandinista front, but in different structures. And during this period each one of these structures developed not one-man but collective leaderships. The GPP (Prolonged People's War tendency) had for leaders Henry Ruiz, Bayardo Arce, and Tomás Borge. The same thing occurred in the tendency that has been called Insurrectionalist or *Tercerista*, where the Ortega brothers and Víctor Tirado played a similar leadership role. In the Proletarian tendency, the same thing; there was no chief leader.* So when we concretized the unification we found there were nine of us who were leaders of the Sandinista front, that no one of us could be singled out, for one reason or another, as the main leader. This was a quality, a contribution, of *sandinismo*.

This very peculiar absence of an individual leadership is a product of concrete historical conditions. By that I mean that it is not a deliberate principle of organization. If Carlos Fonseca were still alive, he would without doubt be the uncontested leader. We say in fact that Carlos is the chief leader of the Sandinista revolution. Today, the National Directorate is recognized by our people, by our militants, as their uncontested leadership.

HARNECKER: Can you tell me how you function, concretely?

WHEELOCK: We have attained a collective way of function-

---

* The leading figures in the Proletarian Tendency were Carlos Roberto Huembes, Jaime Wheelock, Luis Carrión, and Carlos Núñez. Huembes was killed by Somoza's National Guard in November 1976; Wheelock, Carrión, and Núñez are currently members of the FSLN National Directorate.

ing in which the National Directorate is the leadership, and each one of us has more or less the same weight within it. This is not to exclude, in the course of the development of our process, the institutionalization of a one-man form of leadership. But if that happens it would be an organic leadership selection, not the product of some subjective conditions that might single out one of the members above the others. It would be the National Directorate itself that would, for reasons of its own functioning, begin to single out in rank one of its members, in relation to the others.

I would like to point out here that this situation of collective leadership, a situation that has arisen in practice, has been something positive for us. For that reason we think that so long as we can function as a collective leadership, we should continue to do so.

HARNECKER: What are its positive aspects?

WHEELOCK: One of its most positive aspects is that when we discuss any given topic in the National Directorate, we do it on the basis of absolute equality and initiative. All of us state our opinions on the topic under discussion. This is highly positive for it greatly develops the powers of analysis. No point of view can be imposed because of external factors, because of the weight one leader's views may have. Instead, a point of view carries because of its own absolute logic. We improve and gather together the best thinking in order to reach a collective point of view. Our thinking, in reality, takes shape as the thinking of a collective. In this way, it is harder to make mistakes.

HARNECKER: What happens when a group in the leadership holds minority positions?

WHEELOCK: Our experience, over all these years, is that except on very rare occasions the National Directorate has always reached consensus. Taking a vote is an exceptional procedure. On the few occasions when we have had a vote of, say, five to four, we decided there was no consensus and returned to discussion of the question.

HARNECKER: Is it possible, with a leadership of this type, to have the agility required to confront a revolutionary process that is so complex, so dynamic, with so many problems, problems that grow increasingly sharper with the accelerating open intervention of imperialism? Can you respond quickly enough?

WHEELOCK: In practice our leadership functions very dynamically. On the one hand there is the National Directorate, which functions as a collective decision-maker. We meet once a week to review major questions, with a prepared agenda, focusing on matters that have come up in the government, defense, or in the area of politics and the party. But this doesn't mean we don't have a more dynamic manner of day-to-day functioning. For this, first of all we have the Political Commission. It is made up of executive cadres of the Sandinista front, who, between meetings of the National Directorate, carry out its decisions and also make some of their own that are to be ratified later. When a serious problem comes up we convene an extraordinary meeting of the National Directorate.

HARNECKER: How is the Political Commission set up?

WHEELOCK: It is not a body separate from the National Directorate. If we were to depict it in a drawing, it would be a circle inside another circle. The National Directorate has three compañeros who serve on this body. They complement each other in terms of viewing the problems of government, defense, and the party.

HARNECKER: Has this Political Commission had the same members since the revolution, or is membership rotated?

WHEELOCK: Each year it must be ratified or altered. Since the triumph of the revolution we have had two. The last has been functioning for nearly three years.

Our being nine members equal in rank has its advantages. It multiplies the possibilities for carrying out international missions, for internal propaganda, and for being at the front of different areas of national life.

The National Directorate of the Sandinista front has participated actively, through each one of its members, in defined strategic tasks since July 19 to assure the construction of the principal axes of power of the new revolutionary state—the organization of the people, the construction of the armed forces, and the organization of the FSLN as the vanguard capable of leading our people toward a new society.

2. WHO HOLDS POWER?

"The axis of our policy of alliances was not the bourgeoisie but the people. Our assessment of the relationship of forces is based on a reality: we have the arms, and the people are with us."

HARNECKER: The FSLN came to power through the development of, among other things, a broad policy of alliances, both national and international. Today, however, the spectrum of allies has diminished, perhaps more inside the country than abroad. Did you realize that the decision of the FSLN to march alongside some national sectors was going to be ephemeral?

WHEELOCK: This question has to be answered historically. There was a moment in the struggle against imperialism, in 1927, when Sandino stood practically alone. This was at the end of the civil war, following the treason by Moncada in the Espino Negro pact, when the Yankees offered to buy the soldiers' rifles for $10 apiece. Sandino decided not to turn over his arms and to continue the struggle in defense of national sovereignty. But nearly his entire general staff left, accepting the pact of surrender agreed to by the dominant capitalist groups and the bourgeoisie. Sandino's army was reduced from 600 to sixty men. A few days later, when the fighters who remained with Sandino realized that the struggle he was proposing was against the North American government, the majority of them withdrew. This left him with only twenty-one men, nearly the same group that Sandino recruited at the mines—that is, almost all workers.

Following this decision, with determination and for a just cause, Sandino began with very unequal forces to carry out the struggle and initiate the first actions. His decision and the correctness of his political line resulted in the fact that the ranks of his army began to grow, drawing recruits from the humblest sectors, and eventually in the expulsion of the North American army from Nicaraguan soil. We learned this lesson. We began to develop the revolutionary struggle on the basis of a very small nucleus of combatants, and in extremely adverse conditions.

Formation of the Sandinista front was carried out in close connection with the humble classes of the population, not simply for practical reasons but for ideological and historical reasons as well. We needed to create an updated version of [Sandino's] Army for the Defense of National Sovereignty. For that reason we didn't begin by forming a party but rather an army. We tried to reinsert ourselves into the struggle of Sandino, to expel the local expression of North American power, the *somocista* dictatorship.

For many years the Sandinista front was involved in opening up a political space, at the cost of many sacrifices. First we had to act to be felt, then to be believed, and finally to be transformed into a hope for redemption. I can tell you honestly that when I joined the Sandinista front in 1969, I had no idea how small an organization it was. It was a great surprise when I realized that we were really only a dozen militants, that most of the others had been killed. But the front already had a great impact on a national level. The

FSLN was gaining political space in a country that up until then had been monopolized by the so-called historic parallels of the two traditional parties, exercised through a military, ideological, and political dictatorship.

By the 1970s the Sandinista front was the force that had arisen as the most concrete alternative to the *somocista* dictatorship. We had displaced the traditional opposition parties, which in reality had nothing to do with opposition but rather with connivance with the system and its structure of power.

In 1970, the struggle began to be developed and extended. The Sandinista front, starting out with a small military force, began to become an organic force that was to grow among the masses—a mass force that would become manifested in growing military strength. The FSLN accumulated political-military potential and assembled, over a more or less lengthy period of time, the factors that were indispensable for presenting itself as an alternative: audacity, discipline, spirit of sacrifice, heroism, conspiratorial skill, etc. These accumulated qualities were demonstrated in action December 27, 1974: the taking of the house of Chema Castillo to win freedom for the political prisoners.* This action against the dictatorship was widely supported by the masses. Its main significance was political, not military: a serious revolutionary organization had shown itself capable of militarily challenging, in an audacious way, not only the army but the entire dictatorship. The successful conclusion of this action set off a national celebration in Nicaragua. And this was something that was felt by Somoza and everyone else.

---

* Timing the action to coincide with a posh Christmas party, an FSLN commando team of ten men and three women occupied the house of Somoza associate José María "Chema" Castillo. To secure release of the hostages, Somoza was forced to free eighteen political prisoners, publish and broadcast lengthy FSLN communiqués, and pay $2 million.

The political crisis of the Somoza dictatorship was already beginning to be felt by 1976. The ruling classes began to see clearly and with concern that the political instrument that had served for so long to assure their mode of economic power was beginning to erode. They set themselves the task of trying to find a replacement for it. A sector of the population saw this effort to find a replacement as a struggle against *somocismo*. But in reality it was of assistance to *somocismo*, an effort to sustain *somocismo* without Somoza, though of course contrary to what Somoza may have desired. The bourgeoisie formed an opposition front called UDEL (Democratic Liberation Union) that included the Conservative Party, the Social Christian Party, and a few labor organizations from the center and the right. As the political crisis deepened, and as the Sandinista front's confrontation with *somocismo* grew in scope from the end of 1977 on, the bourgeoisie tried to strip the FSLN of its role as the vanguard force of consistent opposition. In effect, we began to compete with them.

The point behind my saying this is that the axis of our policy of alliances was not the bourgeoisie but the people. This is not demagogy; that's exactly how it was. Our program and assessment of the relationship of forces was based on a concrete reality: we had the arms and we had the people with us. It was an anti-imperialist, antidictatorial, popular, and revolutionary alliance.

The bourgeoisie, on the other hand, was terrified by the fact that the two extremes in the conflict were the people, with the Sandinista front as their vanguard, on the one hand; and on the other, the *somocista* dictatorship as the vanguard of the Yankees. They tried to persuade the United States to stop supporting Somoza—who had become a sort of cancer for imperialist domination—and to support them. But it was already quite late. Somoza had no intention of resigning, and the bourgeoisie, in that period, did not have the strength to pull itself together and assume a role of dynamism and legitimacy in the eyes of the people.

A factor in this delay was the very nature of the Nicaraguan bourgeoisie, which as a political class practically didn't exist. The effort here to form a national bourgeoisie was cut short by the United States, when it overthrew the progressive bourgeois Zelaya government. It coincided with an economic crisis that impoverished everybody, and this in turn did not permit the accumulation of national capital. And when the economy revived a little, the Somozas were already in power, not as representatives of the bourgeoisie but as representatives of the Yankees, who stood above the bourgeoisie. Somoza used this power to build a fortune, shared with just a few other families. This was done in such a way as to give us an oligarchy at the top, made up of just a few families, along with a poorly formed, very North-Americanized bourgeoisie that could not survive without foreign capital. For that very reason Nicaragua's bourgeoisie did not have a national program to defend; it was denationalized and weak to boot.

The only forces in contention, therefore, were the *somocista* dictatorship and the Sandinista front. This made it very difficult for the bourgeoisie to gain a political space. It is true that economically, above all after the [1972] earthquake, they began to gain more strength. To the point, in my opinion, that at that moment they had possibilities for beginning to implement a national program of bourgeois economic development. But the popular classes and their vanguard, the Sandinista front, were already far ahead. So when the crisis of the dictatorship came, it was first of all provoked by the revolution, and secondly taken advantage of only by the revolution.

Later the bourgeoisie set out to organize a force called the FAO (Broad Opposition Front) that had its own projects and which, as the continuator of the UDEL, wanted *somocismo* without Somoza. For a few months the FSLN called for participating in the FAO, while at the same time the United People's Movement (MPU) was being formed as the political expression of a broad popular alliance. The MPU was made up of about twenty popular organizations, all of them ready for war. It included the Sandinista front and all the left parties, including the Independent Liberal Party and a sector of the Socialist Party. The FAO was made up of the right-wing parties, plus a small faction of the Socialist Party.

When the FSLN called for participation in the FAO, it was not calling for tail-ending the bourgeoisie or granting them concessions. It was trying to prevent sections of the bourgeoisie and the petty bourgeoisie from taking advantage of the crisis of the dictatorship to convert themselves into an alternative to Somoza for imperialism.

We could have taken power without this alliance, but we made an effort to draw these forces closer when we called for the formation of a National Patriotic front. Because of this approach, one wing of the FAO withdrew and joined the Patriotic front; the other remained in the FAO. The sectors that came over to the Patriotic front were petty-bourgeois—parties made up of professionals, doctors, lawyers, artisans, like the Independent Liberal Party and the People's Social Christian Party. In practice, these were the two parties that came over to the National Patriotic Front. The rest of the FAO stayed where it was. On July 20, when we were in the plaza celebrating the victory, they were in Venezuela, trying to sell their program, a program different from that of the revolution.

That's in relation to alliances before the triumph of the revolution. Now, we have pledged ourselves to a broad program of constructing a new society. Our aim is to integrate all sectors of the nation under revolutionary hegemony. We begin from the basis that we have to develop a process of democratic transformations. For that reason we have set up a system in which power is shared among the organizations that made up the Patriotic front. We formed the Council of State with them; they have people in various ministries. The minister of labor is the president of the Independent Liberal Party. There are vice-ministers who are members of the Socialist Party. There are people in the Supreme Court from the Liberal Party, others from the People's Social Christian Party. That is to say, this is a government of the Patriotic front.

Who are those who have withdrawn? Those who were never with us and who, through the generosity of the Sandinista front and the very broad appeals for integration into the process that we launched, latched on at the last minute—that is, after July 20. Even those who worked against us up until July 20 were later integrated. We united all the forces of the nation to liquidate *somocismo*, but we committed ourselves only to the humble classes. It is logical that people who didn't share our program before the triumph also wouldn't share it when it was being put into practice. In fact it was a very short period of time before they left the country or renounced a role in the process, demonstrating their lack of consistency.

HARNECKER: You mean, then, that the revolution has not lost support?

WHEELOCK: I don't think you can say we lost support that we never had. If these people, at a given moment, participated in the revolutionary process it was first of all because they had lost their battle, and secondly to try to influence the revolutionary process, to derail it. But when they saw the firmness of our determination they left. It's not that they stopped supporting the revolutionary program but rather that they returned to work against the program.

3. THE ROLE OF THE BOURGEOISIE

> "That the bourgeoisie simply produce; that it limit itself as a class to a productive role. That it use its means of production to live, not as instruments of power, of imposition."

HARNECKER: Returning to the theme of the bourgeoisie, do you think there can be an alliance with the bourgeoisie in a country where the people clearly have hegemony?

WHEELOCK: We have begun to carry out a program that seeks to genuinely construct a country, and in doing so we have strictly followed national interests. First, we are seeking to guarantee its sovereignty: that the country be sovereign, that it exist as such. Second, that it exploit its resources as a function of national, not foreign, interests. We are speaking here of things that are really profound, for this is the fullest sense of what the revolution is for Nicaragua: that it can be Nicaragua, a Nicaraguan Nicaragua and not a U.S.-style Nicaragua. To be able to really exist as Nicaragua, in a way that it never existed before in the sense of a sovereign state. And around this program we have organized the population in forms that provide them more favorable living conditions and, at the same time, give the country durable and stable peace. We have here a peasantry that was impoverished to the extreme, a proletariat that was semiproletarian, classes that were not completely formed, including a bourgeoisie that was not completely formed. We have here a capitalist system that was not fully formed, uneven, poorly constructed—a system that no longer served us.

We want to construct a real, genuine social system in Nicaragua, and we want to complete it. In a way, we have begun to do this. We are trying to take the best that existed in our society's natural social tendencies and give them such a form that in the future they can be in accord with national interests.

We think the peasantry has to be grouped together in associations, that the working class has to be converted into a genuine working class with its own specific interests. We think also that the sectors of the bourgeoisie coexisting alongside ought to be given opportunities, but in such a way that their continued possession of means of production—within the limits imposed—does not become a means for calling into question our process or become incompatible with our program for building a new society.

After all, what actually happened here? In the final analysis, there arose a social system of a capitalist character, in which the bourgeoisie was supposedly the dominant class. But in fact they did not dominate, because this bourgeoisie never held in its hands the system's centers of rationality and logic. Those were in the hands of imperialism and its local expression, *somocismo*. The latter two forces represented a power that defended the interests of the local bourgeoisie, but was not a power *of* the bourgeoisie. In a way, Somoza himself was also a major capitalist.

One of the first problems we encountered in trying to incorporate the bourgeoisie into the process was that the power that we represent, revolutionary power, broke with the former logic for constructing the society. So the question that had to be asked was the following: Is it possible for the bourgeoisie as such, or a system molded along bourgeois lines, to exist alongside revolutionary power? I don't think it's possible. The fundamental, characteristic element of capitalist society is the power of the bourgeoisie, the military power of the bourgeoisie—that is, the power to do whatever they have to do, including breaking the rules of the game whenever necessary.

Here what has to be posed theoretically is whether it is possible that the bourgeoisie simply produce, without power, that they limit themselves as a class to a productive role. That is, that they limit themselves to exploiting their means of production and use these means of production to live, not as instruments of power, of imposition.

I think it is possible in Nicaragua. We inherited a country in which neither capitalism nor the capitalist class was fully formed and, on top of that, did not directly hold political power. But the revolution broke the logic of imperial domination in one Latin American country, and when that logic was broken, so too were other very important factors—the psychology of security, for example. The bourgeoisie was accustomed to being the belligerent and dominant force in ideology, culture, and society, but today they are not the ones who dominate. Here those who speak, who set the tone, are the workers and peasants, the student leaders, the union leaders, the ATC, the CST, the Sandinista front—none of which represent the bourgeoisie.

It is a complex problem. But we have not renounced the search for forms in which we can integrate the more or less big individual producers who live in the Nicaragua of today into a social formation dominated by revolutionaries. The conformation of society in the countries of the Third World is somewhat peculiar. The possibilities for social development are not determined by an extreme contradiction between the forces of production and the relations of production. Rather, they are often the product of other circumstances that have to do with a country's national liberation. I believe that in these conditions it is possible to find ways in which a social organization under revolutionary hegemony can maintain forms of production, groups of capitalist production relations, that are not dominant but subordinate. At this moment in Nicaragua, this exists, but without the consent of part of the bourgeoisie. In any event, our program for social construction seeks a peaceful path in which we, in a persuasive manner, seek to integrate all these sectors into national production, into national life.

HARNECKER: Of the existing bourgeois sectors, what percentage, more or less, has remained in the country, working?

WHEELOCK: Here the financial bourgeoisie, which dominated the rest of the economic structure, was cut off at the roots.

HARNECKER: You mean, what is usually called the "oligarchy" has disappeared?

WHEELOCK: Yes, disappeared. What remains are unorganized sectors of the industrial bourgeoisie, and the agrarian bourgeoisie of a local character: the cotton growers of Chinandega and León, the coffee growers of Matagalpa, the sorghum growers of Granada, the rice growers of Nandaime. I would say that the great majority of the direct agricultural producers, that is, the private producers who own 100 or 200 manzanas, say 160 hectares, have stayed in the country. Cotton is the most dynamic sector of our agricultural production, and the medium and large private producer dominates in this crop. This year these growers have great enthusiasm for production, for increasing the crop area, because last year was a good year. In addition, there are incentives from the government, and we have just wiped out their debts.... This year we are thinking about increasing cotton production.

Our political economy seeks to give incentives to this type of producers, to assure them of the security of their property, that it will not be affected in an arbitrary manner. Land is taken over only for reasons that are strictly logical and technical. So a certain understanding has been reached. If the rules of the game hadn't been accepted, production would have fallen. And the state does not have the installed capacity to replace these producers in the short term. So we are not seeking to replace them but rather looking for forms of cooperation, of integration. We would like them to work economically for a project that, over the long run, will give both them and their children stability and security, but within a logic dominated by the forces of the revolution. We have, for example, just finished setting up a number of mixed enterprises in which the state is associated with private interests. One was for a well-drilling outfit whose equipment is part state-owned, part private.

We are thinking about encouraging more of these enterprises. In cotton, for example, in areas where the state has a parcel of land on one side and private producer on the other, we are thinking about joining the two parcels and forming a mixed agricultural enterprise. We can take advantage of the experience they have, and they can take advantage of the capital we have in land. After all, they were a minority, in some ways weak; the old society wasn't theirs. Now we are giving them the possibility of being genuine Nicaraguans, of being national producers, not "dollar-drainers," that is, pro-Yankees who live with their heart in Miami and their whip in Nicaragua. We have opened up a space for the bourgeoisie, in córdobas. If they accept, this space can be kept open indefinitely.

HARNECKER: And how will the problem of the workers who work under these capitalists be resolved?

WHEELOCK: Here the working class works under the perspective of a national program. A little while ago the workers from the San Antonio sugar refinery came to the Ministry of Agricultural Development and presented me with the final sack from production, in testimony of the fact that they had worked for the revolution. They told me: "We work in a private enterprise, but we are not 'private.' We are workers of the revolution, and we work in these production units in the belief that we are helping the revolution." This refinery has not had a single strike in two years. And this refinery, which is privately owned, for us is part of the national patrimony, for it produces a great part of the sugar we export. We help it by subsidizing its costs of production, which are higher than the world price of sugar. But in turn, the profitability of this enterprise is extensively controlled through the credit, fiscal, and pricing policies set by the revolution.

From the economic point of view, the San Antonio refinery does not introduce an element of great lack of control but rather serves as a major source of circulating capital. At present, moreover, we are in the process of reaching agreement on expanding its facilities. This is happening with other industries as well. The important thing is for the working class to be aware of what is being done.

I think if you have a revolutionary government, and if you have a political economy that is clear on how you are going to move forward, it can be quite simple to transform the social structure without always having to resort to expropriation of the means of production. That doesn't mean we won't expropriate, in certain circumstances, especially when what's involved are production units in remote locations where the producers are either decapitalizing or trying to influence the minds of the workers against the revolution. When that happens we expropriate those owners, not because they are private producers but because they are counterrevolutionaries.

HARNECKER: This collaboration by the bourgeoisie, did it begin at the outset of the revolution or is it something that has occurred in the last few years?

WHEELOCK: I don't think you can say that they collaborate with the revolutionary process. The important thing is that they are not in a position to break with the national program. They work in the ambience of a nation that is producing, and that is what, in the last analysis, interests them.

HARNECKER: If they can't take their profits out of the country, if they don't have the means to travel abroad, if their ability to buy hard currency is restricted, and if their properties are limited—doesn't all this have an effect of destimulation?

WHEELOCK: Yes, obviously. That's why, beginning last

year, we gave them certain access to hard currency for useful purposes, including recreational, with certain limitations.

HARNECKER: Does that mean there has been a change in policy in regard to treatment of the bourgeoisie?

WHEELOCK: In 1980–81 we had a level of agricultural production that was acceptable in view of all that had been destroyed. There was an accelerated recovery. Farm production rose by 37 percent. That was the year of the expropriation of Somoza. We were reorganizing that entire sector; we didn't touch the rest of the agricultural producers. In 1981–82, there was a certain decline in production. At that time there was already some uncertainty, because after 1980 we had begun to touch their interests, to strike a blow at the big land owners, and to expropriate non-*somocistas*. It was a year of economic crisis, of a drop in international prices. So there was uncertainty, frictions, and struggle between the bourgeoisie and us on a political level, a struggle between the bourgeoisie's economic associations and us, a struggle in which what was at stake was whether they would produce or not produce. In that context we decided to issue a law stating that those who did not produce would be expropriated.

HARNECKER: You mean that the threat of losing their property weighed more heavily than the destimulation created by other circumstances?

WHEELOCK: Exactly. In 1982–83 the incentives were introduced. Production was granted a margin of profitability, efficiency was rewarded, certain access was given to hard currency. In the agricultural sector, still greatly influenced by the laws of market economy, we practically assured profitability. I don't think anyone would be interested in producing cotton if he knew he was going to lose money. It was a good year in terms of the amount of land planted but a very bad year in terms of the climate and agro-ecological conditions.

For the latter reason it can't be taken as an indicator of the level of production attained.

I think the positive thing has been that we have generated economic policies that have barred the way to the negative tendencies of private production. Thanks to this policy we have registered, despite all the problems we've had (destimulation, problems in the countryside, insecurity), a final result that is more positive than negative. National production has increased, not fallen. At the same time we have given a big push to state production, to cooperative production, and to the peasantry. We have given support to the four sectors that make up agricultural production, which in turn is the economic base of the country: state property, the cooperative sector, big private property, and small private property.

Now some producers, cotton growers for example, have left the country because they did not accept working under these conditions. Here the cotton producer was an entrepreneur in the most dynamic sector of the economy. He had a lot of money, he grew rich, but he consumed rather than invested. He had yachts, bought expensive new cars every year, went on trips with his whole family, spent with great ostentation, bought houses. . . . So some of them did not accept the more humble role that was now theirs to play in this society—a more subdued, more subordinate role—and they left. But there are a lot of people here with experience in raising cotton, and those who left were immediately replaced. For the land is excellent, and since the equipment was already here in the country, a certain amount of experience was all that was required. It was no problem. There was an intermediary base of technicians, with mid-level management capacities, who immediately replaced these producers. The state rented them the land that had been abandoned by its owners.

4. THE CHURCH

"On July 19, 1979, we found Monsignor Obando in Venezuela, working as a politician, not as a bishop, trying to use the influence of religion in support of a political solution."

HARNECKER: The religious phenomenon is a phenomenon extremely widespread in Nicaragua. This, in a certain way, is reflected in the government itself; two of its members are priests, which is quite exceptional. The Catholic church was an element that played a role in favor of the struggle against Somoza, but today it serves more as a brake than as an impulse for the construction of the new society. How is this to be explained? Do you think it is possible to make a strategic alliance with the Christians and, specifically, with the Catholic church, for the construction of the "new society"? Or is it the case that they represented a positive factor only in the struggle against the then-existing tyrant, and that they have now become the main bulwark of bourgeois-democratic values, becoming in effect a brake on the revolution?

WHEELOCK: It is true that there were expressions of support to the revolution and participation in it by religious sectors. But I would say, to start, that the question of religion is not quite the same as the question of participation by Nicaraguans in the Sandinista people's revolution.

Nicaragua was divided, from the point of view of the struggle, between *somocistas* and Sandinistas, between revolutionaries and counterrevolutionaries. The Sandinista front emerged as a political organization that raised economic, social, and political objectives. It emerged fundamentally as an armed revolutionary organization and, in the course of its development, grew to include, was joined by, very diverse sectors of national life: university students, high school students, women, peasants. At a certain moment, as part of the development, as part of the dynamic of the deepening of the struggle, we also saw the incorporation, in an organized way, of young people who had come together around a Christian movement that was active at a student and neighborhood level and included a few progressive priests. We understand their participation to be political, not religious, and also that the participation of the priests was of a strictly political and not religious character. We did not give either the students or the priests the task of using their religious message to gain sympathy. What we did do was to link up with them as combatants, as representatives of part of our people.

So first I would like to make clear that the reason for the participation by the Christian youth and a few priests was that we agreed on common objectives. We did not propose an alliance with the Christians. Certainly the participation of Christians was very important in strengthening the struggle. These were Christians who, from my point of view, were participating in the struggle as Nicaraguans, but with their own perspective. They also participated because of a certain morality, an authentic Christian morality that forms part of the reexamination of what it means to be a Christian in the moment humanity is living today. There was a coincidence of views with the Christians, in that the just cause of, the demand for, national redemption raised by the FSLN was also the aspiration of a more militant and renewed Christianity. So I would separate the question of the institution from the question of the human individual.

In the framework of the currents inside the church as such, we can say that the Christian sectors, if it is possible to speak of Christian sectors, have two attitudes—some are opposed to revolution and others support it. But this attitude, at bottom, is an attitude of class. It is not a stance based on religion, but a stance based on the assessment each individual makes of his role in society. Monsignor Obando [archbishop of Managua] for example, represents bourgeois ideology from his post in the church hierarchy, an ideology that supported nonrevolutionary alternatives for replacing Somoza. So one can ask, Is the Catholic church hierarchy the bearer of Christianity, is it fulfilling its pastoral mission? Or is it simply defending a given political option, an option that is the same as that of the former director of the Banco de América or of a colonel in the *somocista* National Guard.

Furthermore, there existed an entire earlier ideological current that linked the church to the state, to the regime, and to the established order. That current has been present in all the churches in Central America, in a backward, marginalized, underdeveloped, and extremely impoverished Central America. And precisely because of these conditions of injustice and oppression, after Vatican Council II Christian currents arose and flourished here that were opposed to this concept—which they called "collaborationist"—of the hierarchy's relationship to dictatorial governments. The existence of such progressive currents facilitated the incorporation of Christians in the revolution.

HARNECKER: You told me earlier that Obando was in Venezuela as one of the leaders of the FAO when the revolution triumphed. . . .

WHEELOCK: Yes. Obando and the church hierarchy, with rare exceptions, assumed a bourgeois position. They defended the option of *somocismo* without Somoza so as to try to safeguard the existing order, an order that had served to entrench them securely.

HARNECKER: In other words, he wasn't with the revolution; he was against Somoza, which is something different. . . .

WHEELOCK: That's it. When Somoza was capable of preserving *order*, the church was with Somoza. Almost all the bishops, including Obando y Bravo, were *somocistas* in their early years. But the time came when Somoza became an obstacle to preserving order. The bourgeoisie then sought another way out; they became anti-Somoza, but the aim was still to preserve bourgeois order. That's the attitude the church hierarchy was to adopt. And that's why on July 19, 1979, we found Obando in Venezuela, working toward a non-revolutionary option. He was working as a politician, not as a bishop. Clearly, however, he was trying to use the influence of religion to gain support for a political solution of a certain sort. That is where the problems with the church-as-institution originated, that is where they developed from.

HARNECKER: The effort imperialism and the counterrevolution are making today is to try to force a confrontation between you and the Christian population. They characterize you as atheists, as people opposed to the Christian conception of the world. How do you respond to the ideological use imperialism is making of religion?

WHEELOCK: I think you can take as a concrete example what I said to the peasants yesterday, in the ceremony where land titles were given to several cooperatives in Nueva Segovia:

"The *somocistas* say we are atheists, that we don't believe in God; they certainly don't tell you that we are the ones who are living up to the commandments, to the Bible, working toward the well-being of all. We prefer to say, let's look at deeds, not words. Blessed are the poor, the Bible says. But who are we helping? Isn't it the poor, with land, work, loans, schools, the campaign to teach reading and writing . . . ? We say, yes, we are living up to this teaching. Blessed be the poor, and they will be, despite *somocismo* and despite the counterrevolution. Blessed be the meek, the peaceful, for they shall inherit the earth. These words must be familiar to you. Aren't they? Who spoke those words? (A peasant replied, 'He who was on high and who now is here among us.') Yes, he who is here and has given you land.

"So who represents the sentiment of fraternity and love toward the peasants? It is *sandinismo* that represents genuine love here, love of the poor and the peasants that is deep and real. Shut the door to those who say that we are against the ideas of Christianity, because we are living up to these ideas. Not only do we live up to them, but we go beyond them. We do more than just live up to them because we are prepared to shed our last drop of blood for you. How many died in the war that made this triumph possible? Thousands. Why did Carlos Fonseca die? Carlos Fonseca fell and shed his blood for the Nicaraguan people. Where did he die? In the heart of the mountains, at the side of peasants. Julio Buitrago was a student. He wasn't fighting for himself or for his own happiness. If he had wanted to fight for his own happiness he could have remained a law student rather than dying for the people. And Edgard Lang, who was the son of a very rich family. Why did he want to fight, since he already had everything? He fought for a higher purpose—to die and give his life for the people. That is why we are fighting. That is why we will go to the end. And that is why we are invincible."

5. FREEDOM OF THE PRESS

"We do not limit freedom of the press; it still exists. What we limit is the ability to destabilize."

HARNECKER: Isn't it a sign of weakness of this revolution that in the midst of armed counterrevolutionary aggression, periodicals like *La Prensa* are still published?

WHEELOCK: To take this up you have to begin with our revolution's concept of pluralism. From the outset we clearly established the rules of the game. We gave every sector the opportunity to become integrated into the revolution. Our program is a democratic-popular program. There has to be a revolutionary transformation, and above all else, national sovereignty must be defended. These are, shall we say, the basis of the new social leadership. We accept the existence of other political parties. The only thing we prohibit is the organization of supporters of *somocismo*.

But what has actually happened? Under the instigation of imperialism, a series of reactionary sectors within the right wing have begun to violate the peace of our society. To what aim? To facilitate the return of North American imperialism and the enslavement of Nicaragua. They are therefore antinational sectors.

Reagan is the main enemy of Nicaragua's mixed economy. He doesn't want pluralism here, he doesn't want to see us carry out this very important program, for it is full of promise for the rest of Latin America. He doesn't want to see us succeed. So part of his general plan for destabilization here is to try to impede, attack, and destroy our program. That's what lies behind the fact that the newspaper *La Prensa* at a certain point began to be converted into the general staff of reaction. It stopped being *La Prensa* of Pedro Joaquín Chamorro, or *La Prensa* of the first few months of the revolution. It was taken over by sell-out and reactionary sectors, led by the CIA, and they began to use it as an instrument for shaping public opinion as part of their destabilization plans.

What has our response been? We have limited the right wing's use of a public means of communication for spreading their destabilizing message, something they usually try to accomplish by falsifying or distorting news. We have set certain norms.

HARNECKER: What are these norms?

WHEELOCK: There are two main laws. One says that economic and social data must be attested to by official bodies. The other states that news about defense of the country can come only from the Ministry of Defense. Both laws are connected with national defense. It was necessary to discipline the news a little with a sense of responsibility.

With these laws we limited not freedom of the press, which still exists, but rather the ability to destabilize.

In any country in the world, in the United States, for example—if the *New York Times* were to try to publish an article saying the Chase Manhattan Bank was on the verge of collapse, it would be stopped because that's a news item that acts against the system. Freedom of the press, as conceived by bourgeois democracy, means you can make as many criticisms as you like so long as you don't call into question the basis of the regime. When a piece of news or a periodical threatens the system, it is simply suppressed. Our freedom of the press exists within the framework of a new system in which education, participation, and the formation of opinion must have a strong national, moral, and constructive character. We permit citizen pressure of any type whatever as long as it is within the framework of the rules of the new economic, social, and political system we are seeking to build. These even include the right of the opposition parties themselves to aspire to take power.

We are at present discussing a law on political parties in the Council of State where that is made explicit. Our responsibility as a political party is to make every effort to retain power, but from the point of view of the nation we have to acknowledge that there are citizens who have a totally different point of view, and that they have the right to hold this different view. Our task is to persuade and convince them. But if they are not convinced, they have the right to fight for their ideas as long as these ideas are not contrary to the historic necessity to create a new society. They can be anti-Sandinista, they can be opposed to the Sandinista front as a political party, they can criticize us. But they cannot attack the bases of the new society that are in the historic interests of the people of Nicaragua, that are part of their patrimony. Such people can be nonrevolutionary, but they cannot be counterrevolutionary. Against them the revolution does not attack, it defends itself. So it is within these limits, which are quite flexible, that we are moving.

6. WHAT IMPERIALISM FEARS

"Our revolution shattered a general model of imperialist power. If the United States occupies Central American territories, there will be many Sandinos in the area around Managua."

HARNECKER: I understand that you were a student in Chile during the Popular Unity government, and that you are well informed about that experience. Do you think imperialism is using the same methods here? How did it achieve its aims there, while it has not been able to do so in Nicaragua?

WHEELOCK: In Chile imperialism began to organize the removal of the government fundamentally by using the power of economic influence retained by the bourgeoisie and the oligarchy and at the end by using the armed forces, which had a reactionary organization and ideology.

We didn't come to power through elections, nor through the support of a fraction of the electorate, as was the case in Chile. We came to power through armed struggle; we defeated the army of the dictatorship and the Yankees. That enabled us to establish an armed, people's government, based on a very broad national consensus. That's why imperialism is using a multifaceted strategy of struggle against the Sandinista people's revolution. Diplomatically, they are trying to isolate us. Politically, they are trying to incite to action all the domestic and international subversive forces that are disposed to question our holding power. Economically, they are trying to strike a blow at us through sabotage and efforts to discourage the private productive sector. And above all militarily, which is the spearhead of all the rest.

The strategy of imperialism is not the same one we know from the past, that is, destabilization as such, as was the case in Chile. There the aim of destabilization was to bring about the disintegration of the elements that made up the ideological, economic, and political system of the people's government. They tried to separate the people from Allende through ideological and economic, not military, tactics. The military was used for the final blow and brought about the removal of the government in a matter of four hours. Our case is different. The axis of aggression against Nicaragua is military because they are trying to overthrow an armed people's revolutionary government. It can't be destabilized by economic or political measures alone, because we can counteract these. They have to overthrow us militarily, impede the consolidation of our process, impede the consolidation of our people's armed forces. That's why they are resorting to Somoza's army, which is what they have closest at hand for the task.

So our case is different from that of Chile, though to be sure there are some similar elements as well. The tactics imperialism applied in Chile, it has to be acknowledged, were successful. They were based on the class struggle. Imperialism clearly identified which classes were allies, which classes were in conflict, the enemies, the nature of the government, its limitations, its strengths. Imperialism used the weapon of ideology. All of this is being used against us as well.

HARNECKER: Do you think the military aspect was, in your case, present from the beginning?

WHEELOCK: When they saw it was going to be hard to salvage their army, the first thing they tried to do was to work out a governmental compromise with us. We'll give them the government and keep the army, they thought. These negotiations were never negotiations with Somoza, but rather with intermediaries of the United States and the United

States itself, because it was the U.S. that held power here in reality. Their position was that they could remove Somoza at any time, in exchange for our agreement to discuss with the National Guard a way of integrating them into a new army. We could have accepted this, for we were working with the idea that any soldier who hadn't been involved in crimes could be integrated, in one form or another, in a new revolutionary army. However, for a series of reasons that it would take too long to discuss here, this discussion was not able to continue and Somoza's army fell. After Somoza left and we made a very strong military push, the National Guard simply disbanded. They dumped their weapons, their uniforms, everything . . . Somoza's army was finished. All the officers fled, to embassies, in small planes, in big planes, in every direction. So a period of time passed in which the imperialists had no alternative to employ. Of course, they tried to see if they could intervene militarily against us. Somoza's army had been dismantled, not because they wanted that to happen but because of factors beyond their control. Later they began to develop an overall strategy with military aggression as its axis—as I mentioned earlier—to try to cut down our revolution.

HARNECKER: Did you understand clearly from the beginning what was going to happen, that you would have to devote such efforts and resources to militarily strengthening the revolution?

WHEELOCK: We understood that the struggle against Somoza was a struggle against imperialism; not a struggle against the United States as a country but a struggle against an imperialist concept held by the United States government, for Somoza was a creation of imperialism. They are the ones who proposed arming and training the National Guard. The National Guard was the National Guard of the United States. All its officers were trained in North American schools, with a totally imperialist ideology; they spoke

English, they wrote in English.

We knew that at a given moment imperialism was going to try to destroy the revolution, to regain the piece that it had lost. Nicaragua was a country that belonged to a scheme of power that had been created over a long period of time, with a lot of work and with a lot of resources, by the United States. The Central American countries are dependent countries that are located very close to the United States and above all serve it as sources of supply. The countries here have been shaped in accordance with this logic. They supply coffee, minerals, rubber, and cotton. Such countries require a large working class to pick coffee, extract rubber, mine minerals—and a small, simplified administrative structure. So what happened? There were no national classes capable of managing this type of society, because they had never been able to develop. At the same time there was great popular pressure, stemming from the struggle for economic and social demands by thousands of impoverished wage workers. That was a product of this brutal system of oppression in which the administrative layer received a share of the wealth produced.

Consequently, the United States was compelled to create strong dictatorial governments and impose them on top of these conditions of exploitation and oppression. For the local bourgeoisies could not guarantee the stability of societies that were explosive by their very nature. This is what happened in Guatemala, El Salvador, Honduras, Paraguay, Bolivia, Haiti, and the Dominican Republic. All of these countries have dictatorships organized by the United States, conceived within the framework of imperialist economic relations.

The intrinsic contradiction within the North American scheme was the brutality of these dictatorships. That's why they always tried to introduce cushioning elements like elections, with the aim of providing a certain democratic varnish. And they also talked a little about progress, peace, and democracy. These were dictatorships that, paradoxically, talked about democracy. Somoza declared himself a democrat and held elections every five or six years, like Stroessner [of Paraguay].

The Somoza dictatorship was a classical, typical form, a model of imperialist domination in the situation of Latin America and especially in the Caribbean. When the Nicaraguan revolution broke such a model, something qualitative was shattered. Something of the utmost importance for the security of the reproduction of the imperialist model had been lost. This is destabilizing for imperialism's global scheme of power relations.

We are a danger for the United States; not only because we are a country with an independent foreign policy that it considers negative for its interests; not only because they see us as a "Soviet base"; but fundamentally because we represent the shattering of its classic model of domination for Latin America. And that model consists precisely in the coincidence of three systems of power: the oligarchy, the reactionary church hierarchy, and the military gorillas. All their power, draped with pseudodemocratic ideology, was cemented atop that triangle. The Sandinista revolution broke with the oligarchy, with the reactionary church hierarchy, and with the Somoza military dictatorship. It broke with the pattern that brought profound distortions to our history: poverty, brutal oppression, dependency. We are a response, a promising synthesis that is moving away from the past. In reality we are carrying out for the first time in Central America what the United States and its model always promised the people. Under revolutionary hegemony we are attaining peace, stability, progress for the people, and a more perfect democracy. I can tell you that a rupture of this classic model has global effects, for this North American model is in crisis, is being broken, and is being weakened. And we are a proof that revolutionary hegemony does not lead to all the things the United States has said. For example, to totalitarianism, to that communist society bogeyman the United States is always trying to peddle, to persecution, to cruelty, to executions—the notions they also tried to peddle in Chile.

What has happened here? We have had, on the part of revolutionaries, on the part of a "leftist" regime, a whole series of responses that are totally contradictory to the image the United States is trying to create. And, yes, this does have subversive power. It has more subversive power than the arms we are supposedly sending to El Salvador. For it is a general message that has to do precisely with what we could call the crisis of the imperialist model and, for that very reason, the crisis of imperialism. What Reagan and his administration fear the most is that here we are developing an authentically national model—national, Latin American, and in addition a continuation of the work of Bolívar, Martí, and Sandino.

That's also why they isolated Cuba, attacking the Cuban people who, in 1959, were the first to triumphantly break Yankee domination in America. And since then they have not ceased their entire campaign of aggression, lies, and blackmail against the Cuban revolution. That is why we feel ourselves to be brothers of the Cubans. We are sons of America, suffering together the painful birth of liberty in America.

The appeal and attractiveness of a revolution like this—humanist, generous, antidictatorial, participationist, popular, involving social transformations, with economic successes, with great support worldwide—is a defeat for imperialism much greater than the defeat we handed them in battle. It is something bigger than Nicaragua, something more important than a local revolution. This revolution shattered a general model of imperialist power, and for that reason some of the imperialists think that the end is near, that this is the beginning of the end for imperialism.

HARNECKER: How far do you think imperialism will go? Will there be direct intervention?

WHEELOCK: We have never discounted the possibility of direct intervention. If we go by the lessons of our own history we would have to conclude that imperialism is already putting into operation an escalation that will lead, at a given moment, to direct intervention by U.S. military forces in Nicaragua.

We have to remember that Nicaragua fought the United States at various times in the past. They sent troops here before the Bolshevik revolution, before the Cuban revolution. And we are probably going to fight the United States again. Not precisely because of the fact that we are continuing the Bolshevik revolution, that we are continuing the Cuban revolution, but because this is something that is part and parcel of the struggle for freedom and sovereignty in Latin America—you have to oppose imperialism to be free. The case of the Malvinas is an example. If we want there to exist someday a free and sovereign Latin America that follows its own path, that has the right to its own development, to its own prosperity, it will have to be accomplished by fighting North American imperialism.

The countries most subordinated to the United States were precisely the countries of Central America, because they were located along the U.S. spinal cord—the isthmus for an interoceanic canal, a factor that has been a part of our entire history. At one point there were plans to build a canal across Nicaragua, and the United States wanted to maintain this in reserve. Control over the canal means control over their naval and commercial traffic. Through the canal pass all their raw materials, all their fundamental flow of commerce. They must have thought, How are we going to instill confidence in our allies on other continents if we can't exercise meaningful control over something so close?

In reality we are already at war against imperialism. They have organized a secret war against us, but when all is said and done it is a real war. There are Yankee marines and advisers behind this war, serving in its command posts. But the type of soldier involved is less important than the aim and objective being sought. The objective is not to prevent arms from being passed from Nicaragua to El Salvador. This is a justification Reagan is trying to sell to the North American people and Congress, to portray us as an aggressor country. The real aim is to overthrow the revolutionary government. It is to prevent a deeper fissure in its pattern of domination. They claim we are a threat to U.S. security. But this is absolutely false. Nicaragua doesn't represent a threat to the North American nation or people. What it does threaten is imperial will. For that reason our struggle is part of the struggle of the North American people.

An idea of what Reagan is capable of doing has been given by recent developments. We discovered here that agents of the CIA were organizing a plot to murder our foreign minister. In a step that was both prudent and responsible, we expelled only the three North American embassy employees who were most deeply implicated. In reprisal the United States expelled thirty Nicaraguan functionaries, enormously increasing the difficulty of continuing the business arrangements we have with hundreds of North American companies. It was a measure way out of proportion. It shows the intent of the Reagan administration, when it can find an iota of justification, to hit us hard. All that has kept Reagan from implementing even greater aggression against Nicaragua has been international public opinion and domestic pressure inside the United States.

HARNECKER: And the situation in Central America, what role does it play?

WHEELOCK: With the government of Guatemala we really haven't had any problem. We are not in agreement with the type of regime that exists there, from a political and ideological point of view, but this has not led us to break commercial, economic, and cultural relations with the Guatemalan government. With the government of Costa Rica, we have a policy of friendship and cooperation. We were beginning to have good relations with the Salvadoran junta, following the coup against the Romero regime in 1979. We even received a member of that junta here. And in regard to Honduras, we looked quite favorably on the initial neutral and prudent position of the Policarpo Paz government.

But what has happened? Aggressive U.S. policy has taken hold of Honduras, creating a situation of tension, practically a war, in Central America. Why? Because the United States is reacting violently to events that are going to change the relationship of forces and that are going to modify their model of domination in the region. To begin with they opposed the existence of a progressive government in El Salvador, conspired against it, and unleashed internal persecution against all progressive elements in the country. What have they done in Honduras? They are sustaining a military dictatorship that has now come to be a replacement for Somoza's. They are converting Honduras into a U.S. military base and from Honduran territory are constantly provoking hostile actions against the Nicaraguan revolution. In Costa Rica they are trying to influence, pressure, and blackmail the government, to turn it against Nicaragua. They have formed "democratic ententes" with reactionary governments against Nicaragua. They would like to revive CONDECA [Central American Defense Council] to set us fighting against each other to serve their interests. They have gone so far as to bring Israel into the picture. They have carried out several large-scale military maneuvers. They have opposed a peaceful solution in El Salvador. They are arming Somoza's guardsmen. With the result that we, who would like to be a factor for peace and stability, are accused of preparing more than one

Central American country for slaughter. We are accused of being aggressors, and we haven't attacked anyone. We are the ones who are being attacked, as a function of imperialism's aggressive will. All this while the Contadora group continues a discussion that is multilateral and, in a certain sense, bilateral with us.

As long as the U.S. government exercises such a decisive influence over the governments of Central America, there really can be no solution. What the Reagan administration wants is the return of right-wing and fascist military dictatorships, not only in Central America but in the whole world. It seems that these are the only governments that can maintain a stable alliance with the United States, which itself is ruled by irresponsibles and fascists. That is the problem.

We, on the other hand, despite the past, encountered a constructive interlude with Carter, for Carter understood that the United States had to make a certain shift. Reagan supposedly is seeking to protect the United States, but he is leading it to its ruin. Reagan's war policy is not only beyond the control of the United States but of all humanity. It means encouraging the massacres of Palestinians at the hands of the Israelis, encouraging centers of tension everywhere. They want to destroy the Nicaraguan revolution, fill the entire world with arms, stuff themselves with arms, force every country in the world to arm itself. This is going to lead all of us to death. There is another, more secure, way to protect the United States. That is through coexistence, and this was Carter's thesis. Carter said, in effect, let us acknowledge that we can no longer remain friends with the Anastasio Somozas, the Alfredo Stroessners, the Augusto Pinochets. That was more intelligent and forced us to be more prudent. It led us to make a series of commitments, including with the United States. It made us more receptive to proposals they might make. Carter sent us a few important messages at certain times, messages whose considerations we listened to and accepted.

On the other hand, when the [1979] change took place in the Salvadoran government, we asked for the opinion of the revolutionaries of that country. They were enthusiastic because they saw the possibility of embarking toward the beginning of a solution to the conflict. In other words, if deep social changes were to take place in Central America, there would be no revolutionary struggles.

The great majority of the people of Central America, and this includes all layers of society, even progressive sectors of the bourgeoisie, are in favor of such changes. They are changes that are conducive to durable peace and stability.

If deep social changes were to take place, and if a possibility for participation were to open up for those who are today fighting with arms, there would be no problem. But this is not what the present government of the United States wants. It is the United States that is really fostering external and internal violence. It is the United States that is really the origin of violence. They are simply trying to deceive people when they say it has to do with the Soviet Union and the security of the United States.

HARNECKER: If the United States attacks Nicaragua, what will happen with the revolutionaries in the rest of the countries of Central America? Won't the struggle become regionalized?

WHEELOCK: If the United States attacks Nicaragua I see a very high cost for the Nicaraguan people, and I also see a very high cost for the North American forces that penetrate into the country. They paid a high price fifty years ago when Sandino fought them, with few weapons and from a very disadvantageous position. Today, however, the United States will not be fighting a guerrilla liberation movement but an entire country that is prepared to battle to the last man. This is another element that has slowed down imperialism. It has made them take the route of destabilization, of preparing better internal subjective conditions so as to be in a position to mount a more rapid, violent, and shattering attack. And this is where their calculations go wrong. For it is going to be very difficult to do this in Nicaragua, where the great majority of the population are poor and humble people, people who have made gains with the revolution and who are going to defend it with determination.

If the United States intervenes militarily, they are going to compel us to make use of the relations and resources we may find in other countries. It is certain that they are going to have to intervene in other Central American countries to intervene in Nicaragua. In fact they are already building a big base in Honduras for aggression against our country. If this aggression takes place and the United States occupies Central American territories, there will be many Sandinos in the area around Nicaragua. We want to avoid this intervention to the maximum, but we will not sidestep our duty to resist it to the last drop of blood.

7. THERE WILL BE ELECTIONS

> "Imperialism is demanding that we hold elections, because they think the revolution can be overthrown through elections. But our first task is to create an irreversible model of people's power. The forms will come later."

HARNECKER: The question of elections is one of the arguments most used by imperialism against you. If you had carried out an electoral process immediately after the triumph over Somoza, you would undoubtedly have won by a wide margin. Why didn't you do this?

WHEELOCK: We knew perfectly well at the time of the triumph of the revolution that if the Sandinista front had called elections it would have won a resounding victory. However the fact that revolutionary power had emerged out of a massive armed struggle with participation, in one or another form of struggle, of the entire Nicaraguan people gave us a legitimacy of greater quality than a new civil election could have. From the juridical point of view, even bourgeois law recognizes that revolutions are a source of rights and legitimacy, for they are the work of an entire people. When the will of the people is expressed in an armed struggle against an antipopular government, the government that emerges has a historical basis that requires no other source of legitimacy.

A revolution that arises out of armed struggle, and armed struggle itself, is in a certain sense a test of opinion, for it implies a relationship of forces tremendously favorable to a cause. So we could say, therefore, that Nicaragua had "elections" in the period leading up to July 19, but in a military fashion; in contrast to the negative, false, artificial, and deceitful legitimacy *somocismo* tried to cloak itself in, for *somocismo* too had its elections. But those elections under Somoza did not necessarily imply a genuine test of public opinion. They were elections intended to deceive the Nicaraguan people and to cover up the dictatorial and unjust character of the Somoza regime. Somoza always won the elections, and by an overwhelming majority; that's what appeared in the vote results. You might ask, How is it possible that Somoza could win? But it is easy to answer. First, there was no system of national identity cards here, but rather a process of registration for each election. So Somoza could arrange for the vote of nonexistent citizens, including even the dead. In addition, since there was no national identification system, no identity card of any sort, one person could vote fifty or as many times as necessary under different names. Second, the boards of elections were totally controlled by the *somocistas*. And the final tally was taken by an electoral tribunal that was also dominated by the *somocistas*. In short, elections here had absolutely no prestige.

The Sandinista front did not think it was necessary to hold elections because it felt, in the first place, that the revolution had been a perfect test of opinion, of much greater democratic content. And secondly, because this was not the task of the moment; the number-one task then was national reconstruction. For that reason we suggested elections for 1985.

We ourselves called for elections in our program, and we maintain this position. However, a series of situations, linked to the aggression, have made it more difficult and complex to begin to prepare for elections. Not to mention a series of uncompleted technical tasks, such as a census and a national registration of the population, and this too may hold things up. We remain, however, of the opinion that it is necessary to consult our people on most decisions. And in point of fact we maintain ongoing consultation with the different social sectors, sometimes informally and at times in a formal manner. In this area we have developed, from the bottom of society on up, a set of norms and systems of participation that, taken together, are a prefiguration of a new democracy. Above and beyond the Council of State, we hold continual discussions with the people, one example of this being public meetings with the national junta in different parts of the country—in neighborhoods, in factories, in the countryside—in short, throughout the whole country. Workers participate in the management of enterprises. Local areas are governed by the ranks of the population. The people's organizations participate in the formulation of major government measures through committees for the discussion of political questions. Such committees discuss agrarian reform, industrial production, agriculture, and cattle raising and are part of practically every government body that can make important decisions.

HARNECKER: Can you explain how this actually works?

WHEELOCK: I'll give you an example. Our agrarian reform policy—that is, the transformation and development of agriculture and cattle raising—is formulated in consultation with a body called the National Council on Agrarian Reform. There are also regional councils of this type. Every proposal for development is brought for discussion before this council, which includes representatives of peasant organizations, workers' organizations, municipal and regional organizations, and state institutions.

That doesn't mean that we're satisfied. We are working toward the construction of a new society. This implies first of all building the central apparatus of a new state, a task that we are at present still carrying out. In a second phase we will assimilate and analyze our accumulated experience and on that basis continue working toward the institutionalization of the revolution. That will require, first of all, participation in that work by the popular organizations and all sectors of the population. In our draft plans for this, we have talked about a national constituent assembly. It is likely that an organization of this character will work for some time, perhaps for years, laying the basis for what will be a new republican institutionality of a democratic and popular character. Although elections need not necessarily be linked to such a constituent assembly and to such an institutionalization, we have thought about the possibility of linking them—that is, of using elections to initiate our institutionalization. What is likely, in the framework of all the aggressions we are suffering, is that institutionalization will proceed in an autonomous manner, and the question of elections will be dependent on a return to a minimum normality. It makes no sense for us to be trying to organize a big election campaign at a time when we are being brutally attacked.

Imperialism is demanding that we hold elections, not because they are convinced that elections are the guarantee of a government's legitimacy, but because they think the revolution can be overthrown by elections.

Now it wouldn't be of much help, and in fact would be a grave setback, if we were planning to repeat something like the worn-out electoral maneuvers of the *somocista* past. In Latin America, elections in general have been discredited; they don't correspond to the growing political maturity of our people. The ruling groups in general employ this type of elections to confuse the people with promises and manipulative campaigns, so as to perpetuate regimes that can no longer respond to the masses' needs.

Our duty as Nicaraguans and as Latin Americans is to seek to overcome historically, within the framework of democracy, the contradiction inherent in traditional elections—namely, that they are antipopular. This is the challenge. We are studying, we are examining history, we are examining the past so as to recover it, so as to become the continuators of the vanguard of republican forms of government that were once part of this continent but have since been eroded away. We want to help bring solutions.

In 1830 in Nicaragua, only those who owned property could vote. The responsibility of citizenship was measured according to your pocketbook which meant only the wealthy sectors had the right to vote. The Liberal revolution of 1893 institutionalized universal suffrage. That was a conquest, but a relative one, for Nicaragua was still a country that was illiterate in its great majority.

I think we must study universal suffrage, in the sense of assuring that citizens can effectively vote in accordance with their authentic interests. It is a question of consciousness, of political maturity, of more advanced popular and social organization. To assure that in Nicaragua the workers and peasants make use of the right to vote, we have to find new forms of participation, of state leadership. The first thing we have to do is to create an irreversible model of people's power; the forms will come later. There is nothing simple about this. It is a theoretical and historical problem that hasn't even been sorted out yet. The challenge for us is to sort it out. If we don't, what will be the use of the revolution? To return to the past?

The ridiculous thing is that others reproach us for moving slowly in carrying out the pledge to hold elections. It's ironic that in circumstances in which no one, from Plato's utopia on down, can boast of having attained democracy, we, the Sandinistas, are criticized for not having attained it in three or four years.

8. AGRARIAN REFORM

"We are carefully seeking the best land for the small producers and the cooperatives"

HARNECKER: Can you tell me the main measures that have been taken in the field of agrarian reform and how they have affected the peasant population?

WHEELOCK: After practically four years of agrarian reform we can say, in general terms, that we have completed a quite acceptable process of transformation of the property structure we inherited from *somocismo*. At the same time, the drastic revolutionary measures that we have taken have not resulted in a decline in agricultural production. To the contrary, year after year there has been an increase in the recovery and growth of the agricultural sector.

In my opinion, it's not always so easy to combine two such sets of circumstances. It is the result of applying the fundamental political principles of our revolutionary program to agrarian reform and of a program of transformations that has taken into account the socioeconomic conditions that characterize Nicaragua. Nicaragua's agrarian reform is, for that reason, peculiar to it.

I will explain, first, the main political factors.

We worked out a program based on pluralism and the mixed economy, but with a content that is profoundly popular, revolutionary, and anti-imperialist. That is the framework from which all our practical steps in agrarian reform flow. Agrarian reform, therefore, is a means, an instrument for attaining these objectives, and not an end in and of itself. To understand this, it is important to see how its different phases developed.

There was a first phase that I would call anti-*somocista*, in which we recovered all the land that *somocismo* had accumulated through robbery, extortion, eviction, etc. Our first agrarian reform law was in fact a decree—the now-famous Decree Number Three of the Junta of the Government of National Reconstruction—that confiscated the *somocistas*. It was complemented by Decree Number Thirty-eight, which extended the measure to Somoza's associates.

That gave us about a million hectares, nearly 20 percent of the land owned in the country. These properties had to be organized in the form of state enterprises because the great majority of farms were in reality agro-industrial plantations. They included sugar refineries, coffee plantations, and modern rice plantations that were not susceptible either to being distributed among small producers or ceded to cooperatives.

In this first phase there arose what we call the people's property sector, which had in particular the task of initiating a process of incorporating agricultural workers into the administration of the enterprises. Formation of this sector gave the state an important control over the strategic section of the economy.

We quickly realized that what we had recovered from *somocismo*, given its technological nature and its territorial magnitude, left us rather limited in terms of resolving the problem of peasants without land. To be sure we issued laws forcing landlords to rent out land, and at lower prices—a measure that benefited thousands of peasants, squatters, and small renters. We also initiated a credit policy that was so extensive that, in comparison with the last year of *somocismo*, it multiplied by ten the amount of agricultural loans given to peasants.

These measures, however, were insufficient, and we began to work on a more integrated agrarian reform law. The aim of this law, which was to mark the second phase, was to take idle or insufficiently exploited land out of the hands of the big landowners and turn it over to landless peasants, so as to form small units of property, in some cases individually owned but fundamentally cooperative. I would call this the antilatifundist phase. In applying this law we expropriated some 600,000 hectares for the benefit of both the peasantry and the state enterprises.

The overall result of these two phases was a very important change in the structure of agricultural property in Nicaragua. Before the triumph of the revolution, 2,000 landowners owned 50 percent of the land while 120,000 peasants owned barely 3 percent of the national territory.

Because we acted fundamentally against the *somocistas* and owners of idle land, those 2,000 have been drastically reduced, to the point that today they control no more than 13 percent of the land. The state controls 23 percent, and the cooperatives and small producers another 20 percent. We have succeeded in establishing a vast cooperative movement, made up of more than 2,500 associative groups, including nearly 70,000 peasants.

There is an extremely broad layer of medium-sized producers—made up in its majority of humble peasants, but including some who are relatively well off—that owns more than 30 percent of the land. There are also properties of 100, 200, and 300 hectares that belong to big private landowners. They are modern plantations, generally are irrigated, and have certain characteristics of landed property. But because of their efficiency and their size, they have not been brought under the agrarian reform. Finally, the state owns the national land—that is, land that has not been claimed or parceled up—which amounts to half the total area of the country.

We are working today on the third phase, oriented toward consolidation and rationalization of what has already been accomplished. This phase gives particular emphasis to cooperative development and to answering the demand for land on the part of peasant communities in various parts of the country.

I spoke first of the political principles because of the importance they have had in guiding—and in the last analysis, conditioning—our program of transformation. Our agrarian reform, while taking into account national unity and the mixed economy, has struck a blow at *somocismo* and at ownership of idle land. But it has also left space for private producers if they are efficient and, of course, if they assume a role that is consistent with the revolution. At the same time poor and landless peasants have benefited from a series of policies aimed at helping them and providing them with incentives such as cheap credit, subsidized inputs, advantageous prices for corn and beans, grocery supply centers in the countryside, social and housing programs, rural electrification, health care, literacy instruction, road construction, etc.

To be sure, we have segregated what had to be segregated—the cancer that had to be cut out. We are working within a model of agricultural development in which the state, acting as the spearhead of production and the pacesetter of norms, is backed up by efficient private production, by the cooperatives, by the thousands of peasants, today with land, who are together increasing national production, both for domestic consumption and for export.

That doesn't mean that the job is finished. We have much further to go, not only in regard to the process of transformation of agrarian structures, but also in establishing a new economic development that will have as its axis precisely this agricultural sector. It is certain that this last task is going to be very hard.

First, because the socioeconomic formation of Nicaragua is very uneven. There is a pole of modernization, formed by the extensively upgraded plantations. But this coexists alongside considerable holdovers from the aristocratic economy of colonial origin that functions under a pattern of land use that involves extensive idle terrain. This is especially true in the case of primitive cattle raising of the kind that dominates great expanses of land in the center of the country. Alongside these big cattle ranches there exists a minuscule, subsistence peasant economy that is in a certain sense an annex or tributary to the aristocratic haciendas. This peasant community is made up of settlers, squatters, and so forth.

Second, because Nicaragua is a poor country, with weakly developed forces of production and does not have its own technological base for carrying out a project of development based on mechanization and irrigation, which is what we would like to promote.

However, on the basis of international cooperation and the support of the socialist countries and of countries friendly to Nicaragua—such as Mexico, the Arab countries, the Netherlands, France, and Spain—we are carrying out projects that could be characterized as ambitious and whose completion will represent a qualitative leap for the country. In the agricultural sector we are carrying out more than twenty projects totaling some $1.2 billion. These include a sugar refinery, two African palm plantations, four projects for production of blond tobacco, a project to provide 20,000 manzanas of irrigated land for basic foodstuffs, two modern dairy projects that will provide 100 million liters of milk a year, big poultry complexes, rice fields, etc.

We are making all these investments in the midst of an international economic crisis. For us, this is not anything unusual. We have to rebuild what was destroyed and cover the basic necessities that were never covered under *somocismo*. Moreover, we have to take into account the future needs of a population that is increasingly demanding.

HARNECKER: The fact that there was a delay in distributing land to the poor peasantry, didn't this give rise to discontent in that social sector and provide a weapon to the counterrevolution?

WHEELOCK: There was a period between the first and second phase in which we left ourselves, in effect, somewhat exposed in regard to the speed with which land was distributed to the peasants. However, from the promulgation of the agrarian reform law until today, we have distributed hundreds of thousands of hectares of land to the peasants. We are carefully seeking the best land for the small producers and the cooperatives because, in their majority, they are producers of cereals and they need flat, rich land.

Somocismo drove these small producers to poor and marginal land. Humid, tropical land, which is quite extensive in Nicaragua, would be of no use to them for it serves best for perennial crops. So we are giving the peasants some of the best land on the Pacific Coast, where they can attain high crop yields. Of course the counterrevolution has raised as a banner the claim that the revolution is expropriating everything for the state, and that eventually the last peasant with any land left will be affected. But the truth is that we have only hit the big landowners, and among them only the ones who weren't producing. It's also true that some landowners who were producing were affected, but this was done on the basis of previous agreement and cash compensation.

And it was done mainly to acquire land destined for peasant production.

If the revolution has benefited any social sector in this society it has been the peasantry, and they have benefited greatly. That is why the great majority of those who defend the revolution, with arms in hand, against the *somocistas* are peasants. In the north the *somocista* counterrevolutionary bands have murdered more than 200 peasants, both members of cooperatives and individual producers, and they continue to carry out a campaign of terror to frighten and divide the peasants. Nonetheless, in the midst of regions that are at present genuine theaters of full-scale war, there are functioning agricultural communities that have not stopped work and that are armed to defend their land.

HARNECKER: And if you compare the yields on state land and the land distributed among the peasants, which are more productive?

WHEELOCK: State production in Nicaragua is characterized by high efficiency and high technology. In almost all the branches of agriculture that we share with big private production, the state has the best yields. That is nothing out of the ordinary, because in underdeveloped societies the size of the holdings of native landowners does not allow the possibilities of development, of mechanization, of intensive use of technology, that an agricultural enterprise managed by the state has. I don't say that to try to glorify state production. In fact I think if you compare Nicaraguan state production with that of some of the transnational enterprises, you'd probably find they have higher yields. But, if we compare them with big native producers, the state is more efficient, and it can be even more efficient if we reorganize production.

Peasants in a cooperative, or individual peasant producers, work the land provided by the agrarian reform, with the support we have made available in terms of loans, inputs, improved seeds, prices, etc. They have registered a level of production higher than that of traditional peasant production and are moving in the direction of nearly attaining the production levels of the big private producers. This we can see, for example, in cotton.

HARNECKER: While you were speaking about state enterprises with high technology, I was thinking about the problem of how to make high technology compatible with the unemployment that normally exists in an underdeveloped country. . . .

WHEELOCK: OK, we have some examples. There are certain technologies that were employed here by capitalism to reduce the labor force. We are completely against the use of technology as an instrument for reducing the labor force and, as a consequence, increasing unemployment. We use technology for three purposes. First, to obtain better yields. Second, to create sources of employment on the periphery of the cities. And third, to resolve the problems of labor shortages that we are already beginning to encounter in some sectors of agricultural production.

In the first case, it is absolutely necessary that the production of corn, for example, attain a higher degree of technology. The production of basic foodstuffs in Nicaragua has to be modernized because there are limitations in the amount of land available for both export and food crops. The same land has to be used by the country both for domestic consumption and to meet the need for foreign exchange. We believe that the only way we can obtain both corn and cotton at the same time is to irrigate and sow the same land with both crops, one after the other. At present corn, although the basic food of Nicaragua, is a marginal crop. It is planted in the mountains of the interior with very rudimentary techniques that are in no way suitable from an agro-ecological point of view.

In the second case, we view technology as synonymous

with increasing the number of jobs. That is the case, for example, with the banana plantations, which provide employment for some 4,000 people. In the north, where there is little land and much unemployment, raising tobacco has generated jobs for some 6,500 heads of families. This is despite the fact that we have only planted some 1,000 manzanas of tobacco.

In the third case, there are crops such as cotton that have to be mechanized. Cotton requires thousands of pickers, and we are already starting to run short of such labor. The same thing is happening with the sugar harvest.

HARNECKER: That is from the point of view of the peasantry and the agrarian question. But if you look at the country as a whole, aren't there unemployed sectors, originally from the countryside, who would have work if you didn't modernize the cultivation of certain land so much?

WHEELOCK: I think the answer to this problem lies precisely in agro-industry. That is, using the countryside as the basis for an industrial transformation that will enable us to bring economic development both to the rural population and to the population on the periphery of the cities. From the point of view of unemployment, it is this latter layer that presents the greatest problem. Furthermore, it is a layer not easily subject to change in its occupational structure. There is a resistance on the part of unemployed industrial workers and small artisans to taking up agricultural labor.

In a certain sense, among the urban population agriculture has the connotation of degrading and servile labor. To be sure, it is work that is sometimes hard, as for example cutting sugarcane. It is not easy for us to change the structure of employment. It seems it would be easier if we were to advance the entire structure, developing it toward the top, vertically in other words, and promote it as a source of geometrically progressing employment. A move in this direction, however, requires intensive use of capital, and our economic limitations prevent us from doing it in all projects. But we are not going to renounce development. We do not want to be a country based on what others may consider "appropriate technology," that is, technology that institutionalizes underdevelopment. At present we are, for example, building a poultry processing plant that is going to be the biggest in Nicaragua. This project was planned with the aim of providing work for 500 families, and for that reason deliberately employs an intermediate technology. What lies behind this is the need to employ the technology most adequate to each concrete case, according to the needs, to the regional particularities, etc.

9. INTEGRATION OF ARTISANS

"We can't force the nationalization of tortilla production. That would be absurd."

HARNECKER: When you visit Nicaragua you realize there are a great number of small producers and small businessmen, what we could call self-employed workers. What is the revolution thinking of doing with this sector? How does it intend to incorporate it into the project for the new society that's being constructed?

WHEELOCK: The model of capitalist exploitation that imperialism imposed in our country determined that there coexist, alongside the big, high-technology agro-export operations, an enormous sector of primitive, backward, almost subsistence agricultural production. This same process developed in industry. Nicaraguan industry is something relatively new. A certain process of industrialization began in 1960, in keeping with the policy of the so-called Alliance for Progress put forward by the United States to try to lessen the impact of the Cuban revolution. It sought to encourage a process of import substitution, related to the creation of the Central American Common Market. Actually this process didn't amount to much more than setting up some rather obsolete plants, brought over from the United States, to mix raw or semirefined materials supplied by the U.S. In reality our fundamental industrial base was, and continues to be, the artisans.

We have vast production by small agricultural producers, along with vast industrial production by artisans. I am going to give you two facts. In agriculture, large-scale production existed in only 2,000 production units. Of these, no more than 400 used some degree of technology, mostly in coffee and cotton production. Cattle raising was extensive, rather than intensive. At the same time there were more than 130,000 small production units, working the land with the most rudimentary means. In industry there aren't more than 120 plants with more than fifty workers. At the same time, there are more than 15,000 small shops with fewer than five workers. Our artisan-based agriculture and industry are overwhelmingly of a local character. All this adds up to demonstrate that this country is heavily under the influence of what you could call a precapitalist economy. The more underdeveloped and backward a society is, the greater the influence of the mercantile-artisan economy. Therefore, in our revolutionary projections, we must adjust to all these artisanal forms, creating development plans that emphasize cooperatives and associations rather than the state. This means, for example, adopting intermediary technologies.

Our present rhythm and models of economic organization are influenced by the way in which productive forces were developed by our country's dependent capitalism. We have to combine two things in the process of change. First, the formation of a sector of state production that brings together the most developed and strategic areas of the economy. Second, the strong presence of an artisan economy, on which we are trying to impress a certain degree of association; for example, the transformation of family farm production into cooperative production.

This artisan economy has communal roots that originate in primitive society. It is based on the participation of the entire community, under very primitive reciprocal mechanisms of cooperation. For example in a locality (one of the many formed by the development of the peasant economy) specialized occupations—barbering, for example—develop aimed more at cooperation than exploitation. The same is true of the emergence of the small, very primitive shop for making tortillas. The feature of "simple" cooperation and specialization is more a product of the communal economy of Indian society than of the development of capitalism. We can't—in any way—force the nationalization of tortilla production. That would be absurd.

It's important to take into account that the socialist model is a solution for contradictions that are found only in developed capitalist countries.

For a series of reasons, many of them political and others which have to do with hunger and desperation, some peoples have made revolutions on the basis of the existence of the very worst conditions of progress and social development—to try to modify their society greatly and get it on the track of real development. This is our case. Although we may have socialist principles—and we do have them—the solution to transforming our society does not lie in expropriating all the means of production. This wouldn't lead to socialism but rather to its opposite. It could even lead to the destruction and dismantling of society. What we are searching for is a way to combine, on the one hand, a plan in which the starting point will be the strategic and most developed sectors of the economy, and on the other, the organization of a social plan in which cooperative forms of work—even if of a rudimentary character—will predominate.

So a significant sector of self-employed workers and small businessmen exists in our country. But it is the new relations of production created by the revolution that dominate the process of economic development. This domination was achieved by the nationalization of foreign trade, natural resources, the strategic industrial sectors, and the banks. With these steps we have created a system of production and management that is predominant and has hegemony—but that also coexists to an appreciable degree with forms that we could call capitalist and with forms that are backward or precapitalist.

Inside what we call a regime of mixed economy, we have formed various sectors: state property; large, medium, and small private property; and cooperatives. Our tendency is toward having state and cooperative property predominate but at the same time coexist with medium, small, and even large private production. Over time, property relations of backward capitalism will surely become secondary, subordinate. This is our conception of how we must march forward. The pace, however, is determined not only by technological questions but also by political questions. . . .

HARNECKER: And perhaps by what happens in Central America, right?

WHEELOCK: Right. The situation would be different if a federation of Central American states existed, with a division of labor, etc.

10. DEFENDING OUR ECONOMY

> "We want to be an industrialized country that sells manufactured goods; we want to process our agricultural products, can and sell our foods, and make furniture out of our wood."

HARNECKER: Today, when the world capitalist crisis is greatly affecting the underdeveloped countries, could you tell me what Nicaragua's economic situation is compared with the rest of the Central American countries?

WHEELOCK: Nicaragua has been hit hard by the international capitalist crisis, and this shows up in a reduction in the amount of hard currency available to us. It's one of the countries that is most vulnerable to being hit by the crisis. It's a very fragile country. In the first place, this fragility lies in the fact that Nicaragua was originally built up—after its independence—as a country that was to produce cheap consumer goods for countries that already specialized in producing the means of production (industry, machinery), such as England. We were inserted into the dynamic of industrialized economies that had already reached a very high level of development. And because of this very specialization, they needed food for the former peasants who now were workers producing manufactured goods for the world. They also needed raw materials for these industries. So we began to produce wood, minerals, coffee, sugar, etc. In this international division of labor between producers of the means of production and the producers of consumer goods, our job was the latter. But this international division of labor, which is technical, came to be in a certain sense social, because the remuneration between the two economic sectors was always unfavorable for the producers of consumer goods. So Nicaragua throughout its history lost a great deal of value and its capacity for accumulation, leaving it a primary country, with what's called a simple development—without possibilities for growth. We . . . what were we? A country of cotton pickers, coffee pickers, and cane cutters, with a small administrative structure of bookkeepers.

Previously, the country had a certain layer of artisans, and there were close links between the artisans and the farmers. Local artisans produced for the farmers, and the farmers produced for the artisans, although the artisan production really only consisted of carts, wooden drinking vessels, horse harnesses, hats, etc. It was a local, cottage industry but one that wound up being a genuine industry after all. But when Nicaragua began to devote itself to production of primary materials, its incipient industry was replaced by imports. This brought about our first major insertion in the international division of labor, a situation that produced only underdevelopment and growing poverty for the great majority of urban and rural workers.

Imperialism later realized, following the triumph of the Cuban revolution, that this model had entered into crisis, that it allowed for revolutionary explosion. So it was necessary to make some adjustments. That's how all the ideas about the Alliance for Progress developed. In the case of Central America this resulted in their encouraging the Central American Common Market, agrarian reform, and import replacement. So in a manner of speaking, we were to industrialize a bit—instead of just being sellers of cotton and buyers of Colgate toothpaste produced in the United States, we were to sell cotton and at least produce a little toothpaste as well. El Salvador was supposed to produce toothpaste; Guatemala, juices; Costa Rica, tires; Honduras, plastics. And so, what began here was called import-replacement industrialization. But what was import-replacement industrialization? It was simply the acquisition of plants that, while they turned out the final product in our countries, didn't replace the need for the flow of intermediary goods. It's true that now we weren't importing toothpaste, but we were bringing in all the ingredients required to make the product. We were even sent toothpaste we were supposed to package here and label "Central American product, made in Nicaragua." That is, it was simply fiction.

What happened and what is happening now? Prices of raw materials our industries need to turn out finished products have risen enormously. Neither the commercial agro-export model established at the end of the last century nor the import-replacement scheme put forward in the 1960s produced well-being for our people. The latter was just a new way to drain hard currency, because all the dollars brought in by agricultural production were taken away by industry.

Nicaraguan industry produces $80 million in exports and requires $160 million in imports. It imports more than it exports, and agriculture is eaten alive in the process.

The effects of the crisis on our country were that the prices of all the consumer goods we produced were dirt cheap and the prices of everything we needed to produce these consumer goods were sky high. At the same time, the prices of raw materials for the import-replacement industries had increased a lot. The present crisis is the sum total of the crises of the agro-export and import-replacement models. It has left us a deficit of $400 to $500 million, year in and year out, in our balance of payments. And now they're beginning to talk about the "nonviability" of our economies.

The revolution is beginning to develop a new economic model. It is based on the search for a different role in the international division of labor. We can continue producing consumer goods, but it's not the same to produce raw consumer goods as it is to produce them with a certain degree of processing. We want to be an industrialized country that sells manufactured goods. We want to process our agricultural products, can and sell our foods, make furniture out of our wood—this is the deep nationalist sense of the revolution. This can only be done if we become a sovereign nation that doesn't have an economic model contrary to its interests imposed on it from outside.

During the Somoza period the Nicaraguan economy

was structured to complement the U.S. economy, based on its interests and not ours—meat for Puerto Rico, wood for building houses in Louisiana, cotton for U.S. soldiers' uniforms in Korea, a sugar industry to make up for the quota they took away from Cuba. Today, however, with the revolution, Nicaraguans can begin to decide something as basic as *what to produce*. The country can consider other markets, friendly countries, socialist countries, Latin American countries. We can construct a new type of commercial system and trade with those who will give us greater advantages.

One result of the fact that this new model is beginning to be implemented is that the crisis in our country is not as sharp as it is in the rest of Central America. It's true that it shows up in a lack of available hard currency, but we haven't closed plants. We haven't thrown workers out of work. Instead we are moving forward with important development projects of a kind that Nicaragua never before had in its history, projects that provide a lot of employment. As a result of the revolution we have been able to develop a series of cooperative economic relations—not only with friendly nations in Latin America and other continents, but also with the socialist countries.

So this crisis isn't translated into unemployment, or into falling investments, or runaway inflation, as exist in Costa Rica. Because the state—with a package of economic measures—has taken steps to confront the crisis.

What's really in crisis in Nicaragua is the *somocista* model of development. The revolution works in a new model, which is already beginning to respond well. With this model we can begin the march away from poverty, backwardness, and inequality, and we can play a more dynamic, more realistic role in international economic relations—a different role from being the producers of the optional dessert for the industrial economies' banquet—coffee, cacao, sugar, bananas.

11. PLANNING THE UNPLANNABLE?

"It's difficult to plan in a dependent country, in the midst of an international economic crisis and military aggression."

HARNECKER: Concerning this new model—didn't you adopt very hasty measures that you had to revise later on?

WHEELOCK: In general I believe we've followed an adequate pace with regard to almost all the problems—precisely because of the fact that in our discussions there are always different opinions and we end up adopting a position that is a synthesis of the various contributions. The result is a balanced opinion of the majority, which in general is the opinion of everyone. So I'd say that the National Directorate is a rather cautious leadership. It's not adventurist or voluntarist. And of course we have certainly made some mistakes. For example, in the beginning here in the [agrarian reform] ministry, we tried to introduce an excessively rigorous planning system, and this brought on some problems. After that, we tried to introduce a rather complex accounting system, and that turned out to be quite difficult too. Efforts to introduce a total planning system didn't work out either, because the society has strong mercantilist traditions that don't easily allow for planning.

HARNECKER: Does this mean that you rejected all economic planning systems?

WHEELOCK: No. We can develop good planning by beginning with a macroeconomic balance sheet. That's feasible—what to produce, how, how much, where, and for whom. It can be done by drawing up a balance sheet of the existing resources and of those required to guarantee our technical and material needs. By projecting an investment portfolio, introducing accounting measures within it, and distributing the resources among the various sectors of society. This is feasible. I would say we have no problems at this level.

We can carry out detailed technical and economic planning in the people's property sector, and we are already doing this in agriculture. In cooperative production, when it's a question of production cooperatives, we also have the capacity to work with technical and economic plans. We haven't done it because for the moment we're working more to organize this sector than to introduce planning into it. But these sectors of private property are subject, in a way, to certain planning mechanisms—land registration, financing, production contracts, etc.

But the extensive sector of artisan production, made up of small industrial producers and the service sector, permits planning of no more than an indicative nature. In this area we utilize levers of a market nature, such as credit policies and financial incentives through pricing and subsidies. In the beginning we talked about an obligatory plan, but the society wasn't ready for this. On the other hand, the people's property sector was just barely being established, and it couldn't be sufficiently planned out either.

In general terms, I believe we've reached a good understanding of the laws of exchange and functioning of an economy that's in an intermediary—transitional, let's say—situation. So it doesn't frighten us if the law of value is mentioned here. The laws of development are, in general, independent of the will of men. The important thing is to recognize this, master the laws, and not try to make them disappear in a voluntarist manner. At one time we, along with other sectors of commercial production or regulation, tried to get rid of the law of value. What actually disappeared was almost all basic foodstuffs. We tried to set a fixed price for beans and force everyone—including the peasants—to sell them at this price so that there would be a bean market at a very cheap price. What happened? Not only did the price rise even higher because of the shortages, but the product disappeared from the market. This was a voluntarist incident inside a system that works by laws of a market nature. We use the laws of the market and in this way—as if they were a cart horse—we pull all the strings we need to pull. We combine an almost-obligatory technical and economic planning with planning that is more of an indicative nature.

Our experience has been that each time we concretize a plan we also have to draw up an emergency plan. Because, besides the military aggression we suffer, in a certain sense our variable factors—since we are such a dependent country—are a function of the international market. We are part of a general market system in which our planning capacity alone doesn't determine whether the plan will work or not. We can draw up a plan based on a set price for the sale of our products—for example $90 for a bale of cotton. But if these prices are not maintained—something that doesn't depend upon us—if instead of selling at $90, the cotton sells at $60, and that has happened with other export products, the plan is shot. It's difficult to plan in a dependent country that has open-ended international relations. And it's even more difficult if the economic factors, including the international economic crisis, are aggravated by the political problems and military aggression our country suffers.

Nevertheless, we continue to perfect the planning mechanisms. We have a national system made up of the sum total of the sectoral units: finance, agriculture, industry, construction, etc. We have regional planning that reaches as far down as units of enterprises. And we have contingency plans, which are a substantial part of planning in our particular conditions.

Right now the Ministry of Planning is working on an overall system. The will to plan, to bring order and proportional balance to the economy, is being imposed against the tendencies—call them objective, if you like—of the old, anarchic free-exchange society.

12. AGGRESSION AGAINST NICARAGUA

"As I said earlier, the historic struggle of Nicaragua has never been anything other than the struggle of the people against imperialist aggression."

HARNECKER: The FSLN—supported by the entire population—won a war against Somoza and his army. But today a good part of the National Guard—perhaps half of it—is once again fighting against you, trying to regain the power they lost. Why wasn't the massive flight of these elements stopped? Didn't you foresee their possible return?

WHEELOCK: Right after the last Nicaraguan war against imperialism, in which Sandino drove the U.S. Marines out of Nicaragua, the United States carried out a political maneuver in which it withdrew its army while maintaining political and economic intervention. During that seven-year struggle with Sandino, the U.S. Army organized an armed force that later—when they left—would become the National Guard. That's why, when we said that the *somocista* regime was the local expression of imperialism, we had put our finger on the historic reality against which the Nicaraguan people had struggled. This is why our revolutionary triumph in fact meant a defeat for armed U.S. intervention carried out, under cover, by the *somocista* National Guard.

In the final analysis, we were not fighting against Somoza, but against imperialism. But to convince our people of the justness of the struggle, we had to bring them together to struggle against the immediate and most dangerous enemy. That is, against the concrete, visible expression of imperialism in our country—*somocismo*. That is what our people lived with daily—not the abstract concept of imperialism. For a time we made an error in this regard, an error of strategic importance. By not clearly differentiating between these two things, we weren't able to correctly single out the enemy. At one time we said that the principal enemy here was imperialism and that for that reason an armed struggle couldn't be developed in a single country. We said it had to be developed on a world scale, creating one, two, three, four, five, ten Vietnams, and that the war was going to be a people's war throughout Central America. In the context of such a view, it made no sense to fight against Somoza. It was through Carlos Fonseca that we began to carry out all our work on the basis of the peculiarities of the struggle in our country.

So we can say that, while we did not defeat the historic will of imperialism to maintain a grip on Nicaragua, we did win a very important battle by defeating its local army, the National Guard. But this army did not disappear, nor did imperialism's will to try to reconquer lost territory.

Now, what happened after July 19? The National Guard was defeated politically and militarily. We didn't defeat this army by annihilating it physically, but by removing its capacity to attain strategic objectives. The majority of the soldiers of the *somocista* guard remained alive. Some 6,000 left for El Salvador, Guatemala, and Honduras. They had time to get out. Others simply dispersed, and we were able to capture some 3,500.

In order to obtain an effective force that would serve as the backbone of all its aggressive plans against Nicaragua, the United States then sought out guard members who had left the country. And just as they did in 1927, they again reorganized the guard—arming it, revitalizing it, and reassembling it as the axis of a larger plan.

HARNECKER: The fact that the imperialists would have

to resort to the National Guard, to *somocismo*—a phenomenon so hated by the people—didn't this demonstrate a great weakness on their part? The fact that they weren't able to obtain the support of other sectors that could have given greater legitimacy to their cause, that they had to wave such a soiled flag. . . .

WHEELOCK: As I said earlier, the historic struggle of Nicaragua has never been anything other than the struggle of the people against imperialist aggression; the struggle of the Nicaraguan people against the local political, economic, and military expression of imperialism—*somocismo*.

July 19 dealt a deathblow to *somocismo* but not to the imperialists' plans. On the other hand, as I also mentioned before, no matter how hard the bourgeois groups and reactionary parties here tried to present themselves as an alternative, they had neither the economic and social strength nor the historic opportunity. They had already been completely cornered by the revolutionary forces. Here the bourgeoisie never had the belligerency, strength, and experience, nor does it have the desire, to come back and reconquer Nicaragua. The bourgeoisie left for Miami. Perhaps the bourgeoisie could lend out some of its active agents to be directors of the counterrevolution, as if they were managing a bank—but that's all. Imperialism knows perfectly well that a bourgeois army ready to fight against the people of Nicaragua can never rise up here. That's why they find themselves compelled, against their own interests, to resort once again to that contingent of mercenaries—the National Guard.

HARNECKER: How is it possible that the counterrevolutionaries were able to penetrate so many kilometers inside Nicaraguan territory?

WHEELOCK: There are three factors that explain why the bands were able to move so far into our territory. First, Nicaragua has a 580-kilometer border with Honduras, and this border area is quite cut off from the rest of the country. There are hundreds of kilometers where communication and transportation facilities do not exist, because the area is too mountainous. In addition, the Nicaraguan side is more underdeveloped than the Honduran side and has a very low population density. It is a region that is not really solidly integrated into the rest of the country.

The second factor is the complete support imperialism has from the Honduran armed forces and government, which have provided the bands supplies, logistics, matériel, border territory, bases, etc. This is another factor I consider fundamental—the fact that they permit a well-trained, well-armed force to penetrate whatever territory they like and carry out combat tasks.

There's a third factor of a more technical dimension. The United States has developed—in the theater of operations by these bands—an intricate network of apparatuses that enable them to know the exact location and movements of our forces. They are constantly photographing our territory, and through radar and other sophisticated techniques they monitor all our movements. This enables the bands to carry out work and infiltrate very deeply at times—wherever they know they aren't going to find our forces stopping them.

HARNECKER: Can it be said that they don't have the support of the local population?

WHEELOCK: Regarding that, it's necessary to point out that many National Guard members have relatives in the area bordering Honduras. This is taken advantage of by the counterrevolution, which takes these family ties into consideration in forming its bands. In addition, the National Guard officers leading these forces are very familiar with the region, because it was the site of past counterinsurgency action against us. They know each one of the collaborators they had then who we still haven't won away from them—those who ruled the cattle trails, who adhered to the old order. In addition, they have found support among some landowners and rich peasants linked to *somocismo* and among some backward sectors of the poor peasantry. But this support isn't a key factor, because we have been able to make them withdraw completely from all sites where they have penetrated. Lately they've been forced to use tactics more like those of a regular army than of a guerrilla force. That was when they encircled a relatively small area—Jalapa and the surrounding region.

13. BACKWARD OR FORWARD IN POPULAR SUPPORT?

> "There are even certain sectors who are drawing closer to the revolution as they see our country is being attacked."

HARNECKER: One last question—has the revolution lost or gained support among the population? Has there been some erosion of support because of the inability to respond to all the people's expectations?

WHEELOCK: In this regard, we have many advantages. First, the Nicaraguan people were a people living in poverty, in growing poverty. Each year more people joined the ranks of the poor, the dispossessed. Even middle layers of the population were being incorporated into the ranks of the unemployed. The poverty in the countryside was terrible. The infant mortality rate overall was 130 per 1,000, and in the countryside it was 200 per 1,000. No light, no water, and no more than huts to live in. Almost all women in the countryside were illiterate. In the cities, there was high unemployment, a lot of poverty, and a social niche of relative comfort only for the limited middle-class layers that had developed in Nicaragua.

So I can tell you that the revolution has brought only

benefits for the great majority. We have hurt only a minority. Our economic policy favors the middle sectors in the countryside and guarantees stability to urban middle sectors, who are fundamentally dependent on the revolutionary state.

Politically we have the capacity to mobilize 600,000 persons—the great majority of them members of the revolution's mass organizations. This is quite a lot if we take into account the fact that the economically active population of Nicaragua is 900,000 persons.

But it's not easy to lead a country in the middle of an economic crisis. We have struggled to defend workers' real wages with large subsidies, food imports, maintaining all jobs, subsidizing companies, working twenty-four hours a day to adequately distribute all the hard currency so that the plants don't close—that is, to defend the people's economy.

Our people know that we've maintained the price of a liter of milk within the reach of every pocketbook: three córdobas—that's five U.S. cents. This at a time when in Costa Rica, for example, milk is sold at a price twenty times higher. Almost all the products of basic consumption are cheap here in Nicaragua. And the family budget—to give you an example—is based on more income now than in the past. In a family that before had only one member working, now four out of five are working, and sometimes five. So family income is much higher.

That's why, even though production is higher than it was in Somoza's time, we have problems with food supply. Many who didn't use to consume are now part of the picture because they now have more income, or more stability in their work, or because we have put more rural stores in the interior, mountain regions. We have brought goods to a population that before now did not consume them. In this sense we have doubled the number of consumers, while production has grown slowly. We produce three times more chicken and three times more eggs. Nevertheless, eggs are still scarce here because the demand is much greater. The population has also grown 20 percent in relation to 1979 figures. And international conditions are not the best for economic growth.

There's discontent. There is uneasiness throughout the population because of food problems. But these problems aren't much different from the inconveniences I see in my own house—when there's no laundry soap, when you have to go looking for it in four different places. This uneasiness, however, does not represent a lack of support for the revolution, because support for the revolution in all fundamental matters still remains. There are even certain sectors who are drawing closer to the revolution as they see our country being attacked. The tests this country is being put through have consolidated that support. Reagan's aggressive policies have actually helped to consolidate the revolution.

Nicaragua is a country that keeps its borders open, its immigration offices working hard, its airlines connected with the United States daily, and its doors open for anyone who wants to leave. It is a country that is functioning perfectly smoothly in the midst of aggression, in a situation of war, in which growing ranks of youth, workers, and professionals are being incorporated, because they feel a great readiness to defend their nation, their revolution. It is a country where there are big private producers who decide to go through all these difficulties because they are Nicaraguans.

Of course if we were to propose that our minister of internal commerce be the candidate for mayor of Managua, he surely would not receive a single vote. But if our people knew that the CIA was preparing to assassinate this very same minister of internal commerce, as it did with [Foreign] Minister D'Escoto, this minister would have the entire population behind him for defense.

Finally, I just want to add one thing. Imperialism thought

that by introducing the task forces they were going to produce uprisings and insurrections here. What they actually produced, to the contrary, was a great national mobilization against the bands. Who are the ones fighting the bands? The youth, the working class, the peasants, the intellectuals, everyone. . . .

In addition, they are fighting as a class because the youth participate as an organized force; the same with the peasantry. We don't organize our battalions with indiscriminate levies as they do in El Salvador, or as was done here in Somoza's time, and as all bourgeois armies have done. Rather, we do it through the conscious and voluntary participation of combatants who are organized in one or another of the country's mass organizations.

It is the entire people who are fighting; the same people who produce; the same ones who study. All Nicaraguans must simultaneously carry out the various tasks of the revolution: defense, production, progress, development. This small population must multiply its efforts to confront the historic challenge of carrying this revolution through to the end.

This is a revolution of working people

Interview with Tomás Borge

The following excerpts are from an interview conducted in June 1983 by a group of Canadians. Their tour, organized by the Toronto-based Latin America Working Group, was sponsored by the Sandinista Workers Federation and the FSLN. Both the transcript of the interview and the translation are by the tour group. The text originally appeared in the September 19, 1983, issue of *Intercontinental Press*.

TOUR MEMBER: We have met with a lot of groups since we arrived in Nicaragua. And many of these groups refer to the FSLN as their vanguard. We know that you will be entering into the electoral process in the next two years. We wonder if we might get some sense of your guiding principles in this respect?

TOMÁS BORGE: Obviously, an electoral process is essentially a political act. Our desire is that this electoral process be as broad-based and democratic as is possible—much more broadly based and democratic than the majority of the electoral processes which take place in Latin America, or in the Americas in general.

Just limiting my comments to the Latin American continent, obviously you already realize that all the electoral processes in this region for the most part are simply electoral processes already precooked, prefabricated, that bring to the leadership groups, minority groups, that control the privileges in the country. That is why the largest parties in Latin America are the parties of those who have abstained from voting. And I think we can also include the United States in that.

Here, our people will, through a formal electoral process, determine what they have already decided through their blood. Our people have already voted. They didn't vote with ballots and ballot boxes. They voted through the trenches. And the largest vote that our people cast for the process was the number of martyrs they gave to the revolution. Perhaps at the time of voting, when the electoral process actually takes place, we should add 50,000 martyrs and heroes who fell at the time of the insurrection. However, I can assure you that the majority of the working people in this country completely support the Sandinista National Liberation Front.

What maintains this revolutionary process at an ideological level? Our revolution, like all revolutions, has its own roots. Sandino, as a thinker, was way ahead of his time. The thinking and ideas of Sandino are like an encyclopedia for the Sandinistas of today. After that follows the thinking of Carlos Fonseca. Carlos's thinking enriches Sandino's thinking, putting it in the context of his time, putting it into the reality he was living. But rather than use ideological names or categories, it is the content that is important.

All revolutions throughout history are revolutions whose subjects come from a particular social class. I will not give names to the revolutions. However, I will say of this revolution, that it is a revolution of the working people. It is not a revolution of the bourgeoisie. It is a revolution of the poor. It is a revolution of the workers and the peasants.

To this revolution of workers and peasants—you can give it any name you want, you can brand it any way you want—it will always be a revolution of the workers and peasants. Regardless of the outcome of the electoral process, we are sure it will be the outcome that the workers and peasants want.

A famous German writer asked me, "well, what would happen if the FSLN didn't win the elections? Would you hand over power to another political party?" "Why should we discuss things that are impossible," I said.

TOUR MEMBER: We are aware that the aggressions in the country have been escalating in the past while. Could you give us an overview of the military situation at the present time? We are also wondering if you might share some of the front's reflections on what the possible options are in the light of these increased aggressions?

BORGE: First of all, we would have to say that the situation is becoming more serious every day. There is a lot of talk about the possibility of peace. And we have made substantial efforts to prevent war. Such efforts as we have not allowed ourselves to be provoked. Such provocations are being carried out from Honduras, and there have been other provocations. We have had limitless patience in order to prevent a confrontation. But from a pragmatic point of view the efforts we have undertaken, and also the efforts of other countries in seeking peace, have not been realized, given the unwillingness of the U.S. to answer for peace.

What is the point of continuing to struggle for peace if the U.S. is committed to fighting a war? The tremendous military might represented by the U.S. must be limited or it will be fatal. What can we do to limit or at least postpone a war?

The only thing we have is pressure—by all peoples of

the world. And I think particularly of the North American people.

The pressures of the governments of the world . . . there are many congressmen . . . the problem is that there are many congressmen, in other countries as well, who want to do as much as they can to prevent the war. But what are they faced with? They are not acting energetically enough to prevent a war in Central America because they are afraid that Reagan will use their efforts to seek peace in Central America and accuse them of being Communist. This is in view of the fact that the U.S. is moving into an electoral process. So they are not being energetic enough. They are afraid. And there are pressures. This is unfortunately the situation.

However, we see that the peoples of the world, through their own organizations, trade unions, political parties, and other associations, the populations of Latin America, North America, Europe, can apply pressure so that the demented mind of Reagan—can put certain limitations on his desire to inflame all Central America.

We have to do a logical analysis of Central America. Reagan wants peace for Central America? It's obvious he doesn't want peace.

He wants peace on the basis of us turning ourselves in. He wants peace, as long as we don't carry out our revolution. He wants peace on the basis of turning the Nicaraguan people into slaves. He wants peace, as long as we go down on our knees. That is to say, he doesn't want peace. Because we are not going to go down on our knees. We are not going to stop the revolutionary process. And we are not going to stop being in solidarity with other peoples of the world. And we will not allow imperialism to dominate our countries again. So, he doesn't want peace.

He sent Mr. Stone here. Stone? What the hell is he doing here anyway? Has he come with a peaceful banner? No, he comes as a judge. He doesn't even come as an intermediary.

He comes as if he doesn't see any of the problems in Central America—he's above all the local problems—as if it wasn't the United States who started all these problems in the first place. He comes as an arbitrator.

We are prepared to speak to Mr. Stone as many times as is necessary. But he must understand, and the U.S. government who sent him must understand, that he is an intermediary. He is not a judge. Because if we were to be strictly realistic, he should come as the accused rather than as a judge.

There is absolutely no way that the U.S. government is going to solve the problem in Central America . . . only international solidarity of the people. The position of certain open-minded governments that can pressure the U.S. government *may* avoid the war.

We are not saying the prospects for peace are totally negative. But solidarity doesn't yet have the dimensions, the magnitude and force necessary, to pressure the U.S. government.

Personally, I believe there will be a serious increase in U.S. aggression. It wouldn't be surprising if in the next few days there was a serious provocation. We're not sure what form this provocation will take against Nicaragua. It would not be strange if this war, which we have tried to avoid, were to happen.

OK. So the counterrevolutionary bands have penetrated. They have their own strategic plan. First of all, they are trying to test the military might of the revolution. First, they speculated, they thought these penetrations would weaken our defense lines. And it was a surprise to them to learn that they did not weaken our other defense lines. In fact, they strengthened them.

They have also been trying to carry out an analysis of the correlation of forces. They have been doing their own calculations. They say, "well, they have so many tanks, so much artillery, so much infantry, so many planes." So they have done their own calculations of how much we have, and how much they have, how many soldiers, etc. They have done a mathematical calculation of the correlation of forces.

But the idiots don't know that this kind of calculation is useless, that there are other factors that go beyond questions of how many munitions we have, how many meters of cannons. What they have forgotten is the will, the commitment, the morale, the combativity, of a revolutionary people.

How many people could we put under arms? We could put as many people under arms as we have arms. Here we don't lack people. We lack guns. How many people can the Honduran people arm? Several tens of thousands, but can they arm the people of Honduras? If they arm the people of Honduras then the problem between Honduras and Nicaragua is over.

What is the most serious aspect of this problem? First of all, the military advice that is being given to the Salvadoran, Honduran, and Guatemalan armies doesn't concern us. We're not particularly opposed to the advice they give to the Salvadoran army—I'm speaking about the U.S.

We haven't opposed their military advisers to the Guatemalan army. Nor to the Honduran government. Because, after all, they advise and train the Salvadoran army, and that army is being beaten. After all, they advised and trained the Somoza army, and we defeated it. So we're not too concerned about that. Because they are destined by history to be advisers to military defeat.

But, there is quite a difference between their military advisers and the fact that they are building a military base in Honduras. That is no longer just military advice. That is the installation of a different kind of military support. What would they say if we placed a Soviet military installation here?

So, we're not so concerned about sending military advisers to train the Central American armies, but we are seriously concerned about their establishing a military base in the territory. The military base in Honduras is aimed against El Salvador and against Nicaragua. This is a qualitative step in the aggression against Nicaragua. This is the most dangerous situation that has happened so far.

What is going to happen? They are going to increase the activities against Teotecacinte and Jalapa, that's one thing we are certain of. If they try . . . they are going to try to create some kind of international provocation between the Honduran army and ourselves in that area. Because they have artillery set up there and they are using it. And Honduran troops have entered into that part of the territory.

Now we don't have any notion about the nature of that provocation that's going to take place. But we know they are planning the provocation to inflame some kind of war.

Also, in the area of Northern Zelaya there are counterrevolutionary forces; however these forces don't have combativity, they aren't as cohesive, they don't have the moral strength that the ex-National Guardsmen have who are attacking the Jalapa area.

In the southern border, the characteristics are similar. There is not much of a possibility that the aggressions on the southern border will have the characteristics of that in the Jalapa area. They don't have the same constituency, the same moral support in the south.

The supposed increase in aggressions in the southern border is mostly something being promoted in the newspaper *La Nación* of Costa Rica, and other media. What has happened there, the Costa Ricans who are our brothers, our neighbors, through those newspapers, through that media, they believe that Managua is going to fall any day. Or León, or Rivas. It's quite a surprise for the Costa Ricans to come here and see that things are pretty quiet . . . and yet these towns are supposed to be taken over. And nothing is happening here.

I'm not optimistic in regards to peace. But I am absolutely optimistic in terms of victory.

TOUR MEMBER: We understand that up to 80 percent of the economy is still in private hands. We were wondering, how do you see class conflict, particularly in terms of the popular classes and their needs and those who still privately own businesses?

BORGE: I expect that you got quite a technical explanation at the Ministry of Planning. Perhaps they forgot to tell you that a mixed economy in Nicaragua is not the same as a mixed economy in Costa Rica, or in Uruguay and other countries of Latin America. This is a mixed economy within the revolution. In other words, a mixed economy at the service of the workers. Because in other countries it is a mixed economy at the service of the bourgeoisie.

It's certain that most of the land is still in private hands, but the productive part of the agricultural economy is in the People's Property Sector area. And the mechanism for export and trade is in the hands of the state. And the banks are in the hands of the state.

There is not so much of a problem in what you would call the industrial, manufacturing area. Perhaps the most serious difficulty is in the commercial area, because this is where speculation takes place, hoarding, artificial shortages of consumer goods.

But perhaps the most important problem is that Nicaragua is very backward. It's not just that we received an obsolete and noncompetitive industry, but also the monstrous decapitalization, capital flight. . . . Not only have we inherited tremendously heavy debt, but we are also victims of the international economic crisis.

And that we are victims of, what you would say, tremendous, brutal unequal exchange between "first world" and Third World. In this sense, there are common interests among all Third World countries, and specifically all peoples of Latin America suffer from this unequal exchange. And all the people of Central America.

We have won the right to transform this reality.

We have to pull ourselves out of this dependence. And in some ways the U.S. is helping us do this because they are closing off their markets to us. And we will now be obligated to find other countries to carry out trade with. Although our problem is not fundamentally that of markets. Really, the cotton we produce, there's more countries that could buy it than we can produce. And really, most of our agro-export production, cash crops, there's more countries to buy it than we can produce. Our problems are not our buyers. Our problem is production and technological dependence.

Our main strategic line of development in the economic sector is agro-export and production of food. And of course, our problems have been aggravated by the military problems we have been undergoing. The aggressions.

And really, it is virtually a miracle when you think of it, that despite the debt we have inherited, despite the obsolescence, the dependence, the aggressions, etc., we are living better than any other Central American country.

I'm going to give you some examples. . . . In other countries, very nearby countries, consumer prices are much higher. Large unemployment, services cut back, tremendous inflation (inflation . . . . like a woman about to give birth). It's a very serious and painful situation. Here there are no social disturbances.

If you go to other countries nearby they'll say of course there are all these problems. They have a dictatorship, a Marxist-Leninist dictatorship, which prevents workers from striking. That's what they say. But here, the workers haven't the least fear of the police. What worker here is going to be afraid of the police? The only fear we would have is that the police would join the workers. [*Laughter*]

It's not for fear, but for commitment, that people aren't

striking. Because the working class here is the most revolutionary class, which has gained consciousness tremendously rapidly, because of its own history. And how could it be that the Nicaraguan working class would not develop a revolutionary consciousness? It's not only that they are the ones who struggle, but they also triumph.

And I don't remember who said it, that the people learn more in one minute of revolutionary experience than they can in a decade or more of other kinds of experience: Maybe somebody here knows who said that?

TOUR MEMBER: During our last two weeks here, we have had the opportunity to meet and talk with representatives and members of many of the mass organizations, including AMNLAE, CSN [Nicaraguan Trade Union Coordinating Committee], UNAG [National Union of Farmers and Ranchers], CDSs. Since we haven't had the privilege of living in a revolutionary society, or have experience with a revolutionary vanguard, I think some of us are having difficulty understanding what the relationship is between the FSLN and these mass organizations, and what the interaction is between the two.

BORGE: The mass organizations have their own life. And the natural leaders of these mass organizations are the people who have been the best. People who lead these organizations are people who these mass organizations, perhaps, have given birth to. These are the best people. And the best people in this country, the greatest people, happen to be members of the Sandinista National Liberation Front.

And so, the mass organizations are led by the best of the people in the country, who have emerged out of their own organizations. And because they are people who have given such sacrifice, they are members of the front. But they have their own autonomy as mass organizations, they have their own capacity to struggle, their own demands. They struggle, they push, they carry out their own activities. But neither am I saying that the FSLN is apart from this.

We are not an organization that is blind. We are always listening to the desires, the will, the cries of the people. We also have an obligation to help orient the mass organizations. There is a dialectical relationship between the mass organizations and the vanguard. There is a coming and going. The FSLN learns from the masses. And the FSLN also teaches the masses.

And that is why there is such a close interrelationship between the front and the mass organizations, although large numbers of people in the mass organizations are not necessarily members of the FSLN. But those people who have emerged as natural leaders of the mass organizations, for the most part, are FSLN people. But there is this constant dialogue between the mass organizations. This is what gives life to the FSLN.

What would the FSLN do without the mass organizations? What would the masses do without the FSLN?

That's why once we said the FSLN is the people, and the people became the Sandinista front. Was it me who said that once? [*Laughter*]

TOUR MEMBER: Just a follow-up on that question. Can we ask how one becomes a member of the FSLN?

BORGE: In the case of . . . those who are not Nicaraguans, it has to come from the National Directorate. And they have to come and live in Nicaragua and be here for quite some time.

And those who are Nicaraguan are people who have had to go through a very difficult stage. First of all, card-carrying members of the FSLN, if you like—we don't want these people to have privileges. It represents a large packsack, that has been carried over a big mountain—a pack-sack filled with many, many duties and responsibilities. With more responsibilities than rights and privileges.

How should a Sandinista be? A person who must forget

himself. Capable of loving profoundly, other human beings. Could a Sandinista be an egotistical person? First of all, a Sandinista must be generous. He must be courageous, happy, very brave. He has to be the best, and not wait for someone to recognize these values. Sandinistas must be prepared to give up their lives, but must be prepared to defend their life. But most important, to be prepared to defend the lives of others.

Can a Sandinista be a thief? An assassin? A coward? Servile? A Sandinista that's afraid of imperialism? A Sandinista that begins to shake like a wet dog in the rain? [*Laughter*]

No, the Sandinista has to be the opposite of these. But at the same time a Sandinista must be simple and humble. He has to be a good father, a good mother and father, a good friend, and a good lover. Can a Sandinista be useless? [*Laughter*] A Sandinista has to be the best in everything.

TOUR MEMBER: We qualify in all of them except one—we're not Nicaraguan. [*Laughter*]

BORGE: A Sandinista has to be a Sandinista in their own country. Struggling for their own people. Identifying themselves with the interests of the workers in their own countries. And courageously opposing all injustices. Fighting against the corrupt, discrimination, consumption, being in solidarity with all the peoples of the world, struggling for their liberation, because these are also victims of imperialism.

Perhaps the Sandinistas in Uruguay, they might be called Tupamaros. It doesn't matter what they are called. The Sandinistas in Canada, I don't know what they are called . . . [*Laughter*] . . . it doesn't matter. The Sandinistas in Peru . . . the Sandinistas in El Salvador are the revolutionaries fighting there. At one time, we were the Tupamaros of Nicaragua.

So you could be Sandinistas, too. And we could take your spirit of struggle and solidarity in your own country, we could learn from your experiences so we could become better revolutionaries in our own country. Solidarity is the most elevated expression of the revolution.

If you want to know if someone is really a revolutionary or not, ask them if they are in solidarity with other people? If we just wanted to do our revolution here and forget about the problems of other peoples around the world, we would not be revolutionaries. We are not prepared to negotiate with anybody our feelings of solidarity toward our brothers in El Salvador . . . and many other things.

Many things we are doing here are for the peoples trying to liberate themselves in Latin America. And we have paid a high price because of this solidarity. I say this to you, if all the Nicaraguans would have to die, as a price for the solidarity that we feel for the Central American, for the Latin American revolutions, we would, without vacillating, give our lives. Imperialism doesn't understand that. And how is this Mr. Stone ever going to understand that?

TOUR MEMBER: We wondered if the FSLN was aligned to any international bodies, and if so, what countries, ideologically, or geographically.

BORGE: We are nonaligned. We are aligned to just causes. We have expressed our nonalignment in different fashions. But some people have such a narrow way of looking at the international questions. And their way of looking at it is that to be nonaligned means you have to be aligned to the United States.

Of course, the United States is not a country that is aligned. But they want everybody aligned to them. And so that when all the countries that they want . . . when the countries that are aligned with them, are aligned with them, then they say, "these countries are nonaligned." Because "we are not aligned, right."

We maintain friendship with the Soviet Union, and with Mexico, to give you two examples. We have friendship with Cuba, and we feel proud to be friends with Cuba. Because Cuba has been extraordinarily generous with Nicaragua. A generosity with no conditions attached.

We would be demagogues, hypocrites, if we didn't tell you that we were very true friends with Cuba and we are very grateful to Cuba. In the most difficult moments we have faced, Cuba has given us a great deal of support. And perhaps one of the qualities I failed to mention in terms of qualities of Sandinistas . . . is gratitude.

But the fact that we have this special friendship with Cuba, and that we are also friends with the Soviet Union, does that mean we are aligned? We take our own decisions. Sometimes the decisions we take may not please our brothers and sisters in Cuba. Other times, we agree. And so what we have here is more a coinciding of interests. They are not things that are imposed on us. In any case, we have been accused of being a satellite.

First they said we were a satellite of Cuba, which, in turn, was a satellite of the Soviet Union. So we were a satellite of a satellite. This was the accusation. So now we're the satellite of the Soviet Union.

I've always asked myself, do we have satellite faces? [*Laughter*] Do we have faces of pets? Pet dogs? Because if we want to be pet dogs and if we accepted the very undignified position of being a satellite, it would be much easier for us to decide to be a satellite of that cowboy, Ronald Reagan. We would be saving 200,000 headaches. Because after all, one thing is clear, if we decided to become a satellite of this cowboy, we would not only save these headaches but we would also have saved ourselves all the aggressions from the National Guard. Because the U.S. wouldn't have bothered to arm them and create aggressions against us. And these aggressions they are carrying out against us are precisely because we are not satellites of anyone.

Even if we wanted to be a satellite, we couldn't. We couldn't because of geographical impediments. But we do not want to be a satellite. But we do have friends. And our friends are our friends, and our enemies are our enemies.

A U.S. congressman was telling me—I had just seen his face, and he told me finally he had found the excuse, the reason, the proof to show that Nicaragua was a satellite of the Soviet Union. And this proof was regarding the declaration by Andropov, who had made a statement in respect of national sovereignty of Nicaragua—the right of Nicaragua to self-determination—congratulating Nicaragua for its reconstruction efforts, etc. And it reiterated, reemphasized, that the Soviet Union was going to continue to help Nicaragua in the economic field. So the congressman told me, "there's the proof."

So I said, "let's do something. Let's take this statement and let's take where it says the Soviet Union, and we'll say the United States. And where it says Andropov, we'll say Reagan." And we would be absolutely delighted that Reagan would say that he is going to respect our national sovereignty, that he identifies with our desire for peace, and that he expresses his desire to help us in the development of our country. What Nicaraguan is going to oppose that?

However, if this statement that was said was a U.S. statement, would that then mean we would be accused of being a U.S. satellite? Why? Why would we be accused of being a satellite of the U.S.? On the contrary, we would be delighted if every country in the world would have these same desires toward Nicaragua, respecting our national sovereignty, or wanting to help in the economic development of the country. What has Reagan said exactly? And the situation in that sense is very sad.

Well, then, welcome to Nicaragua, happy trip. We are very sorry that you are leaving so soon. And it would be unforgivable if you didn't come back to Nicaragua later.

TOUR MEMBER: Commander. We are first very honored that you would come and speak to us. It was very unexpected. We'd like to give you a little memento from the group—to the FSLN from the Ontario group. I know that you are in a hurry, but I only want to make one comment.

When we first came here, as you know we had been reading the press of the United States and they put a label on the revolution. One of the things that they say, Commander, is that this is a totalitarian state. The second day we were here we visited the Victoria Breweries, and they were very proud to show us their arsenal of rifles. And we had a great problem immediately. We could never figure why the authorities of a totalitarian state would give the workers arms.

BORGE: You have learned the essence of the problem. [*Applause*]

Our promises were made to the poorest of our country
by Sergio Ramírez

The following speech was given July 14, 1983, to a Conference on Latin America held in Managua. The conference, sponsored by the Nicaraguan Artists Association, was attended by more than 200 writers and artists from Latin America, Canada, and the United States. In the speech, Ramírez poses and answers three of the major charges the U.S. government has raised against Nicaragua: that Nicaragua is exporting its revolution, that the Sandinistas have betrayed the revolution, and that the Sandinista revolution is totalitarian. The translation for this volume is by Michael Baumann.

Like the rest of Central America, Nicaragua has had a disadvantageous relationship with the United States, almost since the United States appeared as a nation and replaced its original aspiration for freedom and democracy with Manifest Destiny.

Because of our unfortunate geographic proximity, and because of the possibility of Nicaraguan territory being used for the opening of an interoceanic canal, we have been under the gaze, both geopolitical and in terms of conquest, of successive North American administrations. This proximity, and the insatiable thirst for domination encouraged by the imperial vision held by those who encouraged the perpetual expansion of U.S. borders, and who in fact sought to expand them, created a fundamental historical contradiction. To survive as a nation, Nicaragua has had to fight for decades against the imperialist ambitions of the United States—from 1855, when we were invaded by the first filibusters, to 1979, when the revolution definitively proclaimed national independence. This includes the rejection of intervention in 1927 by General Sandino who, arms in hand, drew together the ideological underpinnings of this age-old struggle, a struggle of all of Latin America that today we are carrying on, once again, from this small but solid trench.

This is also a political and ideological struggle, and the arguments of imperialist propaganda merely seek to mask and justify the military aggression that is armed, organized, directed, and financed by the Reagan administration. It is therefore worthwhile to examine some of the most widely publicized lies that are being intoned like songs of death and treachery against our right to independence. We should examine them in the light of our reason, which is the thinking of poor people fighting for their national identity in face of increasing blows from Manifest Destiny: to see the falsity behind the lies and fallacious arguments that have been repeated so many times.

1. *The serious error of the Sandinistas is that they are trying to export their revolution.*

Revolutions throughout history have always been "exportable," if we wish to use this somewhat mercantile term when discussing the dynamic by which ideas circulate beyond borders. There never would have been a French revolution without the revolution in the thirteen North American colonies; the ideas of Jefferson would never have existed without the inspiration of the French Encyclopedists; General Lafayette would never have left France to fight in the hills of Virginia if he hadn't believed that revolutions have no borders; and Benjamin Franklin wouldn't have spent so many years hatching conspiracies in the European courts if he didn't believe the American revolution was exportable.

The fact is that the revolution that gave birth to the United States as a nation was the most exported revolution of modern history. It was moreover the revolution that imported the most in terms of ideological elements used as a basis for its thinking, its war of liberation, and its novel laws.

In face of the absolutism of the Spanish monarchs in Hispanic America, equal to the colonialist absolutism England exercised over the future United States, our native-born liberators found that the most seductive and dazzling formulas for doing away with the colonial yoke came from the north, just as later all our calamities were to come from the same place. These included the example of a bloody and implacable war carried out by men committed to replacing the colonial regime with a new political and social order; the crystallization of the utopian ideas of democracy of the European Enlightenment, which were to be tested for the first time in practice in the New World. The New World was the Promised Land for those philosophic dreams that up until then had been extravagances: constitutional government and balance of powers. These were extremist and subversive concepts in the eyes of the monarchy, and spreading them clandestinely in Hispanic America led to persecution, imprisonment, and exile. To read James Madison in those days was a crime against the state, just as today reading Marx can cost your life in Guatemala or El Salvador.

The constitution of the new United States and the explosive ideas that inspired it were carried by mule back throughout all Central America, like a smuggled item. That emerging republic, led by wild-eyed radicals—extremist exporters of revolutions who believed only in their own model and rejected any other opposed to it—represented a threat to the internal security and strategic interests of Spain in the New World; the great imperial power began to crack. In 1823, after Central America won its independence, the first federal constitution adopted in the effort to provide a foundation for the ephemeral dream of a united, Morazanist Central America began with the same preamble, copied word for word, from the constitution drafted by Madison in 1787.

The United States was exporting a model in those days, and it was also exporting a blood-drenched example of the fact that such a profound change, the defeat of the British empire in American territory, could not be carried through without rifles, without militarily crushing the enemy, and without emulating the Minutemen, guerrilla combatants as valiant as those of the Salvadoran Farabundo Martí National Liberation Front (FMLN). In face of the insurgency of a new order based on new ideas, necessarily subversive, the old order and old ideas were destroyed in war. Thousands of counterrevolutionary Tories fled in a massive exodus to Canada; revolutions always produce exoduses.

The first armed revolution on the continent took place in the United States. The United States exported its revolution to Spanish America. And as much as the crown tried to repress those clandestine ideas that circulated persistently and secretly through the Vicekingdom of Guatemala and through Nueva Granada, it was impossible that they not take hold in the minds of thousands of other bearded, shoeless, hungry, and impoverished extremists who trafficked in books and pamphlets containing those incendiary speeches and subversive laws, and who also trafficked in rifles and ammunition to impose by force of arms ideas that already had the force of reason. Men who did not hesitate, as Bolívar said in his speech at Angostura, to seek and accept the arms necessary to assure the victory of their liberating army: "Our army lacked military equipment. It had always been without arms. . . . Now the soldiers of independence are armed not only with justice but also with force. . . . Such great advantage we owe to the unlimited liberality of some generous foreigners who saw humanity groan and the cause of reason go under, and who did not remain passive spectators but arrived with protective aid. . . . These friends of humanity are the guardian spirits of America. . . ."

Neither Jefferson nor Washington nor Bolívar nor Morazán could have avoided, in those days of the forging of a new world and of a continent in revolution, having their revolutions exported. It was not a matter of tricks or devices to impose a model by force, but of leading a historic crusade of radical changes that was to bury the old colonial world.

Morazán, ideologist of the great dream of a federal republic of Central America, never thought in provincial terms nor believed that his liberalism came to a halt at the borders of Honduras. To the contrary, his political and military movement, the most formidable of the nineteenth century in Central America, gave rise to a great revolutionary party in the entire region. This party counterposed ideas to ideas and carried through its conception of change by force of federalist arms. The struggle then was not between Hondurans and Salvadorans, or between Guatemalans and Nicaraguans, but between liberals and reactionaries, between the armed revolutionaries of those days and the obscurantist clergy and feudal landowners, between the new Central America that was beginning to emerge with new ideas and the Central America of darkness, of the monks of the Inquisition, of the men of the gallows and the knife. And Morazán, like Washington and Bolívar, was a great exporter of revolution, of subversion, of extremism, because he wanted to change reality.

In the same way it is impossible for the Sandinistas, who

in the twentieth century repeat Morazán's revolutionary deed, to prevent their idea of revolution from being exported. We export new ideas, ideas of change and renovation, ideas that lay the foundation of a new world that is being born; we export the proven possibility that a people in arms can, when they set out to do it, defeat a tyranny and establish a new and resurgent world on the remnants of that tyranny; we export the news that in Nicaragua the revolution has brought with it literacy, agrarian reform, the end of polio, the right to life and to hope. How can it be avoided that a peasant in another country in Central America would not hear, not know, not realize that in Nicaragua land is being given to other poor and shoeless peasants like himself. How can it be avoided that he not realize that here other children, who are not his, are being vaccinated, and that his will continue to die of gastric illnesses, of polio?

Now, as in the past, the struggle is not between Nicaraguans and Hondurans but rather between landless laborers and political bosses, between new men and specters of the past, between those who are fighting for a better order and those who are trying to maintain forever a worse order.

In this sense, we export our revolution.

2. *The Sandinistas have betrayed the original program of their revolution.*

The original program of the revolution in the United States began to be betrayed quite quickly. James Madison himself, the father of the American constitution, expressed fear as early as 1829 that perpetual expansion of the new nation, under the control of factory owners and businessmen, would put an end to the experiment of republican government.

Madison's fears became reality shortly afterward in the doctrine known as Manifest Destiny. America in revolution, the continent set aflame by the bonfires of change, soon became the America of the haves and the America of the have-nots, of the oppressors and the oppressed, of the despoilers and the despoiled, of the expansionists and the fenced-in. And the sons of Washington and Jefferson not only expropriated from us great territories of Mexico in the first big step toward enslavement, but the name America as well. From then on the dream of liberty and justice became a nightmare of domination. The United States of 1898 was no longer the United States of 1776. It had left behind its original revolutionary program, initiated an expansionist counterrevolution that swallowed Cuba and Puerto Rico and prepared to assault the entire Caribbean, including Nicaragua and Panama. It did this not in the name of the old republican ideal for which so many soldiers of independence shed their blood on snowy battlefields, but rather in the name of that imperialist ideological aberration Manifest Destiny, an aberration over which was later to be drawn the veil of Pan-Americanism—that is, the United States allied with the rest of the continent in a sly and opportunistic way, so as to kill the possibility of identity and identification of the nations that are today actually or potentially subjugated. All the scaffolding of constitutional laws, division of powers, and courts of justice began to fall under the weight of imperialist interventions, of the most sordid alliances with the worst these poor and weak countries were able to provide—with the political bosses and obscure exploiters wearing presidential sashes they had secured through deals with the grandchildren of the founder of that first liberating republic that history had already hidden in its shadows.

We know what the original program of the revolution in the United States was. But when the Sandinistas are told they betrayed their original program what program is being discussed?

During Reagan's election campaign in 1980, the spokespeople for the New Right, who had already gained the positions of leadership in the Republican Party, said that the United States would never again commit the error of not fighting to the end for an ally like Somoza, and expressed feelings of guilt and shame of having abandoned him. Later they said they preferred Somoza a thousand times more than the Sandinistas. Later still they armed the old supporters of the *somocista* regime, the National Guard no less, to destroy the Sandinista revolutionary program and retake power with the weapons of counterrevolution.

The aim of the United States is to seek reinstallation of the National Guard as the decisive force in Nicaragua, faithful to North American interests in the region, just as the army of General Alvarez in Honduras is faithful to those interests.

Why do they want the National Guard to once again occupy the territory of Nicaragua as it did for fifty years in the past? To give us the constitution of Jefferson and the political model of Washington? To complete in Nicaragua the American dream of 1776? That dream does not exist. But the National Guard does, thanks to the Reagan administration.

The sleight-of-hand artists of the Reagan administration cannot really believe we have betrayed an original revolutionary program because they reject any idea of revolution, in a radical and visceral manner. The word revolution is incompatible with their vision and conception of the world. The "revolution" that, according to them, we were unable to name and are drawing away from, is going to be entrusted to the colonels and hired assassins of the *somocista* National Guard who murdered thousands of young people and peasants, who bombed *barrios* and hamlets, who raped women and filled the jails.

But Reagan's ideologists aren't the only ones who claim that we are betraying the original program of the revolution. Those who believe they have been adversely affected materially or ideologically by the revolution say they do not see, either in its direction or its actions, what they conceived as the original program. That is to say, an original program in which the winds of revolution did not so much as rustle their privileges of so many decades, their extravagant riches, their feudal haciendas, their dealings and corporate links with the dictatorship. It would have been impossible to make a revolution with such sacrifice, at the expense of so much blood, and cut it to such a pattern—a pattern that is egoistic, hardly Christian, and certainly not altruistic. This idea of a revolution without consequences, we have genuinely betrayed.

But don't forget that the fundamental promises of the Sandinistas weren't made to the United States, to whom we have never made any promises of any kind, or to privileged groups in Nicaragua. The fundamental promises were made to the poorest of our country, the promises that they defended with arms and heroism. And the original program continues, growing and multiplying for them, in cooperatives, in schools, in health-care centers, in land, in dignity, in national sovereignty. There was never any other program but that, which was the original program.

We believe that it is the United States that should return to its original program of freedom and democracy, the program of Washington, Madison, and Jefferson, whose beautiful revolutionary program was betrayed by capitalist greed, by unbridled accumulation of riches, and by that aberrant will to expansionism that has so many times pushed the borders of the United States toward our own borders, as it is pushing today once again toward the border of Honduras.

3. *What the Sandinistas have done is to copy a model of revolution, a totalitarian model.*

The same ideological cunning that justified the invasion of these American territories and the confiscation of our own free destiny also believed in the pretext of the invader's racial superiority, in the pretext of the racial inferiority of the people being invaded: that if we as marginal people were perpetually condemned to live from the crumbs of wealth, it was because of our own historical impossibility. The adventure of the Yankee conquest was thus converted into an adventure of the white race, possessor of all initiatives and spirit of conquest, capable of dominating nature and creating all science and technology, the machine, and ceaseless progress. Not only were we converted into the conquered but also into the crude and lazy half-breed, illiterate by choice and inertia, poor by irreparable destiny, violent and anarchic, quarrelsome and revengeful.

God was on the side of the United States, of its prophetic mission to conquer the world, of this people of the Second Coming who were to find their promised land wherever they liked, establish borders, and domesticate the turbulent savages who, according to the canons of William Walker, were worthy only of slavery because they were racially inferior.

From then onward not only a submission dictated by divinity, but a model of political conduct was imposed on our country as well. And that was to accept foreign domination, along with all the excellencies of that conquering race and all its never-attainable advantages—civilization and progress offered to us, like chimeras, through culture, but impossible to reach under the ideological penalty we were sentenced to.

This dogma of political and cultural domination left us not so much as a chink to breathe through and nothing in the way of independence or our own thinking. The North American political system our heroes sought, and for the adoption of which they fought, became converted into the perpetual expansion of armed puritans toward conquest, toward a destiny that we were supposed to accept no matter how bitter. The triumph of this effort at domination presupposed emptying all our national identity, all our own thinking, of any aspiration to elaborate a political model, to develop our own creative capacity. The powerful, strong, and learned Yankees were masters of all initiatives and of the entire future. We, the cause and product of underdevelopment, could not be masters even of our own organic poverty, of our own poverty that only generated more poverty. We were condemned to live on the ideological leftovers of the model of perfect Yankee democracy that every four years elected its presidents amidst colored balloons. These presidents prepared, nonetheless, to tighten the screws of domination in our countries in the name of bankers and financiers whose clutches neither Jefferson nor Madison foresaw.

So when the New Right, which today governs the United States, hears talk of Nicaragua's own model, they raise their eyebrows in disdain and discontent, in an attitude that changes quickly from surprise to fury. Their own model? Those who don't have the historical capacity to generate models, those who can only aspire to an eternally fixed role in the ideological and political division of labor! For such mentalities initiatives of whatever sort, not to mention historical programs, are elaborated only in the metropolitan centers and never in the periphery; as if the United States itself was not, at its origin, the periphery from which a new model of bloody revolution surged forward.

But political models waste away when they begin to serve interests for which they were never destined, as Madison himself bitterly lamented. For us the effectiveness of a political model depends on its capacity to resolve the problem of democracy and the problem of justice. Effective democracy is what we are seeking to practice in Nicaragua, with broad popular participation, with a permanent dynamic of involving the whole people in multiple political and social tasks. This is a people who state their opinions and who are listened to; a people who support, who build, who lead, who mobilize, who take care of communal problems, problems in the neighborhood as well as problems in the nation; a sovereign people who are prepared to fight for defense and also to spread literacy, to teach, to vaccinate. This is a democracy that exists every day and not once every four, five, or six years in formal elections; a democracy not for the minority but for the totality, in which votes are cast consciously and the best is chosen—not a candidate sold like soap powder or deodorant but a conscious leader. Here a vote will be freely given and not manipulated by a public relations company; it will be a vote to change, to improve a country, and not in favor of transnational financial interests or military-industrial trusts.

Perhaps when Madison wrote his constitution he was thinking of that type of democracy, which no longer exists in the United States.

Moreover, for us democracy is not merely a formal model but rather a constant process capable of resolving the fundamental problems of development and capable of giving the people who vote and participate the real possibility of transforming their conditions of life—a democracy that establishes justice and does away with exploitation.

Because a political model emerges from a concrete reality and from the necessity this reality imposes for change. The Sandinista model, our own model, emerged from the lengthy U.S. domination in Nicaragua, a domination that was political, economic, and military, as well as social, and even cultural. It is to this domination that our model responds and establishes as a vital necessity, in order to be our own model, ideological independence. And along with national independence our model establishes the recovery of our natural resources, the recovery of our will to develop an economic program that in transforming the country gives us the possibility not only of generating riches but also of distributing them justly.

When there's talk about copying a model, it's well to remember that what *somocismo* did, for half a century, was to copy in a servile manner the model imposed by the

United States. Nicaragua was welded into the most radical capitalist model, a market economy that impoverished the country and further distanced the possibilities of its real development. And along with this extreme capitalist model, Nicaragua suffered extreme dependence on the markets, raw materials, and resources of capital. Nicaragua, a satellite of the United States; Nicaragua, behind a genuine iron curtain, with a solid grating and triple-locked. And of course we also imported the Somoza family and the political model of elections every four years, a two-party system, a two-house legislature, a supreme court, constitution, and laws. And it was all a cruel joke.

This model, imported, copied, and imposed, was a historic failure: and we are now seeking our own model. We are no longer a satellite of the United States, we are no longer behind the iron curtain of the United States. We are free, sovereign, and independent, something that was always falsely inscribed in the *somocista* constitutions but is today true even though we have not yet written our own constitution.

To consolidate this national program, this model of our own sovereign revolution, is why we are prepared to face any challenge and any sacrifice. To make this idea possible and nurture it permanently is why the people of Nicaragua are prepared to defend, arms in hand, their revolutionary program and model. And it is why they are prepared to attain a definitive peace that will enable this model to flourish, a model they do not seek to impose on anyone. Because it has its own real political borders, which are those of Nicaragua. We are in no way the people chosen by God to fulfill any manifest destiny. We have no capital to export, no transnational enterprises to defend beyond our borders. Our dreams are not of domination, expansion, nor conquest. They are the humble dreams of a humble people who aspire to full justice and independence.

For that we wish to live in peace, to grow in peace, and

multiply in peace the example of our sovereign people who never considered asking permission of anyone to make their revolutions, and will never ask anyone for permission to defend it.

Free homeland or death!

We are a very small country confronting a truly colossal force

Interview with Daniel Ortega

The following interview originally appeared in the July 18, 1983, English-language edition of *Barricada International*.

QUESTION: Some of the political groups that supported the revolution at the time of its triumph are now among the opposition or have joined the counterrevolution. To what extent might this situation be due to a shift from the original program of the Sandinista popular revolution, which everyone supported in one way or another?

DANIEL ORTEGA: At the time of the triumph, we had at hand a program which had been proposed, drafted, developed, and then made public and guaranteed by the Sandinista National Liberation Front. It's important to make clear that the program which we are calling the "original" program was entirely prepared, discussed, and approved by the FSLN. This completely refutes the maneuvers made by some groups to give the impression that the original program was the result of pacts and agreements made with other political groups and in the presence of foreign heads of state.

That is to say, at no time was any agreement or political pact made with another political force; even the composition of the Junta of the Government of National Reconstruction was not decided as the result of any pact or agreement made with another political group. Rather, we called upon persons who were well-known nationally, and naturally they were involved in some political activity.

In this way, we called upon Violeta Barrios de Chamorro as well as Alfonso Robelo, Sergio Ramírez, and Moisés Hassan. In the case of Sergio Ramírez and Moisés Hassan, they were representing social and political groups which adhered directly to the FSLN line.

Sergio Ramírez was the head of the Group of Twelve and Hassan was one of the leading figures of the United People's Movement. They were asked: "This is the Sandinista front's program, do you support it?" It was the same program which was later applied immediately after the revolutionary triumph on July 19.

Of course, in the application of a program the interests of different sectors participating in the country's political life come into play. And the FSLN, in this case, was going to apply a program which had the national interests at heart, the people's interests, the revolution's interests. This clashed with the interests of people such as Mr. Robelo, who tried to steer the government in a direction which was more in line with his own interests.

When we began confiscating all of Somoza's properties and those of his associates, as outlined in the program, contradictions emerged. There was no problem with Somoza's personal properties, but among the *somocistas* there were people closely linked to Mr. Robelo, who had a personal relationship with him; when the application of the specific provisions contained in the program were discussed, Robelo's personal economic interests came to the fore.

This conflict arose on repeated occasions, in relation to different matters. When the nationalization of the banks was put forth, which was a significant measure, and the nationalization of exports, they prompted heated discussions.

From that moment on, conflicts arose within the government junta. And Mr. Robelo, above all, was the most belligerent. There was a time when he opposed a whole series of measures but always accepted the junta's majority decision in the end.

The minutes of the junta's meetings show that from the very beginning, when the revolutionary program went into effect, Robelo opposed it. And this had to do with his economic interests, with his understanding of political pluralism and mixed economy, since he actually wasn't viewing the program as a means to transform, to change the existing structures of the country, to improve it substantially, and to seek justice in the distribution of wealth.

He was fighting to maintain the existing forms of exploitation, and this totally violated the spirit of the revolutionary program. We mention Robelo because he was the prototype of this kind within the country's highest governmental body, and he represented—although not formally nor as a result of any alliance or agreement—the interests of the sector of Nicaraguan society which refuses to accept revolutionary change which benefits the majority. On the contrary, he was in favor of getting rid of Somoza but controlling the revolution.

From that point on, Robelo did nothing more than gather that sector's criticisms, which were logically in complete agreement with the criteria of the revolution's external enemies. In other words, the arguments Robelo raised within the junta were those of the political and economic groups here in the country and were the same arguments used by the ousted *somocistas* residing outside the country. They were also the same arguments echoed by the revolution's enemies in the U.S., Latin America, and other places.

A campaign was developed to portray the revolution as betrayed, as having cast aside the spirit of the original program, and as having radicalized the process to its own detriment.

In reality, the original program demands a radicalization of the process—that is, a deepening of the process. Measures such as nationalizing exports and banks are radical; striking blows at the large economic holdings of *somocistas* and at latifundists with idle lands, by means of the agrarian reform, are all profound measures which logically come into conflict with the interests of those who had another type of program in mind.

The FSLN has consistently applied the original program. It has not been diverted from its course for a moment.

QUESTION: The state of emergency decreed in March of last year imposed a series of restrictions on civilian life. To what extent was this measure really necessary? Don't you think there might be a serious risk involved in maintaining a measure like this?

ORTEGA: I think the FSLN's great desire to achieve stability in the country immediately was demonstrated a few months after the revolutionary triumph, while there were still barricades in the streets and signs of the insurrection were still fresh; it began to normalize life in the country and suspended all the existing emergency measures; the administration of cities and towns were transferred from the FSLN military commands to local governments; censorship of the mass media was lifted; and full freedom was given to political parties. Legal requirements were observed, to the degree possible, in the trials of all the detained *somocista* criminals captured by the people.

But what happened? That effort to normalize life in the country began to be frustrated almost immediately as armed activity against the revolutionary process was unleashed.

The first such actions occurred in 1980 and were directed against the literacy teachers.

With great effort, we launched a literacy campaign. Young Nicaraguans went to the countryside to teach the people to read and write. And they became the first victims of armed counterrevolutionary attacks.

But the situation had not yet become highly dangerous. It began to be so as groups of *somocista* guards in exile, already linked to the CIA, developed ties with groups of Nicaraguans inside the country who opposed the Sandinista revolution and were often members of political parties, trade unions, or coffee growers' associations: for example, businessmen like Jorge Salazar.*

When an administration determined to give open support to these enemies of the Nicaraguan people took office in the U.S., the situation became even more dangerous. This foreign interference began to be evident in the concentration and regroupment of *somocista* guards in Honduran territory, the incursions of *somocista* bands, and the formation of conspiratorial groups inside the country. These were organized by the CIA to carry out terrorist activity—such as the bombing of two bridges,† and concrete criminal actions against the civilian population and production activities.

For that reason, we were obliged to make a series of decisions in order to defend the revolutionary process and with

---

* Jorge Salazar was a leader of a small counterrevolutionary group who was killed in a confrontation with the authorities while he was transporting arms in 1980. At the time of his death, he was president of the Agricultural Producers Union of Nicaragua, an organization of the country's large-scale agriculturalists. His widow is presently one of the heads of the Nicaraguan Democratic Force, a counterrevolutionary organization mostly comprised of Somocista ex-guards. [footnote in original]

† On March 14, 1982, two bridges near the Honduran border were blown up by CIA-armed and trained commandos. [footnote in original]

it the people's conquests. And that led us to establish the state of emergency in the military and economic spheres, since we are suffering both economic and military aggressions from the United States. The Reagan administration's hostilities against Nicaragua are well known.

We are a very small country confronting a truly colossal force—U.S. power—and, honestly, the only way to resist those attacks is to close ranks, strengthening the country's defense at all levels.

QUESTION: Do you think it will really be possible to carry out elections in 1985, since neither a prompt solution to the Central American crisis, nor the possibility of lifting the emergency measures established in Nicaragua is in sight?

ORTEGA: In spite of the state of aggressions, of the war, we are committed to continue the process of institutionalizing the revolution. We will have to take into account the immediate conditions at the time of elections in 1985. We believe that the efforts of the revolution's enemies are aimed at making us say: "Because of the terrorist activities, the destabilizing activities, we will suppress elections." But we're not going to fall for that provocation.

While conditions permit, we will continue building schools, hospitals, sugar mills, and hydroelectric and geothermal plants in this country, and we will continue defending the revolution with arms. As the aggressions become more serious, to the extent that they affect all these economic and social efforts, we will have to adapt ourselves to those conditions and confront the difficulties of development and, ultimately, of survival.

QUESTION: To what extent might the decisions made by the revolutionary government be affected by the shortage of certain basic food items? Do the economic problems work in favor of the counterrevolution?

ORTEGA: In the first place, we have to take into account that the crisis that affects Nicaragua must be seen within the context of world economic problems, the greatest victim of which are poor, Third World nations. The countries of Central America are the main victims of the world economic crisis. Large, market-economy nations unload the weight of their crisis on countries like ours and make us pay with the blood of our peoples. This is a central element necessary to understand the crisis Central American nations are enduring.

The problems of high prices and scarcity of foods are problems that other countries are feeling acutely. But there is a substantial difference in the case of Nicaragua: here, there is a revolution, and this has allowed the population to become aware of these problems and familiar with them, to discuss them, and make demands and criticisms.

The situation is totally different in other countries where the people are not aware of those problems, and government policy is not aimed at resolving them. Rather, the people are sacrificed to safeguard the interests of those who enjoy better economic conditions.

So, in Nicaragua there is a different situation, where criticism and even discontent produced by shortages are expressed *within* the revolution.

Here, there are very concrete factors that have worked to worsen this situation. This year, above all, climatic problems have taken their toll. We suffered a drought that seriously affected the production of basic grains, plantains, and other products which are needed by the population. On top of this, demand increased automatically, given the government's decision to guarantee the consumption of basic foods to large sectors of the population which previously did not have access to them. We are speaking of the high percentage of our population who are peasants, farm workers, and rural workers who previously lacked the benefits of basic nutrition.

Then, we must add the aggressions and the mobilization of the country in order to confront them. Human resources are involved in defense activities. Many join reserve battalions and often have to leave their lands for several months.

On the other hand, all these thousands of mobilized men and women must eat, and there goes another large amount of resources. The economic crisis is compounded by the U.S. government's determination to damage the Nicaraguan economy, to affect the Nicaraguan people's possibilities of consumption in order to turn the population against the revolution.

The aggressive economic pressures the United States has unleashed against the Nicaraguan people are common knowledge. They decided to cut off our wheat and cooking oil supplies, then they reduced the sugar quota, which, at its advantageous price, was a source of foreign exchange for the country.

On the other hand, the United States decided to block all loans and aid to Nicaragua in international bodies and it has cut all forms of economic support it had maintained in the past for the *somocista* regime.

On top of this complex situation, there is another destabilizing factor: trade. This plays a negative role in terms of price increases, and, logically, this provokes discontent within the population. But, as I said before, what is important is that this population criticizes, shouts, complains, and expresses discontent, but within the revolution.

Only a minority is shouting in discontent outside of the revolution and against the revolution. A superficial viewer might speak of discontent upon observing this active population that criticizes and makes demands, but the revolution also teaches that one must criticize and make demands, and organize to do so.

Yes, there is discontent with this situation, and we are all discontented. But this is a nation which, faced with *somocista* guards and the United States' hostile military and economic policy, in the face of all this, responds as one clenched fist. It supports the revolution.

QUESTION: Also in the framework of the economic situation, there are those who refer to the Nicaraguan revolution as state-controlled. Others, however, speak of the need for a larger state participation in the economy. What is the future of the Nicaraguan economy, of the economic sectors which today exist in the country: the private sector, the mixed sector, and the state sector? What role will these be given in the future?

ORTEGA: The guidelines that the revolution has set in that sense are aimed at achieving a unified direction for the economy. We cannot function here with a fragmented economy, acting anarchically and responding to the interests of merely utilitarian factors, which were what carried the most weight in the past, instead of development factors, which are the most important.

So, there are some guidelines that have the purpose of setting the bases for an economic take-off in the country. This means transforming the bases of the economy and mobilizing all sectors to carry out transformations in agriculture, in industry, in construction, in all areas required for the country's development.

This, of course, to a certain degree affects the false freedom that these groups had—and here, we're speaking of the private sector—to get involved in any business, without concern for whether it might be detrimental to the country's future, to development, without thinking about popular sectors, the working class. In the past, there really wasn't even an economic policy that favored strengthening a truly national bourgeoisie; that sector was totally neutralized, splintered, anarchic, and served as a mere instrument of foreign economic interests.

Now the revolution proposes to drastically change this situation. It proposes to develop a planned economy that will respond to the need for change and development in the country. There is a place in these plans for small, medium, and large-scale producers, industrialists, artisans, etc. The private sector at large has the opportunity to play an active role in the development of this economic model.

QUESTION: Exactly what kind of role? One of their main complaints is that they are denied the opportunity to participate in decision making.

ORTEGA: That complaint must be viewed from a political perspective. Some private producers are linked to political groups which oppose the Sandinista front, and it often becomes hard to tell whether they are speaking as producers or as politicians. They generally speak as politicians. They say they're excluded, but in reality a series of mechanisms has been established here in the various sectors of production, particularly in the agricultural and commercial sectors, in which they all participate directly.

They are able to participate as representatives of an economic force in the nation. As politicians, they can go argue and complain in the Council of State, where they have a place. As producers they can form part of the different commissions that have been created.

The private sector is present on all these commissions. This is where their demands for foreign exchange are considered, to see if these demands respond to the country's development needs.

In any case, the underlying problem here is the huge limitations the country faces in its efforts to reactivate the economy. These limitations are imposed, in part, by the continuous U.S. aggressions which affect the economy, as well as the world market structure. While developed nations buy our export products at the prices they choose, we have to buy their products at their ever-increasing prices.

On the other hand, we are vulnerable to powerful U.S. economic aggressions, which include pressures to cut off the loans and aid that constitute an important source of foreign exchange for the country. Distribution of this foreign exchange is a very difficult and complicated matter, but we are just as strict with state enterprises as we are with private businessmen.

We find that those businessmen are manipulated politically or they intentionally act in a negative manner, even though they are aware of these problems, simply because they want to give the impression that the state is denying them foreign exchange and thus is harming private enterprise, seeking to make the private sector disappear.

But the truth is that if someone is harming the private sector here and dealing it a hard blow, for example, by cutting off the sugar quota, that someone is the United States government. It is harming everyone in the country equally, including the private sector.

QUESTION: Nicaragua has declared itself a nonaligned nation. However, in international forums as well as in its economic, political, and diplomatic affairs, it has deepened relations with socialist countries. Nicaragua is accused of having joined the socialist bloc. To what extent has Nicaragua maintained its original policy of nonalignment? To what extent does government policy respond to that principle?

ORTEGA: Nicaragua really does sustain and defend the policy of nonalignment. This is so evident, so clear, that Nicaragua has achieved a leading role within the nonaligned nations movement, and is greatly respected among its members.

How else could you explain Nicaragua's election to the United Nations Security Council, in spite of the U.S. opposition and campaign to block that election? The fact that Nicaragua has established relations at various levels with the countries of the socialist community does no harm to its policy of nonalignment. On the contrary, it reinforces that policy; the past regime was completely aligned with the United States and rejected relations with the socialist, Arab, and African countries.

When the revolution triumphed, it never considered breaking relations with the United States, but, at the same time and consistent with its policy of nonalignment, Nicaragua sought to open itself up to all the countries of the world.

The extensive relations with various countries of the world have brought about a diversification in our economic and trade relations. That means we are beginning to break our traditional dependence on the United States and to maintain our own identity on the international level.

Naturally, for a country which in the past could not even imagine having relations with a socialist country, this step sounds extremely significant, but it is something Nicaragua set out to develop since July 19, 1979.

This fourth anniversary is demonstrating the possibility of establishing and consolidating a revolutionary process in Central America. But we are also celebrating this anniversary at the most critical moment for the Central American region; this moment requires responses soon: responses that will help us overcome the confrontation promoted by the U.S. government. We must develop a new kind of relationship with the United States.

The crisis we mentioned reflects the fact that the policy promoted by the United States in the region is really obsolete and worn-out and should thus be replaced.

The U.S. government is not yet conscious of this. On the contrary, it desperately clings to its policy, trying to revive a corpse, and cannot see the need for a change, which is the only way to save the future relationship between the Central American peoples and the United States. This has been demonstrated in the recent case of the Malvinas Islands, where U.S. policy was made totally clear: it is a policy that does not adapt to the new mentality, to progress, to development.

The Sandinista people's revolution is an irreversible political reality

by Daniel Ortega

The following speech was given July 19, 1983, before a crowd of more than 150,000 gathered in León to celebrate the fourth anniversary of the revolution. The mobilization for the rally was carried out under the slogans "All arms to the people! Everyone to defense!" The speech was originally published in the July 20, 1983, issue of *Barricada*. This translation is from the August 8, 1983, issue of *Intercontinental Press*.

Many of you have been here since last night. Our visitors will be asking themselves if you are tired? *["No"]* Our visitors will also be asking themselves if you have been brought to this plaza by force? *["No"]* Our visitors will be asking themselves if you want the traitor Edén Pastora? *["No"]* If you are Sandinistas? *["Yes"]* *[Applause and slogans]*

One cannot be in this city of León without a remembrance of [Rubén] Darío, and we cannot hold this meeting without a remembrance of Bolívar. *[Applause]*

From this always heroic and combative city of León, on

the twenty-second anniversary of the Sandinista National Liberation Front and the fourth anniversary of the triumph [of the revolution], we welcome the representatives of friendly governments and peoples and, in particular, the delegations of citizens of the United States, and delegations and individual figures who are friends of our revolution and have come here from different and distant places. [*Applause*]

We have among us two of Nicaragua's very dear friends. One of them is Julio Cortázar, who at the beginning of this year received the recognition of the people when he was awarded the Rubén Darío Order. [*Applause*]

Our greetings on this glorious day go out to the men who are on our borders, in the front lines of battle, defending the integrity of our territory, the sovereignty of our homeland, and the revolution. [*Applause and chants of "They shall not pass!"*]

Our greetings on this glorious day go out to the inhabitants of the small villages, districts, and towns in the border zones; to the men, women, children, and elderly who confront the enemies of the people with a rifle on their shoulder and a machete in their hands.

Our affection and respect go out to the heroic people of Teotecacinante, to the heroic people of Jalapa, to the heroic people of San Francisco del Norte. [*Applause*]

We celebrate this anniversary remembering those men who with determination left us a legacy of dignity, bravery, love of the people, and love of the homeland. Men like Andrés Castro, men like Benjamin Zeledón, men like Rigoberto López Pérez, men like Carlos Fonseca, and men like Augusto César Sandino. [*Applause*]

They are the eternal makers of our history. The revolutionary triumph attained on July 19, 1979, belongs to them. They are present in the small and large tasks. They are alive in our slogans. They are people's power. [*Chants of "People's power!"*]

León was the first territory liberated during the final offensive and during those days it was made the provisional capital. The Junta of the Government of National Reconstruction was installed here.

Here, they fought with Sandinista boldness; here the red and black drums resounded in Subtiava, El Coyolar, La Ermita, El Laborío, La Estación, La Cartonera, Zaragoza, San Carlos, San Felipe, in all of León's neighborhoods. [*Applause*]

All of the fury accumulated during long years of struggle, all the thirst for justice stored up from the times of Pedrarias, who was the first Somoza and who—drunk with ambition and rage—sent his dogs to destroy the Indians. All the accumulated fury took the form of the people organized into the Sandinista front, which in its final offensive buried once and for all Somoza and *somocismo*, the [National] Guard, the exploiters, those who would sell out the country, the enemies of the people.

A new consciousness flowered on July 19. A consciousness that tells us that individualism, selfishness, greed, overbearing arrogance, demagogy, and lies must be eradicated. A consciousness that tells us that the love for the people rises above material goods. A consciousness that readies us to work at any time, in any place, and on any task. A consciousness that tells us, as Che did, that we cannot feel totally happy and tranquil while there are barefoot children without schools in our homeland or in any corner of the world. A new consciousness engaged in a limitless war against the vices of the old consciousness. A new consciousness that readies us to give our lives in defense of the interests of the people. A new Sandinista consciousness that makes us worthy sons of Sandino.

And this new consciousness is seen in the tasks taken up with revolutionary enthusiasm, even under the worst circumstances, by men, women, children, by young and old, organized in the Sandinista Workers Federation, in the Association of Rural Workers, in the July 19 Sandinista Youth organization, in the Luisa Amanda Espinoza Nicaraguan Women's Organization, in the Sandinista Defense Committees, in the National Union of Farmers and Ranchers, in the National Employees Union, in the Sandinista Children's Association, in the Sandinista Cultural Workers Association, in the Heroes and Martyrs National Professional Confederation, in the National Association of Nicaraguan Educators, in the Health Workers Federation, in the Nicaraguan Journalists Union. These are the organized lifeblood and energy of the new Sandinista consciousness.

And this new consciousness is the Sandinista National Liberation Front, the political vanguard of the Nicaraguan people, whose members and candidate members become daily more disciplined, daily more humble, daily more ready to face long hours and sacrifices, daily more self-critical and critical, daily more brotherly with their brothers, daily more Sandinista.

And just as the Sandinista front knew how to lead the people to reach victory, today—in the tasks of defense, in the tasks of education and culture, in the tasks of production, in the social programs, in the organization and mobilization of the working people, in the ideological struggle, and in international policy—the Sandinista front is present as a guide of the revolution, with the National Directorate as its highest leader. [*Applause*]

The Sandinista front is present in the revolutionary state through the government junta, through the ministers, through the technical cadres and state workers, all of whom carry out the state's policies within the state.

The Sandinista front is present in the armed forces through the heads of the Ministry of Defense and the Ministry of the Interior, who are responsible for carrying out the revolution's policies of defense and security.

In the prorevolutionary professional associations, in the

auxiliary apparatuses, and in the ongoing organization and mobilization of the masses, the Sandinista front is present to carry out ideological struggle, to support state measures, to support defense plans, to support foreign policy.

We can state that, in these four years of revolution, the Sandinista consciousness is the strength of the people synthesized and organized in the Sandinista front and by the Sandinista front. This Sandinista consciousness has been reflected in the goals that were met and also in the goals which were not fulfilled.

Today we derive pleasure from the great victory of the literacy campaign, which reduced illiteracy from more than 50 percent to 12 percent. But we cannot sit back while 12 percent of Nicaraguans cannot read or write and, therefore, cannot be considered totally free men.

We have created 2,639 educational centers; 1,252 new school buildings have been built and 16,975 Popular Adult Education Collectives created. And compared with the 500,000 students in 1978 in the *somocista* past, we presently have 1,005,318 students. [*Applause*]

It is true that a great effort has been made. But on the other hand, the achievement level of the students is low, and in this area we all have a degree of responsibility: the Sandinista front, the Ministry of Education, the teachers, and the students. This is a situation we can improve and which must be improved.

In the area of health care, there has been an increase throughout the nation, with a doubling of the number of visits, that is, a doubling in service to the public. Also, for the first time in Nicaragua's history, not a single case of poliomyelitis has been reported, and measles has been reduced from 3,784 cases in 1980 to 226 cases in 1982. We could list other successes, which have especially lowered infant mortality.

But we will not hide the serious and grave deficiencies

that still exist in the health sector, in the supply of medicines and, above all, in the poor service to the public. These deficiencies must be overcome.

In the industrial sphere, we have reached an acceptable rhythm of production and we must acknowledge the high level of consciousness and the discipline of the workers and of the technicians, who in the midst of big limitations—above all of parts and raw materials—have been able to maintain production.

It is clear that profound changes are called for in the medium and long term. In the meantime, it will be necessary to continue struggling to maintain production, raising the levels of efficiency and providing more vigilance to prevent robbery and misappropriation of the people's property.

In the agricultural sector, we have advanced in the recovery of national production. The coffee harvest was an exemplary effort of mobilization by the working people. Under the criminal gunfire of the *somocista* counterrevolutionaries, we brought in the largest harvest in history, some 1,420,000 quintals [1 quintal = 100 pounds].

As for cotton, due to the problems imposed by the floods, the goal of 130,000 manzanas was not met. But a high yield was obtained. For this year we set out to plant 150,000 manzanas; this figure has already been exceeded with the planting of 171,800 manzanas. [*Applause*]

Four years after the revolutionary triumph, the unjust agrarian structures inherited from *somocismo* have been pulled out by their roots. Under *somocismo*, 1,700 landowners had stripped the peasants of their land, and ended up controlling almost 3 million manzanas, which represented 41 percent of the land. In the meantime, more than 100,000 small producers who had farms of less than fifty manzanas owned barely 1 million manzanas, that is, 15 percent of the land, which was also of poor quality.

The agrarian reform has completely transformed this unjust panorama, opening a new future for the farm workers and peasants. The *somocista* landowners have passed into history and the idle and unproductive system of latifundias has been hit hard. Through the confiscation of *somocista* latifundias and the application of the Agrarian Reform Law, 2 million manzanas have passed into the hands of the people to establish agrarian reform enterprises or to strengthen the cooperative movement.

The eighty agrarian reform enterprises that make up the people's property sector have played a decisive role in reactivating production,* in improving the standard of living of farm workers, and in developing new investment projects.

The cooperative movement, which has the firm support of the revolutionary state, is already emerging as a powerful source which will play a very important role in the future of our agrarian production and in the organization of self-defense in the countryside.

To support this vigorous movement which brings together more than 60,000 peasants, the revolution has given agrarian reform land titles for 237,209 manzanas to cooperatives as well as 63,352 to individual producers—a total of 300,561 manzanas benefiting 20,236 peasant families.

On the other hand, we must criticize the abuses to which some small and medium peasants have been subjected, having seen their property invaded with no justification. We must reaffirm here that the revolution guarantees ownership of land to those who work it and does not permit these unjust and illegal occupations, just as we must also have the necessary resolve to start production on the idle lands.

There has been much talk about the debts of the peasants. It has been a much-discussed question. We all know that

---

* At this point *Barricada* indicates that the speech was interrupted by wind. This paragraph and the two that follow it are based on the summary of the speech issued by the Nicaraguan press office.

during the time of *somocismo* the peasants became badly indebted and that now, after the triumph of the revolution, they have continued to pile up debts.

Therefore, as the revolution increased credits to the peasants, their debt expanded, because it came on top of an old debt, the old debt from *somocismo*.

The National Union of Farmers and Ranchers [UNAG] has been spearheading a whole movement to have the situation of the debt revised, particularly the debt of those peasants who are involved in the productive area such as in basic grains, and especially the debt of the peasants who are organized in cooperatives.

A few days ago the government junta received a delegation from the UNAG. The National Directorate has been keeping abreast of this problem, and has supported the demands of the peasants because it feels that these are just demands. But we feel that here we also have to make a just decision. A just decision must not be paternalistic, but rather fraternal.

Therefore, the government junta is directing the National Finance System to proceed to carry out an overall financial restructuring of the debt of the cooperative and small individual producers of basic grains who have used their credit responsibly.

How will this restructuring be carried out? We have not wanted to use the word "cancellation" because we feel that this is not what is involved. The restructuring of the debt will take place in the following way: for the Sandinista agricultural cooperatives or production cooperatives all debts accumulated up to the 1982–83 growing season will be taken into account, that is, will be considered, and all the debts they have accumulated up to that date will be lifted. [*Applause*]

For the credit and service cooperatives the debts accumulated up to the 1981–82 growing season; and for the individual producers the debts accumulated up to the 1980–81 growing season will be lifted, that is, all debts from those dates back will be lifted. [*Applause*]

Also, the revolutionary government will assume the debts of peasants integrated into defense in the reserve battalions, the Sandinista People's Militia, self-defense settlements, or cooperatives that have been damaged by the activities of the *somocista* counterrevolutionaries. [*Applause*]

We must mention here the problem of food supply. This is a daily problem that cannot be looked at apart from the difficult circumstances under which impoverished countries like ours live, countries that, because they want to be free, are economically, militarily and politically attacked.

We must also bear in mind that the productive sector has not fully recovered from the destruction that took place during the war and that the great efforts that have been made to raise production are still insufficient. In addition, there are the effects of the prolonged drought that affected our harvest of basic grains and also profoundly affected grazing lands and other livestock feed, resulting in a drop in production of meat, milk, cheese, chicken, and eggs, especially in May, June, and the beginning of July.

The revolution has expanded consumption. The sectors that did not consume, especially in the countryside, the agricultural workers who were superexploited in the time of *somocismo*, have begun to consume since the revolutionary triumph due to all the laws that have been aimed at the nutrition of the agricultural workers.

We won't say that it is optimal nutrition. We won't say that it is first-rate nutrition. But it is nutrition that takes place within the measure of our possibilities.

This means that consumption has been expanded, while supply has not grown as fast as consumption, and therefore we have this problem. But in addition to this there have been added problems from nature like the drought, as well as problems of economic aggression, because this too affects production.

And there is another problem—the problem of the monopolizers, of the speculative hoarders, of those who have a *somocista* mentality and continue making money on the hunger and needs of the people. When we import food to help resolve this, the monopolists and the speculative hoarders run up the prices on the product.

It is a problem we must find some solution to, even if temporary. The National Directorate is looking into this problem, and the government junta is meeting on this problem. We feel that serious measures of a political type, an administrative type, must be taken, in which everyone participates.

Those who don't participate will not have the right to complain later. [*Applause*]

Among other things, we say that it is necessary to stimulate more energetically the production of foodstuffs and basic goods. You know that perspectives have been laid out and we have been stressing them. But many times due to human failures, weaknesses, and errors, these aims have not been fulfilled.

It is necessary to increase vigilance so that these perspectives are fulfilled, so that we can produce beans, rice, and corn in abundance, and eggs in abundance, and meat in abundance. [*Applause*] So that we can have everyday food.

Other things can be lacking. Chewing gum can be lacking, but we cannot lack beans. [*Applause*]

We must punish [*Applause*], we must punish with real severity the speculative practices of monopolization and, generally, all trafficking in the hunger and necessities of the people. The laws are there. The decisions are there. But we need the energy of everyone to force compliance with these decisions. Meanwhile they have continued playing with the people's hunger.

We must in the first place guarantee the nutrition of the

children, and the nutrition of men, women, young people, and old people mobilized in armed defense of the revolution. [*Applause*]

Today as we commemorate this twenty-second anniversary of the Sandinista front and the fourth anniversary of the revolutionary triumph, humanity is living through decisive moments, in military terms and in the economic sphere.

In military terms, there are those who would advance a policy of hegemony, which means investing billions of dollars in ever more sophisticated atomic weaponry. Not long ago a United Nations body said that if one-tenth of these resources were used to combat hunger in the world through development programs, hunger could be eliminated, it could be defeated.

They are increasing the resources allocated to the industry of death. They are rejecting reasonable proposals that are made to put a stop to this irrational arms race. While billions of dollars are invested in armaments, they are cutting aid, they are cutting credits for the poor countries. They are keeping us subjected to economic exploitation in international economic relations, in which the industrialized market-economy countries place the whole weight of their crisis on the poor countries like ours.

This hegemonistic policy, which the present U.S. administration is trying to impose in the military and economic spheres, has meant a larger quota of sacrifices for the people of Nicaragua.

So far this year, the attacks by the *somocista* guard and the traitor Pastora, directed and coordinated by the Central Intelligence Agency, have already cost more than 600 Nicaraguan lives and $70 million in losses.

To these economic losses caused by the direct military attacks, we must add the loans to Nicaragua that the U.S. administration has cut; and the blockade it is pushing for in the multilateral international bodies like the Inter-American

Development Bank; the cut in our sugar quota to the U.S. market, which we are all familiar with—bringing the total loss to $354 million.

In addition, we would have to add the losses that Nicaragua suffers with the drop in the prices of our principal export products, which in the past year alone meant losses of $180 million compared with the prices in 1980. This brings it to a total of $534 million that Nicaragua has stopped receiving.

But there's still more. If we add the credits that have not gone to Nicaraguan farmers due to shortages in foreign exchange; the roads that have not been completed; the schools that couldn't be built because of suspended loans; the rural development programs that were not carried out, also because of suspended loans; and other such essential productive activities that would have been financed by the blocked loans, the damage caused could be multiplied by as much as five times.

Everyone knows that we are not oil producers. Although multinational companies have made some explorations in the past, the reality is that at present we are not oil producers.

In order to bring an energy plant into use we need bunker fuel, which is an oil derivative. To light a lantern we need gas, which is an oil derivative. To light a kitchen stove we also need this gas, derived from oil. To operate the tractors, the jeeps, transportation in general, we need diesel fuel or gasoline, which are derived from oil.

Despite the efforts made with geothermal and hydroelectric power, we depend on oil. We want to thank Mexico and Venezuela for the support they have given and continue to provide to the Central American countries in terms of oil. [*Applause*]

We want to use this opportunity to become totally aware of the delicate nature of the situation. We must make a greater effort in saving energy and saving oil. We should, with Sandinista firmness, face up to the extremely grave situation that this presents us in the economic sphere.

We were saying that the economic crisis is not the only thing hitting us, and in fact there is a whole campaign of aggression against Nicaragua being mounted by the United States.

In the midst of the military, political, and economic aggression, we have been making great efforts in institutionalizing the revolution. The Council of State has already discussed a law on political parties, and the majority of its articles have already been approved. Commissions from the Council of State have also been sent abroad to study the experience of other peoples in regard to elections, so that we Nicaraguans can be the ones to decide the type of elections we will have in 1985. [*Applause*]

But the enemies of our revolution are trying to sabotage this effort. They have not been convinced that they will not be able to defeat this revolutionary power, this Sandinista power, this people's power, with bullets or with ballots. [*Applause and chants of "People's power!"*]

We said that we are subjected to military, political, and economic aggression. They have launched many aggressions, including from the north and from the south.

The first attempts have failed. They launched the *somocista* guards, with the support of Honduras's army chief. They launched the traitor Edén Pastora. But the guardsmen and the traitor have ended up like Uncle Coyote, with their teeth broken. [*Applause and chants of "One single army!"*]

The U.S. administration is bent on a military solution and has given no sign of an alleged readiness to negotiate.

Nicaragua has always been ready to seek a negotiated political solution to the region's problems. We have shown our readiness on numerous occasions, especially by supporting the Contadora group. [*Applause*]

We also give our support to the call for peace recently made by the bishops of Honduras, which, we are sure, has been well received by the fraternal people of Honduras, who do not want war and who do want peace. [*Applause*]

Today when the threats of aggression seem very close; today when the dangers of war engulf the region; today when the heroic Salvadoran people are being attacked and the U.S. military intervention in Central America is increasing, the National Directorate of the Sandinista National Liberation Front wants to make public the following basic points for overcoming the crisis that afflicts the region.

We do not want war. We want to avoid greater sacrifices by the people and therefore we are obliged to make the greatest efforts in a responsible manner. The National Directorate makes the following declaration:

"With responsibility before history, taking into account the grave situation the Central American region is going through, having been turned into an important focus of international tension as a result of the present U.S. administration's policies, the National Directorate of the Sandinista National Liberation Front feels that it is the inescapable moral obligation of all the governments of Central America and of the political leaders of the United States to spare our peoples the tragedy of a generalized war.

"Therefore, due to this pressing as well as noble objective, it recognizes the value of the positive proposals that came out of the meeting of heads of state of Mexico, Colombia, Venezuela, and Panama last weekend in Cancún, Mexico, which gives a big impetus to the search for peace that motivates the Contadora group.

"The National Directorate of the Sandinista National Liberation Front shares the criteria expressed by the heads of state of the Contadora group, that 'the use of force as an alternative solution does not solve but rather aggravates the underlying tensions. Central American peace will be a reality only to the degree that the fundamental principles of coexistence among nations are respected: nonintervention;

self-determination; [*Applause*] sovereign equality of states; [*Applause*] cooperation for economic and social development; peaceful solution of controversies; as well as the free and authentic expression of the people's will.'

"We share these criteria because our ideals and principles—people's power, the socioeconomic transformations to benefit the great majority of the nation, the sovereignty and full independence of our homeland, the determination to build a new free, democratic, and pluralistic society without exploitation—are facts and convictions deeply rooted in the hearts of millions of Nicaraguans.

"The Sandinista people's revolution is an irreversible political reality, with national and international repercussions recognized by the whole world.

"Nicaragua has no expansionist ambitions, nor does it want to impose its sociopolitical system on other countries. We have no economic investments abroad, nor do we have dreams of imperial domination. Therefore our people do not need and do not want war. For Nicaragua the commitment to *never* attack any country is a matter of principle.

"The Sandinista National Liberation Front, which has fought and will continue to fight to assure our people an existence of peace and security, is conscious of the deterioration that has taken place in the situation in the region. In line with the latest constructive steps of the Contadora group, it has decided to make a new effort to contribute to peace, despite our absolute conviction that the greatest threat to the peace of the region requires bilateral solutions.

"The Government of National Reconstruction will accept that the initial phases of the process of negotiations sponsored by the Contadora group would have a multilateral character, in order to put an end to the excuses, [*Applause*] and so that those who claim to be interested in peace should take concrete steps to develop the process that can lay the foundation for peace. [*Applause*]

"Furthermore, taking into account that the heads of state have entrusted their ministers of foreign relations to work out specific proposals to be presented for consideration by the Central American countries at the next joint meeting of foreign ministers, and taking into account that the biggest dangers to peace in the region can arise out of the worsening of the already existing military conflicts, the Sandinista National Liberation Front proposes that a discussion immediately begin on the following basic points:

"1. A commitment to end any existing warlike situation through the immediate signing of a nonaggression pact between Nicaragua and Honduras."

Brothers and sisters, do you agree with this proposal? [*The people answer, "Yes!"*]

"2. The absolute end to all supplies of arms from any country to the conflicting forces in El Salvador, so that these people can resolve their problems without outside interference."

Nicaraguan brothers and sisters, do you agree with this proposal? [*The people answer, "Yes!"*]

"3. The absolute cessation of all military aid—in the form of arms shipments, training, use of territory to launch attacks or any other form of aggression—to the forces opposing any of the Central American governments."

Nicaraguan brothers and sisters, do you agree with this proposal? [*The people answer, "Yes!"*]

"4. Commitments to ensure absolute respect for the self-determination of the peoples of Central America and the noninterference in the internal affairs of each country."

Do you agree with this point? [*The people answer, "Yes!"*]

"5. An end to aggressions and economic discrimination against any Central American country."

Are you in agreement with this point? [*The people answer, "Yes!"*]

"6. No installation of foreign military bases on Central

American territory and the suspension of military exercises in the Central American area with participation of foreign armies."

Are we in agreement with this proposal? [*The people answer, "Yes!"*]

"Progress in the solution of these points will automatically contribute to the discussion of other points that also worry the Central American states and that are included in the agenda of the Contadora group in order to find an acceptable and lasting solution for the security and stability of the countries of the region.

"If agreements are reached with the help of the Contadora group and with their approval, the United Nations Security Council, as the highest international body charged with overseeing international peace and security, would have to supervise and guarantee compliance of these agreements by all countries.

"Nicaragua states in advance its readiness to accept with full responsibility all commitments that flow from such accords. And it demonstrates this by accepting the view of the heads of state of the Contadora group that the task of settling specific differences between countries must be initially undertaken with the signing of a memorandum of understanding and the creation of commissions that would allow all parties to develop joint actions and guarantee effective control of their territories, especially in border areas.

"While these initiatives are being worked out in practice, the people of Nicaragua will remain completely mobilized, ready to raise a wall of patriotism and rifles, against which all the aggressors will shatter. [*Applause*]

"León, July 19, 1983, Year of Struggle for Peace and Sovereignty" [*Chants of "They shall not pass!"*]

This is the peace proposal the National Directorate submits for the approval of the people of Nicaragua. Are we in agreement with this peace proposal? [*A unanimous "Yes!"*]

A peace proposal that the Junta of the Government of National Reconstruction will take up. [*Chants of "People's power"*] We make this proposal because we really want peace. To continue building schools, we want peace. To continue raising production, we want peace. To improve attention to the people's health, we want peace. To wipe out hunger and poverty, we want peace. In order that mothers, children, brothers, families do not live through the martyrdom of war, we want peace.

But we want an honorable peace. We don't want the peace of the tomb, we don't want a cowardly peace. Rather than that, we would prefer to suffer, we would prefer to fight, we would prefer to die, but never to yield. [*Applause and chants of "They shall not pass!"*]

In the meanwhile, we must prepare ourselves to defend the revolution from the new attacks our enemies are organizing. The government of the United States is behind those plans, in which the *somocista* guards and the traitors are in the first rank, followed by the army of Honduras, and behind it the U.S. soldiers.

We must prepare ourselves to repel them and defeat them with the fighting spirit of Pedro Aráuz, of Germán Pomares, of Selím Shible, of Hilario Sánchez, of Oscar Danilo Rosales, of Gilberto Rostrán Barvis, of Guadalupe Moreno, of René Carrión, of Fanor Urroz, of Félix Pedro Picado, of Marcos Somarriba, of Felix Pedro Carrillo, of Mauricio Martínez, of Erick Ramírez, of Sergio Saldaña, of José Rubí, of Luisa Amanda Espinoza.

We must prepare ourselves to fight and win with all the formidable strength of the organized people, and it is the decision of the National Directorate, which has been accepted by the government junta, to submit as soon as possible for its approval the draft of a law establishing patriotic military service. [*Applause and chants of "They shall not pass!"*]

And it is the decision of the National Directorate, accepted by the government junta, to deliver in an orderly, organized manner—to the furthest corner of the country—all arms to the people [*Applause and chants of "All arms to the people!"*] so that the people, organized territorially in the Sandinista People's Militia, can have their combat weapons to defend the land; all arms to the people to defend the gains of the revolution; all arms to the people to defend people's power; all arms to the people to defend this new society; all arms to the people to defend peace; all arms to the people to defend this Free Homeland or Death; all arms to the people. [*Thunderous applause and chants of "We are fighting to win! They shall not pass!" "National Directorate, give the order! They shall not pass!"*]

U.S. destabilization in Nicaragua
Interview with Sergio Ramírez

The following interview conducted by Carlos Rincón was released by the New Nicaragua press agency on August 13, 1983.

CARLOS RINCÓN: There exists a notorious telegram sent in 1970 by the general headquarters of the CIA to its station in Santiago, Chile: "High authority in Washington authorizes you to propose to the AA. FF. of Chile any material aid, including armed intervention, if they make a move to impede the election of Allende by Congress on October 24." Later Nixon and Kissinger, out of fear of the demonstration effect in the Third World of the "Chilean way," designed a medium-term strategy to transform the economic, social, and political order in Chile before precipitating the use of military force against the Popular Unity government ten years ago. Are there parallels between that process of destabilization and the policy advanced by the United States government of Carter and Reagan toward Nicaragua?

SERGIO RAMÍREZ: I think that the first similarity that we

could note is in reference to the imperial will of the United States—or of a North American administration at a given moment—to prevent a government from taking power or to overthrow this government once it has taken it, whenever it considers that such a government, because of its ideology or its composition, does not correspond to the interests that the United States says it defends—that is, its political, economic, and strategic interests of a geopolitical or military character. This happened in Chile even before the rise of Allende, as this telegram proves, when they attempted to prevent the head of the government from taking office. But there is also a basic difference with the case of Nicaragua. In the case of Chile the destabilization was virtually an initiative of the large transnationals, especially ITT and other U.S. companies prejudiced by the process of revolutionary transformation in Chile. With the full connivance of the State Department and the CIA, these multinationals encouraged the coup d'etat, financed it, and, in alliance with the political right, created all the internal conditions for carrying through the coup.

Even though there is a difference between the Chilean case and the present situation in Nicaragua, however, it is similar to an earlier situation, when the liberal-reformist government of General Zelaya was overthrown in 1910 by the State Department—the CIA did not exist then—and by the mining company of the Bucanans family, the Rosario Mine Company, whose lawyer was the United States secretary of state and whose head accountant was the one who would later be the president of Nicaragua, Adolfo Díaz. We find here more or less a likeness with the coup d'etat in Chile in 1973.

The fundamental element in these comparisons, then, is the imperial will of the United States to reject the existence of all governments extraneous to its interests or its strategic designs. Between Chile and Nicaragua, therefore, there is this similarity; the similarity is also in the emphasis in which the United States dedicates economic investments in human material, propagandistic, and international agitation resources, etc., to this subversive project.

But we can also note another important difference, in that in Chile what was being dealt with was the conquest of the government by Popular Unity, and not the taking of power; they didn't even have the parliament. This is extremely important in understanding the difference, the obvious difference in the present situation. In Chile, the rightist sectors that never accepted the fact that Popular Unity won the elections of 1970 and assumed the executive seat, always had the army as their principal support. This is an army that was doing nothing more than playing a "democratic" role, a front, respectful of institutions, of the constitution, of the laws, of parliament. It was seen that all of this was a pure lie.

RINCÓN: In reality the Chilean army had always intervened throughout the entire republican history of Chile each time that the hegemony exercised by the bloc in power had been brought into question.

RAMÍREZ: Yes, this is what has happened in the great majority of the Latin American countries. That is, the bourgeois-democratic project is supported until class domination is at stake. And then comes the army, the great regulator, which is what happened in Chile. There are these democratic armies, civilized, constructed in the image and likeness of the European armies. This is the case of the Chilean army, which is very Prussian, or other armies that have notable French or Belgian traits. The Salvadoran army itself—at least the rural guard—has its roots in the Spanish civil guard. But when the time arrives these armies throw away their mask and convert into what they are—veritably fascist armies.

But I was telling you, the difference between Nicaragua and Chile of the Popular Unity resides in the fact that Allende barely had one part of the mechanisms of government. He didn't really have power, the power was in the hands of the rightist parliament, of the army. And here in Nicaragua, in turn, the destruction of the *somocista* guard—which was the same fascist army that I was speaking to you about, just without European tradition since it was always an army of intervention—is one of the basic conditions of our ascendance to power. Therefore, our most basic task in the face of the North American aggression is to defend this power, and not to defend the government, in contradiction to other sectors that share a part of this power, as in Chile. The Sandinista front has the power here. It is people's power and therefore, although in those terms the task is more difficult, the challenge is also greater. It is that confrontation that we are facing at this time.

RINCÓN: The picture of arrogant imperial will that you are drawing seems accurate to me. At any rate, in policy, the time periods and dates are key. On April 1, 1981, barely one and a half years after the overthrow of Somoza, the United States cut economic assistance to Nicaragua and began to apply pressure on international financial institutions to block credits. With these measures of intimidation and harassment, what the *New York Times* has called the "secret war so poorly hidden" was then declared.

RAMÍREZ: The United States ill will toward this revolution reaches its highest point with the Reagan administration. Of this there is no doubt. In Reagan's political discourse, in his electoral campaign, in the proposed policies toward Central America, in the works of the Heritage Foundation and from all those elements that come out of the universities to govern the United States, Nicaragua has always been a focal theme. That is, within the definition of its policy and strategies, Nicaragua plays a crucial role, considering that after Nicaragua come El Salvador, Guatemala, and shortly—as Mr. Shultz recently said in his vision of the situation—we will have the Communists fighting at the United States border with Mexico. This vision is absolutely determining for them, and it allows us to say that the Reagan government is an extremist government. The extremists are very dangerous in any context and the extremists that constitute the Reagan government are applying that extremist policy to Nicaragua.

There is a considerable difference with what the policy of Mr. Carter was, a more peaceful policy we might say, although during the latter part of his government Carter moved in to tackle the tasking of tightening the screws against Nicaragua. There came a moment in which he surely believed, from the electoral point of view, that it was appropriate to take measures against Nicaragua that could help him in an electoral triumph. In reality, it was the Carter administration that began to pressure us with accusations that we were militarily aiding the Salvadoran guerrillas, something which they could in no way ever prove. But our confrontation has evidently been with the Reagan administration. On that date that you mentioned, after assuming power, it effectively decided to cut all economic aid to Nicaragua, including food, even though this aid had already begun to be cut by Carter.

As part of these same pressures, and little by little, the Reagan administration decided to destabilize us economically—not just by cutting bilateral loans to Nicaragua, but also trying to influence the multilateral organizations to which Nicaragua has access, such as the Inter-American Development Bank (IDB) and the World Bank. In some of them it has had success, and in others it has not. This does nothing more than demonstrate an aggressive will against Nicaragua, and it is one of the ways that they attempt to twist the arm of the revolution. To this extent, however, one has to see the equilibrium of forces in the world, a correlation that until now has never been favorable to the interests of the United States, and this is what has helped such a small and weak country to navigate successfully in so difficult and stormy an ocean.

RINCÓN: During February and March of 1982 the *Washington Post* and *New York Times* made known the approval of a $19 million fund to finance covert operations against Nicaragua. The *Miami Herald* of February 15, 1983, also reported that CIA Director William Casey had made a new demand for funds. What are the real sums? What is the real amount and who has received it?

RAMÍREZ: The secret in the amount of these finances is found in the fact that the North American government—or the various North American governments, since in essence they are ideologically the same—has never learned the lesson of history. I think that I learned more reading a book called *The Fish is Red*, on the CIA's scheme to try to overthrow the Cuban government throughout the decade of the 1960s, than what they have learned in a century, because all of the errors that they have committed with Nicaragua are already clearly described in full detail in that book. The same errors that are made on the basis of that policy in the failure of the Bay of Pigs.

I think that $19 million is a symbolic figure that they themselves are putting forward in order to convince the world that, in the end, the question is not how many millions of dollars; but this operation involves a whole lot of money, and it is money that is aimed at different objectives. In the first place we have the internal economic destabilization, taking into account that Nicaragua is a country with extensive frontiers and that it is therefore easy to carry out operations of this type. We have still not seen the effects that a deepening of this policy might have, for example, in the counterfeiting of córdobas, the counterfeiting of dollars in order to provoke shortages, which is something that was also used in Chile: draining the market, buying great quantities of foods and basic consumer items, inflating the domestic market by putting into circulation millions of bills in the currency. This is a weapon which they surely still have in reserve and for which they must have many millions of dollars waiting.

In the second place is the destabilization of economic objects through such terrorist acts as the blowing up of bridges, the plans to blow up the oil refinery, the cement factory; that is, plans against the nerve points of the country's economy. This is a part of their plans because for them everything is legitimate, all these are methods of struggle. Another equally key area is the financing of the internal rightist elements, the leaders of private enterprise, the ecclesiastical hierarchy, sustaining their activities in many ways; from donating vehicles for their activities to donating paper to the daily *La Prensa*.

All this is articulated with the central plank, the large-scale financing of the counterrevolution: the financing of the entire operation staged from Honduras with support in Miami and with representatives in other countries. This enormous operation involves paying military advisers, technicians, terrorists; transporting arms and war supplies from the United States to Honduras; daily flights; training; arms to thousands of men, paying them salaries because they are mercenaries, supplying them with equipment for military operations; constructing camps; the funds that are set aside for Edén Pastora in Costa Rica—which is still handled apart from the former *somocista* guards in an effort to save this alternative for the last moment—and the money that they inject into the newspapers, radio stations, and television programs throughout Central America, Latin America, and Europe in order to finance the propaganda against the Sandinista revolution.

It is an operation that costs millions of dollars, that has many edges, not just the military, which is aimed at besieging this country, at trying to overthrow this revolution, taking into account that the United States can use all the resources it wants. The United States is the central bank for the entire Western world and it can print all the dollars that it wants and send them all around the world without anyone asking why its money circulates beyond its own borders. This immense destabilization campaign, this immense campaign of aggression applied against such a small country as Nicaragua, is a totally disproportionate task and depends upon covert, clandestine financing that means millions and millions of dollars. It also implies having to roar like a lion in military maneuvers near our borders, the presence of boats carrying missiles in Nicaraguan territorial waters, of sophisticated electronic spy boats, of clandestine flights over Nicaragua, of U-2 planes photographing national territory inch by inch. All this also costs many millions of dollars.

RINCÓN: The photographs that Assistant CIA Director Bobby Inman exhibited in May 1982 only proved the practice of spy flights over Nicaragua with Lockheed SR-71 planes. As is already well known, the Bay of Pigs operation was prepared like this. But we were speaking of costs.

RAMÍREZ: Yes. The last Big Pine operation alone (maneuvers close to the border), cost $5 million. An empire puts into play all its financial, material, and economic resources against a small country that barely exports $500 million a year.

RINCÓN: In view of this absolute disproportion, the problem that you mentioned earlier is that of legitimation, which is of great significance for a thinking consistent with law. Where does the United States regime find a legitimation for the intimidation, harassment, destabilization, and aggression, the same legitimacy that it comes up with in diplomacy, when dealing with a sovereign country such as Nicaragua? How does it legitimize this action, the framework of which is the game of the present international correlation of forces?

RAMÍREZ: I told you earlier that the Reagan administration is an extremist one. It is a government of ideological extremists who apply that extremism not only to Nicaragua and Central America, reviving obsolete ideological ghosts of the beginning of this century, such as the firm control that the United States has to exert over its commercial maritime routes, over the canal routes, over the Caribbean as a "mare nostrum," but also to its confrontation with the USSR, to its relation with Western Europe. It is the way, I wouldn't say unpolitely but rather roughly, of dealing with its own allies in Western Europe: to the imperial plan of Caesar arriving in Gaul. Really, to impose the installation of missiles in the European countries against their own people's will, is a mental insanity.

Reagan's impudence is incredible when he says that an atomic response from the USSR would be limited to Western Europe, which would be the only theater of nuclear battle. He simply declares the Europeans cannon fodder, and the United States is always sure to remain in a safe place. To think that the United States can survive, with its freeways, its skyscrapers, and its wheat and corn fields in Iowa and Nebraska, without having any blade of straw moving after the atomic war, while Western Europe and the USSR would be destroyed, is part of an extremist delirium. To impose on European countries the embargo on parts and supplies for the Soviet pipeline is against reality, against the European countries' dignity, even as military allies of the United States. All this is part of an insanity, of a mad unbalance applied to world policy.

I think that the world should become aware of this, of who the people sitting in the White House are, of who holds the atomic buttons as well as the capacity to attack such a little country as Nicaragua. Well, someone who is capable of thinking of this major madness is capable of thinking of the minor one. It is madness to want to destroy this revolution. And it is a madness because it is historically proven that these attempts have always failed; it has never been possible to destroy a real revolution.

RINCÓN: In this general situation we find that the Reagan administration is using Honduras, the second-poorest country in the entire hemisphere, as a bridgehead for its policy of aggression against Nicaragua. According to a November 8, 1982, *Newsweek* report, United States Ambassador Negroponte is the coordinator from Tegucigalpa, and Argentine secret service agents and army members are also present. On the other hand, there is a series of new developments within the Latin American situation, among them the significance of the general break from the Monroe Doctrine in the Malvinas Islands War.

RAMÍREZ: I was speaking to you about the United States imperial insanity carried to its extremes in its relations with Western Europe, with the socialist camp, with the Soviet Union. The total botching of its Latin American policy is part of that same alienation and power. In the nineteenth century the United States invented the Pan-American theory as a rhetorical wrapping for its policy. They continued speaking of this even when they invaded Nicaragua, Haiti, Honduras, the Dominican Republic, Mexico—without interrupting that Pan-Americanism lecture for an instant. But when United States strategic interests are threatened, that is when the interests of England, its principal NATO ally and the country with which the United States has the greatest affinity, are threatened—and at least with the Conservative government the ideological similarities are clear; Mrs. Thatcher is a Reagan wearing a skirt—the United States throws to the side all of its enormous Pan-Americanism rhetoric without a second thought. It treats all of Latin America with imperial political scorn. After having cultivated its relationships with Latin America for so long, the United States turned its back on the continent, hoping for continental acceptance and complacency in the face of the turned back. This is a misunderstanding of the reality of all that has happened in

Latin America, not since the Nicaraguan revolution, but before, and of how each Latin American country has its own profile. Latin America is not the grey and dark region that the United States has always pretended it is.

At the same time of the Malvinas Islands War the United States rejected Latin America, even though it was a member of the Organization of American States (OAS), and the Rio de Janeiro Mutual Defense Pact, which the United States had signed, was in effect. Thus, the situation in Latin America qualitatively changed. We can say that after the Malvinas Islands War, Latin America and its relations with the United States will never be the same.

Reagan tried to recoup his lost territory after this enormous United States strategic error in Latin America with his imperial journey, but United States policy only suffered more for it. When he arrived in Brazil, he didn't even know where he was. He thought he was in Bolivia, and so he toasted Bolivia at the state banquet, which says a lot about his senility, or his disdain, and his trip to strategically important Brazil ended in a fiasco. He also failed above all in Colombia, because President Betancour had already determined Colombian policy toward Central America before Reagan arrived, and in Costa Rica Reagan put on a third-rate show and took off for Honduras. His stops in Central America may have been successful relative to the circumstances; but in Colombia and Brazil, where he had hoped to be successful and where he could have gained the most, his visit was a true failure. Two things were important here: the United States position in the Malvinas Island crisis, which all Latin American countries rejected to one degree or another, and the Central American situation. Reagan was going to Brazil and Colombia to ask for support for his position on Central America, a position which isolates Nicaragua and reinforces the aggression from Honduras, but his calls were not answered. This is why I tell you that the international balance of forces is not in favor of the United States with respect to its Central American policy, or with respect to its policies for Nicaragua and El Salvador.

Everything that the United States is doing in Central America is truly insane; if you want to have good relations with the United States you have to stoop to the level to which the weak Honduran government has sunk.

Washington is using Honduras because its geographic position favors United States interests. It has subjected this country to an abject and humiliating policy. That is, they praised General Alvarez as the great savior of Central America, the leader of the noble anticommunist crusade. The United States convinced him that with an army he was going to end the communist threat in Central America, that he is the holy crusader of Christian civilization, and at the same time they pushed the president, elected in "free elections," into an impotent post of little dignity. All of this creates for its part potential factors of destabilization for this country, which are very dangerous and whose effects have not yet been seen. For example, another army is being armed inside Honduras besides the Honduran army, that is the *somocista* guards. So there they have 8,000 *somocistas* armed to the teeth with items such as heavy artillery, all caliber arms, logistics, communications, provisions, camps, landing strips, highways. They have created an armed force inside Honduras that is aligned with the Honduran military Right, principally with Alvarez. But if the correlation within the army should happen to change, and this is perfectly likely, the *somocistas* would immediately become a factor of instability in Honduras. Honduras has the worst role because besides having the *somocistas* it will soon have the Salvadoran guards as well, so that it would have three armies . . . because in accordance with the ideologically stupid policy institutionalized in the United States the next step would be to arm the defeated Salvadoran army in Honduras to try to recover power in El Salvador, in accordance with the course of events there.

RINCÓN: The new escalation of aggression against Nicaragua which was announced in a press conference on March 21 was initiated in early February from Honduras with the consent of the United States government. At the [head] are known members of the *somocista* guard, many of whom have been linked to that military organization since the 1970s. I think the significance of this continuity is very much connected to Nicaragua's history.

RAMÍREZ: The fact that the United States military instrument is the former National Guard has really profound significance. We could say that the United States began its history of dominance over Nicaragua in 1855, when William Walker attempted to take Central America, and established himself in Nicaragua for several years. But it essentially dominated the country from 1910, when the Yankee marines first intervened in Nicaragua, until 1933 when they were dislodged by Sandino. The entire history of the dictator is also a history of intervention—the United States aligned itself with the worst in the country. It was allied with a backward, abject, and vulgar minority which had the economic power, contradicting the people's interests. Those interests of the people were always defended by the purest and most honest men that the country could give at the moment. We are speaking of General Estrada and the peasants who defended the sovereignty of San Jacinto, of General Zeledón who opposed the intervention of 1912, and later of Sandino and his men. Our history has been a chronicle of the conflict between the best of the Nicaraguan nation and the United States, allied with the most abject of the country. I suppose that all military occupations are like that; they must be so. But here the dominant class developed a political, ideological, and cultural identification with the United States and the North American lifestyle to shelter their conviction that the military occupation here was privilege, a great advantage for the country, a factor of civilization. Nicaragua was an underdeveloped country which had to be civilized, by force if necessary. The admiration for the progressive Yankee—the skyscrapers, the machines, the superhighways—all of this had to be transplanted from the United States. That was the great dream of the bourgeoisie. Somoza was the most degraded expression of that bourgeoisie, in a perfect state of mediocrity. He represented that degradation, and the United States-organized National Guard was his instrument of power. A direct complement of power.

Today, when Reagan speaks of us as the "fourth border" of the United States, the *somocista* guard is their key strategic instrument. It was created here during the North American occupation and continued as the instrument of Somoza's power until the dictator's torturous final days.

After the United States had created the National Guard in order to defeat Sandino and assure the maintenance of their strategic interests in Nicaragua, they left the country. The United States continued to consider the National Guard as a security factor in the preservation of their strategic power in Nicaragua, and they never abandoned that factor. They really have never disowned it, for when the Sandinista front was militarily defeating the guard in July 1979, it was none other than the powerful Carter administration which decided that, whatever the cost, the guard had to be saved. They tried to preserve it as an armed institution, so that they could return later to reconstruct it, wash its bloody hands—that is, purge from its ranks all of the publicly known assassins and criminals—and try to create from who knows where the new facade and social acceptance. Thus, with its slate wiped clean, the guard was to continue as *the* factor of stability in the country.

That same National Guard continues as a major element within the current United States policy of complete domination over Nicaragua. Washington knew that the moment Somoza fled, this continuation would be the decisive factor. Somoza could run, but if the guard stayed United States strategic interests in the country would remain guaranteed. But we also knew this, and for this reason we acted against the will of the United States and destroyed the National Guard. Mr. Bowdler was trying to make us agree to an incorporation of the guard into a reorganized power structure, but this arrangement would have allowed it to seize power, sidestep the Sandinista front, and create an alliance with Somoza's successors—the nonuniformed Somozas who remained in the country. I am referring to the landowners, the big industrialists, coffee growers, and cotton growers who were going to replace Somoza. United States domination could be guaranteed only by an army loyal to its class interests, the political interests of the United States.

That was the great debate over Nicaragua. And what happened after history lashed out at the guard and the Nicaraguan people's vanguard took power? The *somocista* guard which Carter couldn't save is reinstalled on the Honduran front by Reagan. His administration collects the *somocista* guard soldiers, noncommissioned officers, and officers; retrains them in Miami; sends them to Honduras; protects them; and gives them salaries and all of the economic resources needed for training, arms, and logistics. Reagan is reconstructing the National Guard, just as was done in 1927, 1934, in 1956 when the "stability factor" that was present in the old Somoza disappeared, and once again in 1979 when the bolstering of the guard was the central axis of United States political action in Nicaragua.

The United States government continues to follow this pattern of reliance on the National Guard. During the liberation war the guards murdered hundreds of youth here. They littered the hill named "Head Count" in Managua with corpses, and they dragged youth out of their homes to torture and kill them in their parents' presence. The jails were overflowing. Now they rape women and burn peasants' farms up north. These are the people who Reagan wants to reinstall here in Nicaragua. He arms them so that they can retake power and then defend it in the name of the United States. In Honduras there are thousands of those *somocista* guards who have been convinced that a triumph is inevitable, that the United States guarantees that triumph.

The bourgeoisie knows that it is the same murderous National Guard, but in its naivety, in its assessment it thinks that the United States is only using it as an instrument for the destruction of the Sandinista front in order to put it, the civilian bourgeoisie, into power. That is their great illusion. They think that it is possible for a separation to exist in that sense (between the National Guard and the bourgeoisie), or they pretend to think so. Or maybe I am the naive one, for since the revolution here many things have changed, as they did in Chile, as they did in Uruguay, and in Guatemala when the dominant class feels that it has lost everything, or that it is about to lose everything. It bares its claws, foams at the mouth, and is capable of murdering. Maybe some of these people who claim their innocence here, who consort with the religious groups, believe that the guard has a necessary role to fulfill in Managua; to exterminate us all, murder, and destroy in order to reconstruct the former order. That would be the other alternative possibility.

These are the forces on which the United States leans. Perhaps the State Department strategists think that the *somocista* guard has no name, or that its bloodied name can be hidden by such figures as Calero Portocarrero, Pastora, or Robelo, who will govern the country with the support of the National Guard, which is the vital element. All the plans for the political recovery of the country by the imperialist power involve the National Guard. This is, therefore, the great element which sustains the counterrevolution. There is no counterrevolution without the National Guard, and therefore we do not accept that there are two or three or four counterrevolutions. There is only one counterrevolution, which responds with different faces to the same necessity to reestablish the same project, the same domination that the United States lost over Nicaragua.

Nicaragua has won its right to be free
by Daniel Ortega

The following speech was given September 27, 1983, in New York before the Thirty-eighth General Assembly of the United Nations. The translation is by the Permanent Mission of Nicaragua to the UN.

Our concern knows no limits, for it is obvious that in a Third World conflagration there will be no winners, only losers, including those who seek military hegemony and who fan the flames of war. It is impossible to underestimate the consequences for world peace and security that stem from the proliferation of nuclear weapons since they were first dropped on the peoples of Hiroshima and Nagasaki.

The report by Secretary General Javier Pérez de Cuéllar on the functioning of the organization reflects this critical international situation that is deteriorating more and more.

The efforts of the peoples in search of justice, freedom, and peace clash with those defending monopolistic interests and denying the legitimate aspirations of the peoples.

The results of this monopolistic policy are in violation of our peoples' human rights, for while $800 billion are wasted on weapons and efforts are made to increase their number and especially their sophistication, 46,000 children die each day of hunger, malnutrition, and lack of medical attention.

Those who dream of breaking the strategic balance and impose an arms race are committing genocide!

Those who are using scientific knowledge, which is the patrimony of all humanity, outdoing the Nazis in the macabre task of spreading death, and now even taking care not to destroy buildings or other physical objects, those whose latest nightmares foresee an arms race in space—they are committing genocide!

Those who remain inflexible in the search for mutual security, stability, and world peace—they are committing genocide!

Those who invoke the name of God and human rights in order to justify a climate of cold war, larger budgets for nuclear weapons, and more aggressions against peoples around the globe—they are committing genocide!

They are participating in the murder of millions of children who die each year, victims of the economic injustice that has been imposed in the world, but above all, they are threatening humankind with extinction.

Today, when the threat of nuclear war takes on uncontrollable dimensions, it has become an urgent matter to reach realistic accords in the Geneva framework. Let no more death-bearing missiles be stationed! Let the nuclear arsenal be frozen in its development, production, accumulation, and stationing! Let the nuclear arsenal be reduced and eventually eliminated!

Only when disarmament is universal, only when disarmament is complete can there be international security. Let us station missiles of peace and bury once and for all the missiles of war!

In the wake of this policy of arms build-up, an escalation of aggression has been unleashed in different parts of the world, victimizing the peoples of the Third World, some of whom have attained their liberation and others of whom are still fighting to obtain it.

The racist regime of Pretoria, with the approval and encouragement of the United States government and other governments that, paradoxically, claim to be concerned for human rights, attacks and invades Mozambique, Angola, Zambia, Zimbabwe, Seychelles, Lesotho, Botswana, and Swaziland, in an attempt to consolidate and perpetuate apartheid and racism. Nicaragua condemns the racist South African regime and voices its solidarity with the front-line states in their decision to support the total liberation of southern Africa.

By the same token, we support the struggle of the people of Namibia and their legitimate representative, SWAPO [South West Africa People's Organisation], and we demand the speedy implementation of Security Council Resolution 435, just as the Organization of Africa Unity demanded in its most recent summit meeting.

We also express our solidarity with the African National Congress, which has seen many of its courageous members fall waging a just struggle, among them the three South African antiracist militants, amidst the guilty silence of governments maintaining excellent relations with that regime.

Amidst democratic and humanistic claims, assumed from monopolistic and demagogic positions, the peoples find themselves subjected to colonial and neocolonial rule imposed by those so-called democracies. Such is the situation of the peoples of the Western Sahara and Puerto Rico, whose inalienable right to self-determination continues to be trampled; of the Palestinian people, whose right to form their own state continues to be denied; of the Korean people, still artificially divided; of the Cypriot, Cuban, Argentine, and Panamanian peoples, part of whose territories are either occupied by or under the control of foreign countries, and of the Honduran people, whose sovereignty has been undermined and whose territory has been occupied by the U.S. armed forces.

Nicaragua repudiates the situations faced by these territories. It therefore supports the struggle of the Saharan people and their representative, the Polisario Front. Nicaragua demands the decolonization of Puerto Rico and considers as unacceptable any measure aimed at changing this sister nation's political status without its consent and explicit participation. Nicaragua reaffirms its support for the Palestinian cause in its just struggle to recover the territory that has been taken away; we also support the holding of an international meeting on Palestine with the full participation of the Palestine Liberation Organization, the United States, and the Soviet Union. Nicaragua supports the reunification of Korea and the withdrawal of all foreign troops from the area.

Nicaragua reaffirms its support for the independence, sovereignty, and territorial integrity of the Republic of Cyprus. Nicaragua demands the return of the occupied Cuban territory of Guantánamo, the lifting of the blockade, a halt to the spy flights that violate its airspace, and an end to violations of its territorial waters.

Still present on the Latin American scene is the military aggression that was carried out in the Malvinas Islands, which attempted to eternalize colonial domination over this territory that is part of the Argentine nation. Nicaragua demands that the decision by the Decolonization Committee on the status of the Malvinas Islands be implemented, and we totally support the Argentine people in their just cause.

Once more we reiterate our support for the legitimate and just demand by the Republic of Bolivia to recover a direct and useful sea route to the Pacific Ocean, with full sovereignty over it. We appeal to all states to voice their solidarity with the Bolivian people's inalienable right.

With respect to the tragic and dangerous conflict in Lebanon, the current crisis there is a direct result of the Zionist invasion and expansionist and hegemonic ambitions in the area. We appeal for respect for the cease-fire so that progress can be made toward reconciliation among all forces and sectors of that country, in order to safeguard the nation's sovereignty and to end the increasingly direct intervention of the powers currently involved there.

This policy of U.S. military escalation can also be seen in major, ongoing provocation against the Libyan Arab Jamahiriya. Nicaragua denounces and repudiates these actions, while expressing its support to the people and government of Libya.

This aggressive policy is also manifested in Southeast Asia, where plans are being hatched against the peoples of Vietnam, Laos, and Kampuchea. Nicaragua ratifies its solidarity with the heroic peoples of Vietnam, Laos, and Kampuchea; condemns those destabilizing plans; and welcomes the efforts by the secretary general of the United Nations and the Movement of Nonaligned Countries to promote unconditional dialogue among the countries of the region.

Meanwhile in Afghanistan the United Nations has also made considerable efforts through its secretary general in the search for a political solution to the situation in that region. The Movement of Nonaligned Countries has made similar efforts, issuing appeals that Nicaragua supports.

Among the most painful problems of the critical world situation is the war between Iran and Iraq, brother nations and members of the Nonaligned movement. We join in the calls for an end to this war so that both sides can reach an honorable, just, and lasting peace, through negotiations.

There should also be a dialogue and a peaceful solution among the parties involved in the conflict in Chad, safeguarding this people's right to freely determine their own future.

We extend our support to the efforts being made to attain a solution within the framework of anticolonialist principles and the Organization of African Unity.

This aggressive and militaristic escalation manifested in Africa, Asia, the Middle East, and Latin America is also expressed in overt and covert actions promoted by the government of the United States against the people and government of Grenada. Nicaragua condemns this policy of destabilization and demands respect for the self-determination of the people and government of Grenada.

This aggressive escalation also aims through the Central Intelligence Agency at overthrowing the revolutionary government of Suriname, which is facing destabilization. Nicaragua condemns the aggressive actions of the CIA and supports Suriname's right to determine its own future, free of all foreign interference and pressure.

In its seventh summit meeting, the Movement of Non-aligned Countries reaffirmed its support for the social and economic transformations that were begun in the Republic of Chile by President Salvador Allende. Nicaragua, in homage to President Allende, supports the legitimate aspirations of the Chilean people for a reestablishment of their basic freedoms, human rights, and the policy of nonalignment that President Salvador Allende and the Popular Unity government defended until the very last moment.

After the long struggle led by Gen. Omar Torrijos, the people of Panama obtained the signing of the Torrijos-Carter treaties. There have been attempts to violate and block the implementation of these agreements, and the United States government also continues to use Panamanian territory in the so-called Canal Zone to train soldiers and mercenaries who are later employed against the people of El Salvador and the people of Nicaragua. Also abusing its presence on Panamanian territory, the United States uses the bases of the Southern Command for the transshipment of tons of weapons, for the transport of U.S. soldiers, and for spy-flights of U-2, SR-71, and RG-35 planes, all with the intention of strengthening its policy of aggression against the Central American people.

Nicaragua demands the full application of the Torrijos-Carter treaties and demands that the government of the United States stop utilizing Panamanian territory in the so-called Canal Zone for launching aggressive actions against the peoples of Central America.

Mr. President:

Distinguished delegates:

This international situation that constitutes ever greater threats to peace is related directly to the inequality and exploitation suffered by our peoples at the hands of the developed countries with a market economy, which have imposed an unjust international economic order.

This economic order has fed the prosperity of those countries. This economic order has expanded at the price of our underdevelopment and is facing a crisis of its own making, the cost of which it is shifting to our nations. This economic order reactivates its economy through restrictive economic adjustments and industrial redeployment, which has exacted a high social price from the inhabitants of those countries, with corresponding effects in the economies of our countries. In the last four years this economic order has meant a drop in real per capita income of 19 percent for the countries of the Central American region.

This economic order has meant a drop in export prices as large as 3.5 percent in the year 1982 for the developing countries that do not produce oil, while in that same year the industrialized countries' trade advantage grew by 1.5 percent.

This economic order has meant for the non-oil-producing countries of the Third World a growing balance-of-payments deficit, which in the year 1982 reached $90 billion. This economic order sharpens our countries' foreign debt problem, now reaching $664 billion. This economic order establishes the logic of the minority. It expresses itself through stabilization programs imposed on Third World countries as a precondition for the renegotiation of their debts.

This economic order pursues a strategy that attempts to reduce the public debt, especially in terms of social services and subsidies for production and consumption, freezing salaries and increasing the cost of public services, thus reproducing an older model of growth.

This economic order, while fomenting and imposing restrictive measures on our peoples in an economic policy that can only be termed antidemocratic, antihuman, and irrational, disproportionately inflates its fiscal deficit in order to produce more and more weapons by investing billions in the laboratories of death.

This economic order, irrational and contrary to our peoples' human rights, invests millions in subsidies to farmers so that they produce less, in a world that is hungry and that requires more and improved agricultural production.

This economic order has restricted our countries' access to financing. The international banks, which in 1980 gave up to $160 billion in new loans, in 1982 have reduced the granting of new loans to only $95 billion.

But in the face of this unjust economic order, in the face of this logic of the minority, the logic of the majority emerges with greater strength and demands:

- A reduction in the development gap between the industrialized countries with market economies and the countries of the Third World;
- A renegotiation of the terms of exchange in order to establish a new international economic order, a new order that includes a strategy for food production to obtain Third World food self-sufficiency, with the collaboration of the developed countries and the international agencies.

The economic needs of the impoverished countries must no longer be manipulated through economic and military blackmail. The international community must reject all forms of discrimination and economic aggression. We repeat that "in the face of the strategy of the wealthy lenders a strategy must be found by the impoverished debtors."

We have a duty toward our peoples to establish an organization of debtor countries that would enable us to unite in a single forum. In that way we could move toward the formulation of a world economic policy in line with the logic of the majority. The problem of debt is not a unilateral problem, and that is why we must unite our efforts.

This struggle must encompass:

- The establishment of fair commercial prices and sufficient credit at reasonable interest rates to promote a massive transfer of resources;
- The opening of possibilities for development and the possibility of fulfilling our obligations with dignity;
- The attainment of a suitable level of dialogue between the wealthy and the impoverished;
- The establishment of permanent means of consultation among debtor nations;
- The establishment of a point of reference for the activation of mechanisms of reciprocal assistance and solidarity.

In this way we will be taking concrete steps in favor of peace and stability without sacrificing the well-being of the peoples. Above all, this requires an understanding of the need for a process of integral development for humanity and therefore a change in the attitude of the lender nations.

Mr. President:

Distinguished delegates:

The Central American region is not exempt from this upsurge of military, political, and economic tensions. Our peoples, historically deprived of the benefits of development, victims of injustice and a lack of freedom, are today assertively demanding these rights.

The current struggle of the Central American peoples has its roots in the expansionist policies of the United States of America. In the year 1855 this expansionist policy, which was grabbing extensive territory from Mexico, had a military presence in Nicaragua through William Walker and his mercenaries, who were finally defeated and expelled after a bloody struggle. Since that time the different U.S. administrations would endeavor to stabilize brutal regimes in the region, which were to become their principal instrument of domination. Since that time in the history of our peoples there would be one landing of U.S. soldiers after another—direct interventions aimed at propping up tyrannical governments and drowning the peoples' struggle in blood. That was how the government of the United States became the best friend of tyrants such as Somoza, Ubico, Carias, and Hernández. And that was how the United States government became the greatest enemy of our peoples.

U.S. democracy has meant in our region hunger and exploitation for the peasants and for the workers. And it has meant fabulous wealth for the exploiting minorities.

The triumph of the Nicaraguan revolution was but the result of this long struggle against U.S. domination, which began in 1855 against Walker and which culminated on July 19, 1979, with the overthrow of Anastasio Somoza.

Our revolution triumphed over this unjust U.S. policy and while it is true that in the months following this victory the possibility of new relations with the United States opened, the taking of office of the new administration in 1981 cut short this effort—once more it was the policy of the Big Stick, the policy of gunboats, the policy of terror.

We could say that from that moment on, since January 1981, the new U.S. administration declared war on the people of Nicaragua. The strategy was a clear one: military aggression, more economic aggression, more slander campaigns, more attempts to isolate us internationally—all with the goal of destabilizing the Nicaraguan revolution to bring about its destruction.

Thus they proposed to undermine the struggle of the peoples of the region and in particular the struggle of the people of El Salvador. Crushing the Nicaraguan revolution would mean crushing the possibilities of change in Central America and would maintain the situation of injustice and lack of freedom—according to the thinking of the U.S. administration's strategists.

They decided, therefore, to implement a military encirclement of the fighting people of El Salvador and against the liberated people of Nicaragua. From that time on the U.S. military presence in the region has been on the increase, openly in El Salvador and Honduras and covertly in Costa Rica.

There immediately followed actions by the guardsmen of the Somoza regime. Armed, financed, and directed by the U.S. government through the CIA and Pentagon, they began their criminal operations against our people from their bases of operations in Honduran territory.

Joining these aggressive actions from Costa Rican territory were foreign mercenaries, counterrevolutionaries of Nicaraguan origin, and more Somoza guardsmen. From its military base in the Southern Command in Panama, the United States began spy flights over our territory with RC-135, SR-71, and U-2 planes. To date there have been 203 spy flights and 512 violations of our airspace by Honduran air force planes and others provided by the CIA to counterrevolutionaries who have penetrated our territory on supply, information, and attack missions from their operational bases in Honduras and Costa Rica.

In the same period, between 1981 and 1983, on thirty-four occasions we have detected the presence in our territorial waters of U.S. naval vessels totaling fifty-six violations of our territorial water: twenty-four from Honduran territory and thirty-two from Costa Rican territory. These activities are for the infiltration and supplying of counterrevolutionary groups. These operations by the U.S. administration, for which $19 million was initially appropriated, were of a covert nature at the time. In the first months of 1982 the Central Intelligence Agency had already designed a plan for military escalation, one that would be put into operation toward the end of that same year.

The response of our people was immediate. Between December 1982 and January of this year these aggressions were defeated. In the month of February the United States carried out joint military maneuvers with the Honduran army, in order to provide support for the counterrevolutionaries who had embarked on a new invasion. They were again defeated.

In the months of July and September the government of the United States would undertake new attempts at invasion through the CIA, relying on the counterrevolutionaries and the Honduran army. At the same time, they would continue conducting joint maneuvers with Honduran armed forces in the area bordering on Nicaragua. In September they began an exercise called "Ahuas Tara II" (Big Pine II), with the objective of creating a military situation involving the Honduran army in the support of the army of El Salvador, on the one hand, and to threaten our revolution with a show of force that in no way rules out a blockade and direct aggression.

These "Ahuas Tara II" military maneuvers have been accompanied by naval maneuvers without precedent in the region, involving nineteen warships with 16,484 troops on board and 5,000 more operating on Honduran soil.

These systematic military aggressions by the government of the United States have become increasingly overt and have taken a toll from 1981 to 1983 of 717 Nicaraguans killed, including civilians and members of the armed forces.

Forty-one of them were teachers; 154 were workers linked to production centers. On the other hand 529 people—workers, students, and technicians—have been kidnapped; 514 have been wounded. In defense of their sovereignty our armed people have annihilated 1,636 counterrevolutionaries and wounded 280.

As a consequence of this policy of the United States we must add the losses our country has suffered due to the destruction of ports, damages to production facilities, destruction of construction equipment, health centers, schools, and day-care centers—representing a total of $108.5 million in damages, amounting to one-quarter of our annual investments.

This month a new modality of attack began to be employed in an attempt to "normalize" its escalation against Nicaragua. Rocket-equipped planes coming from Costa Rican territory as well as Honduran territory have dropped 500-pound bombs on the Augusto César Sandino International Airport, schools, houses, and fuel tanks in the Port of Corinto. These bombings continue occurring. Also part of this new U.S. escalation was the blowing up of an oil-receiving station located two miles from our shores in the Pacific Ocean and other criminal actions aimed at seriously affecting our economy.

As we pointed out before, this aggressive activity was part of the increase of U.S. military presence in the region including the establishment of military and naval bases with new airports in Honduras, the organization and direction of the Salvadoran army in its military operations against the Salvadoran patriots, and an increase in pressure on the governments in the region to involve them even further in the current actions against Nicaragua.

Mr. President:

Distinguished delegates:

The efforts carried out to contain the aggressive policy

of the United States in the region, to promote dialogue and negotiation in pursuit of a political solution, have also been significant. This organization, through the Security Council and the secretary general, has watched the situation closely and been active in these efforts. The Movement of Nonaligned Countries has also assumed a position clearly condemning the aggressive, destabilizing, and interventionist policy in the region and has given its support to the efforts aimed at finding a political solution.

In this peace effort, Mexico and France have made a valuable contribution in promoting dialogue. The activity undertaken by Mexico, Venezuela, Panama, and Colombia in the Contadora group has been solidly supported by all those genuinely interested in the search for peace. The position assumed by members of the U.S. Congress and by important sectors of the U.S. media, intellectuals, the religious community, and the public at large is consistent with the desire for peace on the part of the peoples of Central America who reject these aggressive policies.

We can say that from very different ideological positions throughout the world there is agreement in condemning an aggressive and bellicose escalation in the Central American region and in demanding that dialogue be the means of resolving the problems. But the U.S. administration tramples on all these efforts, rejecting them in practice, and is swiftly carrying forward its aggressive plans.

The U.S. administration is trying to ignore the defeat that its policy has suffered in the region. It has failed in its attempt to destroy the Salvadoran patriots. It has also failed in its attempts to send thousands of Somoza mercenaries against the Nicaraguan people. Our people are inflicting more casualties on them every day, and more of them are deserting.

Where are the successes of U.S. policy in Central America? Where are its victories in El Salvador? Where are its "freedom fighters"?

The policy of military attacks and aggressions has already failed and the only alternative left to the U.S. administration is greater and ever more direct involvement.

This explains the presence of the U.S. warships: the presence of the U.S. soldiers; the visit by Mr. Weinberger; the statements by Mr. Iklé; the demands made by Mr. Shultz, Mr. Clark, and Mr. Casey; and the approval of a new appropriation of $19 million to continue the covert operations against Nicaragua, despite the House of Representatives' vote against these operations.

Mr. President:

Distinguished delegates:

Nicaragua struggled against imperialist domination and the Somoza dictatorship in search of peace, in search of justice, in search of freedom. Nicaragua cultivates and defends this vocation for peace, which is nothing more than the sacred right of our peoples to demand peace, win peace, and defend peace.

Yesterday we heard President Reagan state that in Central America, as in southern Africa, the United States is trying to be persuasive regarding the need not to depend on the use of force. We also heard him say that the United States is trying to construct a framework for peaceful negotiations, thereby pursuing a policy of keeping the major powers out of the conflicts of the Third World.

We must expect therefore an immediate halt to the aggressions, the immediate withdrawal of the U.S. warships from our territorial waters and from the region, the withdrawal of the U.S. soldiers from the region, the withdrawal of U.S. government support to the armed activities of the Somoza guardsmen and the other counterrevolutionary mercenaries, and an end to the covert operations.

Only concrete steps such as these would provide proof of the existence of a genuine political will in support of the peace initiative, the process, and negotiations in order to ensure the security of all the Central American states, and the strict fulfillment of Resolution 530 of the Security Council of the United Nations. Nicaragua believes that so long as these concrete steps are not taken there will be no way to find a solution to the region's crisis.

Allow us to reaffirm what we have stated before: in the first place an attempt must be made to win security for those states that feel threatened. Nicaragua is the most threatened and attacked country of this continent, threatened and attacked by an extraregional power that openly defends such a policy. It is therefore our right and sovereign obligation to provide our people with more and even better weapons to defend the nation under attack—an aggression that grows with each day.

We reiterate that the United States must withdraw its aggressive forces from the region and desist from its policy of aggression. Accords must be reached offering security to the states of the region first and foremost. Then we will be able to discuss problems of weapons and advisers.

The U.S. government has gone along offering different pretexts to justify its aggressive policy in the region. It has called Nicaragua a threat because of alleged arms traffic to El Salvador. On other occasions it has come down to the alleged East-West confrontation under way in the region. They have also voiced concern about the state of democracy in Nicaragua. Most recently, however, they have stated quite clearly that the problem is the very existence of a free Nicaragua.

What all of this does is indicate the lack of consistency and instability of U.S. policy. And they should be told that they are unable today, as they were unable yesterday, to see the root of the problem: the expansionist policy they first employed in the last century and which they continue defending at the present.

Nicaragua has won its right to be free and this right must be respected. Nicaragua has defined itself and therefore acts as a nonaligned country, and this way must be respected.

Nicaragua is constructing its democracy. And its sovereign right to choose its own internal system, its own brand of democracy, is a right of our people that cannot be negotiated, cannot be discussed, that must be respected.

Mr. President:

Distinguished delegates:

How to avoid a conflagration in Central America is an obligation that concerns the entire international community, defenders of the principles contained in the charter of the United Nations. In the course of this year the Movement of Nonaligned Countries, meeting first in an extraordinary ministerial meeting of its Coordinating Bureau in Managua last January, and then in March in New Delhi during the Seventh Summit of Heads of State and Government, has manifested its resolute support for the efforts that are under way to attain a peaceful solution to the problems of our region.

The Security Council, in its resolution Number 530, also issued an urgent call to all states to support the efforts of the Contadora group aimed at resolving differences by means of frank and constructive dialogue.

Despite the appeals and the efforts, the situation in Central America becomes more complicated every day. The aggressions against Nicaragua resume and intensify. Threats, intimidation, intervention occur. There is an attempt to place the so-called vital interests of a great power above the delicate efforts being made to achieve peace and coexistence in Central America on the basis of full respect of all the nations of the region.

Nicaragua will never attack any country but it will defend itself from all aggressions no matter how big or powerful the aggressor may be. And we know that the United States, that great military power, is threatening Nicaragua.

Whenever Nicaragua has been attacked or invaded it has

defended itself. It has fought, and we Nicaraguans will always be ready and willing to resist and defeat future imperialist interventions.

In the face of this situation, this assembly must give new impetus and backing to the efforts in search of peace, by means of a new and urgent appeal to all states to refrain from taking actions and to rescind decisions already taken that worsen the situation in the region.

Toward this end, today Nicaragua is requesting that the "Matter of Central America: Threats to peace, sovereignty, and the exercise of the right to free self-determination of the Central American people, and the peace initiatives" be considered as an urgent item on the agenda of the plenary of this Thirty-eighth General Assembly.

Mr. President:

Distinguished delegates:

This Thirty-eighth General Assembly of the United Nations has brought us together in moments of greater pain and suffering for our peoples and of unprecedented threats to the future of humanity.

There is still time to avoid a catastrophe. Voices, but above all actions, will have to be mobilized to denounce and unmask the irrational positions and strengthen the rational ones. This is not the time to ignore the situation. This is not the time for timid or wavering positions. Even at the risk of facing yet more difficult situations, what is at stake goes beyond individual interests. It is an obligation of all—and in this case of those of us who do not possess atomic weapons or economic power—to demand peace and to struggle for peace with all the moral strength of our peoples.

Thank you very much.

Nicaragua's proposals for peace in Central America

The following is the text of a full-page advertisement placed in the December 11, 1983, issue of the *New York Times* by the Nicaraguan embassy in Washington, D.C.

Realizing that war among brother nations is a real possibility at this moment in Central America, Nicaragua wants the American public to understand its position and not be misled by the confusion of reports or the campaign of misinformation directed against a nation that truly wants peace.

Nicaragua is a small country of only three million people. We are struggling to build democratic structures and to restore an economy devastated by forty years of Somoza dictatorship. We want the right to freely determine our own future in peace and security. We do not want or admit interference or direction from *any* foreign power.

As your neighbors on this continent we seek a relationship of mutual respect and cooperation with the United

States. But for the past two years our citizens have been subjected to acts of sabotage and terrorism, including aerial bombings. A covert war is being waged against the people of Nicaragua.

Our people are united against this "covert war" and unflinchingly defend Nicaragua's sovereignty, independence, and territorial integrity. Foreign-backed mercenaries have not been able to capture and hold a single village in our country. Thus, our generous amnesty decrees and offers of demilitarization among Central American nations are not a sign of weakness, but of strength.

With tensions increasing and the threat of a wider war all too real, the people of Nicaragua are addressing the American people. It is our hope that you will seek ways to make your government understand that military solutions are not the path to peace. It also is our hope that the Reagan administration understands that a war in Central America will have no winners and that not only our people but also the people of the United States will suffer the consequences.

Nicaragua was the first nation to make concrete proposals for peace in Central America. The following facts attest to Nicaragua's recent initiatives and its desire for a peaceful solution to the crisis:

Fact one:

October 15, 1983—Nicaragua presents the drafts of three separate treaties and an accord on El Salvador to the Contadora nations (Mexico, Venezuela, Colombia, and Panama). These agreements contain concrete and detailed solutions to the problems of transshipment of arms, foreign intervention, support of subversion, etc. The proposals require a commitment to *on-site inspection* and other guarantees that will be supervised by Contadora. October 20, 1983—These proposals are presented to the U.S. State Department.

Fact two:
November 30, 1983—Interior Minister Tomás Borge is scheduled to arrive in the United States with a series of new announcements on concrete steps Nicaragua is taking to decrease tensions. His visa is denied by the U.S. government using invalid and tendentious arguments aimed at manipulating the right of its own citizens to be duly informed.

Fact three:
November 30, 1983—Three more draft proposals are presented to Contadora. These agreements include specific exclusions of foreign arms importations into the region and the withdrawal of foreign military advisers, as well as a combined social and economic development plan for the region.

Fact four:
December 1, 1983—Amnesty is declared for Miskito Indians and other citizens of Nicaragua engaged in acts of insurgency in Northern Zelaya.

Fact five:
December 4, 1983—Amnesty is announced for exiled nationals of Nicaragua, including those who have taken up arms and have been engaged in illegal activities against Nicaragua since July 19, 1979. Nicaragua pledges to return agricultural lands abandoned by their owners or to adequately compensate them for those lands.

Fact six:
The Nicaraguan government calls upon the Council of State to hold extraordinary sessions to finalize the formulation of the election laws. At the same time the government states that the election process is to begin January 31, 1984, with a 1985 election date to be announced on February 21, 1984.

The following are the complete texts of three recently promulgated decrees intended to continue the process of democracy in Nicaragua:

THE DECREE OF AMNESTY OFFERED BY THE GOVERNMENT OF NICARAGUA FOR CRIMES COMMITTED AGAINST IT

The Junta of the Government of National Reconstruction considering:

1. That it is the will of the revolutionary government to guarantee the normal development of the electoral process that will culminate in the elections of 1985, and that will commence on January 31, 1984, in accordance with the provisions of Decree Number 513 of September 10, 1980;

2. That the present North American administration is promoting a cunning campaign of armed actions carried out principally by the genocidal former Somoza guards, directed against the Sandinista people's revolution and its will to assure internal democracy and pluralism;

3. That, despite these actions, the revolutionary government wishes to create the necessary conditions that will permit the participation of the greatest possible number of Nicaraguans in the electoral process;

Therefore, in use of its faculties, decrees:

Art. 1—The citizens who may have left the country on any date subsequent to July 19, 1979, and who may have been involved in illegal activities contrary to public order, even those of an armed nature, shall have all the guarantees that this decree confers in order to return to the country and incorporate themselves into civic life and the electoral process, with full right to elect and to be elected.

Art. 2—The consulates of Nicaragua in North America, Honduras, and Costa Rica shall issue respective safe conducts to the nationals who decide to accept the benefits of this decree.

Art. 3—The citizens who may have been involved in the activities of counterrevolutionary bands organized from abroad, upon laying down their arms, shall have, in addition to their respective safe conducts, the option of being incorporated into land distribution programs of agrarian reform.

In the case of agricultural proprietors who may have abandoned their lands, and which later may have been occupied, their lands shall be restored to them or adequate compensation made.

In the cases foreseen in this article, the safe conduct may also be issued by delegates of the Ministry of Interior in the respective zone.

Art. 4—The following shall be excepted from the benefits and guarantees referred to in Articles 1 and 3 of this decree:

A. Officers of the extinct National Guard and members of the Somoza security force involved in repressive acts who have not surrendered to the tribunals of justice;

B. Those who have been condemned by judicial processes for acts against public security and order without having been pardoned by a resolution approved by the Council of State;

C. Those who, acting as counterrevolutionary chiefs or ringleaders, have publicly or privately requested the intervention of a foreign power in Nicaragua and the provision of funds by this same foreign power to finance counterrevolutionary actions in Nicaragua, or those who have accepted such funds;

D. Those who, in the same situation described in the previous clause, have directed or planned terrorist attacks to cause damage to the Nicaraguan population or the economic resources of the country.

Art. 5—The persons who decide to receive the benefits and guarantees of this decree may do so within a term commencing with publication of the same and expiring on February 21, 1984.

Art. 6—The dispositions of this decree shall not affect those contained in the law of agrarian reform (Decree Number 782) and those of Decree Number 1352.

Art. 7—The present decree shall be effective upon its publication in the *Gazette,* the official journal.

Given in the city of Managua on December 4, 1983, "Year of Struggle for Peace and Sovereignty."

THE DECREE OF THE GOVERNMENT OF NICARAGUA REGULATING THE ELECTIONS OF 1985

The Junta of the Government of National Reconstruction considering:

1. That, in conformity with Decree Number 513 of September 10, 1980, in January 1984 the electoral process must be initiated by means of which Nicaraguans must choose the government that shall continue constructing the new Nicaragua;

2. That, despite the difficult circumstances through which the nation is passing as a consequence of the imperialistic aggression, it is the will of the Sandinista National Liberation Front and of the government of the republic, that the necessary steps continue to be taken to carry out the electoral process;

In use of its faculties, decrees:

Art. 1—The electoral process shall commence on January 31, 1984, for all effects foreseen in Decree Number 513 of September 10, 1980.

Art. 2—To the end of concluding the discussion and approval of the electoral law and other laws and regulations that form the juridical framework of the electoral process, by means of this decree the Council of State is called into extraordinary sessions commencing on January 4, 1984, and shall function uninterruptedly until the convocation of its ordinary period of sessions.

Art. 3—The proselytizing activities of electoral character shall be authorized by the competent electoral organisms contemplated in the electoral law.

Art. 4—The date for the holding of elections shall be determined by the Junta of the Government of National Reconstruction and announced on February 21, 1984.

Art. 5—The present decree shall enter into effect upon its publication in the *Gazette,* the official journal.

Given in the city of Managua, on December 4, 1983, "Year of Struggle for Peace and Sovereignty."

THE DECREE OF AMNESTY FOR NICARAGUANS OF MISKITO ORIGIN AND OTHERS INVOLVED IN CERTAIN AGGRESSIONS IN THE PROVINCE OF NORTHERN ZELAYA

From the Junta of the Government of National Reconstruction:

1. Whereas: The Junta of the Government of National Reconstruction gathers from the historic program of the Sandinista National Liberation Front the commitment to struggle for the true recovery of ethnic minority rights and incorporates them into the statute on the rights and guarantees of Nicaraguans.

2. In the statement of principles regarding indigenous communities of the Atlantic Coast, both the Junta of the Government of National Reconstruction and the National Directorate of the FSLN recognize that this people has traditionally been exploited, oppressed, and submitted to savage colonialism.

3. The government of the United States has fomented

counterrevolutionary activity developing a campaign of confusion intended to impede the government of Nicaragua, together with authentic indigenous representatives, from advancing the solution to the difficult and complex problem inherited from the past.

4. Zelaya, the traditional site of settlements of indigenous communities, has been a zone of special interest for the development of counterrevolutionary plans.

5. The level of counterrevolutionary aggressions to which the zone has been submitted, together with the secular underdevelopment and exploitation and lack of progress of the communities, has made them open victims to the manipulation, deception, and terror of the counterrevolutionary bands.

6. Taking into account the special circumstances under which the Miskitos have lived and considering that it has been deception and coercion that has led them to commit crimes, the National Commission for the Protection and Promotion of Human Rights has recommended revolutionary generosity to the Junta of the Government of National Reconstruction.

7. The Sandinista people's revolution is the product of the uninterrupted struggle of our people to recover the interests of the oppressed and exploited. Since July 19, 1979, for the first time, the people of Nicaragua, from diverse exploited sectors and ethnic groups, have had the possibility to participate in the construction of the new society.

Therefore, in use of the Junta of the Government of National Reconstruction powers and in exercise of the right of pardon, decrees the following:

Art. 1—Amnesty is granted to Nicaraguan citizens of Miskito origin who have committed crimes against public safety and order and any other related crimes between December 1, 1981, and December 1, 1983, and who currently are in any of the following situations:

A. Under detention, whether already sentenced, pending sentence, pending trial, by order of the attorney general's office or detained for investigation.

B. At large, either inside or outside national territory.

Art. 2—Amnesty is also granted to all Nicaraguan citizens who, because of the events that occurred along the Coco River or whatever other event that has occurred as a consequence of the aggression that has been imposed upon Northern Zelaya between December 1, 1981, and December 1, 1983, have become involved in the criminal activities referred to in Article 1.

Art. 3—In order to partake in the benefits of this law, Nicaraguan citizens who are outside national territory may freely return and join in the tasks required by the revolution.

Art. 4—The delegation of the government junta in the Northern Zelaya region is empowered to adopt the appropriate procedures to facilitate and expedite the reunification and reincorporation in daily activities of all those beneficiaries of the amnesty.

Art. 5—Upon publication of this decree, the police and authorities of the judicial, penitentiary, and security systems must immediately release the persons who benefit from the amnesty.

Art. 6—This decree, published in Spanish and Miskito, will enter into effect from the moment of its publication in any collective mass media organ, without prejudicing subsequent publication in the official register the *Gazette*.

Decreed in the city of Managua, on December 1, 1983, "Year of Struggle for Peace and Sovereignty."

Junta of the Government of
National Reconstruction
Daniel Ortega Saavedra
Sergio Ramírez Mercado
Rafael Córdova Rivas

We speak to you from a country at war
by Tomás Borge

The following speech was given in December 1983 to a group of U.S. citizens in Managua. Borge had been scheduled to tour the U.S. at the end of the year, but on November 29, less than twenty-four hours before his scheduled flight, the U.S. government denied his visa. The speech originally appeared in the January 27, 1984, issue of the *Militant*.

Before the visa to visit the United States was denied us, we intended to travel to educational centers that had invited us as well as to meet with congressmen and journalists from various North American news media.

Everything seems to indicate that Mr. Reagan's administration feels that U.S. citizens have no right to listen to voices of Nicaraguans.

We wish to speak to you from a country that is at war: not only the single war we would have wished to wage, which is the war against underdevelopment, but also a war against military forces organized by the U.S. administration.

U.S. governing circles openly discuss the amounts to be assigned to covert operations against Nicaragua: operations that to us signify air raids, sabotage of production centers, and that also signify death, massive migrations, and economic losses.

What does not seem to be much discussed is the "right" of one country to attack another, or the "right" of a powerful country like the United States to decide the destiny of a country that is nearly eighty times smaller in size and in population.

There is much discussion about the internal situation in Nicaragua. The Sandinista revolution is placed in question, but there is little discussion about the presumed right to intervene in Nicaragua.

This war, in which the United States is directly involved, today costs the U.S. taxpayers millions of dollars. Tomorrow this war may cost the people of the United States thousands of lives, as it is costing us Nicaraguans now.

The United States public is daily presented with a series of assertions about Nicaragua that are plainly and simply false, or else are half-truths. On the basis of these assertions an attempt is made to justify to the North American people an increasing involvement in a war against Nicaragua.

We would like to briefly analyze some of the principal claims that the Reagan administration presents concerning Nicaragua. Each of these claims is utilized to create a sentiment in U.S. public opinion to support the action the administration has taken to destroy the Sandinista people's revolution.

Let us see what these claims are.

First claim: Central America is the arena of an East-West struggle

It is true that Latin America, in its entirety, is poor and backward. Central America is poor and backward even with respect to the rest of Latin America. The per capita income of Latin Americans is $1,554 per year; that of Central Americans is $472. That of North Americans is approximately $10,000. Some 6.7 percent of Latin Americans live in Central America, but they produce only 2 percent of the gross national product of Latin America.

Life expectancy in Central America is about fifty years, according to the fraudulent official data that Central American governments have traditionally provided. Central Americans live an average twenty-three years less than persons born in the United States. There are places in Central America where infant mortality reaches the figure of 200 per 1,000 births. In the United States, infant mortality is only thirteen per 1,000 births.

Five percent of the population—the richest sector—appropriated, until the revolutionary victory, 43 percent of everything our country produced. These figures are not much different from other existing realities in Central America. When I say that there are areas in El Salvador where there is one medical doctor for every 4,000 inhabitants, I am citing a figure that is more or less the same for the rest of Central America. I am sure that you are not unaware of the fact that in developed countries the proportion is one medical doctor for every 520 inhabitants.

Central America has been victimized by dictatorships, each of which might have provided a verse for the Apocalypse. The last dictatorship suffered by Nicaragua lasted nearly half a century. It has been conservatively calculated that the National Guard, Somoza's army, murdered more than 300,000 Nicaraguans. Since 1954, more than 100,000 persons have been murdered in Guatemala, and the Salvadorans, since 1979, have paid the same quota that we did in the final stage of our struggle against Somoza: nearly 50,000 human lives.

Hunger, dear friends, is not a conflict between East and

West; hunger is a conflict between the dictatorial regimes and our peoples, who are hungry as well for justice. "Commander Hunger" is the commander in chief of Central American peoples.

This sophism concerning East-West conflict is, therefore, a deliberate lie to justify aggression against our peoples.

The problem must be posed in other terms. Ours is a struggle of national affirmation and it is a struggle that has the objective of ending underdevelopment, social injustice, and oppression.

Would it not be more logical if, rather than making and unmaking dictators, rather than arming and training oppressive armies, rather than supporting selfish oligarchies, rather than perpetuating underdevelopment by means of a profoundly unjust international economic order, the United States were to support profound social change, stop opposing peoples, stop arming oppressors? Would it not be more logical if the United States were to orient its gigantic technological proficiency toward overcoming hunger and misery, not only in Central America, but among two-thirds of humanity?

Second claim: Nicaragua threatens the national security of the United States

We did not know we were so great and powerful.

Nicaragua is eighty times smaller than the United States, and it has almost ninety times fewer inhabitants. The total cost of manufacturing the U.S. B-1 strategic bombers alone is sixty-two times greater than the annual budget of the Republic of Nicaragua.

How can we be a threat to the national security of the United States? It is absurd to attempt any military comparison. Besides which, our doctrine as well as our armament is of a strictly defensive character.

It has even been stated, defying all logic, that we might

threaten the Panama Canal, as if we had either the desire or the military capability to do so. Some maintain that this danger derives from the fact that we "export" the revolution—as if revolutions were cotton or coffee.

Faced with the evident weakness of all these arguments, at one point it was said that nuclear missiles aimed at the United States would be installed in Nicaragua. Nobody has asked us to install missiles in Nicaragua, nor have we requested missiles of anyone.

Third claim: a civil war is under way in Nicaragua

An attempt has also been made to create the impression that a spontaneous conflict has developed in Nicaragua, in which a part of the population is fighting against revolutionary power.

It is enough to have a minimum of common sense, enough to visit Nicaragua, to realize the extraordinary degree of popular support that our revolution enjoys.

What then, is the origin of the war? It has become axiomatic that the military forces that attack Nicaragua come from Honduran and Costa Rican territory and that the mastermind and supplier of this invasion is the government of the United States. To state the contrary is to reduce the obvious to a scandalous lie. Of course, the lie bears fruit, and this was the philosophy of the German Third Reich when it upheld the maxim: "Lie, and lie again: something will stick."

On the other hand, it is a law of history that revolution necessarily produces counterrevolution. When the United States won its independence, there were also some 100,000 opponents who went to Canada. In Nicaragua, this counterrevolution, though weak, is inevitable. The strength acquired by this counterrevolution originates with a political decision by a government which, while maintaining diplomatic relations with Nicaragua, has determined to make war on Nicaragua.

The United States government, acting through the Central Intelligence Agency, reassembled members of Somoza's former National Guard who were dispersed throughout Guatemala, Honduras, El Salvador, and the United States, forming them into what was ultimately called the Nicaraguan Democratic Forces. These former members of Somoza's army were concentrated by the United States in Honduran territory. The counterrevolutionary forces commenced harassing our military installations. At the same time they were able to draw a sector of the Miskito Indian population into counterrevolutionary activity, using radio broadcasts and agents who based their appeal on the separatist leanings of some of the Miskito leaders.

These forces act from bases located in Honduran territory. Their activities on our soil depend on the rearguard and logistical support of the Honduran army and the financing, planning, and intelligence supplied by the CIA.

None of this is rhetorical excess. The so-called Nicaraguan Democratic Forces function out of Honduras and have three command echelons: the lowest, composed of former officers of Somoza's National Guard who are in turn commanders of the principal "task forces"; an intermediate command level made up of Honduran army officers, one former officer of the Somoza army, and the CIA station chief in Tegucigalpa; and the high command, made up exclusively of North Americans—officers of the CIA and of the Southern Command of the U.S. Army located in Panama. This latter sets the strategy of the armed aggression against Nicaragua.

Is this a war between Nicaraguans? Or is it an external aggression? Can there be a civil war when one of the bands is organized, directed, armed, and financed from abroad?

Civil war in Nicaragua? A civil war is what exists in El Salvador. The assertion that there is a civil war in Nicaragua is an effort to legitimize a cynical ploy. It is an attempt to create the illusion that there exists in Nicaragua a situation analogous to that of El Salvador; it is a useless attempt to use blackmail to put forward a possible solution in Central America from a position of strength.

Fourth claim: Nicaragua today is a satellite of the Cubans and Soviets

It is still fresh in the memory of Nicaraguans that the highest authority in our country during the time of Somoza was the ambassador of the United States. We are struggling, fundamentally, to be our own masters and make our own decisions. This is an elementary principle of national honor.

The assertion that Nicaragua is dominated by the Cubans and the Soviets seems to be based on an ignorance of the pride and power of national feeling among Nicaraguans. Out of respect for the truth and with full knowledge of the facts, I can affirm that neither the Soviet ambassador, nor the Cuban ambassador, nor Fidel Castro—with whom we have frequently conversed—nor the Soviet leader, Yuri Andropov—with whom we have also spoken—has ever told us what we must do. To think otherwise would be to acknowledge that we have no judgment of our own, that we have no respect for the blood of our martyrs, that we are simply puppets. All the North American friends with whom we have spoken can bear witness to our national pride.

Who among you can believe that we lack the audacity and courage to make our own decisions? If we were sufficiently dishonorable to surrender, there is no doubt whatsoever that it would be much easier and much more comfortable to surrender to the government of the United States.

Our international policy is nonaligned and pro-Third World, and this cannot be gauged only through occasional votes in the United Nations, but in the wide variety of relations we maintain with European, Asian, African, and, naturally, with American nations.

Only 8.8 percent of our foreign commerce in 1982 was

with socialist countries. We trade twice as much with Western Europe or with the United States as with all the socialist countries combined.

Where is the Soviet and Cuban domination? In the political sphere we are extremely jealous of our independence. In the economic sphere we have relations four times greater with nonsocialist countries than with socialist.

We have received respectful treatment from Cuba and the Soviet Union, without any sort of conditions attached. This is the same treatment we would like to have from the United States, a relationship of mutual respect and cooperation.

Fifth claim: There is a totalitarian dictatorship in Nicaragua

Constructing a new state is like erecting a new structure on the ruins of a building that has been struck by a cataclysm. In Nicaragua we have to change everything down to our very mental attitudes, inasmuch as this was a country ruled by indifference, corruption, and selfishness. Although it seems hard to believe, in Nicaragua under the Somoza dictatorship honesty was looked on askance.

With our feet firmly planted in the reality of our country, with all its contradictions and incongruities, the Sandinista National Liberation Front designed a policy of alliances to confront the Somoza tyranny: a policy that saw its continuation in a pluralistic and participatory conception following the revolutionary victory.

The concrete expression of this pluralism and participation is the Council of State. In the Council of State are represented seven political parties, seven labor organizations, five private enterprise organizations, diverse religious sectors, universities, youth and women's organizations, and so on.

In this same context, we have committed ourselves to holding elections, opening the electoral process in 1984 that is to culminate in 1985. In this way we are accomplishing what was promised in 1980, a few months after the triumph [of the revolution]. On February 21 the exact date of the elections—which are scheduled for the first months of 1985—will be announced.

During these years we have carried out a series of reforms whose only objective has been to advance on the road to democracy: teaching 40 percent of our population to read, creating a totally new judicial system to replace the dictatorship's corrupt system, and stimulating a people that was oppressed for a half century to organize itself and to participate in the decisions that affect its destiny. All of this has been accomplished in five years. Has the United States forgotten that in its country the first elections were held in 1789, thirteen years after the Declaration of Independence?

How easy it would be for us, goaded by the slanders of each morning and each afternoon, harassed from all angles, to toss overboard the positions and principles enunciated by our revolutionary National Directorate. Nevertheless, we have demonstrated irrefutably that we continue to be a nonaligned nation with a commitment to pluralism.

In our country a law on political parties has been approved that assures the right of all these parties to seek power.

The level of popular participation has no precedent in our history. More labor unions have been created during these four years of revolution than in all preceding Nicaraguan history. The entire people is organized: agricultural workers, owners of small- and medium-sized businesses, women, youth, city dwellers, businessmen, professionals, students—all these have a voice in a country that was always starved for words. The decisions of our revolutionary directorate are as closely linked to the sentiments of our people as blood is to arteries. This too is democracy. The accusation of totalitarianism has sought arguments in a supposed suppression of freedom of the press. In Nicaragua there are nine newspapers: three dailies and six weeklies. Of the three daily newspapers, one is the official organ of the FSLN; the other two, *Nuevo Diario* and *La Prensa* are private. There are forty-six radio stations, of which twenty-five—or 55 percent—are privately owned. Through these and through *La Prensa,* the declarations and analyses of parties opposing the FSLN are transmitted every day. What is being censored? That which every state censors when confronted with a war situation, as was the case with the North American state during World War II.

How can we avoid censoring news items that promote speculation in basic goods with the purpose of distracting our people from defense tasks? How can we avoid censoring news that attempts to confuse the population and has as its end the obstruction of military service in a situation that requires the defense of the homeland?

Defense of the homeland is also a democratic act.

Sixth claim: Nicaragua violates human rights and practices repression against the Miskitos

It is necessary to start by saying that the U.S. administration had contentedly proclaimed that there is a notable improvement in the observance of human rights in Guatemala, El Salvador, Chile, and Paraguay, but that in Nicaragua the respect for human rights had deteriorated and continues to deteriorate.

The comparison is odious because they speak of the improvement of human rights in countries where genocide has become commonplace, and they say that human rights have deteriorated in a country where there are no executions, where torture has been virtually eradicated, where prisoners, including *somocistas,* have been located in work centers where they have a continuing relationship with their families and with many of them under a regime of what we call "open farms." Open farms in which there are no guards, other than moral suasion and our confidence in the prisoners, that are without police and without bars. And if this audacious measure raises some skepticism, I invite anyone who holds doubts to visit Nicaragua and observe this beautiful, profoundly humane, project in action.

Witness to the treatment we grant prisoners are the International Red Cross, Commission of Human Rights, a group of North American jurists headed by Mr. Ramsey Clark, writers of worldwide prestige such as Julio Cortázar, Carlos Fuentes, Gabriel García Márquez, Gunter Grass, and Graham Greene, among others.

Have there been abuses in Nicaragua? In the first weeks after the triumph, when there were still no police, no judicial system or laws, the people in various cases took justice into their own hands. The accumulated hatred against those who had murdered, raped women, stolen with impunity, was great. But within a few weeks effective control was established throughout the country, putting an end to this type of practice.

There have been other cases of abuses, of mistreatment of prisoners, of some murders, of robberies committed by members of our armed forces. But we have been implacable in judging them. Today there are many Sandinistas completing sentences in our jails . . . and nobody abroad raises a voice on their behalf!

When the revolution triumphed, the Miskito population of the Atlantic Coast was submerged in centuries of historic backwardness, not only with respect to developed countries, but with respect to the population of the rest of Nicaragua.

The Somoza dictatorship never made the slightest effort to bring education or health care to its population. Tuberculosis decimated lives and illiteracy blotted out minds. Neglect was the policy toward the Miskitos.

We wanted to resolve this historic backwardness, having a great deal of will, but with little knowledge.

We committed errors, many errors; many times no account was taken of the cultural particularities of the Miskitos; at other times there was no emphasis on learning their language, and basic aspects of anthropology were unknown. Such errors were committed in good faith; they were taken advantage of by the bad faith of the counterrevolution.

Many of the former Miskito leaders, such as Steadman Fagoth, who had been an agent of Somoza's security office, commenced working with the CIA to divide the Miskitos and prevent them from supporting the revolution. An enormous campaign was launched, including radio broadcasts from Honduras, in which he urged the Miskitos to "flee" to Honduras because "the Sandinistas will kill you" or "they'll send your children to Russia so they will deny their parents," and so on.

Many Miskitos were deceived and left, becoming objects for recruitment by the counterrevolution on the Atlantic Coast. In Honduras they lived in virtual concentration camps. Many of them stayed there, and others were resettled in zones [within Nicaragua] that a number of you have certainly visited, where they have everything that our scanty resources can provide them.

But since we are conscious that the Miskitos who committed crimes against order and public security were deceived and manipulated, the Junta of the Government of National Reconstruction recently decreed a total amnesty for them. All those who are outside the country may return to the bosom of their families, as well as those who have been released from prison, where they had been sentenced or were detained in the course of police investigations.

Seventh claim: in Nicaragua there is religious persecution

We have affirmed, and we repeat once more, that the Nicaraguan people are revolutionary and Christian. Numerous priests, pastors, monks, and nuns participate fully in the revolutionary process. This participation had its origin in the old nightmare of injustice and exploitation that our people endured, in the rejuvenating ideas of Vatican Council II, and in the flexibility and vision of Nicaraguan revolutionary leaders.

Many Christians participated as militants in the Sandinista National Liberation Front. There were Christians who gave their lives for our revolution, including some priests who fell in combat, such as Father Gaspar García Laviana. Various Catholic priests are ministers of state, others are diplomats. The spiritual guide of Nicaraguan youth is a Jesuit priest, Fernando Cardenal.

I will not point out the variety and number of religious people in the intermediate level of revolutionary power, though it might be well to mention that some ministers of state, such as those of education and housing, are militant Christians. There are institutions such as the Valdivieso Center, the Central American Historical Institute, and the Center for Agrarian Studies and Development under the responsibility of religious personnel.

Part of the Catholic hierarchy is opposed and politically hostile to the revolution. They adopt positions that go beyond the religious sphere and in this sense there are conflicts, but on the level of freedom of religion, they have never suffered any interference from our authorities. During the past weeks we have had a series of discussions with the bishops, which have served to improve relations with the Conference of Bishops.

Eighth claim: Nicaragua foments an arms race in Central America

Let us start with a fact: Nicaragua was first threatened and then invaded. We have the right and the obligation to defend ourselves, and we also have the duty to not attack other countries. We do not propose to invade Honduras, and obviously we do not propose to invade the United States.

Therefore, our arms and our military doctrine are of a defensive nature.

We must ask, who is attacking Nicaragua? Is it not the United States? Did they not recently approve $24 million for what they call "covert operations" against my country?

Is it not the United States that presently has 5,145 soldiers in Honduran territory?

Is it not the United States that constructs radar stations, that has spy planes crisscrossing our air space and great fleets patrolling along our coasts?

Is it not the United States that promotes the reactivation of that alliance of repressive armies called CONDECA, from which they wish to illegally exclude Nicaragua? They attack us on all sides, then they accuse us of arming because we are preparing for our own defense.

Honduras now has a great quantity of sophisticated armaments: Scorpion tanks, A-37B aircraft, several dozen fighter bombers and helicopters, plus a training program and organization of a clearly offensive character aimed at Nicaragua.

We are not worried by the quantity of arms possessed by Honduras, inasmuch as it has a perfect right to have them so long as they are not used against another country.

We also, naturally, have a perfect right to have them so long as they are not used against another country. The danger, therefore, lies in the decision to attack, that is to say, in the decision to make war. We are more worried about the enormous military arsenal that the United States has in the Panama Canal Zone, which is a sort of small capital of aggression against Latin America.

We lack airplanes, and we do not have enough weapons for each Nicaraguan to shoulder a rifle. That is to say, our problem is not one of a lack of people willing to fight, but a lack of arms. We are convinced that the problem of other Central American countries is not one of arms, but of men.

We know what war is, because we have made war in order to achieve peace. We know what war is, because we are at war to defend peace. This explains why we arm ourselves, and this explains why we go about the world demanding its intervention on behalf of peace. We grasp the steel of war in our country because no alternative exists, and we have been disposed to come to the United States to engage in a dialogue for peace, because it is the best alternative.

Our revolution continues—despite pressures, despite economic boycotts, despite war—along the road of institutionalization that we have proposed. From the first moment we said that elections would be carried out in 1985, and we are keeping our promise.

On September 17, 1980, the Council of State, by means of Decree 513, approved the inauguration of the electoral period in 1984 and elections in 1985. This was preceded by an official communiqué of the National Directorate of the FSLN on August 23, 1980, which also proposed the carrying out of the electoral process in 1985. This decision has been reaffirmed again and again by the leaders of the revolution.

The decisions announced a few days ago reaffirming the inauguration of the electoral process on January 31, 1984, are simply the continuation of a decision made more than three years ago.

Because of this it is paradoxical that these decisions of ours are attributed to pressures and to the covert war against Nicaragua. As it is also paradoxical that the decisions we have taken on different occasions to prevent the Miskito population from becoming the victims of an artificially imposed war, are likewise interpreted by the Reagan administration as a consequence of the covert war against Nicaragua. Are they perhaps ignorant of the pronouncements made by the FSLN since 1981 in which the respect for the traditions, culture, and rights of the indigenous population of the Atlantic Coast are affirmed?

All of that is paradoxical, as we have said. They make war on us—which is the only thing that could make an electoral process difficult—and then say that, thanks to this war, we are holding elections. They set their millions of dollars and an enormous propaganda apparatus in motion to deceive the Miskitos and use them as cannon fodder in their wide-open "covert war," and then they say that the revolution's amnesty is a consequence of their war. What a way of falsifying reality!

We granted amnesty because we are strong. We will hold elections because we are strong; we are generous because we are strong. We are strong because we are right; we are strong because here the people have arms; we are strong because here democracy, justice, respect for human dignity, national dignity, and national honor predominate.

In the peace proposals for the Central American area, we have included the question of military advisers and that of armaments. We propose the withdrawal of all military advisers in the area and the freezing of armaments in the entire region. Would not this be an effective step toward achieving peace?

The North American people have the right to be well-informed; they have the right to demand that their rulers present them with real facts rather than lies or half-truths to justify actions against other peoples. They have the right to listen to the victims; they have the obligation to judge the victimizers. Nicaragua is never going to attack the United States. Nicaragua is being attacked by the United States. The North American people have the right and duty to know this.

The U.S. administration has two options: either it continues along the belligerent path that only presages an enormous cost in lives, not only of Central Americans but also of North Americans, or else it decides to engage in dialogue, to understand our peoples, to collaborate with social changes and with the possibility of development.

We women learned what we were capable of doing
by Magda Enríquez

The following speech was given February 29, 1984, to a meeting in San Jose, California. The meeting, attended by 150, was sponsored by several local union organizations, women's liberation groups, and church organizations. The speech originally appeared in the March 30, 1984, issue of the *Militant*.

To talk about the participation of women in Nicaragua today we must talk a little bit about the extraordinary history of the participation of women in all of Nicaragua's struggles.

When the Spaniards came to conquer our lives the Indian women refused to bear children in order not to give the Spaniards any more slaves.

That example was followed by many women throughout our struggle for independence from Spain. It was continued in the struggle from 1927 to 1934, the struggle of Augusto César Sandino, who led an army of barefooted men and women against the occupation of Nicaragua by the U.S. Marines.

In that struggle, women participated—not by following their men to help them with the dishes or the laundry but by picking up weapons and being guerrilla fighters.

By the time of the Sandinista National Liberation Front victory on July 19, 1979, many women had joined the struggle on an individual basis.

However, we had not been able to organize as a women's movement. We tried to do it in 1969. In fact, we called our first national women's meeting in a little town called Juigalpa in the Department of Chontales. The meeting was called for one in the afternoon and when the time came only three women showed up.

One of these women was the first woman member of the FSLN. She was already a guerrilla fighter in the mountains. Her name is Gladys Báez and fortunately, she is still alive today. Gladys insisted that the meeting should go on.

We went into the theater. She went up to the stage before the audience of two women and she delivered a speech, which, in short, said that the day was a very historic day for Nicaraguan women because for the first time in our lives we had called upon ourselves to meet as women to discuss our role in Nicaraguan society. And, secondly, because the empty theater certainly showed us how much work we had to do.

A few years later, on September 29, 1977, we met in a church called Las Palmas in Managua. We didn't even fit in there. There were wall to wall women packed in that church. That was the birth of the Association of Nicaraguan Women Confronting the National Problem (AMPRONAC).

On the one hand we were organized and founded by the men and women who belonged to the FSLN, although we did not organize as a party organization or as the female branch of the FSLN.

Not only were we not a party organization, but AMPRONAC was organized as a very open group where women from all different political parties participated. In fact, the great majority of women did not belong to any party at all.

This organizing of AMPRONAC by men and women responded to a principle that for us is still valid—the fact that we do not believe that women's problems are the problems of women but rather the problems of men and women. Therefore we were setting the basis of working together to solve our problems.

Also, we did not organize to struggle exclusively for women's issues. Again, for very specific reasons: First of all, because we knew, and history has proven us right, at least in the Nicaraguan situation we could not talk about the emancipation of women without talking about the emancipation of men—men and women of a society that was certainly not emancipated, but under oppression and repression.

So, we organized to be a force in the liberation struggle and we understood again, that for us to struggle on the political program of AMPRONAC, the first thing we had to do was to topple the dictatorship.

Since we were living in a society where we could not organize without being put in jail, or tortured, or killed, we had to find other ways to struggle.

We started as a human rights group. We kept going from jail to jail, working with lawyers to get the prisoners out of jail.

From the human rights activities, we went into hunger strikes. We went on to take over churches, lead strikes, and mobilize in the streets. We learned how to fight back against the National Guard.

But, most importantly, we learned how to overcome fear. We learned that fear was a very valid feeling. But we learned that the important thing was to overcome fear and to work jointly in the struggle that was a matter for us of life and death.

In doing so, an extraordinary learning experience took place in Nicaragua. We, as women, learned what we were capable of doing. We learned that we had been born for other things besides the roles we had been taught—that is, to be a good woman, you had to be a good wife and a good mother.

To be a good wife and mother you had to be feminine enough to be successful in the marriage market. And then, feminine meant Revlon, Max Factor, and so on. The women in Nicaragua who are brown as I am, began dyeing their hair blond. In 1971 when hot pants and boots were in fashion in the United States, the Nicaraguan women were wearing boots in 90° or 100° weather.

Only a small number of females could afford Revlon and Max Factor, hot pants, and boots. The majority of women in Nicaragua could not afford these things. They were second-rate women.

Enclosed within four walls in the cities, or at the hearths in the rural areas, in her wooden kitchens, the woman had the role of servant, actually, to the husband. In fact, when you came to the hut of a peasant woman in Nicaragua, she would not even come to talk to you if the husband did not invite her to.

She was not even considered a worker. She worked, but only the husband received the payroll. After he got the money he would give her an allowance if he felt like it.

Illiteracy among the rural women in Nicaragua was nearly 100 percent. Those families who could afford to send to school one of their children, sent the boy because, after all, he was going to have to support the family, so let him learn.

And, since the woman only had to make sure she got a husband, she had only to learn to cook and wash, do the dishes, and take care of the children.

This was the picture in Nicaragua in 1977 when we started to organize women with the objective of becoming a political force in the liberation struggle.

We as women were feeling probably more than anybody

else the repression of one of the most brutal dictatorships of the Latin American countries. We not only suffered being raped by the National Guard. We also suffered seeing our children being killed because they were young and therefore possible guerrilla fighters.

All of these things started to accumulate to the point where we understood that the revolution in Nicaragua could not be made without half of the population of the country—women. So, we started to organize.

We started to learn how to organize a community. We learned that we could lead a battle. We learned we could lead a front.

In fact, the western front of the Sandinista revolution, one of the most important fronts of the struggle, was led by a woman, guerrilla Commander Dora María Téllez.

Throughout all of this practice, not only did we learn what we were capable of doing, but the image of women in Nicaraguan society started to change. Our people began to learn what we were capable of doing, as women.

We never entered into a lot of theoretical discussions about women's liberation or the emancipation of women. In fact, we never said that we were equal—we simply demonstrated it, in the battlefields, on the barricades, in the mountains, in the cities.

In doing so, at the time of the victory on July 19, 1979, not only had the Nicaraguan people achieved its first major victory, but we as women had also achieved one of our major victories.

I would like you to reflect on what it was like for us on July 19, 1979. I want you to imagine what a country is like when there is a complete vacuum of power and a bunch of young people who are experts on guerrilla fighting—we did it successfully for over twenty years—take over the power. We certainly knew nothing about organizing a democratic government. Not because we were young, but because we had no history of democracy. We did not even know what a democratic government should look like.

We also had to face the fact that we had to get an economy going. And we had inherited an economy in complete bankruptcy. Banks full of paper, with no money. A treasury robbed by Somoza, the gold taken out, only $3 million left. A dependent economy. We depended on the United States for raw material and technology.

But there was another blow that was even greater. The human cost of the war. Fifty thousand Nicaraguans dead—1.5 percent of our entire population. If we apply that percentage to your population, it is equivalent to 3,390,000 people. That was our human cost, which also produced 40,000 orphans.

But why am I talking about this if I am supposed to be talking about women? Because we are part of the whole thing. Because if we were going to make a democratic government, we had to make sure that through the structuring of that government, the political will for the emancipation of women was getting its due.

That's why we struggled for a seat on the Council of State. That's why we struggled for the women's office under the executive that coordinates all the different programs that benefit women and also deals with the female labor force.

That's why we struggled for a legal office for the woman, so that her legal rights will be protected, so that she will be counseled and advised of her legal rights and will have a team of lawyers to help her in court, if that becomes necessary.

That's why we struggled also for a Family Protection Office, so we could deal with family problems sitting around a table before we took them to court. That's why we have been changing the laws from the Council of State. From that seat on the Council of State. AMNLAE doesn't only change or make laws, but also makes sure that no discriminatory laws are passed.

The laws that we inherited from the dictator Somoza, of course, were very discriminatory laws. In fact they were based on the Roman law and I don't know how much you remember about your history, but the Romans weren't very keen on women.

So, we had to change the patriarchal laws and instead of those, we now have a law which regulates the relationship between mother, father, and children, giving equal rights to all the members of the family, and of course, putting the mother first as recognition of the participation of women in the liberation struggle.

We sit on the Social Security and Welfare Council where we decide where the child-care centers are going to be and how they should be. Some technicians get very enthused and want to build these big beautiful elephants that can take care of only eighty children and we need to provide for 200, so we decide how they are going to be.

We also are going to decide how the educational programs in the child-care centers should be, so there is no stereotyping as the children grow up. The little boys and girls should both play with the trucks, blocks, pots, pans, and dolls. And, we also have to of course deal with the books so there is no stereotyping of women.

For us, this is the practice of democracy. When we as women decide where the child-care centers are going to be built, we are participating. When we the women decide we need a hospital to deal with specific gynecological problems, and we get that hospital, we are practicing democracy. When we are able to vaccinate 200,000 children over a weekend and eradicate whooping cough, measles, and polio for the last two years using volunteers, we are building democracy. When the people teach the people how to read and write, we are building democracy.

We also are organizing women at the grass roots level in all the different sectors.

In the factory, for example, we will organize a working committee of AMNLAE. The women in the working committee will mobilize the rest of the women in that factory to make sure that they are aggressive enough in their union so that the labor leaders learn that they are not only the leaders of the men, but the men and women in the union. And that women's issues must be put in the collective bargaining process.

This is very easy to say but much harder to do, because you have to teach women about labor laws and the labor movement, so that they make sure they don't get fooled by false and corrupt leaders. The woman must learn everything about production in her factory and so on, and eventually, she will get elected to office in the union. We work the same way with all the different sectors—farm workers, cooperatives, neighborhood organizations, professional organizations, students, etc.

We don't believe in tokens. We don't want to have a token woman in the government just to say, "Wow, we finally made it to the junta." Unless somebody can convince me that because there is a Margaret Thatcher in England the status of women has changed there—then maybe we'll go for it. Or if you can convince me that the legal status of women has changed in [the U.S.] since you have one woman in the Supreme Court.

The major problem that we have is that all the resources that could be going into continuing the building of our democracy cannot be used for this work, since they must be put into defending our hard-won revolution. The political, economic, and military aggressions from the United States have increased. There are 5,000 U.S. Marines in Honduras and twelve destroyers off our coast. It is a very dangerous situation.

For us it is not a case of paranoia. Since 1855 we have been invaded by the U.S. government. In fact, the U.S. buccaneer, William Walker, had himself elected president of Nicaragua, made slavery legal, and wanted Nicaragua to become a southern state of the union. Since then, twelve major invasions.

So it is not paranoia. It is a fact. That's why we are prepared for the worst. That's why all of the weapons are in the hands of the people, which, by the way, if we want to talk about democracy, is another example. So we are ready to defend every inch of our territory, and we have been doing so.

The counterrevolutionaries have not been able to take over even one single inch of land. They have been able to cause pain and suffering and destruction. They can only hit and return to Honduras, where the U.S. trainers, of course, reorganize them, and give them new weapons, because of course, we take the ones they bring in. So they get ready to come in again.

Think about the fact that the Nicaraguan children last November were playing a game, "how fast can you run from your house to the bomb shelter," when other children were preparing for Christmas. We do not like it. Because we are not warriors. We're being forced to do it.

I don't like to put my uniform on again, leaving my children behind and go to the battlefront. I don't like to see my fourteen-year-old son, who should be playing football and baseball, having to be a member of the militia. He is the head of his squad in a battalion. I am extremely proud of him, but I don't like it.

Of course, I would like it even less for him to be killed or to see everything that we have achieved destroyed because we were not prepared. That's why we do it. That's why a Grenada will not happen in Nicaragua.

At the same time, we continue to hope for the best because we have great faith in the people, the same faith that brought us to victory, on July 19, 1979, and is keeping up the defense of the revolution.

We also have faith in the capacity of your people. I hope that all who struggle for social services in this country—for health, education, child care, for jobs—learn that every tax dollar taken from those programs is being turned into bombs and bullets which then kill Nicaraguans who are educating their people, who have brought health to their people.

I certainly hope that those connections are made, and that the foreign policy of this country is changed, so that we can sit one day as two sovereign nations whose principles are the same as the forefathers of this nation—the principles of human rights and human dignity, not only for the men and the women in that country, not only for the men and the women of that society, but for the dignity of an entire nation. Thank you.

Justice in Nicaragua is no longer the same
by Tomás Borge

The following are major excerpts from a speech given April 12, 1984, to a congress of Nicaraguan judges and court personnel. In the section of the speech not reprinted here, Borge reviewed the escalating U.S. military aggression against Nicaragua. He noted, according to the April 14, 1984, issue of *Barricada*, that "imperialist aggression against Nicaragua compels us to refer in particular to the theme of war. Sometimes 'justice for times of war' is spoken of as if we were talking about a war between the galaxies. Has it perhaps not been understood that we are in a full-scale war?" After explaining that the physical damages inflicted by "CIA mercenaries" in just the two months preceding the speech totaled over $28 million, Borge concluded, "There is only one single war, and it is called Nicaragua. All Nicaraguans are at war against imperialism and its mercenary army." The translation for this volume is by Michael Baumann.

Just about three years ago, in commemoration of Silvio Mayorga, we held the first seminar on justice in the revolution, in a situation of less conflict and difficulty. Today, in closing this new seminar, in a setting dominated by a resplendent drama of blood and heroism, we find ourselves compelled to take note of the responses demanded by this crucial moment for Nicaragua.

On that previous occasion we said that justice in Nicaragua, following such important deliberations and agreements, would no longer be the same. Today we can say that it is no longer the same, and that it is the same. It is not the same because a serious foundation has been laid for making qualitative changes; it is the same in the sense that those changes have not yet occurred in the easy terrain of legal forms.

Our revolution has undertaken a process of institutionalization that will culminate in the task of providing our country with a constitution. And that constitution, on the basis of a political platform, will be the groundwork for one day building a society without either exploiters or exploited, a society that is strong and egalitarian, in which we can all look each other in the eye without guilt complexes, a society as transparent as crystal, a society of all, in which jails have no place, and in which judges serve only to clarify misunderstandings.

In the framework of this task law, as an expression of politics, will represent an important battlefield in which it is necessary to be able to distinguish, in terms of ideology, between Roman candles and artillery shells. Discussions will be held with the judiciary concerning the problems of structuring the state, the legality and scope of state organisms, and other aspects that, in one form or another, you have discussed in your various presentations.

Such discussion poses anew the question of whether it is useful to continue with the ancient concept of a tripartite division of powers, formally maintained up until now in our juridical system. Isn't it perhaps the case that many of the problems raised in this seminar stem from the belief that the state must be compartmentalized so that, speaking euphemistically, the various powers exercise a check over each other?

Anyone who does not understand that in a revolution there is only one power, revolutionary power, has not understood anything about anything. Anyone who does not understand that each and every one of the various state organs—whatever its name, initials, or adjectives—was established with the sole purpose of responding to the interests of the revolution, is outside of revolutionary reality. The bourgeois ideologists Locke and Montesquieu, together with their concept of division of powers that is so often rehashed by theoreticians of formal democracy, are as much out of fashion as chastity belts.

In their day-to-day actions, the states of the old capitalist order completely ignore the famous three powers. Has, by chance, the highly publicized democracy of the United States, with its artificial and complex division of powers, served to stop Reagan from using terrorism against our small nation? Does that "Superman" really need congressional authorization to finance, arm, and protect the counterrevolutionaries?

The millions of dollars approved by the U.S. Senate are a shameless fig leaf designed to conceal shameful intervention in the affairs of Nicaragua. By this I mean that the millions that were approved in the past, along with those that are being discussed today, are scarcely a part of the deadly total of secret funds that "Spiderman" has dipped into to use against Nicaragua.

To assess the problems of juridical superstructure we must reject the sterile rigor of the positivists, the laborious scribblings of the ideologists of natural law, and the impoverished vision of the so-called "realists" or "sociologists of law." We have to arm ourselves with a scientific, dialectical concept that will enable us to understand what these so-called norms really conceal, their origin and nature, and in the final analysis, what class interests they defend.

Within this perspective, we will give our opinion on some of the considerations formulated by the workshops.

We believe that the theme "unity of jurisdiction," put forward by most participants in terms of the formulation "all jurisdiction according to the statutes governing the judicial system," did not succeed in coming to grips with the objective reasons that led the revolutionary state to utilize more efficient and effective mechanisms for applying the type of justice the circumstances demand.

First of all, it appears to us that, as Compañera Zela Díaz pointed out in one of the presentations, there is a confusion between the jurisdictional function and the judicial function. The function of applying justice is fundamentally carried out by the judicial system.

If there are some organs outside the judicial system that also hand out sentences, such sentences can in nearly all cases be brought before the Supreme Court by way of appeal.

In general terms, we have one single juridical system. The fact that other organs have among their powers the right to dictate sentences is a universal practice.

The fact that special organs have been created to hand down sentences, or that this power has been granted to other organs, does not necessarily mean that the powers of the judicial system have been encroached upon, or that its "autonomy and independence" have been infringed, as is often claimed by jurists trained in the old school who frequently, consciously or unconsciously, are bearers of obsolete interests.

It is common practice in many countries, given the complexity of activities the state must carry out, to give one organ a diversity of functions. As an example, we could point out that our judicial system has been given functions that normally would be proper to other state organs. That is, the members of the Supreme Court, whose fundamental activity is to apply justice, have been commissioned by the revolutionary state to select or designate those who will be given responsibility for the task of directing and overseeing the electoral process.

There are objective reasons—at times conjunctural and momentary reasons—that have motivated assigning the power to hand down sentences to other organs that are not part of the judicial system.

First of all, the present capacity the justice system is said to have to apply justice is called into question by practice. An assessment of the activities carried out by the Supreme Court in recent years (an assessment given as a presentation at this congress) makes clear that this high court has not been able to provide an effective response to the great number of cases that have been brought before it.

In something as important as the appeals process, simply submitting papers and initiating the procedures takes 6,700 percent more time than the limit set by law.

The overall procedure of carrying through an appeal, a procedure that is supposed to be flexible and prompt, moves forward at a pace so slow that if not suspicious is at least exasperating. Unfortunately, this tendency appears to be increasing. In 1981 it took eight months for an appeal to be resolved; in 1983, twenty-two months. And we are talking here of a decision that is supposed to be handed down in forty-five days.

And this is for cases that are handled with supposedly efficient procedures. What can we expect to happen with cases that go before the formalist and rigorous Court of Cassation?

If we have the sensibility and political maturity we sometimes brag about, we have to ask ourselves if it is useful, in the conditions we are living in today, for revolutionary justice to submit counterrevolutionary prisoners to a long and irritating trial? Can the agrarian reform wait until the end of the century for unused land to be given to the peasants, while an appeal to the Court of Cassation is being clarified?

Is it useful to require that a mother who seeks for her children the support payments that have been denied by an irresponsible father must embark on the tortuous path of an ordinary trial? Do you think it is just to require that a worker demanding his paycheck—that is, subsistence for his family—submit to annoying procedures, procedures drawn up by the dictatorship nearly forty years ago to favor capitalist interests?

The intention is to attain expedited and simple justice; to put an end to antiquated and annoying procedures and phraseology; to do away with those lawyers, fortunately less numerous every day, who were trained to exploit the unwary and to share the gains of robbers and thieves who were inevitably found not guilty; to attain a system of justice that gives precise and rapid answers, thereby assuring the rights of all parties, impartiality, and respect for the law—but at the same time a system of justice that guarantees peasants full rights to agrarian reform, mothers rights to support for their children, the right to a job and to housing, within the possibilities of the country, and above all the right of the nation to security.

The bourgeoisie set out to eliminate crude injustice, so as to preserve permanent and traditional forms of injustice. They organized tribunals with absolute powers for use against chicken thieves and revolutionaries, so as to protect highly placed robbers and murderers. The judicial system was designed with those aims in mind. They structured a legal system that was uncompromising in applying the law against the poor; at the same time they made law the ultimate protection of the rich. Many of these laws are still on the books. It is now our job to interpret them in exactly the opposite way, so that in the last analysis these laws, like rifles, become an extension of the political consciousness of men.

In reading many of the presentations I came across expressions that seemed to be a slap at the role the Sandinista Police have carried out as an auxiliary apparatus of the judicial system. The fact that the Sandinista Police have been given jurisdictional functions under law does not stem from a whim but rather is something that is required by reality, and the man who says this is not speaking as the highest official of the police but rather as a revolutionary leader. The police statutes we inherited, drawn up more than a century ago by the lords of the gallows and the knife, were insufficient and out of date.

When the Council of State was urged to approve the law on jurisdictional functions, the crime rate, including the incidence of cattle rustling and drug addiction, was enough to curdle your blood. The lack of a legal instrument that would give the Sandinista Police clear powers of investigation was an obstacle to improving the level of operational efficiency. The judicial system of that period, because of the continued existence of institutions such as the grand jury, among other defects, set free more than 90 percent of those brought to trial, many of them dangerous criminals.

What were the results?

In 1981 there were 22,552 crimes committed; in 1983, 8,102. That is, the crime rate decreased by 64 percent, a figure without precedent in so short a period anywhere in the world.

Of each ten crimes reported in that period, only 50 percent were solved. Today the figure is 72 percent.

We ask of the Sandinista Police that they become more efficient and more human each day. They have committed errors, and these errors have been corrected. They have committed some abuses, and we have punished these abuses.

The imperfections, the errors, and the vices that remain—and that have been called to attention with great enthusiasm by some—are exceptions and not the rule. But the fact that they are pointed out requires us to increase our efforts to advance revolutionary legality so that good intentions produce positive results, and the errors do not serve as pretexts for those who remain in the shadows without noticing the light and warmth of the sun.

One aspect of the law on jurisdictional functions that concerns us is the power to impose sentences in the crimes of cattle rustling and drug addiction, a power that has been conferred on the police. We know that in carrying out such activity the Sandinista Police have committed errors. And that at times, aware of the real possibility that a judge would declare a criminal innocent, they themselves have handed out a sentence. It could be said that this is something out of the past and doesn't happen any more. But we believe that such an approach would do no favor to either the system of justice or to the police. The fact is that in some cases we were unable to apply the force of justice, and so we opted for the justice of force.

These errors, which will have to be overcome, were not committed because the military, and in this case the police are—as some participants in the congress would have it—incapable of applying justice; that is, implying that they are individuals who are different from the ordinary person among our people. The Sandinista military—whether they be policemen, state security personnel, or members of the army—are, like the workers, peasants, and students who have joined the people's militia, the voluntary police, and revolutionary vigilance, protagonists of the revolutionary struggle that made possible this discussion on the legal system. They are men and women who confront every day the risk of death. They have demonstrated in practice their revolutionary quality. They differ in no way from other revolutionaries, except that their blood is more likely to be sacrificed. I believe that the soldiers of the homeland, the sentries of the people's happiness, merit our respect.

In regard to the second theme—the experience in applying old law codes and traditional procedures to resolve conflicts arising out of the application of revolutionary principles—we believe that in general the presentations have been correct. The recommendations of the judges and magistrates must be put into practice with boldness. We have to learn from historical experience. Emerging capitalism, in its struggle to the death with the feudal order, did not hesitate to make new use of the old principles of Roman law. It universalized them and counterposed them to the obstacles that blocked the kingdom of commodity circulation.

Legal norms must often, as a political act, be used to defend and sustain the interests of the revolutionary classes. The laws in this country are and must be at the service of revolutionary principles.

Beccaria's [eighteenth-century] dictum that laws are to be applied, not interpreted, is an obsolete axiom even in erudite and elegant bourgeois law, not to mention in the legal system of revolutionary Nicaragua. It is to act like the Pharisees of the Bible to demand progressive laws in order to be in a position to resolve problems, and to argue that without such laws we cannot respond to contradictions. Laws can't be plucked out of a magician's hat, and so long as we do not have a body of revolutionary laws we insist that we must interpret every law on the basis of the politics of the revolution.

In regard to the efficiency of the judges and the judicial personnel, there is much to be said. It is true that the low wages of the auxiliary personnel is a problem. But it is also true that there are residues of obsolete schemas, imprinted on the consciousness by rote in university classrooms where, apparently, reform of the law school was no more than an idle thought up until July 18 [1979].

These schemas not only have an effect in fundamental

aspects, but in matters of form as well. For some, to be a respectable judge means to adopt complicated rites and forms, to repeat Roman law sanctimoniously, and to have at hand the number of some act in our old codes so as to justify a legal decision that goes against the grain of revolution, to postpone decisions, and to make themselves seem important.

We know that the law codes contain much that is unreal, remote from daily practice and common sense. But this does not justify that someone who steals oranges spends three years or more in costly legal proceedings, in actual fact serving a jail term two or three times longer than what he might have been sentenced to, while a gold smuggler is set free by the diligence of an attorney who, to top things off, is paid off with part of the gold that was being smuggled contrary to the interests of the national treasury.

These inconsistencies cannot continue. And so that they do not continue, the Junta of the Government of National Reconstruction has today issued a decree establishing, in the form of a pilot project in Region IV [three provinces south of Managua] popular participation in the exercise of justice.

This project rationalizes resources. It incorporates the masses, giving them—in fulfillment of the mandate "all arms to the people"—the arm of justice. It implements specialization at the level of the Supreme Court, making it more efficient. In place of the schematic, ritualistic, and obsolete present pattern of procedure, it offers principles that are immediate, efficient, firm, flexible, and oral.

Compañero judges, magistrates, and other members of the judicial system: we must continue studying and discussing these problems. In the future, unlike what happened in this seminar, we must give more emphasis to themes that go beyond individual interests of self-preservation.

We have to fight to bring about, in the short term, popular justice, to incorporate the wisdom of the masses in the administration of justice. We have to fight to attain a judicial system that guarantees the dictatorship of justice.

We have to continue to take steps to make a reality of the principle that men are not only equal before the law but also equal in their social relations.

The Sandinista Front is the organization of the working people
by Jaime Wheelock

The following speech was given May 1, 1984, in Chinandega at a rally celebrating May Day. Thirty thousand people, mostly agricultural and industrial workers, attended the rally. The speech was broadcast live on radio and television, and printed in the May 2, 1984, issue of *Barricada*. This translation originally appeared in the May 28, 1984, issue of *Intercontinental Press*.

Members of the Junta of the Government of National Reconstruction; esteemed brothers of the Sandinista National Liberation Front, of our armed forces, labor organizations, guests from the workers' movements who have been visiting here in recent days; brother working people of Nicaragua:

We did not want to deprive ourselves of the heat of the streets, of the heroic people of Chinandega, who were so courageous in the insurrection against Somoza. We wanted to salute the workers, the housewives, those who for many reasons were unable to be present at the combative meeting celebrated in this heroic city. And we are deeply gratified at having experienced the profound affection the people of Chinandega have for the Sandinista people's revolution and the leaders of that revolution.

This means that the National Directorate of the Sandinista front, the Trade Union Coordinating Committee, and the Sandinista Workers Federation made no mistake in celebrating in Nicaragua the International Day of Workers with the heroic people of León and with the heroic people of Chinandega [*Applause*]—a people who all this time have remained at the vanguard in defense of national sovereignty and at the vanguard in national production. [*Applause*]

How fortunate are the people of Nicaragua to be celebrating May Day with a working people who are building their own future, with a working people, with a peasantry, with students, with revolutionary women who today hold the reins of national power! [*Applause*]

How different this is from the situation of other peoples in the world who are also celebrating May Day today. There are peoples who do not even have a homeland, who still do not have a nation, nowhere even to place their remains, such as the Palestinian people, who are still fighting for a country, for a homeland, for a nation. There are peoples who are still subjugated by the repressive and segregationist government of South Africa, peoples who are enslaved but who nonetheless fight as working people to gain a sovereign nation.

We cannot forget now, at a time when our people are building their revolution, that there are in the world exploited and oppressed peoples who are also celebrating this May 1. Who—even among the Chicago martyrs ninety-eight years ago, who fought for the eight-hour day in the United States—would have thought that many years after their sacrifice as part of the working class, in that period of darkness of the first stages of the working-class struggle, that one day in Nicaragua, under a brilliant sun, they would be commemorated by a worthy and valiant people who are marking today something they will never forget? We are here as working people who represent on this first of May the thousands of combatants who, in different parts of the country, are turning back the aggression launched against us by the Reagan administration. We who are here also represent the thousands of workers cutting sugarcane, picking cotton, or preparing land in defense of the people's economy.

On this May 1, 1984, the people of Nicaragua are engaged in struggle, a struggle that is still necessary to attain national sovereignty and to attain a higher standard of living and social progress. How different it is from the May Days of other years, such as in 1963, when worker and student demonstrators were massacred; such as in 1965, when workers were repressed and tortured; such as in 1978 and 1979, when some workers' leaders were murdered, imprisoned, or sent to the torture chambers.

How different it is today, with the people holding a demonstration in freedom, celebrating with joy the Day of Workers. [*Chants of "The people united will never be defeated; the people armed will never be crushed!"*]

What was the reality Nicaraguans faced in the past? Poverty, misery, marginalization, no hope for progress; only the jail cell, repression, sweat, illiteracy, death. The people lived under the most difficult conditions, at times gaining their daily bread in the street, forced to send their children out, unprotected, to work. We inherited a destroyed economy in the midst of a very difficult international situation. And yet how different is the social and political situation of the workers today.

We are carrying out an agrarian reform that benefits the poor peasant. We have given the peasants 750,000 manzanas of land, and by July 19 the figure will have reached 1 million manzanas. [*Applause and chants of "People's power!"*]

What did *somocismo* accomplish in its entire history? It ended up leaving the peasantry as a whole with scarcely

140,000 manzanas. And yet today, in one day alone, we have given the peasants 70,000 manzanas—in one day half of everything *somocismo* left the peasants with! [*Applause*]

This is a factor that explains the genuinely popular character of this revolutionary government and of this revolution. Also a reflection of its popular character are the steps that were taken to nationalize the banks, to eliminate them as speculative and expropriating institutions and convert them into institutions at the service of the people. Institutions to finance workers' housing, to finance the peasants' harvests, to promote the national production of small and medium producers and of artisans; that is, institutions that are at the service of the people and of the nation. What did we do? We nationalized natural resources, we placed their wealth and production at the service of the interests of the people.

What did the *somocistas* and the speculators do in the past with municipal land? They used people's needs as the basis for speculation, forcing our people to wander in search of tiny pieces of land alongside roads, such as in Rancherías or San José del Obraje [two isolated villages in the far north], in search of the last remaining pieces of land, following the advance of the latifundia and of land hoarding in the cities.

And what is the revolutionary government doing? It is expropriating all these centers of speculation in order to return them to the people. It is giving the people lots on which they can build houses. It is giving the people houses, though they are still humble houses because of the country's poverty. But in the future, with the work and sweat of Nicaraguans, these can be turned into dignified housing.

We are poor. We have inherited debts, destruction, and a people living in extraordinary poverty. We still have a long way to go to reduce to zero the number of children who have no shoes, to eliminate the general poverty of the country. But there is a fundamental factor that must be stressed this first of May.

In 1978 the working class, the entire Nicaraguan working class, was organized into only 133 unions that totaled only about 25,000 members. That was all that was permitted by *somocismo*, which in the countryside prohibited the unionization of agricultural workers and peasants. Chinandega is well aware of this, having lived through the persecutions in Santa Rosa del Peñón and the massacre of worker union members in the 1960s. Peasant unionists were hunted down and their leaders were murdered—leaders like Bernardino Díaz Ochoa, who was massacred by the National Guard.

In 1984, instead of 133 unions we have more than 3,000 unions, with 250,000 workers. We have unions through which the working class is organized to improve its working conditions and to hold what are now fraternal discussions with state administrators. We have a Ministry of Labor with which workers can discuss social and wage demands. But what has the revolution done with the workers? Simply organize them in unions? No, we have organized revolutionary power, incorporating into it the working class, because the working class is in power in Nicaragua. [*Applause and chants*]

How do the working people exercise power? First of all the working people, through their labor organizations and professional and peasant associations, legislate, make laws, and make their own voice heard in the nation. The forms of participation the revolution has opened up through the Council of State are a guarantee of the toilers' interests.

Working people participate in all of the state's consultative bodies. There are no decisions on the economy or prices, on subsidies or wages, on which the working people, through their organizations, do not express themselves in a militant way. Workers participate directly in power through the CDSs, through thousands of organizations, and in assemblies aimed at reviving and raising production. But most important of all is the fact that the revolutionary leadership, the Sandinista National Liberation Front, is the organization of the working people, the organization that returned power to the toilers after taking it away from *somocismo*. [*Applause*] The Sandinista National Liberation Front is *the* representative of workers and peasants. It is the Sandinista National Liberation Front that is at the head of power, that is in the vanguard; and with it, the toilers of Nicaragua. [*Applause and chants of "People's power!"*]

And we are going to ensure that our people have a form of participation that is much more perfect than people have in those democracies of ballot slips, those songbook republics that deceive the people in an election every five or six years, that make them vote following campaigns poisoned with lies, from which emerge governments that were supposedly elected and representative but in reality represent nothing more than fraud and deceit. We want the elections here to be a culmination of the people's maturity. We have given power to the working people, and it is the working people that hold power here! [*Applause and chants of "People's power!"*]

After having taken power, we are advancing. Over the last few years, the revolution has really made efforts, despite the limitations and difficulties. And this first of May finds us carrying out two ferocious battles. It is also a battle of the people, who take it up with sorrow and grief; we all take it up with a heavy heart and dismay. It is the same battle as that fought by Estrada, Zeledón, and Sandino. It is the battle to be Nicaragua, a battle for national sovereignty that has not yet terminated, the battle fought by the people and the youth in particular, to be able to be the youth of Nicaragua, to be able to refer to themselves with dignity as Nicaraguans. This is a struggle the people suffer and feel.

Each time that a young person dies—a young person who perhaps could have become a doctor, an engineer, or a technician for production—we know that their lives have been taken in the struggle we are waging against imperialism. [*Chants of "For those who have died, for our fallen, we swear we will defend the victory!"*] This struggle has been long and hard, and it will continue to be hard as long as the United States retains its imperial will. It is a lie that war is being made against us because we are friends of the Soviet Union, because we are communists, because we have installed tyranny here, or because we do not respect human rights—as the Reagan administration claims.

They intervened in Nicaragua in 1856, when humanity had not even dreamed of a socialist revolution in the Soviet Union. They are not intervening because we are socialists or communists; they are not intervening because we are tyrants. For they never intervened against Somoza or Pinochet, against Duvalier, or against Stroessner in Paraguay, against the Israelis, or against themselves, the worst tyrants and fascists on the face of the earth! [*Applause and chants*]

There is another struggle—another struggle, another difficult war—and that is the war against the worker's pocketbook, the worker's wages. The situation of shortages is a war that is much more complex and difficult. And just as we have resolutely confronted imperialist aggression, so too we have confronted valiantly and from the beginning this very complex phenomenon. What do workers feel? Workers feel that their wages are not sufficient to buy indispensable goods. Is that true? Is this what you feel? [*"Yes!" answer many in the crowd*] We began, at the triumph of the revolution, to fight against this, for there occurred at that time a great difference between wages and the prices of essential products.

You will remember the period after the triumph, when Somoza had left us a devalued currency, an economy in ruins, a country in debt. What happened in those first months? There were no beans because nobody had planted any. There was no rice because that had not been planted either. Eggs were in short supply because all the chickens, all the hens, had disappeared. And what happened? The price of eggs tripled or quadrupled. Why? Because there was a shortage. And when goods are scarce but wages continue to be paid at normal levels, when there is no production, the prices of the items that are scarce go up. We were short of certain products. Sugar, for example, was not scarce, because we had sugar. Milk was not scarce, because we had milk. But eggs, meat, corn, and beans were scarce. What did we do? What we could not produce, we imported. During 1980 and 1981 we maintained ourselves on the basis of imports, on the basis of international loans, using our hard currency to buy corn, milk, beans, and rice. And the shortages were not felt; there was no longer a scarcity.

But following these phenomena, we have suffered others. First among them is the fact that the Sandinista people's revolution coincides with a crisis.

The crisis is striking blows at all poor economies. Even some strong ones have had to devalue their currencies and throw thousands of workers out of work. We have been fighting against this international crisis, trying to prevent the workers' economy from being hit.

And what have we done? In the first place, the economic crisis means that we are receiving less money for our products, the same products we exported in 1978 at practically the same levels.

It is not true that the revolution brought about a crashing decline in production. That is a lie of the right wing. Production here has been recovering, year after year, in a modest way, but it is recovering.

Last year, for example, we exported a lot of coffee and we produced more rice, beans, and sorghum than ever before in the history of the country.

But this production is insufficient, because from the beginning we wanted to give our people the best. We wanted to give the peasant more food, the workers more food, and at cheap prices.

The products we sell internationally are going at low prices. The products we buy on the international market are going at very high prices.

In short, compañeros, since 1979, and in particular from 1980 to 1983, Nicaragua has lost in international trade, because of the crisis, about $2 billion. That is what we have lost through selling our products at the prices they impose on us, and through buying expensive goods, again at the prices they impose on us.

Year after year, the country is losing some $400 million. What could we have done with that $2 billion? We could have given more support to health care, we could have built more houses, we could have strengthened our economy more. In other words, in addition to the destruction, in addition to the shortages, it has to be explained that the country has had difficulties in reactivating the economy and raising levels of production so as to satisfy the needs of the people.

That is, in a nutshell, there are today certain products of which there are not enough to meet the needs of all workers.

We produce more rice, but the people are consuming more rice. We produce more eggs, chicken, and beans, but the people are consuming more rice and beans.

The result therefore is shortages that, little by little, are having an effect on prices.

There is another factor of great importance in addition to the destruction left by *somocismo,* in addition to the shortages we suffered after the war, in addition to the economic crisis that has weakened our capacity to produce food, to reactivate production, to increase our capacity for defense, to avoid indebtedness. Those are not the only factors that have had an impact. There has also been the impact of the aggression.

The aggression against our people has had a deep going impact. In the last two years, as a product of the aggression, some 1,200 agricultural laborers and workers have been murdered. This does not include the soldiers of the revolution who have fallen in combat. We are referring only to members of cooperatives, to workers in production units who have fallen and ceased to produce, whose cooperatives and production units have been broken up.

In addition, because of the war, we have had to move 20,000 people from the north of the country, from the south, from the country's border regions. And these compañeros are not producing. They have scarcely been resettled on the land they have been given by the agrarian reform.

This means less production and more consumption. Yet there is still more—there is the fact that it is the policy of imperialism to try to break our economy. Under attack are not only the production units devoted to export products. Also under attack are vehicle storage centers of the Ministry of Construction, which is opening up roads to get products to market. Trucks bringing milk to the cities are being ambushed. Two days ago, while workers from ENABAS [the state marketing agency] were bringing beans from Nueva Guinea that were destined for León, Chinandega, and Managua, they were ambushed and murdered by the counterrevolution. The truck and its entire cargo were burned.

That is, it is a policy to use aggression to strangle us economically and financially, to destroy units of production, to break up the cooperatives, to murder the producers, to destroy efforts at construction, to try to block the arrival of goods at storage centers, and also to mine the ports, to blockade and drown our economy, to bleed the Nicaraguan people dry.

Accordingly, however much effort the revolution makes, we must begin from a starting point that is very difficult to overcome completely—the thousand years of hunger of our people. It will take many years to continue to develop the programs of production that you yourselves see with your own eyes—the plans for basic food items, for rice plantations, for dairies, for sorghum, the agro-industrial plans for the production of vegetables, etc.

This is only a small step toward resolving the problems of the people. The problem of food, of shortages, will be resolved in the long term. But we are not going to be able to emerge from this situation of shortage so long as we have an international crisis that forces us to assign priorities for the hard currency we have left after we pay for the oil, after we make payments on the debt—that forces us to choose between medicine or houses, milk for babies or toilet paper (we have no paper mills here, we just repackage the toilet paper), deodorant or baby toys. We will have to keep assigning priorities for this hard currency.

It is important that the people understand that some elements of the shortages are part of the price the people of Nicaragua have to pay for real development. For we are setting genuine priorities for the use of hard currency. We are going to spend it only on things that fill an effective and fundamental need of the people.

We are using hard currency to buy, first of all, medicine and milk for children, for mothers, for the sick, and for the combatants. Secondly, to purchase oil to keep the economy functioning. Thirdly, for production. How could we not assign hard currency to production? It would be easy not to assign hard currency to production or to the purchase of oil and instead import razor blades, soap, and a host of similar products. We could live off a fabulous bonanza for a year, but we would then fall into a terrible ruin that we could never emerge from. So we have to use the money for spare parts, to bring in machinery, to sow cotton, to buy inputs—the little money the international market leaves us.

We have had to make priorities, and among the things we have prioritized, in the midst of this difficult situation we, our people, face, there is an aspect that is important for all workers to comprehend and understand.

Left, Ray Hooker. Below, July 22, 1984, founding meeting of MISATAN (Organization of the Miskitos of Nicaragua).

Top, March 27, 1982, demonstration of 20,000, led by women whose sons and daughters were killed in recent clashes with *contras*. Bottom, oil storage tanks aflame in Corinto after attack by CIA-backed *contras*.

April 28, 1983, armed demonstration of 150,000 in Managua answers threats by Reagan.

Top, Sergio Ramírez, Pope John Paul II, Archbishop Obando y Bravo, and Daniel Ortega at March 4, 1983, outdoor meeting in Managua where pope refused to condemn *contra* terror. Bottom, U.S. Army 101st airborne practices invasions in Honduras.

Militia members in Bluefields, on Atlantic Coast.

November 1, 1984, FSLN wind-up campaign rally. FSLN candidates won 67 percent of vote in November 4 elections.

Top, soldiers of Sandinista People's Army prepare for defense of Managua. Bottom, U.S. CIA agent leads *contras* near Costa Rican border.

Top, delegation expresses support of people of U.S. at July 19, 1983, demonstration in León. Bottom, growing involvement of workers in fight against Central American war is reflected in union participation in antiwar demonstration in U.S.

This revolution, why did we make it? To remain in misery? To remain an underdeveloped country? Or to resolve the people's problems? We made it to resolve the people's problems. That is why part of the hard currency destined for production is being used for investments whose results we will not be able to see for three or four years. And you know that no country in Central America, and very few in the world, is investing in the future like Nicaragua.

We are investing in agriculture. Last year we invested 10 billion córdobas in agriculture and 5 billion córdobas in infrastructure for production, that is, in works for the future. Where do you think the hospitals are coming from? From investment. Where are the roads and bridges we are building coming from? From investment. Where is the Tipitapa-Malacatoya sugar mill coming from, the Chiltepe [dairy plant], the railroad, the deepwater port, all the schools? From investments the revolution is making to improve people's lives.

Today, despite the temporary and harsh difficulties, the revolution is investing in all ways for the future. The present belongs to revolutionaries who are capable of understanding the difficulties of the revolution, and who later, along with their children and their families, are going to enjoy a future of progress and happiness. So we are accomplishing a lot. [*Applause and chants*]

We have to defend ourselves. This is something we cannot forget. We would like to be able to give you razor blades, soap, deodorant, shampoo, corn, beans, and rice—that is what we would like to do—but we have to do something much more important: to fight for this little piece of land which does not belong to Reagan but belongs to Nicaraguans! [*Applause and chants*]

This is the most profound meaning of this historical moment. We Nicaraguans are defending territory the United States believes belongs to it by right of conquest. This territory belongs to Nicaraguans, to the people! That is why we are defending it, and that is why we have to have 60,000, 70,000, 100,000 men under arms. [*Applause and chants*]

And that is what it costs to defend ourselves, to defend this country, a country that is in the midst of reconstruction, that is trying to forge for the first time a genuine future. The cost is having to have 60,000 working men under arms. What could we not do with these 70,000 or 100,000 men? We could do a great deal. They are not producing. But they are being fed. We have to pay for this. We have to give them medicine, we have to give them food, we have to provide them with transportation, we have to pay them a wage, we have to provide them with fuel. All of this is a tremendous cost for the country, but we have to do it.

So you yourselves speak. Say what you want the Sandinista National Liberation Front to do. What comes first, consumer goods or defense? [*Chants and shouts of "Defense! Defense!"*]

First comes defense of our national sovereignty, for that we can make sacrifices! [*Applause and chants of "Defense! Defense!"*]

What do you want? A comfortable present, with a lot of consumer goods, or a future not for ourselves but for our children? [*Shouts of "A future! A future for our children!"*]

So that means that however many errors we may have made, and you know them well, however many errors we may have made, we believe that in general we have not been mistaken.

We have maintained the country's basic services, what is indispensable for keeping the country going. We have given support to national defense, and that has left us a little weak. We have given support to production, not as much as we would like, but we have done it. And here working people and the industrial workers are managing to resolve the problems. And although we did not have all the cotton harvesters we would have liked, and although we were short 25,000 cotton pickers, what has happened with this revolutionary people that is conscious of its responsibility?

What happened? What happened is that up until today we have picked 5.75 million *quintals* [1 *quintal* = 100 pounds] of cotton, thanks to the people of León and Chinandega. [*Applause*]

Two months ago all that cotton was still unpicked. We had problems with parts for the harvesters, with the harvesters themselves, with spare parts for the crop dusters. And yet with all the effort the people could muster, we came here when the cotton was still unpicked, we made a first effort, we made a second effort, and what was the result?

The result was a landmark in production, because we had 75,000 volunteer pickers from the CDSs, the CST, and the ATC, led by the Sandinista National Liberation Front. The volunteers came from the ranks of government workers, from the armed forces, and from the July 19 Sandinista Youth. And the cotton is now in the port to help resolve the people's needs. [*Applause, chants of "People's power!"*]

So although we did not give enough hard currency to production, and although we still have problems—because we used the hard currency for defense and to buy medicine and milk for the children—when we came up against these problems and had no hard currency to solve them with, we were able to turn to the people and ask them to aid the rest of the people of Nicaragua and the revolution by raising production. [*Chants and applause*]

Now it is for you to say, should we continue investing, should we build more hospitals, or should we not build more hospitals? More schools? [*Many in the crowd shout "Yes!"*] Productive investments? [*"Yes!"*] Okay, we will continue, little by little, building for the future. [*Applause and chants*]

However, there is a problem that remains. What is that problem? [*A voice in the crowd: "Defense of our country!"*]

Defense of the revolution is the life-and-death task of Nicaraguans. [*Applause and chants of "One single army!"*]

And there remains the problem that wages are very low and are not sufficient to buy products of primary necessity. Even with the efforts we made, the importing that we mentioned earlier of many products—this was not sufficient, and we began to introduce subsidies. Okay, we said, we may see a rise in prices here, because there is a worldwide inflation, but we are going to protect workers' wages. We are going to have transportation at rock bottom prices, subsidized electricity, subsidized beans, rice, milk, and so on. How much did a liter of milk cost before the triumph of the revolution? [*Someone answers, "Three córdobas."*] Three córdobas. That is more or less what it costs today, except in a few places where the sale of raw milk is permitted. But this subsidy we have been providing . . . [*At this point, someone on the speakers' stand calls Wheelock's attention to the time.*]

It won't take much time to finish. A little more time to say something about the question of wages and prices, something which concerns us, something that is another part of the war.

The problem persists. Imports to saturate the market will not solve it. Subsidies will not solve it. Because we are in the midst of an aggression. The phenomenon of shortages, compañeros, we are going to have with us for some time.

What has exploded here in the midst of the phenomenon of shortages is the phenomenon of speculation. The Ministry of Internal Commerce says that a pound of corn should cost one córdoba, and yet when you find a pound of corn in the market, what does it cost? [*People in the audience shout different figures they have paid recently.*] Eighty córdobas a *medio* [a five-gallon oil can that holds about twenty pounds], eight córdobas a pound, three córdobas. First of all there is an anarchy in the prices; secondly, the official price is not being respected even though there is a subsidy.

What have we set as the price for a dozen eggs? We set the price at 10.70 córdobas a dozen. Yet in the markets it went up to fifteen, then to twenty, and recently as high as thirty to thirty-five córdobas for a dozen eggs. Some compañeros are saying up to forty.

And milk. It's being sold at seven córdobas, at eight córdobas a liter. Beans are being sold at ten córdobas a pound in some places, at fifteen in others, when we say the official price is 3.50 córdobas a pound. Cans of powdered milk are selling for seventy-five córdobas, when we say the price should be sixteen córdobas.

So we are going to assume the following. We have a situation of shortage, and wages are not high enough to buy products. How could this not create many problems inside the family? So some workers, I imagine some of you who are here, would prefer not to continue working at your present jobs, would prefer to seek some other, more lucrative activity, perhaps in commerce or speculation. That is the worst thing you could do.

And it will in no way help if, in face of this situation, the union tells the workplace that wages have to be increased. Because that is not the problem. Here neither strikes nor work stoppages nor discussion nor getting rid of a director are going to resolve the problem. Increases in wages are not going to solve the problem. Because if we raise wages, then prices will go up. If we raise wages, what will happen? Wages are part of the cost of production of beans, cotton, corn, sugar, everything.

So we have to seek an effective set of steps. Has the [guarantee] card, for example, been effective? [*Shouts of "Yes!" and "You bet!"*] Do you have corner grocery stores where you are sure of being supplied at adequate prices, at the prices we set? [*Someone shouts, "No! Only ENABAS!"*]

Okay, we are going to do three things. The first thing we are going to do is finish the reorganization of wages, so that we do not have one truck driver at a sugar mill making 6,000 córdobas [a month], another 10,000, and another 8,000. All should make the same. There should be uniformity in wages. [*Applause and chants*]

Secondly, we are going to establish realistic wages, not the wages of two years ago. We are going to give a reasonable wage increase, and we are going to give workers a material incentive. The good worker is going to make more money, he who produces is going to make more. So there is going to be a standardization of wages, an increase in wages, and incentives for the better workers. [*Applause*]

The National System for the Organization of Work and Wages is being implemented gradually, and according to the reports we have, there are now some twenty-eight job classifications incorporated into the system. In a few months we will have finished the work of putting the new system into effect, a system that is humanist and progressive. It is perhaps not a system that is going to resolve all problems, but at least it will resolve the anarchy of the past.

The other two measures will be the following. We have to intervene in distribution. We have to direct products through secure channels. We have to remove products from channels where someone is taking advantage of the heroic and patriotic efforts of the people in defense, in the economy, and in work for the future.

How is it possible for us to have here workers who cut sugarcane ten or twelve hours a day, receive their pay, and then have to turn it over to a speculator, to a criminal, to a parasite who cannot even be called a revolutionary? [*Applause*]

So we are going to make an effort to direct through secure channels a large quantity of basic products, so that the people can set their minds at ease, so that people will feel that the work they do and the wages they receive are sufficient to buy the products that are indispensable to them and to their families. [*Applause and chants of "People's power!"*]

We would like, finally, to say a few things about the situation we are living through, and we are going to do it rapidly, in broad strokes. Because—while we are accustomed to having these meetings at ten or eleven in the morning, under a sun that doesn't bother us much—the children, the workers, and the attention—you can already begin to feel the heat, and the attention is dropping off a little. Are you dropping off a little? [*Shouts of "No!"*] What? [*"No!"*] Could you hear that? [*"Yes!"*] Well then, pay a great deal of attention to what you are going to hear.

Nicaragua once again is at war to defend the homeland. It is not a minor aggression at one border; at issue is a war that will be decisive for the liberty and existence of Nicaragua.

The Reagan administration is using the economic and military power of the United States to attack a small people, with few inhabitants, with a weak economy, and still smarting from the wounds left by *somocismo*.

Why has this unjust and immoral war been waged against us? There is one single reason. In the eyes of that government, which has an imperial vision of the world, a government that is national, sovereign, and has dignity is completely incompatible with its interests.

Who did Nicaragua belong to before? To imperialism. What did imperialism impose on Nicaragua? A sell-out government like that of the Somozas that was content to suck the blood of Nicaraguans, but that was also prepared to let the United States count on Nicaragua for military bases, like those on the Gulf of Fonseca. To have in Nicaragua a territory to be used for its strategic, military, and geopolitical purposes. And to remove from Nicaragua its natural and mineral wealth. A dictatorial and tyrannical regime in Nicaragua was a weapon for guaranteeing the political, economic, cultural, and social domination of U.S. imperialism.

The people of Nicaragua defeated *somocismo* and defeated the policy of imperialism, not only in Nicaragua but in Central America. That is why imperialism wants to regain hegemony in Nicaragua. How can it regain it? In two ways. First through treason, through actions like those of Moncada or Edén Pastora, placing the revolution, its thousands, the conquests of the people, at the feet of imperialism. They have been waiting for some time for treason, but the Sandinista National Liberation Front, like Sandino, is not for sale and does not surrender. And we are not going to sell out nor are we going to surrender. We are not going to betray the revolution. [*Applause*]

What then remains? What is Reagan's solution? Military strengthening of the Panama Canal; military occupation of Honduras; occupation of El Salvador with advisers, armed forces, and equipment; pressure on the government of Costa Rica for the right to occupy highways, airports, and zones of Costa Rican territory.

At this moment there is intervention in four countries. Panama, Costa Rica, Honduras, and El Salvador have suffered intervention by the United States.

Why? To attack Nicaragua, which will not sell out and will not surrender. Left to us is but one road, the road of turning back aggression.

But you should not for a moment believe that this plan to force Nicaragua to yield is based only on military maneuvers, two or three airports in Honduras, or military highways in Costa Rica. No. This plan is a diabolical plan. Why do we say this? What have they managed to do? They have succeeded, first of all, in building a powerful and aggressive platform around Nicaragua, using U.S. forces, rearmed *somocista* National Guardsmen, and hundreds, perhaps a few thousand disaffected elements who left Nicaragua because they had been adversely affected by the popular policies of the revolution.

The bands are part of the armed intervention of the United

States. The U.S. objective is to intervene militarily in Nicaragua, and the bands are the bridgehead, the beachhead of that intervention. They represent steps the United States has already taken.

The world, however, has repudiated the U.S. aggression and its military maneuvers. The world is with Nicaragua: the socialist camp, the Western countries, Latin America, all nations—with a very few exceptions, like Israel, for example, which is aiding the counterrevolution—support Nicaragua and are opposed to the policies of the United States. Even allies of the United States are opposed to the policy of the Reagan administration.

And it will cost them to intervene here, because the people are mobilized for defense. He who intervenes here can expect to suffer tens of thousands of casualties, to be buried with marines and flags back in the United States—that is, if they manage to get out of Nicaragua. [*Applause*]

The counterrevolutionary bands are the bridgehead of this intervention; they are also the force being used by the United States to destabilize our economy—as I said before—and shortages are being felt here. But we shall see the response of the people of Nicaragua. We are a people less literate than the people of Chile, for example. There the CIA, following the policy of Henry Kissinger, who has just visited Central America to once again draw up the same plans, imposed a blockade against a government supported by the entire people of Chile. They began to feel the shortages of goods, the problems with medicine. Toilet paper was in short supply. The impression was created that the government was solving nothing, that before the people had everything and never had to form lines. They did not know what a line was, perhaps because they did not know what aggression was, or a war against the most powerful nation on the face of the earth.

Yet when that powerful nation entered the Second World

War, it too imposed rationing on all residents of the United States. And what happened in Europe, which has an enormous economic development? Who has not seen scenes of rationing there in the movies? They had rationing too.

Here the fact is that we are at war. This is not a war between the United States and another great power. It is a war between the United States and a tiny country. However we were not rationing when we should have already started to, two or three years ago.

The people of Nicaragua understand this. They understand that the CIA and the Reagan administration want to strangle and demoralize the people of Nicaragua. They want workers to return home and see a child who needs medicine. They want these workers to think more about their government than about imperialism, more about the National Directorate than about Ronald Reagan, who sits at his desk every day approving plans of aggression against a small nation.

The Nicaraguan people must understand that the shortages are also and fundamentally a product of the war of aggression being waged by imperialism. How much have we lost in the way of products with the blockade of the ports, with all the workers who are involved in defense? We have lost thousands, millions, that could have resolved many of the needs of the people.

Imperialism understands that its main defeat lies in the economic triumph of the revolution, a triumph we are already on the road to attaining. When this revolution, without Yankee intervention, provides justice to the entire nation—something *they* always promised—when it is this revolution that actually does that for the first time, on that day imperialism is going to tremble, is going to be destabilized from top to bottom in its policies toward the Third World.

The plan of the CIA is to use the bands to attack this country economically, to make us feel the shortages, to turn the people against the government. But what will happen here?

Let us suppose that tomorrow Ronald Reagan, acting in one of his roles, orders military intervention against Nicaragua. What will happen? Tens of thousands, perhaps hundreds of thousands of marines are going to die here.

But let us leave aside the question of who is going to die and who is going to remain in the end. What we would like to know is what more than 700,000 Nicaraguans—not counting the youth, the CDSs, the CST, the ATC, or the Sandinista National Liberation Front—what these 700,000 activists are going to do.

Above all when there are 200,000 under arms. Can another government be established when there are 200,000 guerrillas spread around the country? When there is practically no government in El Salvador, where there are far fewer guerrillas, much more poorly armed. No, there can be no other government, and military intervention is no solution. For that very reason they are going to try to turn and separate the 700,000 from the leadership that is defending national sovereignty.

This is where the role being played by counterrevolutionary priests and the right wing comes in. Because, and think about this, can the counterrevolutionaries really do anything on the borders with the incursions they are carrying out? [*Shouts of "No!"*]

So what can an intervention accomplish? What does an intervention require? Bands striking at the economy, combined with an ideological offensive aimed at the minds of Nicaraguans, a target the counterrevolutionary bullets cannot hit. And we are concerned because, whether out of naïveté or a completely calculated plan we do not know, we have the recent action of the bishops. They seem to want to play the role of serving platter for imperialist reaction, for ideological destabilization.

They say: Gentlemen, the problem here is not national sovereignty; the problem here is not with imperialism; Mr.

Reagan has nothing to do with it; the United States is very far away from here; no ports have been mined here; there are no military bases; it is not the United States that is training the counterrevolutionaries; it is not the U.S. that is flying in Cessna planes in the border area; there were never any helicopters that crashed. Gentlemen of the CIA, we have never read in a single U.S. newspaper, including the *Washington Post* or the *New York Times,* that there is a plan of destabilization. We have never heard that the U.S. Congress has made military aggression against Nicaragua a law. No, gentlemen, this is not what has happened in Nicaragua. It is other things that have happened in Nicaragua.

In short, these gentlemen are either confused or part of the plan of the counterrevolution. [*Shouts of "They are part of the plan!"*]

We speak responsibly and with all the authority that comes from our struggle, from our heroes and martyrs, and from our revolutionary program, which we are putting into practice. Let us hear what you have to say. Are the differences religious or political? [*"Political!"*]

They are political, because religious differences . . . what contradictions are there between the principles of religion and everything we have been doing all these years? [*Shouts of "Between Christianity and revolution, there is no contradiction!"*]

But why is there no contradiction? Do you know why? For a few simple reasons. Is this a government of the rich or of the poor?[*"The poor!"*] Who were those who could not enter the kingdom of heaven? [*"The rich!"*] In fact, it seems that first a camel had to pass through the eye of a needle. So who does this revolution defend? The poor. Whatever the right wing says, is it true or false that we defend the poor? [*"True!"*] Who said, "Blessed be the poor for they shall inherit the earth"? [*"Jesus Christ!"*] And who is giving land to the poor here? Who took land away from the *somocistas* and the rich to give it to the poor? [*Applause and shouts of "The revolution!"*]

Teach those who do not understand. Who here is teaching those who do not understand? Who here loves his neighbor? Who here is fulfilling most consistently the principles of Christianity? [*"The revolution!"*] ... And the Sandinistas. [*"The vanguard!"*]

So there is no material contradiction. They may say you are atheists. Okay, we acknowledge this. But here in the past there was José Santos Zelaya, the Masons; that is, atheism. Here in Nicaragua atheism is something of almost folkloric dimensions. And here in the last century they threw out priests, the Zelaya government threw out priests for less than these priests are doing here today. [*Applause and shouts of approval*]

We state openly that there are some in the Sandinista National Liberation Front who, on the basis of their ideas, their ideology, their studies, their questions, have begun to believe that God does not exist. We state this openly. There is no need to discuss it.

But who is it that permits religious freedom here? Isn't it us? There are many more religious schools here now than in the time of *somocismo*. Who led the literacy campaign? A priest. Who is responsible for Nicaraguan culture? A priest. Who is the minister of housing? A Christian.

This is a government of Christian and revolutionary principles, a government oriented by Christians. So there is no contradiction, because the Christians are also in power. The fact is that politically they are with the revolution. [*Applause*]

And yet they tell us: You have to enter into a dialogue, into a settlement, into an accord; you have to have a dialogue with everybody, including those who have "risen up in arms."

First of all, they are ignoring the fact that we are the ones who have most sought peace and not war. We have made dozens of proposals for peace, for dialogue with the United States. But the only response has been aggression. We are the ones who have tried to start a dialogue. But who do they want us to dialogue with? Because I am going to tell them one thing. There are some things we cannot discuss, and some people we cannot hold discussions with. There are some people with whom there can be no reconciliation.

How can there be reconciliation with those who are murdering and torturing our people? Moreover, if in an act of liberalism we were to want to bring about such a reconciliation, the people would not tolerate it. We could not guarantee the security of those people here. [*Applause*]

What is more, these people left, and they are not going to come back. If they did the people would want to bring them to justice. If they come back here it will not be to hold a dialogue but to massacre the people. Haven't we already offered them a pardon, an amnesty? But there are some we cannot hold a dialogue with. Imagine what those gentlemen, the bishops, would say to us if we told them: You have to bring about a reconciliation with the devil. [*Laughter and applause*]

They say the counterrevolution is *our* enemy. So why doesn't God have a reconciliation with *his* enemy, the devil? Or why don't they make an effort toward this reconciliation and convert the devil into an angel? This they cannot do and never will do. [*Applause*]

So with the *somocistas*, the criminals, and the murderers, just like with the devil, there will be no reconciliation. [*Applause and chants of "They shall not pass!"*]

They tell us we are too deeply involved in hatred and struggle. But at the very beginning it was we who let go thousands of National Guardsmen who had well earned being put up against the wall, a wall the size of the stadium here in Chinandega. We could have filled the stadiums with all those *somocista* dogs who made the mothers and the people suffer. But we were forgiving. Acting on the principle of concord and unity, we pardoned them, gave them trials, and set many of them free.

Who granted pardons and amnesty here? ["*The Sandinista National Liberation Front!*"] That's right. And if a counterrevolutionary happens to ask the pardon of the Nicaraguan people, we may adopt an attitude of forgiveness and compassion, but not reconciliation. Because if tomorrow, by some miracle, the devil were to appear at the door of Monsignor Obando and ask for a pardon, at best Monsignor Obando is likely to tell him, quite reasonably, "Okay, come rejoin the flock of the Lord, but we still have a few matters to discuss with you." Let them come here and ask pardon from the people of Nicaragua for their crimes, and then they will learn the response of the Sandinista National Liberation Front! [*Applause*]

The right wing is trying to deceive people through the media, to undermine the people through campaigns of destabilization and lies. Imperialism is directing counterrevolutionary bands with the aim of carrying out destabilization and murder. Imperialism, the church hierarchy, and the reactionary parties all have the same attitude toward our national sovereignty and the conquests of the revolution.

The moment has come to say, *That's enough from the reaction!* [*Applause and chants of "People's Power!"*]

The gains of the Nicaraguan people are under attack. The people of Nicaragua are being attacked by an imperialist nation, by an immoral foreign power. And neither the people, nor the Sandinista front, nor the National Directorate can continue to be flexible with the abuses that are being committed in the name of liberty, of our liberality, of our flexibility. We cannot continue to let them harm the revolutionary project. We cannot, at the same time we are confronting imperialism, have scorpions inside our shirts.

[*Applause*] We are flexible, but we also know how to carry out our responsibilities. And there is a moment when flexibility begins to undermine the responsibility one has to lead the interests of the people. We are going to be inflexible and vigilant toward the attitudes of politicized elements that are mixed up in counterrevolutionary activities, that are using the pulpits that really belong to the Christian people of Nicaragua. [*Applause and chants*]

We are going to act with a heavy hand against the speculators, against those who are causing damage to, who are mining, the pocketbooks of the people who are fighting, of the people who are producing.

We are going to apply the severest sanctions against the speculators and hoarders. We are going to distribute basic products through secure channels, so that the people receive the goods they themselves are producing. [*Applause*]

Today, on this first of May, we must all be united to defend our conquests. We must be united with the revolution in defense, united with the revolution to increase production, united to raise the levels of discipline in work, the levels of fulfilling production goals.

We must have unity with the technicians, with the administrators, for we do not have fundamental contradictions with them. Our fundamental contradiction is with imperialism. We have to unite, moreover, with the small and medium producers, with all genuine producers, with all Nicaraguans who understand that their task is to forge a Nicaragua for the future and for their children.

The other Nicaraguans, those who call themselves Nicaraguans, like the bands, who are no more than mercenaries in the pay of the United States, who of their own accord have stopped being Nicaraguans—these other Nicaraguans will unite with all those who, from the platforms of some professional associations and of the reactionary producers, are trying to destabilize the revolution, like some activists in COSEP, who have joined in the plans of the counterrevolution.

We will deal blows to the counterrevolution, to the mercenary *somocista* bands, to the speculators, to the internal reaction, to the active agents of the sell-out bourgeoisie. [*Applause*]

Will León and Chinandega permit the counterrevolution to carry out its plans of destabilization? [*"No!"*] Will León and Chinandega lend a receptive ear to the deceitful and counterrevolutionary messages of a mistaken hierarchy? [*"No!"*] Will they allow the counterrevolutionary bands to come through here? [*"No!" "Never!"*]

In the last few days, 200 sons of the western region of Nicaragua have given their lives in defense of the revolution. This region also had 800 deaths in the insurrection. We must continue making these sacrifices so long as the aggression by imperialism continues. And we are sure that the people of the west will continue responding to national sovereignty and to the homeland. [*Applause and chants*] And we are sure that you will fulfill the tasks of production.

Long live the unity between peasants and workers! [*"Viva!"*]

Long live the tasks of defense and production! [*"Viva!"*]

Long live the combative unity of the Nicaraguan people! [*"Viva!"*]

Long live the Sandinista National Liberation Front! [*"Viva!"*]

Free homeland . . . [*"Or death!"*]

A dirty war is being carried out against Nicaragua
by Daniel Ortega

The following is the concluding portion of a speech given May 4, 1984, to open the 1984 parliamentary session of the Nicaraguan Council of State. The entire speech was broadcast live on radio and television, and was printed in the May 7, 1984, issue of *El Nuevo Diario*. This translation originally appeared in the June 11, 1984, issue of *Intercontinental Press*.

The Sandinista people's revolution faces a situation of permanent military aggression by U.S. imperialism, combined with the increasing use of new forms of attack. A dirty war, directed and controlled by the U.S. Central Intelligence Agency, is being carried out against Nicaragua. The CIA is using its own air force to attack economic and defense objectives, as for example in the air strikes at Volcán Casita, Potosí, and San Juan del Sur. It is using naval war vessels—such as high-speed launches armed with artillery and mortars—to attack economic objectives, including port installations and fuel depots along the entire Nicaraguan coast.

U.S. ships and destroyers are being used in a more direct way, to back up the high-speed launches. And to top off all this criminal activity, the CIA has laid mines in our country's main ports, establishing a more direct form of commercial and military blockade. These are new elements that have been introduced into the Central American conflict, and as such are a component of the overall conflict in the area.

The attacks on economic objectives have been costly and damaging, resulting in the partial destruction of our material base and in the necessity of reorienting material resources and labor power to defense of the homeland.

An overall assessment of the cost of damage to economic and social activity of both the state and cooperatives—based on figures that reflect only a partial picture of the reality—indicates the following: Replacement costs for damage created in 1981, 2.2 million córdobas [U.S. $220,000]. In 1982, 235.1 million córdobas. In 1983, 1.7 billion córdobas. The increase reflects the escalation of imperialist military aggression. And from January to March of this year damage totaled just under 150 million córdobas. So from 1981 to the present, the total is 2 billion córdobas. The main cost has been in material damage, which in 1983 alone totaled 1.3 billion córdobas, or 77 percent of total damage.

Another 375 million córdobas represents the cost of resettling people from the border areas, victims of the terrorist policy of the U.S. government.

Total material damage for 1983, equivalent to $128.1 million in hard currency, represented 31 percent of our exports. In national currency it represented 3 percent of the Gross Domestic Product, 20 percent of investment, or 6 percent of total consumption by the people.

But an accurate assessment must also take into account the incalculable impact on the cultivation of corn and beans, the delivery of meat and milk to market, the harvest of coffee, fishing, and the extraction of lumber and minerals—all of which suffered as a result of counterrevolutionary attacks on rural municipalities and production units. As is logical, all of this had a negative impact on the revival of production, the effort to increase investment, and the effort to improve the standard of living of the Nicaraguan people.

Damage caused by the mining of our ports—that we have so far been able to calculate—totals 91 million córdobas. This includes 22 million córdobas for the sinking of fishing boats, 28 million córdobas to cover part of the damage done to foreign ships, and 41 million córdobas in lost income, primarily in lost revenue from the fishing catches of the five fishing boats that were sunk.

Our production facilities are another favorite target of the counterrevolution, for the Yankee government believes it can in this way weaken our potential for defense and lower the morale of our people. Physical damage to the infrastructure of the productive sector totals 298 million córdobas; damage to production itself amounts to another 427 million córdobas. It is the productive sector that has suffered most heavily from terrorist activity, with a total of 875 million córdobas in damage, that is, more than 40 percent of the total damage.

Counterrevolutionary activity in the northern region and on the Atlantic Coast has caused great destruction in the sectors of agriculture and fishing. Agricultural activity has decreased because of the displacement of peasants who had to be moved to safer areas. Production of basic food items has been among the activities most seriously affected. Counterrevolutionary attacks on cooperatives located in these zones have caused damage amounting to 192 million córdobas, to which must be added the great, but not yet calculated, losses suffered by small private producers.

In terms of coffee, tobacco, and other crops, damage has totaled 168 million córdobas. Cattle production has suffered losses of 29 million córdobas, primarily through the smuggling of cattle across our borders by mercenary groups. This has affected our population's consumption of milk and meat, as well as our ability to export these products. Agro-industrial production has been affected by the shortage of hard currency, which in turn has made it difficult to obtain spare parts and replace equipment. This has had negative consequences for the production of milk, sugar, rice, and other essential products.

Fishing has been one of the activities most affected by armed counterrevolutionary actions. In 1983, we had a fleet of 116 fishing boats. Only 41 percent were actually able to be used for fishing. The rest were out of service either for lack of maintenance or spare parts or because they were being used for tasks of defense. In recent months we have lost thirteen fishing boats (six were stolen, two were burned, and five were sunk by mines). Their total replacement cost is about 60 million córdobas, to which must be added 100 million córdobas in lost shrimp and lobster exports—catches that never took place because of the destruction of the boats.

In the gold and silver mines, production of industrial gold dropped 11 percent in relation to 1982. The shortage of hard currency, further deepened by the imperialist aggression, resulted in a shortage of raw materials and spare parts. The equipment is obsolete and economic difficulties prevent replacing it or providing the necessary parts or inputs. Energy difficulties at the Siuna and Bonanza mines, a result of the partial destruction of the El Salto hydroelectric dam by the CIA's mercenaries, caused 15 million córdobas in losses and will reduce even further the production of industrial gold in 1984.

The imperialist economic blockade has caused delays in the arrival of raw materials, inputs, and parts for industry. The consequence has been fluctuations in the production of consumer and intermediate goods. This in turn has at times provoked a crisis in the supply of such essential products as cooking oil, soap, toilet paper, powdered milk, and toothpaste. Small-scale industry has also been affected by the shortage of inputs, with negative consequences for the sustenance of thousands of poor families.

Action by the CIA's mercenaries has also noticeably affected the extraction of lumber from the war zones, causing a decline in production of 19 million board feet, a loss of some 60 million córdobas in exports, and delays in the execution of numerous forestry development projects.

Criminal action by the mercenaries has resulted in the destruction of three people's agricultural storage centers, reducing by 8 percent the country's capacity to store basic grains. It has also forced the closing of five people's stores and caused the destruction of transport vehicles. This has reduced the capability to distribute goods in the war zones and made it more difficult to transport harvests to centers of consumption.

In 1984 the mining of our ports and other actions by the CIA's mercenaries cost us 92 million córdobas in delays in the export of our coffee, sesame, and beef. In addition, ships carrying powdered milk and butterfat have been diverted to Costa Rica, delaying the arrival of these products and affecting primarily our infant population.

Attacks on economic objectives have also been directed against the economic infrastructure, causing 174 million córdobas in damage. Among the most important have been the following:

- Destruction of fuel storage tanks, high-voltage towers, telecommunications towers, bridges, dams, and storage yards for construction vehicles.
- Destruction of the fuel tanks at Corinto alone signified a loss of 80 million córdobas.
- Destruction of construction vehicles and yards.
- Blockade of means of communication through the mining and destruction of bridges, the attack on Sandino Air-

port, and the attacks on customs facilities at Peñas Blancas [on the Costa Rican border] and Las Manos [on the Honduran border].

Delays in projects to improve the infrastructure have resulted in additional losses of 260 million córdobas. Taking into account all factors, the effects of terrorist activity on the infrastructure total 518 million córdobas, that is, nearly a fourth of all damage.

One of the first manifestations of imperialist aggression came in the financial sphere. Because the tasks of rebuilding the country are great, and the terms of trade are so adverse, the economy requires a considerable flow of external resources. The World Bank calculated the requirements, for 1982 and 1983, at some $300 million a year, of which $125 million was to come from multilateral sources. But the U.S. government used its political power in financial institutions to block credits for Nicaragua.

Proof of this lies in such concrete facts as the [U.S.] veto of the $1.7 million Inter-American Development Bank (IDB) loan for farm-to-market roads and in the opposition to other loans for road construction, totaling $35.5 million, that were supposed to be provided by the Central American Bank for Economic Integration, with special funds from the IDB. There is in addition an open attitude of opposition to any Nicaraguan request for aid from multilateral lending institutions in which the United States participates.

As a result of this aggressive policy, in terms of loan agreements the participation of multilateral organizations in our external financing dropped from 32.3 percent in 1980 to 15.6 percent in 1983.

Another aspect of economic aggression has been the cutting off of our channels for trade which, for a small country like ours, are the lifeline of the economy. A few examples in the commercial sphere are the following:

- The virtual elimination of our sugar quota.

- The reduction of our meat quota.
- The suspension of credits for the import of wheat and cooking oil.
- The closing of our consulates in the United States.

The mining of our ports and the penetration of U.S. war fleets into our territorial waters make crystal clear that a commercial and military blockade is part and parcel of United States gunboat diplomacy.

In addition to the economic damage caused by the attacks, defense of the country itself has necessarily represented a considerable economic cost. In 1983 we had to devote 20 percent of the national budget to defense and security, in comparison to 18 percent in 1982. In 1984 it was necessary to raise the figure to 25 percent of the total budget because of the magnitude of the imperialist aggression. The financial cost of defending the country has made it necessary to raise taxes, hold back the expansion of health care and education, and has created an inflationary pressure that hits working people above all.

In terms of material goods, defense requires a share of food supplies, construction equipment, fuel, and industrial products. The productive sector has lent its own means of production, including boats and trucks, in support of our Sandinista People's Army. Defense requires the cooperation of workers, peasants, and technicians, of leaders of the people's organizations and young people, and of all who have answered the call for defense, bringing to that historic task the best cadres from our labor force, our principal source of productive strength. All these brothers, the best of our heroic people, could be planning the economy, drawing up projects, building grain silos, and bringing in harvests instead of suffering and dying on the border to defend the homeland from an inhuman and immoral aggression.

From May 4, 1983, until today we have had to mobilize extraordinary resources to confront a criminal and multipronged escalation of imperialist aggression and destruction. Consequently, we have also had to confront serious difficulties in resolving the problems we face in improving our people's living conditions.

The aggression has forced us to slow down the gradual development of health-care projects, close down many units of primary medical care, and hold up the construction and opening of others. Some vaccination campaigns have had to be suspended, and we have not been able to reach the desired intensity in the campaign to combat malaria. The economic situation of war has considerably affected investment for all health services. In the area of health care, the total cost of the aggression has been 25 million córdobas. Seventeen health centers have been destroyed; fifteen health workers have been killed, including one doctor, eleven have been wounded, and thirteen have been kidnapped, including three nurse's aides.

The Nicaraguan people's social security and welfare programs have been struck a dramatic blow because of the need to divert resources to take care of the populations displaced from the war zones, now totaling more than 114,000 Nicaraguans. We have had to move these people to new settlements, which require food, medical care, cooking utensils, and housing. Just this aspect alone will require the expenditure of 530 million córdobas, to cover emergency costs for the next six months.

Our children in the countryside are being deprived of their Rural Children's Services, which have suffered 9 million córdobas in damage. We have also had to set aside large sums for pensions for the family members of heroic combatants, militia members, and reservists who have fallen in defense of the country.

The supply of basic consumer goods to the population has been seriously affected by the aggression. Production of both corn and beans is concentrated in the zones where the bands are active. Delivery of these products, as well as of essential imported goods, has met with great difficulties, resulting in an inescapable decline in the supply of goods available to people. Furthermore, destruction of transport vehicles and storage centers, in combination with giving priority for their use to defense, has disrupted commercial patterns.

Within this framework of generalized scarcity, it became necessary in the final months of 1983 to give priority to the regions in combat when it came to assigning supply quotas. Consequently a serious situation of shortage is being felt in Regions III and IV [the predominantly urban provinces of Managua, Masaya, Granada, Rivas, and Carazo]. This in turn has provoked unscrupulous activities of speculation, complicated by a process of ideological diversion. The intent of the latter is to create confusion as to the real cause of the situation, which is the U.S. war of aggression.

The financial consequences of the situation of war, combined with the problems of shortages, raised the rate of inflation for the market basket of basic goods by 40 percent in 1983. This has had a serious impact on the standard of living of the working people, who continue confronting the shortages with heroism and sacrifice.

Employment has also been seriously affected by the destruction of productive capacity, especially in fishing and the mines, but also because of the shortage of hard currency provoked by the economic aggression. Industrial manufacturing has been hit the hardest. If all these sectors were able to work at full capacity, at least 10,000 jobs could be created. As we mentioned, the aggression has also accelerated inflation and reduced the buying power of wages.

Workers have felt the aggression in their own flesh. The cost in human lives, which have no price, totaled eighty-eight civilian victims in 1982 and 1,550 in 1983. Of the 1,550 in 1983, 605 were killed, 102 were wounded, and 843 were kidnapped. These figures include only government employees and members of agricultural cooperatives.

From January to March of this year, there were 249 victims, of whom fifty-four were killed, twenty-three wounded, and 172 kidnapped. The total number of victims between 1982 and March 1984 is 1,877, of whom 747 were killed, 125 wounded, 1,015 kidnapped. These are the victims of the policy of state terrorism the Reagan administration has unleashed against our heroic people.

Nor does imperialism wish to allow Nicaraguans to enjoy the right to education that was won with the people's victory of July 19. Fifteen schools in the countryside have been nearly destroyed, construction has had to be halted at twenty-seven more, and imperialist criminal activity has forced the closing of 138 primary schools in the zones affected by U.S. state terrorism.

Several thousand children have been left without primary schooling. The number of primary school teachers who have been killed has risen to twenty-three.

Adult education programs have been a target of the criminal attacks, forcing the closing of 647 people's adult education collectives. The state terrorism of the Reagan administration is soaked with the blood of volunteer adult education teachers, 135 of whom have been killed. Their only crime was to dedicate their free time to helping the rural population emerge from illiteracy and ignorance. These are the dividends of the $21 million the Reagan administration has requested from the U.S. Congress.

But while Washington discusses financing the murder of volunteer teachers, 1,800 of them have mobilized in the Reserve Infantry Battalions to hunt down the murderers of their brothers and to defend the gains the people have won through the Sandinista people's revolution.

Our struggle to increase the quality of teaching and to improve academic performance has been seriously disrupted by the courageous and massive integration of teachers and students into the militias and reserve battalions, at the cost of leaving the classroom behind.

Cultural programs have also been affected, and three cultural workers have been murdered.

The programs to extend electric light have been affected by the sabotage counterrevolutionary bands have carried out against transmission and distribution towers.

Construction of more than 2,000 housing units has had to be suspended in order to divert material resources to resettlement areas for those displaced by the war.

Programs to provide drinkable water in Nueva Segovia and Madriz and a drainage system in Corinto have been suspended, affecting health conditions in those areas.

In short, the standard of living of all Nicaraguans has, to a greater or lesser degree, been affected in multiple ways by the U.S. administration's policy of state terrorism.

In face of this policy of war, it is necessary to take concrete economic and social measures to confront the aggression. We must begin building an economy of defense, although we would much prefer continuing to carry out development projects in a climate of peace.

As a first step, we have established better central control over available resources and have raised the population's consciousness of the need for austerity.

Based on the lessons learned during the military emergency in October and November 1983, we have better leadership of the economy at various critical points—above all in the external sector, that is, hard currency, and in the coordination of distribution. We have managed to share out hard currency with greater efficiency, to the sectors that really have priority—such as defense, supply [of basic goods], health care, and priority production—all within the framework of the 1984 economic plan. These sectors have learned how to use their hard currency with much greater efficiency, with the help of workers in maintaining equipment, making their own spare parts, and economizing with materials.

At the same time, we have attained greater budgetary austerity, aimed at making possible greater spending for defense, reducing the budget deficit to one-half the 1983 deficit, and thereby reducing inflationary pressure.

This has required new taxes on services, gasoline, and big business. It has also meant freezing the budget for health and education. And we have to stop the expansion of subsidies to the consumer, subsidies that have been stolen by the speculators.

Secondly, the hard experience of the last year in terms of supplying the public with consumer goods has convinced us of the necessity of attaining greater social control over the process of distribution of items of basic necessity. The situation of general shortage cannot be overcome in the short term, even less so in the present conditions of war. But distribution can be improved greatly. Despite big difficulties, we have established a distribution system that is a little more fluid and better regulated in terms of prices for rice, beans, cooking oil, soap, salt, and sugar. The same cannot be said for other products, where official distribution channels have been affected by speculation.

In connection with the above, the labor power needed for exports, construction, industry, and priority governmental activities is being drained by a dizzying growth in the sectors of small production, petty commerce, and informal services.

In face of this situation, the revolutionary government is taking a series of measures aimed at acknowledging the genuine costs of production: adjusting consumer prices in accordance with those costs; establishing secure channels for distribution, so as to guarantee a minimum of basic products to the urban and rural population; dealing a heavy blow to the speculators; and returning to productive labor the hundreds of persons who, despite being suited for productive labor, have turned to consumption and speculation.

Thirdly, we have learned from the accumulated lessons of what is now three years of active defense. The revolutionary state has made progress in establishing the correct links between defense and the economy, so as to minimize the economic costs. There have been notable advances in the last year in coordination between the Sandinista People's Army and other governmental institutions in regard to distribution and construction. We have also made advances in effectively integrating the tasks of production and defense, as for example in the establishment of self-defense cooperatives and the use of military contingents to help out in the harvests. In this way the national economy has begun to receive effective support from the defense effort.

We must leave behind the individualist criteria of the dependent capitalism of the *somocista* dictatorship and advance further in the social structuring of the economy. We believe this principle is perfectly compatible with the mixed economy, so long as the producers agree to produce what the economy needs, under production contracts with the state, and so long as businessmen dedicate themselves to distribution, in association with the mass organizations, and not to speculation. What we cannot permit is that while the people fight and workers live on insufficient wages, some individuals take advantage of the shortages and the aggression to speculate and enrich themselves.

This cannot be tolerated!

This must be fought!

Defense of the economy requires an extraordinary effort by workers, peasants, technicians, and administrators to maintain production. The revolutionary state does not intend to abandon the priority projects that represent the economic future of our people.

The response of the Sandinista people's revolution to the needs of our people—with or without the aggression—will be to continue to fulfill them to the degree possible. We will satisfy the needs that were for decades denied by *somocista* dictatorship, by political and economic dependence on U.S. imperialism, and by the native oligarchies—in all their political, social, and economic aspects.

The gains the people have won through the Sandinista people's revolution will be defended and consolidated by the people themselves, a people that is conscious, mobilized, armed, and prepared to make the ultimate sacrifice.

Defense of national sovereignty, of people's power, and of the gains won by the people requires, as we have seen, *defense of the economy and an economy of defense.*

It also requires participation of the people in all forms of defense.

The strength of our Sandinista people's revolution lies in the broad social base that sustains it and in the organizational levels that have been attained. We can affirm that the massive integration of the people in the main tasks has already assured the defense and survival of the Sandinista people's revolution.

This May 4, in recalling the heroic act of Sandino, who neither sold out nor surrendered in face of the arrogance and power of the Yankee invader, we want to extend special recognition to the combatants of the Sandinista People's Army, to the Ministry of the Interior, to the militia members, to the thousands of young people who have joined in the defense effort through patriotic military service, to their mothers and family members, and above all to the heroes and martyrs who have fallen in this daily combat against Yankee intervention.

The people are going to defeat and annihilate the mercenary forces

by Humberto Ortega

The following statement to the Nicaraguan and foreign press was made on June 5, 1984, in the name of the National Directorate of the FSLN and the Junta of the Government of National Reconstruction. It was published in the June 6, 1984, issue of *Barricada*. This translation originally appeared in the August 6, 1984, issue of *Intercontinental Press*.

1. Since the last century, the United States of America has aimed at imperial domination of the Central American region and the Caribbean. Faced with this policy, our people have engaged in heroic periods of struggle against the Yankee invader. The acts of Yankee barbarism against our country claimed about 100,000 victims during the first thirty-four years of this century.

   The last Yankee marine—Anastasio Somoza Debayle—and his genocidal beasts were defeated and driven from Nicaragua by the people in arms, during the great national insurrection that took power July 19, 1979, under the leadership of the Sandinista National Liberation Front.

In those heroic days, the downtrodden people of Sandino lost 50,000 lives in driving out the Yankee *somocista* dictatorship and its allies, the bourgeois forces who would sell their country.

2. When Ronald Reagan assumed office at the head of the U.S. government, it meant the beginning of open war—fought in the military, diplomatic, and financial arenas to reassert imperialist domination over Nicaragua.
3. The aim of the open war our country suffers at the hands of the prowar sectors of the Pentagon and State Department is to destroy the popular and anti-imperialist character of our revolution, to destroy the power of the working people, and to attempt to place in power the pro-Yankee bourgeois classes, which abroad and within our country operate under the CIA's direction.
4. The prowar sectors of the U.S. government are also trying to maximize the strength of the genocidal elements of the *somocista* [National] Guard who managed to escape the people's fury in 1979. They are helping these forces, together with those of the traitor Pastora, to become the military apparatus guaranteeing U.S. imperialist interests and the interests of both the reactionaries who would sell their country and the puppets involved in the disinformation campaign. These puppets reveal through their hatred their opposition to the truly popular character of the new Nicaragua that is being rebuilt and is fighting.
5. The field of battle is made up on one side by the downtrodden people—workers, peasants, artisans, students, professionals, intellectuals, patriotic producers in the countryside and the city, young people, children, old people, Indians, Blacks, Mestizos, and whites—who, led by our historic vanguard, the FSLN, consistently defend people's power and their revolutionary government.

Against the people are the Yankee warmakers, their genocidal military agents and the traitor, as well as their political and ideological intermediaries among those who would sell their country.

6. Our revolution is confronting the declared war against our people in the political and the diplomatic arenas. In connection with the recent visit to our country of the U.S. administration's envoy George Shultz, our revolutionary government has reiterated its firm and responsible willingness to reach various agreements with the United States that would ensure a true framework of security in order to work out political solutions that would first of all end the war our people suffer, and also lead to normalization of relations between the United States and Nicaragua.

7. The trend of the U.S. administration's declared war is toward becoming even larger in the remainder of 1984. First of all, they are doing everything they can to strengthen the counterrevolutionary forces. These forces, supported from their bases in Honduras and Costa Rica, have been organized into military units perfectly meshed into the military machinery of the Yankee forces in Honduras and of that country's army. They intend to impose and expand this condition in Costa Rica, whose neutrality policy is already affected by the activities of the Central Intelligence Agency and other forces of the Pentagon and their mercenary forces.

8. The U.S. administration's strategy of open war consists of continually wearing down our country through the counterrevolutionary activity in the extensive territories of Las Segovias, Matagalpa, Jinotega, the Atlantic Coast, part of Chontales and Río San Juan. The aim is to disrupt the country's economy and affect the economic programs and social works that the Government of National Reconstruction is carrying out.

At the same time, using the political and ideological obfuscation of the domestic right wing, the CIA launches campaigns to sow confusion among the people, attempting to blame the revolutionary government for the grave economic problems we are going through. In fact those problems are specifically due to yesterday's exploitation, the declared war we are suffering today, and the world economic crisis that hits hardest at the small and poor countries like ours.

9. In the military arena, the interventionist strategy seeks to spread the Sandinista People's Army thin in order to wear it down and affect the basic structure of the military defense of the entire country.

    The enemy contemplates seizing Nicaragua's Pacific region, including Managua, through massive attacks by the Yankee army. This is part of an overall plan of intervention in which the mission of the counterrevolutionaries is to distract and spread out our forces, in order to make it easier for the interventionist troops to concentrate their actions against strategic objectives in the country.

10. In the arena of sabotage and terrorism, the Yankee strategy this year is to try to step up attacks against the revolutionary leadership and acts of sabotage against various economic structures—in agriculture, factories, energy, ports, communications—and against resources such as trucks, buses, and machines that the people need for work and mobilization.

11. In the international arena, the strategy of war against our country aims among other things to isolate Nicaragua as much as possible from the various popular and governmental forces of the world, to sabotage the peace efforts put into motion through international forums or groups like Contadora, and to try to use threats against those who aid us to make them back off. All of this is to facilitate the present escalation of aggression and justify

the massive intervention of Yankee troops in the grave Central American crisis, and against Nicaragua in particular.

12. In order to ensure the permanent presence of Yankee troops in the Central American region, the U.S. administration has decided to develop combined joint exercises, like "Granadero I" presently being carried out with the Honduran and Salvadoran armies.

    The warmakers are speeding up various military projects on Honduran territory in order to have use of a secure launching pad for the rapid deployment of their air, naval, and ground forces against any country in the Central American region they decide to intervene in, such as Nicaragua and El Salvador.

    There is information that once these exercises are concluded, the U.S. administration plans to carry out "Big Pine II" maneuvers with Honduran troops in the month of September.

13. It has become clear that the objective of the Yankee military maneuvers in Honduras is to turn that country into their main base of aggression for the Central American region and at the same time to improve the combat readiness and firepower of the Honduran and Salvadoran armies, and improve coordination for carrying out joint military operations.

    Such military maneuvers are also useful to strengthen materially and logistically the *somocista* mercenary forces and those of the traitor and to provide them with better strategic and operations information. These forces are the stepping stone or the spearhead of the Reagan administration's war against our people.

14. The mercenary forces run by the CIA have been restructured so that they are more in line with the needs of the Yankee commanders, able to function as real military units of a modern army. The mercenary forces that have been

infiltrated into our country are being resupplied by air and land from more than twenty military bases on Honduran and Costa Rican territory bordering Nicaragua.

In these bases they have established military schools, field hospitals, communications centers, and their propaganda apparatus.

More than 10,000 genocidal troops launch constant criminal attacks against the working people throughout the regions bordering on Honduras and Costa Rica. And the ports have not escaped this terrorist activity, having been mined by the CIA. Air attacks have cost countless losses in human lives and material damage.

15. An end to the war basically depends on the will of the present U.S. administration. Nicaragua contributes to ending the war to the extent that it totally defeats the mercenary forces presently acting against our country from the border territories.

    Nicaragua contributes to making sure the war does not spread to the whole country to the extent that it strengthens its combat readiness throughout the national territory, thereby raising the cost of the Yankee interventionist adventure if one should take place.

16. The Sandinista people's revolution confronts the war strategy directed against us with the revolutionary strategy of people's war.

    Our workers and our battle-tested youth carry tens of thousands of rifles in varied military and security tasks related to the national defense of our homeland and revolution.

    Our glorious Sandinista People's Militias, reserve infantry battalions, and youth doing their patriotic military service, structured into the Sandinista People's Army, ensure the strength of the ground, armored, and artillery troops, the Sandinista Air Force, the antiaircraft defense, the border guards, and the sailors, and carry out the basic missions of military defense of our sacred home soil.

The combatants of the Ministry of the Interior, the State Security and State Intelligence, the Sandinista Police, and the self-sacrificing volunteer police fight the CIA's plans to form a terrorist urban front. They secure the information needed to militarily strike at the enemy, fighting shoulder to shoulder with their brothers of the Sandinista People's Army in the front lines.

The people, organized in the Sandinista Defense Committees carry out vital revolutionary vigilance in defense of the people's interests and gains.

The mass organizations like the Luisa Amanda Espinoza Nicaraguan Women's Association, the Luis Alfonso Velásquez Association of Sandinista Children, and the Sandinista Defense Committees, together with the government institutions, ensure the basic functioning of the diverse civil defense measures.

Through their self-sacrificing work, our laboring people—especially the workers and peasants—maintain the country's production in order to be able to feed our children and provide what is needed for the people mobilized in the war fronts.

The firm and enthusiastic young people of the July 19 Sandinista Youth orient the people to more passionately and fervently counteract the right wing's campaigns of obfuscation and keep the streets and every corner of the country from being manipulated by the reactionaries.

17. The people, massively involved in the homeland's defense—the mothers and their children, the husband and his wife, the child and the old person—want peace, tranquility, normalcy in the country. That is why the people, massively involved in defense, are going to defeat and even annihilate the mercenary forces.

And in this way in the near future they will achieve the tranquility, the normalcy, the peace that our people, today at war, deserve. With the indestructible strength of the workers and peasants, the children of Zeledón, Sandino, Rigoberto, and Carlos Fonseca will crush the mercenaries in order to win peace.

18. The whole country must be turned into the great rear guard of the war fronts. And to achieve that, we will ensure that the whole nation can participate in this patriotic activity, with the people's forces involved in the war fronts and the tasks of production.

    In this way the worker will not only ensure the material needs of the war front but will also carry a rifle against the Yankee aggression.

19. The general line, in the immediate period, is
    a. Break up to the maximum degree possible the mercenary forces operating in the border and mountain regions through the massive and ongoing mobilization of Sandino's heroic people to go to the war fronts.
    b. Neutralize the rightists in our cities and towns who conspire in campaigns of confusion that are an important complement to the military aggression.
    c. Strengthen the country's rear guard in order to:
        - Secure the war fronts;
        - Ensure basic production;
        - Improve and strengthen combat readiness and mobilization readiness. This will ensure that the people are massively involved in the present battle and will fine-tune the country's general defense and its readiness to confront and defeat a possible Yankee intervention.

20. The massive incorporation of the people into defense of the homeland has given rise to a series of problems that have not been properly attended to by the appropriate institutions. The main problems are the following:
    a. The imperialist war has made it necessary to extend the period of mobilization of the reserve and militia

units far beyond what was planned.
b. Payment of the mobilized compañeros has not been carried out in the time stipulated.
c. Compensation for losses resulting from the mobilization of the peasants is not being made as it should be.
d. In some cases there has not been compliance with the revolutionary government's laws regarding the work rights of the mobilized compañeros. We know of cases of compañeros who do not get their job back when they are demobilized.
e. There has been insufficient and very irregular attention paid to families of compañeros who have fallen or been war casualties and to their pensions.
f. The opportunities for the people to permanently honor the heroes and martyrs who have fallen in defense of the homeland have not been strengthened.
g. We have found that the means through which the young people doing patriotic military service can communicate with their families, such as correspondence and visits, have been irregular and weak in their functioning.
h. We have verified that in some cases the methods of recruitment contradicted the norms and procedures designed to treat our people with the respect they deserve.
i. There must be greater creativity and more flexible mechanisms for the basic training of the Sandinista People's Militias.
j. The institutions of the ministries do not adequately ensure that the lines of the revolutionary government are carried out to give priority attention to the needs of the mobilized compañeros and to other lines of support for the defense tasks.

21. Due to this situation, despite the difficulties imposed on us by the mercenary attack, the National Director-

ate of the Sandinista National Liberation Front and the revolutionary government have taken some immediate measures to gradually overcome the previously noted problems:

a. The National Commission of Support for the Combatants has been established. Its coordinator is Compañero Reynaldo Antonio Téfel, minister of the Social Security and Welfare Institute. Yesterday, Monday [June 4], it held its first meeting.

   This national commission is a government body responsible for supervising the implementation of all the special problems that the central government is assigning to the various ministries to give the necessary attention to the basic needs of the combatants.

b. Through the National Commission of Support for the Combatants, the government junta will oversee implementation of the following measures:
   - Solving the human and social problems of the combatants and close family members, especially problems related to pensions, funerals, and disability of the combatants and the most pressing and urgent needs of their mothers, companions, and children.
   - Giving priority attention to health care for the combatants.
   - Strengthening the special agrarian reform programs to turn land over to the families of heroes and martyrs and combatants. The same for lots and basic construction materials so they have a simple but suitable roof over their heads.
   - Speeding up the study on readjusting the status of all those receiving pensions, so that in accordance with the present economic possibilities we can begin carrying out the readjustments in the second half of this year; with an immediate review of the cases of the families of compañeros who have fallen in

combat or been wounded in action so that they get prompt relief.
- Immediately working out a new law of social security benefits for the combatant and his family members. This will include those in the reserve units and Sandinista People's Militia units that have been mobilized, as well as the professional members of the armed forces and those fulfilling patriotic military service.

  This new law will unify all the prior decrees of the government junta and will adjust them to present conditions.

c. Through increased mass participation we will ensure that reserve infantry battalions and Sandinista People's Militia units will be mobilized for training and field campaigns for a period of no less than four months nor more than six.

   This will make it possible for larger numbers of organized patriots to have the opportunity to participate directly in the search and destroy campaigns being carried out this year, in particular to neutralize to the maximum possible degree the mercenary forces of Yankee imperialism.

d. It will be guaranteed that adequate financial attention will be paid to the reserve infantry battalions and Sandinista People's Militia units mobilized for the designated period in the field. In particular, various measures are now being taken by the army and government to see that payments are not delayed, to compensate the peasants for losses in their harvests due to their being mobilized, and increase the financial aid given to patriots without full-time jobs who are serving in the reserves and militias, among other measures.

   In addition, mechanisms will be strengthened to

permit the implementation of the law guaranteeing the mobilized patriot's right to keep his job in state and private companies. The National Commission of Support for the Combatants will be one of the bodies to aid in these tasks.

e. Mechanisms are being strengthened in the Sandinista People's Army to guarantee better communication between the families and soldiers doing patriotic military service.

Due to the increase in the mercenary aggression and the many tasks of defense, during the present year, the system of passes for personnel doing their patriotic military service will not be implemented as would be the case under normal conditions.

As we neutralize the present mercenary activity, it will be possible not only to normalize passes for the patriot on patriotic military service, but also the system of vacations and leaves for all those making up the armed forces.

f. The Sandinista People's Militia has created various special training centers for the patriotic reservists and militia members mobilized in the field. These training centers have infantry, field engineering, and firing ranges, as well as classrooms for tactical, topographical, artillery, and antiaircraft instruction, among other subjects.

For the instruction of the militias in general, the basic conditions are now being created to add new weapons and knowledge to the instruction already received.

The territorial structure of the Sandinista People's Militia will continue to be strengthened throughout the country, while reiterating that in some cases and situations the militia members must carry out missions outside their assigned territory.

g. Coordination between the armed forces, governmental, political, and mass institutions will be increased to ensure the highest respect is paid the combatants who have fallen in the war that Yankee imperialism forces on us. The National Commission of Support for the Combatants will be an important pillar for accomplishing this honorable duty.

We are on a war footing to defend this revolution of the downtrodden and working people to the last drop of our blood.

We are on a war footing to defeat the war that the present U.S. administration has forced on us.

The National Directorate of the FSLN and the Junta of the Government of National Reconstruction are laying out the necessary measures to strengthen the people's organization in order to confront the present aggression of the U.S. military power.

The heroic people of Sandino, imbued with the spirit of the Defense of National Sovereignty and the spirit of the self-sacrificing guerrillas of the Sandinista National Liberation Front who fought the *somocista* tyranny, are fighting the mercenaries, the forward detachment of the Yankee intervention.

And today, the old rifles of the barefoot peasants who fought with Sandino and of the guerrillas of Carlos Fonseca, Silvio Mayorga, Oscar Turcios, Germán Pomares, and Selim Shible have become new and modern rifles, rocket launchers, artillery, cannons, and modest air and naval resources, which are used with fervor, sacrifice, and fearlessness by the sons of Sandino.

It is true that the brutal war the United States has forced on us has taken thousands of victims, has murdered families, has orphaned children, has destroyed homes. But it is also true that this heroic people, who want and desire peace, have the necessary vigor to turn themselves into the best fighters and to defeat and expel the Yankee aggression.

With the permanent and massive mobilization of the people of Sandino: Everyone against the foreign aggression!

Free homeland or death!

The Sandinista Front is the fire of popular justice
by Daniel Ortega

The following speech was given July 17, 1984, to a meeting of the Sandinista Assembly, a broad advisory body to the FSLN's National Directorate. At that meeting the FSLN announced its candidates for the November 4, 1984, elections. This speech marked the opening of Ortega's campaign for the Nicaraguan presidency and it was published in the July 18, 1984, issue of *Barricada*. This translation originally appeared in the September 3, 1984, issue of *Intercontinental Press*.

The Sandinista National Liberation Front is the continuator of the struggle Cleto Ordóñez launched in favor of the exploited classes at the dawn of independence.

The Sandinista front is the unforgettable example of the peasant soldiers who defeated the Yankee filibuster at San Jacinto in 1856.

The Sandinista front is the anti-imperialist stance and social advocacy of Rubén Dario.

The Sandinista front is the heroism of Zeledón, who rose

up in defense of our sovereignty when it was violated by the Yankee marines in 1912. And above all, the FSLN is the immortal struggle of Sandino and his Army for the Defense of National Sovereignty, which from 1927 on, implanted in the consciousness of the workers and peasants the historic program of struggle for national independence and the transformation of our society.

The Sandinista front is the just action of Rigoberto, who launched the beginning of the end of imperialist domination in 1956. It is the heroism of Ramón Raudales in 1958, of El Chaparral, of the Patriotic Youth, of the New Nicaragua Movement, and of July 23 [1959] when the students of León were massacred.

The Sandinista front is the patriotic, worthy, anti-imperialist history of the heroic people of Nicaragua, which Carlos Fonseca with his popular wisdom understood how to synthesize.

The Sandinista front is the program of Sandino, upheld by the sons of Sandino in Bocay, Managua, El Patuca, Coco River, and Walakistán in 1963.

It is the red and black banner of Sandino, defended in blood and fire at Pancasán in 1967; at Zinica in 1970; in the action of December 27, 1974; in the October 1977 offensive; in the popular mobilizations of January 1978; in the seizure of the National Palace; in the September 1978 insurrection, and on the Carlos Fonseca northern front, the Pablo Úbeda north-central front, the Rigoberto López western front, the Camilo Ortega central front, the Benjamin Zeledón southern front, and the Roberto Huembes eastern front.

The Sandinista front is the fire of popular justice in the final insurrection, with the dictatorship's barracks surrendering to the guerrilla columns; it is the general strike; it is the retreat;* it is the heroic battle of the people and the

---

* On June 28, 1979, FSLN units fighting Somoza's National Guard in the eastern neighborhoods of Managua decided to conduct a retreat to

50,000 heroes and martyrs; it is the heroes of San Jacinto, the stirring song of Dario; it is Zeledón; it is Sandino; it is Rigoberto; it is Carlos Fonseca defeating the Yankees and the traitors on July 19, 1979.

Today, history calls upon the people to defend their program, which is the program of the Sandinista front.

Today, when we again face the ever-present enemy, Yankee imperialism and the traitors who would sell their country, this same heroic people is waging the battle—this people of workers and peasants, youth, Indians, Blacks, mestizos, whites, peons, artisans, shopkeepers, market vendors, students, women, small and medium farmers, loyal businessmen, professionals and technicians, religious workers, intellectuals and artists.

This same people will go on waging the battle for the new Nicaragua, with its historic vanguard, the Sandinista National Liberation Front, defending its plan of struggle in the first free elections ever held in the history of our homeland.

There was never any other alternative of power for our people than the FSLN; the options presented by the traditional parties were always lies. We were the choice the people made by taking up the rifles of liberation in order to overthrow the dictatorship and eradicate imperialist domination from Nicaragua.

We are the alternative the people have supported throughout these five years of the revolutionary process, years filled with deep going transformations of the social and economic reality, just as the Sandinista front promised in its historic

---

the nearby city of Masaya. Accompanied by hundreds of the capital's residents, the Sandinistas succeeded in keeping their forces intact and reaching Masaya, already liberated from the dictatorship's army. The tactical withdrawal from Managua proved to be a turning point in the war and a key to the victory of the insurrection three weeks later.

program of struggle, which is now being carried out.

The Sandinista front was forged with heroism and sacrifice in the clandestine guerrilla struggle in the cities, countryside, and mountains. Through wisdom, patience, tenacity, and sacrifice during many years, the road to victory was opened, leaving along the way the blood shed by our best leaders, the leaders of the people.

The Sandinista front, at the head of the people in the struggle and the insurrection's victory, buried the past of betrayals, pacts, and electoral maneuvers by the traitorous parties of Yankee imperialism.

The Sandinista front will remain at the head of this people, who today are struggling without quarter against the genocidal and traitorous mercenaries, paid, armed, and directed by Yankee imperialism in an attempt to bring back the past of imperialist domination and exploitation.

In the first free elections in Nicaragua's history, which only the Sandinista revolution has made possible, this same people will reiterate on November 4, 1984, the vote for the revolution that it casts every day in the factories, trade unions, cooperatives, neighborhoods, shops, classrooms, in the building of the new Nicaragua.

In this way, the people will also be reiterating their daily votes on the battlefronts, in the trenches, in the struggle to the death against the mercenaries and foreign invaders.

The people will vote for their program, their plan of struggle.

The people will vote for their conquests and gains in the revolution.

The people will vote massively for the Sandinista front.

The people will vote for the National Directorate.

The people will vote for their candidates of the Sandinista front.

The people will be voting for the people, harvesting a new victory in defense of peace, national sovereignty, and the building of their new society.

Let's go forward! With the front!*

The Sandinista front will educate the generations to come in respect and veneration for all the men and women of our homeland who, in the course of all our struggles, have shed their blood for the conquest of a future of peace and justice.

They are the ones who died fighting without rest against imperialist domination and its instrument, the genocidal dictatorship.

They are the ones who since the revolutionary victory have fallen in defense of our sacred rights to freedom and independence, in the war we are waging against the invaders and in the day-to-day battle for the reconstruction of our homeland.

They are the ones whom we must emulate in struggle, in everyday tasks, and at the moments of greatest tests and sacrifices. They are the ones who will guide our course toward the future, and their example of sacrifice and heroism will live forever in our consciences and in our hearts.

The Sandinista front and its National Directorate, the top political leadership of the people of Sandino, commit ourselves to guarantee faithful compliance with our historic program and to continue fighting without rest and with all our strength and energy to defend the right of the people to build this new society, free of exploiters and exploited, for which more than 200,000 Nicaraguans have fought and died during the past century.

This is the homeland our heroes and martyrs dreamed of.

This is definitely the homeland for which Zeledón, San-

---

* At this point in his speech, Ortega read the FSLN's election platform or "Plan of Struggle." *Barricada* summarized this section of the speech by listing the headings of the platform's twenty-three points.

dino, Rigoberto, and Carlos Fonseca gave their lives, living up to our slogan of "Free homeland or death!"

Let's go forward with the front!

Sandino yesterday, Sandino today, Sandino forever!

Plan of struggle

by the Sandinista National Liberation Front

The following document was the FSLN's platform for the November 4, 1984, Nicaraguan presidential and legislative elections. Distributed massively throughout the country, it was the subject of intensive discussion in the workplaces, neighborhoods, and farms. Despite attempts to disrupt the elections by U.S.-backed counterrevolutionaries and a boycott by several of the major capitalist parties, the elections marked an advance for the revolution. As another major step in carrying out the democratic program of the revolution, the election of a national assembly contributed to further isolating the bourgeois opposition to Sandinista power both inside and outside Nicaragua.

More than 1.5 million people registered to vote and nearly 80 percent of them actually cast ballots. The FSLN's candidates received 67 percent of the vote, electing Daniel Ortega as president and Sergio Ramirez as vice-president, and filling sixty-one of the ninety seats in the National Constituent Assembly. This translation originally appeared in the October 1, 1984, issue of *Intercontinental Press*.

I. The power of the people

The Sandinista front commits itself to strengthen the power of the people and to keep weapons in the hands of the people in order to uphold and defend that power.

The Sandinista front will guarantee that the inexhaustible source of revolutionary power will always be the trade unions of the workers and agricultural laborers; the neighborhood, women's, and youth organizations; and the unions of small- and medium-sized agricultural proprietors, journalists, professionals and technicians, intellectuals and artists, and religious workers.

II. Defense of the homeland

Weapons will remain in the hands of the people and we will go on strengthening our armed forces so long as imperialism goes on pressing its policy of destroying the power that belongs to the people. Its aim is to force us back into the past of submission and surrender, and that would mean wresting away all our gains, wresting away our sovereignty and independence.

The Sandinista front commits itself to go on defending the country's sovereignty, on the basis of continuing to arm and organize the entire people. The Sandinista front will remain at the head of the people until the final victory over those who are attacking our homeland. Sandinista militants will continue to offer the best example of participation in combat.

We will go on encouraging and instilling in our armed forces the spirit of unshakeable patriotism in the fight against the aggressor, as well as the most absolute respect for working people.

The Sandinista front likewise commits itself to go on developing the policy, initiated by the revolutionary government, of assisting combatants in order to ensure jobs and social benefits for them and their families.

Attention to health care for the combatants will be increased, and full social security benefits will be extended to them. Also, combatants from the towns and cities will be given priority in the distribution of housing lots and construction materials.

Land reform programs will also be extended to benefit the peasant fighters.

III. Security and tranquility for Nicaraguans

The Sandinista front commits itself to go on furthering the professional and technical capacities of the Ministry of the Interior; developing its organizational abilities in order to guarantee the country's internal stability, crime prevention, security, respect, and tranquility for all Nicaraguans; and proceeding with all due energy against foreign aggressors and lawbreakers.

The Sandinista front also commits itself to continue supporting the development of revolutionary night-watch duty and the police volunteers, as exemplary forms of popular participation.

IV. The struggle for peace

The Sandinista front commits itself to go on developing a worthy and nonaligned international policy that corresponds above all to the interests of Nicaragua and Nicaraguans, without thereby infringing on the rights of other peoples.

We will go on exercising our sovereign and irrenounceable right to maintain relations with all the countries of the world and to lend support and solidarity to the cause of oppressed peoples against any form of subjugation.

We will go on struggling for world peace by fighting the hegemonistic and warlike policies that the U.S. administration seeks to impose on humanity even at risk to the survival of the human race.

We will continue to seek peace in Central America, without infringing our own sovereignty and fundamental rights as a free and independent country. We will go on seeking by all means to end the unjust and immoral aggression Nicaragua suffers at the hands of the government of the United States.

V. Human rights and public liberties

The Sandinista front commits itself to incorporate into the new constitution that will be voted upon by the National Assembly this integral set of rights and freedoms that the Sandinista revolution has brought into force through the daily exercise of democracy and public liberties in Nicaragua. For the Sandinista front these rights took on a new dimension with the revolutionary victory:

The right to a job.
The right to land.
The right to organize and mobilize.
The right to housing and a building lot.
Workers' access to the communications media.
The right to education, culture, and sports.
The right to equal opportunities.
The right to criticize, engage in dialogue, and raise demands.
The right to health care.
The rights of women.
The rights of children, youth, and the aged.
In sum, the overall right to human life.

These are rights and freedoms that will be assured to all Nicaraguans. Only constant progress in transformations brought by the revolution will be able to make this fully possible, insofar as we advance in health care, housing, education, and social well-being; and to the extent that there is more and more political consciousness among the great working masses of the nation.

The Sandinista front commits itself to go on encouraging

a new communications policy in Nicaragua, guaranteeing democratic use of the media and the right of the great majority to express themselves freely. Likewise, new ethics in the field of information will be consolidated, according to the principles of respect for the truth and human dignity that the Sandinista revolution promotes.

VI. The new economy

The Sandinista front commits itself to deepen the social and economic revolution that has already been launched, by consolidating our model of independent economic development.

This model will continue to be in tune with the necessity of transforming the social reality of the country. It will have to contribute to meeting the basic needs of the people, diversifying economic cooperation and export markets, and furthering our process of technological assimilation in an orderly fashion.

At the same time, we set ourselves the aim of regulating the participation in our country's development of foreign capital from other states and from private companies so that, in cooperation with our revolutionary state, projects may be developed to make possible the transformation of our raw materials and the development of our resources and wealth without infringing on our sovereignty.

This commitment also calls for ensuring the just and equitable distribution of wealth, and for continuing to fight injustice and social and economic inequality.

Within the mixed-economy framework—which offers room both for the functioning of the enterprises of the people's property sector and for those in the hands of private owners that correspond to the interests of national development—the instruments of governmental economic direction of centralized planning will continue to be strengthened.

Planning leads toward more rational use of all the country's resources, in order to direct them toward the goals of overall transformation of the society and overcoming the model of dependency to which we were subordinated.

The Sandinista front commits itself to go on making use of material and financial resources, including foreign ones, in order to increase our capacity to produce foods and basic goods.

To further this policy, we will continue guaranteeing credit and bank financing as well as capital resources to all Nicaraguans who wish to produce patriotically and efficiently.

We will not spare any expenses or economic efforts to guarantee the defense of our homeland, the material necessities of the armed forces, and the provisioning of the fighters on the firing line.

We will go on fostering public spending aimed at defending the prices of basic consumer goods. We will do likewise in the health, education, housing, and services programs, above all in those regions that have been most affected by foreign aggression.

We commit ourselves to ensure the completion of those investment projects that are of strategic importance to the country's development. These will result in increased food production; in the processing of our agricultural, mineral, and forest resources; in the generation of electric power; and in transport systems and road and highway construction of use for production and defense.

In the same way, we will struggle to ensure the creation of poles of economic development in the various regions of the country, in such a way as to generate productive activities and create better local job opportunities for workers without forcing them to move into the capital.

We will be energetic in combating failures, deficiencies, vices, weaknesses, and bureaucratism in the state institutions.

The Sandinista front commits itself to go on exercising its

legitimate right to obtain economic and financial aid from all countries in the world that solidarize with our revolution and that offer us such cooperation without political conditions.

In dealing with the problem of the foreign debt, we have stated that Nicaragua will remain responsible for its financial commitments, without endangering our economic development and independence. We also uphold the necessity of bringing together the debtor countries in order to confront in a rational and coherent fashion the club that the creditors have organized.

We will also adopt a foreign investments law, with regulations capable of attracting to our country the capital resources necessary for our development while at the same time guaranteeing our interests as a sovereign country.

VII. The peasants and land reform

The Sandinista revolution's policy in the countryside consists of giving land free of charge to the peasants who want to work it and in helping them to organize themselves so as to gain better access to bank credit and technical assistance.

This also means guaranteeing the property of the small- and medium-sized rural producers who were already landowners before the victory, and providing them with support in terms of credit and technical aid.

This policy also applies to agricultural producers who work efficiently and produce good yields, whatever the size of their property holding.

The Sandinista front commits itself to go on developing the agrarian reform as one of the axes of economic transformation.

The Sandinista front commits itself to continue promoting the distribution to the peasants of property titles to the land, and to make sure bank credit and technical aid reaches them in an effective way.

The Sandinista front commits itself to continue encouraging and extending the organization of cooperatives in the countryside.

We will also go on supporting the small- and medium-sized agricultural proprietors, as well as all the farmers and ranchers in general who produce with dedication, efficiency, and patriotism.

We will go on struggling to keep the roads in good condition and to open more; to improve the systems of transport, storage, and warehousing; and to ensure that just and stable prices are paid to producers.

The Sandinista front likewise commits itself to go on guaranteeing access to bank credit for all producers without discrimination, and to provide them with technical assistance, fertilizers, vaccines, seed, and spare parts, taking into account the supply problems brought on by the aggression we are suffering.

VIII. Wages and the supply of goods

In order to deal with the problem of the supply of goods, the Sandinista front commits itself to guarantee to the population access to the principal basic products needed for subsistence, at stable fixed prices, distributed through uniform and secure channels. The list of goods will be broadened to include other consumer products to the extent that the imperialist aggression diminishes and we achieve greater levels of production and organization.

The Sandinista front commits itself to fight for the stability and control of prices of basic consumer goods without exception, in order to safeguard them from speculation and hoarding.

The rights of all those shopkeepers, market vendors, and small merchants who work honestly to strengthen the distribution channels will be protected.

We also commit ourselves to guarantee the supply of goods to all the fighters on the battle fronts and to provide basic goods to the population of all those zones that are directly affected by the war against the invaders.

We commit ourselves to go on developing supply networks in the countryside, installing people's stores and rural supply centers little by little. At these outlets it will also be possible to obtain machetes, boots, files, and other products needed by the peasantry that the country is in a position to provide.

The Sandinista front commits itself to go on applying a rational policy to maintain the stability of prices for basic products and to energetically enforce the laws against speculation and hoarding.

In the same way, the Sandinista front commits itself to go on developing a just and rational policy with regard to wages, according to the principle of equal wages for equal work, as has been initiated with the application of the National System for the Organization of Work and Wages. Moral and material incentives in production and productivity also form part of this policy.

This policy will lead us to periodically adjust wages in relation to the controlled prices of basic goods, and to give priority to the wages of workers in strategic areas of production and services, in both the countryside and the cities.

IX. Workers, trade unions, and jobs

The revolution promotes trade union organizations so that the workers can participate in the management and organization of production and supervise compliance with the labor laws, respect for the norms of safety and hygiene, and food and housing conditions in rural sectors.

In the factories, plants, and workplaces, commissaries, cafeterias, and medical services have been established. Contracts provide for many other guarantees and benefits.

The revolution promotes ongoing technical training of workers. It supports the innovators who help to overcome difficulties in the importation of machinery and spare parts while at the same time creating the basis of a national technology in the midst of limitations.

The Sandinista front has promoted the unity of the working class and will go on doing so, in a constant struggle against divisionism, opportunism, low productivity, indiscipline, and work inefficiency.

All these are vices that the agents of imperialism and capitalism try to preserve among the most backward sectors of the working class. It will be necessary to combat them energetically.

The Sandinista front, as the historic vanguard of the Nicaraguan proletariat, reaffirms its confidence in the workers and commits itself to guarantee their true leading role in the revolution and to go on consolidating the organization of the working class, both in the cities and in the countryside. It will likewise promote participation by the working class in the management of enterprises; its ongoing technical education; and its contributions to the country's technological development.

We also commit ourselves to overhaul the labor laws and exercise special vigilance over compliance with them in all the country's workplaces.

X. Handicrafts and small-scale industry

The Sandinista front commits itself to support the artisans and small-scale industrialists, encouraging them to organize in cooperatives to guarantee access to bank credit at appropriate interest rates and periods of repayment, as well as to provide supplies and raw materials. The distribution centers that already exist for this purpose will be expanded.

Within the limits imposed by the scarcity of foreign currency, efforts will be made to guarantee the basic supplies that are required. Export programs for handicraft products will be promoted.

XI. Professionals and technicians

The Sandinista front commits itself to go on encouraging the organization of the country's professionals and technicians and to establish a more coherent policy aimed at improving their levels of scientific knowledge, developing their political consciousness, and fostering their dedication to serving the interests of the people.

We likewise commit ourselves to broaden the professionals' opportunities for education and updating their technical knowledge, and to encourage their involvement in scientific research and in contributing to the technological development of the country.

We will also continue going forward in the task of establishing uniform wage scales and just payment norms for various professional and technical activities.

XII. The revolutionary state

It is urgent to eliminate the legacy of the past in the administration of justice and to move forward with concrete measures for greater efficiency and less bureaucratism in the administration of the state.

The FSLN will deepen the popular and anti-imperialist character of the Nicaraguan state.

The Sandinista front commits itself to strengthen the role of the comptroller-general of the republic, so that this institution can become the faithful guardian of the conduct of public servants and see to it that the people's funds are scrupulously invested.

It also commits itself to punish in an exemplary fashion all those servants of the state who commit abuses of any kind.

In the same way, we will proceed energetically in the struggle against bureaucratism, with the aim of creating greater levels of efficiency in the government.

The Sandinista front commits itself to move forward in reordering the system of administration of justice, in professionalizing the judiciary, and in elaborating special policies so that the administration of justice can more and more correspond to the interests of the people.

XIII. The Atlantic Coast

The Sandinista front commits itself to continue upholding the territorial integrity of Nicaragua, more and more incorporating the Atlantic Coast into the country. We will continue the process of integration and transformation that has already begun; go on creating new poles of economic development in forestry, mining, and fishing; and develop ports, agriculture in permanent settlements, communications media, and highways.

The Sandinista front commits itself as well to go on respecting the culture and religious beliefs of Creoles [English-speaking Blacks], Miskitos, Sumos, and Ramas, who are all part of the Nicaraguan nationality; to preserve and encourage the preservation of their languages, cultural traditions, and customs, incorporating these into the cultural heritage of the nation; and to go on defending their right to be educated in their mother tongue as well as in Spanish, the national language.

The Sandinista front commits itself to defend the rights that the ethnic minorities enjoy as Nicaraguans to exploit the land and benefit from it, both from the lands they already possess and from those the revolution provides them through the agrarian reform.

The Sandinista front likewise commits itself to go on working to create better living and working conditions for the mine workers, who in the past epitomized the most merciless exploitation by the foreign corporations. The same goes for the forestry workers and fishermen.

We will go on defending the ethnic minorities' right of organization and their participation in running the government.

XIV. Health, welfare, and social security

The Sandinista front commits itself to go on struggling to consolidate the Uniform Health-Care System and to improve the quality of services provided to patients in the hospitals. To go on bringing health-care services to rural areas, especially to those that are under counterrevolutionary military attack, as well as to ensure the supply of medicines, whatever the limitations imposed by the war of aggression.

We will go on making efforts to provide preferential attention to invalids, through various programs of protection and welfare.

We will go on struggling to improve the quality of care and to provide fraternal and humanitarian treatment of patients.

We commit ourselves to go on eradicating infantile ailments, to continue to struggle against childhood malnutrition, to go on fighting infant mortality, and to put priority on attention to mothers during and after pregnancy as well as care to the newborn.

We commit ourselves to support and strengthen the popular health campaigns, so that the organized people may develop and consolidate their participation in caring for their own health and in developing preventive medicine.

Likewise, we will go on training more and more doctors, nurses, and health technicians, with a new consciousness of service to the people.

The Sandinista front will continue broadening social security in the countryside, along with programs to care for the aged and disabled and to protect minors against all forms of abandonment, cruelty, and exploitation. And it commits itself to go on fighting against prostitution, drug addiction, and alcoholism, and to develop rehabilitation programs in those fields.

XV. Education, culture, and sports

The Sandinista front commits itself to consolidate the development of a new, democratic form of education in Nicaragua, one that trains young people in a rounded way and links their preparation for labor to the needs of transforming the country and contributing to its greatness.

We will continue making efforts to reduce the illiteracy rate still further and press the battle to achieve basic people's education at the fourth-grade level for all Nicaraguans of school age. Technical education for workers will continue to be developed.

We will put together a uniform system of education, from preschool learning up to diversified university training, corresponding to the realities and needs of the country.

We will train teachers and professors in a massive way at all levels. We will continue building classrooms and schools, within the limits imposed on us by the war of aggression.

We will go on defending and advancing toward the right to free education throughout the country, putting an end to the expensive education still offered by certain private schools.

We will work toward the transformation of curricula and the preparation of our own textbooks and other learning materials. We will likewise work to improve the country's capacity to generate scientific and technical knowledge, through teaching and research.

We will train new, well-rounded human individuals, through new forms of scientific and humanitarian education.

Aware that there are still children without teachers and schools, we will go on extending education to the masses, taking care at the same time to improve its quality.

We will go on encouraging the participation of the people in cultural activity, in order to ensure the development of a rich and diverse culture representative of our nationality.

In the same way, we commit ourselves to go on transforming television, radio, and other communications media of the revolution into media that are truly educational and informative.

The Sandinista front commits itself to support the process of democratizing sport and bringing it to the masses in a noncommercial way, through the participation of the organized people, youth in particular.

Taking into account the limited resources we have, we will go on promoting sports, broadening such activities and encouraging their growth. Baseball in particular will be promoted without prejudice toward other sporting activities.

XVI. Intellectuals and artists

The Sandinista revolution has enjoyed the overwhelming support of journalists, who are working today to communicate revolutionary truth on the basis of new opportunities and new forms of expression.

Likewise, writers, musicians, performers, film makers, plastic artists, all cultural workers are giving a new creative and popular dimension to the development of art in this country.

The Sandinista front commits itself to go on supporting the development of a new, critical journalism, constructive and incorruptible, and to foster the organization of journalists so as to make possible their professional and intellectual development.

The Sandinista front likewise commits itself to go on guaranteeing the freedom of cultural creation, supporting writers, artists, and other cultural workers so they can go on developing all their creative potential and circulating their works among our people. We will help them to strengthen their associations, unions, institutions, editorial houses, schools, workshops, and centers of artistic education.

XVII. Housing, basic services, and recreation

Workers' brigades have brought roads, water, electric power, and telecommunications to the most remote areas of Nicaragua, opening up contact among regions that previously were isolated. Television and radio have been brought to the northern part of the country and to the Atlantic Coast.

Despite the adverse conditions imposed by the war of aggression and the serious economic limitations, the revolution has launched a program for building popular recreation centers, guaranteeing the people's right to healthy entertainment.

Recreation in decent conditions has ceased to be the privilege of a minority in Nicaragua. We will continue with this effort to broaden tourist and recreational facilities for the people, to the extent that the situation of aggression allows it. Preference in recreational programs will be given to combatants and their children and family members.

The Sandinista front commits itself to go on fighting to assure Nicaraguans the right to dignified housing. We will continue handing out lots and building materials, above all in rural regions affected by the war. And we will go on guaranteeing that housing land will not be the object of speculation or commercial activity.

We will go on bringing electricity, drinking water, and communications facilities to the entire country, above all to the peasant communities and rural workplaces.

XVIII. Transportation

New transportation networks have been set up in rural areas that had remained cut off in the past. The creation of transport cooperatives has been encouraged.

We have made efforts to rationalize the system of urban transportation in Managua and other cities, expanding the number of routes according to the needs of workers, and establishing nighttime service. Hundreds of new buses have been imported, but difficulties persist in maintenance and the supply of spare parts, as well as in the organization of service.

Land transport to the Atlantic Coast has been opened for the first time through the Matagalpa-Waslala-Siuna Highway. The Blanco River-Siuna Highway is also under construction.

A new railroad linking the port of Corinto with the cities of Chinandega, León, and Managua is being built in order to restore the train service interrupted by the floods of 1982. Work has begun to make El Bluff into the first deepwater port on the Atlantic Coast.

The Sandinista front commits itself to go on advancing in the improvement of urban, interurban, and rural transportation networks, making special efforts to connect rural communities.

We will go forward in building the port of El Bluff and the Blanco River-Siuna Highway. We will go on building and maintaining the roads in the productive zones, and we will make efforts to improve transport across Lake Nicaragua and on the rivers of the Atlantic Coast.

XIX. Children

In order to protect the lives of children—the greatest treasure of our homeland—the Sandinista revolution has carried out health programs and vaccination campaigns and has set up diarrhea treatment centers.

Children's parks, preschool and child-development centers, and classrooms have multiplied in the countryside and in previously neglected neighborhoods. Recreation centers have been opened, and there will be more in the future.

We will go on carrying out programs to benefit all Nicaraguan children, with special attention to the offspring of our heroes and martyrs and above all to those orphaned by the imperialist war.

There is still a long road ahead of us before children can fully enjoy all the protective measures and rights that the Sandinista revolution seeks to guarantee. There are still many children who work instead of going to school—children who peddle newspapers, children without shoes, children who beg.

In this regard, the Sandinista front commits itself to work without rest to ensure good health and healthy development for our children, to broaden their educational and recreational opportunities, and to guarantee them happiness and security in order that they can truly be the ones dearest to the revolution's heart.

XX. Youth

The Sandinista front commits itself to go on encouraging the organization of youth in the UNEN [National Union of Nicaraguan Students] and the FES [Secondary Students Federation], supporting them as well in the development of their varied tasks of political and patriotic education.

We also commit ourselves to offer the youth better and more varied opportunities for professional and technical education by means of perfecting the country's educational system, providing opportunities to study abroad in friendly countries, and linking education more and more to labor and defense.

In the same way, the Sandinista front commits itself to make efforts to guarantee to young people the same opportunities in jobs as in education, and to encourage their participation in defense, culture, and sports, as well as expanding recreation and entertainment facilities for young people.

XXI. Women

The family laws adopted by the revolutionary government are aimed at protecting women as mothers and providing them the dignity due them within the family.

The revolution has created equality of opportunity for all Nicaraguans, regardless of sex, and has restored the dignity of women. But social problems persist, and these pose obstacles to full participation by women in the revolution.

The Sandinista front will make greater efforts to overcome these social problems in order that women can achieve full participation. And it will struggle in a more systematic way to eliminate prostitution.

The Sandinista front will go on defending the nuclear family and the integrity of the home. To make it possible for the family laws adopted by the revolution to be fully complied with, education guidelines aimed at fostering greater understanding of this set of problems will be developed.

The Sandinista front commits itself to go on encouraging women's participation in society, opening job and educational opportunities in order to place them on an equal footing with men.

XXII. Religion and the revolution

The Sandinista front will go on guaranteeing the freedom of Nicaraguans to profess a religious faith. No one can be discriminated against for publicly professing or publicizing their religious beliefs. Those who profess no religious faith have the same rights.

The Sandinista front, which has the deepest respect for all the religious celebrations and traditions of our people, will go on making efforts to uphold the true content of such celebrations, attacking the manifestations of corruption and vice that affected these in the past.

The Sandinista front also considers that religious celebrations must not be utilized for political or commercial ends.

The Sandinista front will go on defending a secular state that, like any modern state representative of the entire people, must not adopt any religion in particular.

The Sandinista front will guarantee the right of individuals, churches, and private associations to organize for religious purposes.

The Sandinista front commits itself to stimulate and encourage participation by Christians in the tasks of the revolution, upholding the strictest respect for freedom of worship and the free functioning of the different churches in Nicaragua.

XXIII. Remembering our heroes and martyrs

The Sandinista front will educate the generations to come in respect and veneration for all the men and women of our homeland who, in the course of all our struggles, have shed their blood for the conquest of a future of peace and justice.

They are the ones who died fighting without rest against imperialist domination and its instrument, the genocidal dictatorship.

They are the ones who since the revolutionary victory have fallen in defense of our sacred rights to freedom and independence, in the war we are waging against the invaders and in the day-to-day battle for the reconstruction of the homeland.

They are the ones whom we must emulate in struggle, in everyday tasks, and at the moments of greatest tests and sacrifices. They are the ones who will guide our course toward the future, and their example of sacrifice and heroism will live forever in our consciences and in our hearts.

The Sandinista front and its National Directorate, the top political leadership of the people of Sandino, commit ourselves to guarantee faithful compliance with our historic program and to continue fighting without rest and with all our strength and energy to defend the right of the people to build this new society, free of exploiters and exploited, for which more than 200,000 Nicaraguans have fought and died during this past century.

This is the homeland our heroes and martyrs dreamed of.

This is definitely the homeland for which Zeledón, Sandino, Rigoberto, and Carlos Fonseca gave their lives, living up to our slogan of:

Free homeland or death!

Let's go forward with the front!

The unity of the FSLN cannot be challenged
by Tomás Borge

The following speech was given July 17, 1984, to the meeting of the Sandinista Assembly that launched the FSLN's election campaign. This translation originally appeared in the September 3, 1984, issue of *Intercontinental Press*.

It has been five years since our people brought down the Somoza dynasty. Five years ago hopes replaced repugnance and death. Five dramatic and splendid years. Five years that have brought to fruition the prophetic struggle of that simple worker, that unparalleled guerrilla leader who was and will always be, for ever and ever, Augusto César Sandino.

Five years of bringing to reality in this land the dreams of Sandino's continuator, the clearheaded and wise thinker, the strategist who taught us to summon the willpower to carry out the revolutionary transformation of our national reality—our founder, our chief, our brother, Carlos Fonseca.

Almost two decades of war in mountains, cities, and consciences, with thousands and thousands of dead—this was the necessary price to pay in order for Nicaragua to begin to exist. Without the struggle of those years, pressed forward and headed by the people's vanguard, the Sandinista National Liberation Front, there would have been no July 19.

Our vanguard has grown and multiplied. Since its birth, our vanguard has renounced routine and fear in order to launch itself audaciously into the application of a revolutionary perspective that today is in the process of being fully realized. The results of the heroic prophecy of Sandino and of the correct strategy of Carlos have now begun to make up part of our everyday life.

One million Nicaraguans studying; three million manzanas of land affected by the agrarian reform to benefit the people; infant mortality reduced by at least one-third—these are a few of the conquests that we have the pleasure of celebrating today.

The unity of the Sandinistas was the result of a historic necessity, but it was also the consequence of the political maturity of the leaders of this revolution. During the time of clashes and disputes, the unity of the FSLN came to be a demand on the part of its militants. Today the unity of the Sandinistas is something more than a demand, it is an order that cannot be challenged, an order issued by the entire people of Nicaragua.

It is not a question of artificial unity, forged at the price of cover-ups or falsifications, but rather unity around a clear program and an outstanding banner. It is not a question of some makeshift unity, dogmatically imposed, but rather of a living unity that reflects the contradictions of life and is nourished by them. Therefore such unity is bound to deepen, because our unquestionable National Directorate, the top political expression of the collective character of the Sandinista people's revolution, is working today and will always work to apply and develop constantly all the fundamental principles that have inspired and will inspire our struggle and that are like the air that we breathe.

The challenge presented by the dismantling of the power apparatus of the dictatorship has consolidated Sandinista unity. And the institutionalization of the revolutionary process ought to spur it forward. This institutionalization in Nicaragua is nothing other than a contribution to the essential requirement of deepening the revolutionary process. The complex process of organizing the state apparatus in all its multiple dimensions never broke the equilibrium inside the revolutionary government. Instead, it helped us to gain maturity and confidence. The defense of our homeland, threatened by mortars and slanders, attacked by murderers and liars, has likewise fortified the unity of the Nicaraguan revolutionaries.

These five years in the development of a revolutionary power that grows without artificial fertilizers have enabled a group of young leaders, my brothers of the National Directorate, to become experienced rulers and skilled political leaders. Their work inspires the living hopes of the founders of the Sandinista National Liberation Front.

These five years laid the bases for the accumulated experience to be projected into the immediate future. The birth process that shook the foundations of this land has been accomplished. It is now a question of deepening the revolution, of lending continuity to the historic fact of July 19.

The institutionalization of the process calls for advancing with renewed energy in the development and consolidation of the party of Nicaraguan revolutionaries, the Sandinista National Liberation Front. It is the spinal column of the revolution, the sentinel of revolutionary purity, the guarantee of strategic firmness.

In that way we will consolidate the defense of our right to be ourselves, and the inalterable course toward the construction of a superior social framework. Thus we will ensure that national dignity will remain erect, never to be subjugated. The preponderant role of the revolutionary classes will thereby be guaranteed.

Of all the conquests of the revolution, the most important and sacred one is that for the first time in history, Nicaragua is Nicaragua, and we Nicaraguans are Nicaraguans. Nicaragua had been condemned to be a torture chamber and a theater of fools; a country of men without land, of children without schools, of sick people without hospitals; a faceless homeland.

Now Nicaragua is celebrating its fifth year of life. Nicaragua finally exists, and it is because it exists that we have carried out the literacy campaign and revived cultural life. Freedom to create exists because Nicaragua exists. Because it finally exists, we will be implacable with those who seek to deny to our homeland the right to exist, those who want it to go back to being a humiliated colony, the echo chamber of a foreign voice, the shadow of another body.

Nicaragua exists through the unleashing of the creative energy of its people, who were never sheep and who know very well how to distinguish between fraternal and fruitful criticism and the poisonous work of their enemies. The people have the right and duty to express themselves freely—not only their desires but also their criticisms. The revolutionary who does not exercise criticism and self-criticism is surely a conformist and under suspicion of becoming a counter-revolutionary.

Nicaragua finally exists, and because it exists we have taught half a million people to read and write, put an end to poliomyelitis, saved the lives of many children who were dying like flies from hunger and sickness, and turned over land and rifles and hope to the people.

Nicaragua finally exists, and because it exists we have been able to confront so successfully the tremendous and continual aggressions. It exists because we have been able to face up to our own errors.

Our enemies do not propose to destroy the FSLN as a political party but rather to eliminate from the face of the earth what the FSLN represents as a historic project. But history is stubborn like a Chontales mule, and has pointed like a compass needle in one single direction—so long as the revolution exists, Nicaragua will exist.

So long as the revolution exists, national sovereignty will not be negotiable; nor will the people's economy, nor the democracy of people's power.

The revolution will go on living so long as revolutionaries give it life and remain willing to give their lives for the revolution.

Neither backwardness, nor poverty, nor aggression, nor imperialism, nor anyone can destroy this revolution. The only ones who could ever manage to destroy it—that is, who could allow Nicaragua to cease to exist once again, as the lessons of history show—are we revolutionaries ourselves.

Many have asked themselves, Where does the secret of such power reside? How is it possible that the people of such a small land, impoverished and eaten up piecemeal, manage to survive and triumph? How is it possible that this country of no more than 3 million inhabitants fearlessly confronts the all-powerful empire that fabricates and exports wars and dictatorships, and toys shamelessly with the fate of billions of human beings?

We found the answer in a humble woman of Ocotal, the same day that that city of ours, so close to the border, heroically and victoriously repulsed a counterrevolutionary attack. That woman, Compañera Petrona Zelaya, told us, lifting her rifle and looking up, "They shall not pass this spot. Because here we are—my children, my brothers and sisters, my parents, my neighbors. We shall not let them pass. And if we die, the children, brothers, sisters, parents, and neighbors of other barrios, blocks, and towns shall not let them pass."

That day we felt ourselves once again atop the peak of El Chipote, in Sandino's invincible fortress, and we again lived through the days of hunger and cold on the guerrilla fronts of Río Coco and Bocay, of Pancasán and Fila Grande. "They shall not pass this spot." Yes, compañera of Ocotal, our compañeros everywhere, our brothers and sisters of Nicaragua:

They shall not pass! We are an invincible people, and we have all the moral right in the world to cry, Free homeland or death!

The relevance of Sandino's thought
by Sergio Ramírez

The following speech was published in the July–August 1984 issue of the English-language edition of *Tricontinental*, a magazine published in Cuba by the Executive Secretariat of the Organization of Solidarity of the Peoples of Africa, Asia and Latin America (OSPAAAL).

One of the ways the Right tries to discredit the character and thinking of Sandino is to deny the contemporaneity of this man and his philosophy.

But Sandino is very much a part of the contemporary scene. His actions were not separate from the historical circumstances in which he lived; they were the direct result of a contradiction, a confrontation between Nicaragua and imperialism. And since this contradiction has not disappeared, the man and his deeds live on.

Let's look at the relevance of Sandino's thoughts and actions in terms of three aspects: first, the defense of sovereignty; second, popular democracy; and third, economic change. These three elements comprise an important basis of the Sandinista people's revolution, and they are a direct heritage of Sandino's thought and action.

We've already pointed out that Sandino's deeds were marked by one principal contradiction: the Nicaraguan nation versus U.S. imperialism.

Nicaragua's geopolitical situation as part of a conglomerate of small countries which happens to be in close proximity to the United States is what has determined this confrontation. This was combined with the possibility of a canal route through the isthmus—it could have been either Panama or Nicaragua—which awakened the imperial powers' (especially England's) lust for this territory ever since the nineteenth century. England and the United States squabbled over the Caribbean throughout the last quarter of the nineteenth century.

Related to this was the occupation of Nicaragua by individual filibusters like William Walker in the middle of the last century, and also the expansionist desires of the United States, which tried to take over all of Central America. It was after the defeat of the Paris Commune that England began to consolidate its colonial domain in Africa and Asia. When the war between the United States and Spain for possession of Cuba was resolved in favor of the United States in 1898, this marked the first division between the world's imperial powers. The United States began to fully exercise its rule over the Caribbean.

The war resulted in the United States taking over Cuba, Puerto Rico, Guam, and the Philippines (the last remaining possessions of the Spanish Empire). It was through this first imperialist war that the United States came to exercise its firm rule over the Caribbean, effectively terminating once and for all British interests in this region—including those in Nicaragua and other parts of Central America.

McKinley began the process, taking over Cuba. It was

continued by Theodore Roosevelt, who appropriated Panama, and [William] Howard Taft, who took Nicaragua. One by one the countries of the Caribbean: Santo Domingo, Haiti, Honduras, as well as Nicaragua, Cuba, and Puerto Rico, came to be occupied by U.S. troops in successive landings. The marines were followed by the bankers. The Big Stick policy was augmented by Dollar Diplomacy, giving way at the beginning of the twentieth century to the famous theses of United States national security and strategic borders. All of these rested on the ideological platform of imperialism: the Monroe Doctrine.

These theses (of national security and strategic borders), far from losing their relevance, have cropped up at various stages of imperialism throughout the twentieth century.

This fundamental contradiction between the Nicaraguan nation and U.S. imperialism was affirmed after the war to take over Cuba, led to the occupation of Nicaragua, continued during Sandino's war and throughout the Somoza dictatorship, and was finally resolved in favor of the Nicaraguan people only on July 19, 1979. It was resolved in the sense that when the people took over their government, that changed the correlation of power. But the contradiction itself remained, in that imperialism is still trying to regain its hegemony over the Nicaraguan nation.

The Sandinista thesis of defense of sovereignty, which was Sandino's first principle in opposition to U.S. occupation, has lost none of its timeliness in Nicaragua, since this contradiction continues today.

A Sandinista concept just as important as that of the defense of sovereignty against intervention and U.S. occupation is the notion of the demise of the parallel tendencies: that is, the disappearance of the traditional oligarchic forces represented by the Conservative and Liberal parties. This would make way for new political forces representing new social forces.

These parallel tendencies came into being during the first Central American independence struggles, even before Nicaragua claimed its independence in 1821. They represented what later came to be the Legitimate Party in Nicaragua, the reactionary forces, those of the clerics and monarchists, who opposed independence efforts. Later this tendency was represented by the Democratic Party or democratic faction, which represented the Creole groups—distinguishing between the royalists, who came directly from Spain, and the Creoles, the children of the Spaniards who were born in the Americas.

The Creoles were an emerging force that tried to break the colonial ties to make way for diversification in their trade and economic interests which the colony could no longer satisfy. These were the partisans of independence. This confrontation continued even after independence was gained in 1821. The forces backed by the Catholic church and the big landowners opposed Morazán's proposal for a Central American federation. Morazán led the Liberal movement that called for a federation of Central American republics patterned after the young federation of the United States—which was the political-democratic model for the Central American countries—as opposed to the Conservatives, who wanted a single Central America, but not under a federal system. They wanted a Central America divided into provinces, with each maintaining its own sovereignty.

When Morazán's efforts were defeated, it was the Conservative scheme that won out in Central America. In Nicaragua the Liberal and Conservative factions fought for power until 1854, when President Fruto Chamorro's government succeeded in incorporating its oligarchic, patriarchal principles, which had been hotly debated since the days of the independence struggle, in the Nicaraguan constitution.

The result was a civil war and Yankee intervention.

After thirty years of Conservative governments, beginning with that of Tomás Martínez, the Liberals took power again in 1893 with the Zelaya administration and the Liberal revolution. This time it was the coffee growers, who had been consolidating their power since the end of the nineteenth century, who took power, representing new interests. The Conservative counterrevolution in 1909 did away with Zelaya and put the Conservative Party back in office, with the backing of the interventionist forces.

These two parallel political forces, the Liberals and the Conservatives, seesawed in power throughout Nicaraguan history—coming head-on in the 1927 Constitutionalist War—until Sandino's arrival. When the Liberal Moncada betrayed the cause in Espino Negro it was clear that, under the U.S. intervention, the only difference between the Liberals and Conservatives was their fight over who would bear the "caress of the foreign whip." It was also clear in the Nicaragua of 1927, when a group of men led by Sandino fought for national sovereignty and independence, that neither of these political forces was capable of responding to the nation's needs. Neither of the two parties accomplice and allied to foreign intervention was capable of representing the nation.

Sandino wanted to break forever with these two forces and recover the country's sovereignty. The struggle against the occupation forces necessarily implied a battle against these parallel forces. The Liberal and Conservative parties were inextricably linked, and for Sandino, to do away with Yankee intervention, expel the invader, meant wiping out these parallel parties. Once foreign forces had left the country, when sovereignty and national independence had been assured, the matter of government within Nicaragua would have to be resolved with a new force, opposed to these parallel tendencies.

That is why Sandino's political plans always spoke of a new party, which would represent the emerging social forces.

Instead of representing the Creole oligarchy, the businessmen, the cattlemen, the coffee growers, it would be linked to the middle sectors, professionals and, above all, it would be a party based on an alliance between workers, peasant farmers, and artisans. The party must provide for the political organization of these forces, which are the ones who struggle against U.S. intervention. They are the miners and hired field hands, the small farmers of northern Nicaragua, the banana plantation workers, the ones who work in the lumber industry, artisans and students, progressive professionals. It was in this sense that Sandino often spoke of a labor party, a new democratic party, an agrarian party. Many names have been given to the projected new party in Nicaragua which would represent these new social forces. But its principal characteristic is that it must be an anti-imperialist party.

What are the economic consequences of the foreign occupation of Nicaragua?

First of all, control of national resources, mines and forests, followed by financial control. We shouldn't forget that when the Big Stick policy and Dollar Diplomacy were introduced in 1910, U.S. bankers literally took over Nicaragua. They took the railroads and customs as collateral for the usurious loans they gave the country; they created a national bank with headquarters in the United States. Financial control of the country was thus added to control of mining and forestry, which existed prior to the arrival of the occupation troops. And along with the control of national resources and finances, we have the problem of being tied to the capitalist markets, especially that of the United States, for export of national raw materials such as coffee.

This was the economic relationship established by the occupation, a relationship of control over the country's resources. To this must be added the internal consequences of oligarchic rule over Nicaragua: the latifundia, the limitation of the agricultural frontiers. That is, the lack of exploration and exploitation of enormous amounts of land, the lack of communication within the country, especially between the Atlantic and Pacific coasts, the very slight development of productive forces. Added to this, a marginalized and forgotten peasantry, and poor development of proletarian forces (which were found primarily in the mining sector, the banana plantations, and the lumber industry). This was due of course to the almost total lack of industrial development of the country in that period.

The most important financial resources were in the hands of the imperialists who dominated the economy and maintained the domestic economic backwardness. They gave the Creole oligarchy that was tied to them only the crumbs of their economic exploitation. The most dynamic sectors: banking, mining, railroads, and customs, were all directly exploited by imperialism.

The Sandinista response to all this was, first, the recovery of all national resources: the mines, the forests and, above all, what Sandino considered to be Nicaragua's greatest resource of all: the canal. For Sandino, the building of a canal wasn't only an economic matter, but one of critical political importance for the country's sovereignty. He insisted that the canal should be built by a company in which the majority interests would be held by Latin Americans. Sandino understood that the construction of a canal through Nicaragua could not be carried out solely through national investment, since there were not sufficient resources available.

Second, Sandino's plan called for the development of farming and the means of communication, the national integration of the Atlantic and Pacific sections of the country.

And third, agrarian reform: an agrarian reform based on nationalization of the land and its organization into peasant cooperatives. Following this economic program, Sandino organized the first peasant cooperatives in Wiwilí, whose members were later massacred when he was assassinated in Managua in 1934.

Having recognized these three antecedents: national sovereignty, popular democracy, and economic transformation, it is important to see that these are reflected in today's Sandinista program.

None of these three basic lines have lost their relevance. On the contrary, they remain relevant because there is a program of national transformation in progress.

First of all we have defense of our sovereignty. It is possible to defend it in the context of the Sandinista people's revolution because the hegemonistic force of the revolution represents the interests of the workers, the peasantry—of the revolutionary sectors of the country, which have the same class composition as Sandino's Army for the Defense of National Sovereignty of Nicaragua.

Just as the field hands, the artisans, miners, and small farmers were those who united to defend Nicaragua's national sovereignty in 1927, while the ruling groups of landlords and businessmen were embroiled with the intervention, this same clear delineation of forces has reappeared throughout the revolutionary process that began in 1979.

In the context of revolutionary rule it is possible to defend our nation's sovereignty because the Sandinista front represents the interests of the people, of the working class and peasantry; because there is an army that has this same class composition and perspective; the perspective Sandino had in 1927.

Neither Sandino nor his army represented a mixture of class interests. The Yankee intervention itself had defined the two camps and divided the classes for or against Nicaraguan sovereignty.

In addition to our military defense forces, the development of Sandinista political ideas in foreign policy makes it possible to defend our sovereignty. Throughout his struggle

Sandino formed his own foreign policy based on the concept of a broad, worldwide—but especially Latin American—anti-imperialist alliance.

It would be an anti-imperialist alliance that would allow political space to develop the military efforts in defense of Nicaraguan sovereignty. It would include political parties of various ideological types under one anti-imperialist banner, along with trade unions and workers' groups, and civic organizations from all over the continent. This political force would induce some Latin American governments to act in solidarity with them. The focus would always be on consolidating all forces against the imperialist advance in Latin America, because imperialist control of Nicaragua would lead to its control over all Central America, the fall of Mexico and the rest of the Latin American countries.

Sandino always placed great stress on this. In the face of this imminent danger he wanted one single strategy to confront imperialism with a wide-ranging effort by Latin American and global political forces.

There is a similarity between Sandino's ideas and the foreign policy of the Sandinista people's revolution: that of defending their efforts to consolidate the revolution on the international plane through a broad alliance in support of the revolution. This has been carried out through the Nicaraguan government's membership in the Nonaligned movement and various other alliances the revolutionary government has tried to set up around the world in support of the revolutionary process.

Sandino's idea of popular democracy when he called for the elimination of the parallel parties and the emergence of a new political force is being carried out and developed by the Sandinista people's revolution.

The revolution has at last made it possible for these noxious traditional political forces to disappear. As a new class takes power, the displaced classes, along with the parties representing their interests, are also displaced. And that new emerging force that Sandino dreamed of will replace them. That new force is the Sandinista National Liberation Front (FSLN).

Popular democracy can be developed by the Sandinista front through the bodies of people's power, which include the revolutionary government, the Council of State, and all the other forms of popular government that the revolution promotes through all phases of national life. This possibility of consolidating popular rule has also made it possible to develop and strengthen plans for popular democracy throughout the country. Once freed of foreign domination in national political life, freed from the influence of foreign forms of government and the rule by those parallel parties, it is possible to move entirely toward new forms of organization for running the country, to the benefit of the new class that is now in power.

The Sandinista revolution replaced the foreign and oligarchic interests, which in Sandino's time dominated national life, and which continued to do so in different forms under the dictatorship of the Somoza family. The Somozas ruled over an agricultural-export capitalist economy, followed by an industrial, banking, and financial one. When the Sandinistas replaced these classes in power, they also took over the economic reins of the country. This initiated a Sandinista economic program which also has its seeds in the ideas of Sandino.

It begins with the recovery of Nicaragua's national resources, its mines, forests, and fishing resources which were all in foreign hands. This was achieved through the nationalization of important sectors of the economy, finances, insurance, industry, commerce, transportation—by declaring these areas property of the people. But above all, referring to the ideas of Sandino, it is expressed through the agrarian reform program, through the political preference the revolution has given to the agricultural production cooperatives. To Sandino, these were the core of his agrarian reform: nationalization of the land and the organization of peasant cooperatives.

All of these measures, developed during the years of revolution, are the bases that open the way for a new economy and the organization of a new society.

We can't say that all the ideas that motivate the revolutionary Sandinista program were in Sandino's mind, were part of his plans. We're talking about another period of time, with different circumstances. While it is true that the intervention, the contradiction, and the enemy are the same, the development of productive forces in the country is different. They are of a different quality. The evolution of social forces in Nicaragua also reflects two different eras. But the basic ideas which resulted from that fundamental contradiction have remained unchanged throughout history. They came to bear fruit during the Sandinista people's revolution, beginning with the class concept which Sandino had already clearly established in his struggle. This is the basis of the identity between the two eras. It is in this clear class interest that we find the necessary connection between Sandino's ideas of nationhood, of sovereignty; the Sandinista popular antioligarchic idea, and the necessary scientific conception that the ideology of the revolution must have. That revolutionary ideology is based simultaneously on Sandino's thinking and on the scientific concept of history, on universal scientific concepts.

Economic production is the rear guard of the battle front

The following two documents were prepared in connection with the Third National Assembly of Unions, held in Managua September 8 and 9, 1984. The first, "Base Document of the National Assembly of Unions," was drafted prior to the assembly by the national leadership of the Sandinista Workers Federation (CST) and circulated for discussion to the union delegates. The second, "Resolutions of the Assembly," contains the preamble and ten resolutions adopted by the assembly. The assembly was attended by more than 600 union leaders, including delegates from the CST, the Association of Rural Workers, the National Union of Employees, the Health Workers Federation, the National Association of Nicaraguan Educators, and the Nicaraguan Journalists Union. This translation originally appeared in the November 26, 1984, issue of *Intercontinental Press*.

BASE DOCUMENT OF THE NATIONAL ASSEMBLY OF UNIONS

I. Introduction

Barely four years after the First Assembly of Trade Union Federations and Organizations for the Unity of the Workers, which was held in Managua November 15 and 16, 1980, the revolutionary working class of Nicaragua—the foundation and motor force of the whole process of economic, social, and political transformations in our country—confronts new situations and larger and more serious problems that require of us higher levels of consciousness and organization, greater united efforts, and a more active, dynamic, and combative presence of the unions.

In that historic assembly, all the union federations shared a basic concern: to economically revive the country, to achieve traditional levels of production in the shortest possible time, to push forward a powerful development of the productive forces, and to lay the foundations for a truly national economy that serves the toiling majority.

In the five commissions that were created at that assembly, important aspects such as the following were analyzed and discussed in depth, starting from the proposition that "the economy was the main problem of the revolution" (conclusions).

1. Increase production and productivity.

2. Improve the working conditions and social services and increase wages in line with Nicaragua's economic situation.

3. Maintain strict revolutionary discipline in the work centers.

4. Settle labor conflicts without halting production.

To a great extent these proposals retain their validity, and to some degree the proposals and conclusions of that first assembly have set the guidelines for our trade union and labor activity in the four years since then, along with the policies implemented by the revolutionary government. In a summary and descriptive analysis we can point to some advances in the road traveled since then.

1. In many places, even having sufficient inputs and parts, we still have not reached the historic levels of production and productivity.

2. From 1981 to the middle of 1983, our working conditions and social services underwent important growth, which is now being pushed backward due to the aggression.

3. Our union forces have not actively closed ranks around labor discipline.

4. Despite our commitment to resolve labor conflicts without halting production, it is true that strikes have persisted, including in centers that are very vital to defense.

II. Principal achievements and difficulties of the revolution

The fundamental achievement of the revolution is the maintenance and defense of revolutionary power.

The policy of agro-industrial development of the country is the basis of the transformations in economic activity, expressed in the agrarian reform.

A total of 1.6 million manzanas of land have been turned over to cooperatives and individual producers, benefiting more than 30,000 families. This has reduced the latifundist sector, typical of the backward and dependent economy of Latin America, from 41 percent to 11 percent, and led to setting up a cooperative movement with more than 3,000 cooperatives covering 10 percent of the land.

Accompanying the transformation in landholding has been technical assistance, rural credit, and cancellation of peasant debts in the amount of 328 million córdobas.

Agro-industrial and infrastructural projects are moving forward and are at various stages of completion:

• The Tipitapa-Malacatoya sugar mill, with advanced technology, which will mean jobs for 5,000 workers when fully completed.

• Chiltepe project, aimed at increasing cattle production, based on advanced techniques and obtaining purebred cattle.

• The African Palm project, in Cuckra Hill and El Castillo and exploitation of coconuts and rubber.

- An increase in "Burley" tobacco production and completion of the Sébaco Valley Agro-Industrial Complex.
- Regarding infrastructure and energy development, in addition to finishing the first unit of the Patricio Argüello Geothermal project, the second unit is moving ahead, as are the Mojolca-Copalar, Asturias, and Lareynaga hydroelectric projects. Some 2,260 kilometers of electrical power lines have been installed.
- The MASA project, with the construction and expansion of storage depots for basic grains, to facilitate their distribution.

The total investment planned for 1984 reaches the sum of 6.65 billion córdobas, of which 73.9 percent is destined for infrastructure and the productive sector, and the remaining 26.1 percent for the social sector.

Regarding the volume of agricultural exports, while it is true that there will be a slight growth in nearly all the products, this will not meet the requirements in hard currencies we need in order to survive. As a result of the fall in the price of exports and the rise in the price of imported products, between 1980 and 1983 Nicaragua lost a total of US$764 million, putting our trade balance in deficit and raising the foreign debt.

Regarding manufacturing production, the ongoing problem has been the lack of foreign currency for imports of raw materials and parts.

Regarding social improvements—housing, health, education, existing social security, and all policies aimed at benefiting the workers—the economic budgetary limitations mean that their effects do not reach everyone nor do we reach the levels desired.

Nonetheless, due to the war, we are going through an ever more critical situation that strikes at the aspirations of the working population for a better material and spiritual life.

- The relative reduction in the supply of products resulting from increased demand, the shortage of hard currency, and inflation have led to a rise in the prices of basic and nonbasic products, hitting at the wages of workers.

- The commissaries in the companies and work centers and the Rural Supply Centers no longer guarantee a practical and efficient supply of goods. But they have not been replaced by the network of local outlets and grocery stores organized on a territorial basis. This network displays organizational weaknesses and shortcomings and does not even guarantee the availability of basic necessities.
- The lack of medicines is negatively affecting the population, despite the achievements in preventive medicine, the extension of health services into the countryside, etc.
- Transit systems, both within and between cities, and freight transportation cause problems for riders and in supplying the population.
- The lack of spare parts, inputs, and raw materials makes it difficult and sometimes almost impossible to meet goals and sometimes jeopardizes jobs.

III. We are at war

Today more than ever, above and beyond the problems of the economy is the problem of imperialist war. The main problem facing the revolution is not the economy, as was the case in 1980.

We are waging a war to the death in defense of our sovereignty and independence, to safeguard our gains and revolutionary power.

This aggression is being waged by a great economic and military power against a small country that must make extraordinary efforts to repel it and survive. We are forced to pay a big price in blood and sacrifice in order to maintain our dignity and national honor, and we pay a big price in material resources we are forced to invest above and beyond our economic possibilities.

The aggression goes beyond financial and commercial strangulation. It uses ideological campaigns of defamation and disinformation. It makes use of national and international reactionary political forces, sabotage, and destruction of economic and social objectives. All this has the aim of breaking up the revolutionary power, weakening our defensive capabilities, and creating the conditions for a direct military invasion by the United States.

In addition to the high defense expenditures used to confront the aggression, we have suffered losses of $1.04 billion through the destruction of productive centers, the mined ports, the sabotage, etc. This is $200 million more than the value of exports in the years 1982 and 1983 taken together. In a period of world crisis and recession, this drain is hard for any country's economy to withstand.

The human losses, counting combatants and civilians, are approximately 9,000 dead. At the same time hundreds of Nicaraguans, especially Miskito Indians, have been kidnapped and forced to join the counterrevolutionary ranks. Many others have been displaced and forced to leave their homes and fields to be resettled in more secure zones, thereby affecting production. In two years the area harvested has declined by 11.6 percent, and perspectives are not good.

The aggression will not stop, with or without elections, nor will the Contadora or Manzanillo negotiations stop it. However, the solidarity of the peoples of Asia, Africa, Europe, and the Americas, and within the Americas the support of the Contadora countries, will serve as a containment wall against the warlike policy of U.S. imperialism. At this very moment the United States has laid down all the logistical and infrastructural preconditions for a direct invasion of El Salvador or Nicaragua, which could take place at any time, even before the U.S. presidential elections.

The revolutionary forces and the working class must marshal all their energies and be prepared to fight and produce in line with defense needs without sparing efforts, risks, or sacrifices. All this makes our economy an economy of resistance in order to survive and triumph. An economy subjected to ever greater tensions.

In the face of the sharpening problems, the working class, the organized laboring people must fundamentally utilize resources of a moral and ideological type. In the face of the impossibility of satisfying material needs, their convictions are put to the test. Today the working class of Nicaragua, the unions, have before them the following challenges:

1. Strengthen and consolidate the military defense forces ranging from the Sandinista People's Army to the revolutionary vigilance.

2. Work for the approval in all work centers of norms of production that would allow us to reach the historic output, guarantee the achievement of the planned goals, and make up for the compañeros mobilized at the battlefront.

3. Resolve labor problems and conflicts through negotiations without halting production.

4. Seeing the possibility of pockets of hunger as a result of scarcity and the escalating war, we support distribution on a territorial basis, ensuring a correct distribution of existing supplies.

5. We ask the revolutionary government to finalize the application of the first subsystem of the National System for the Organization of Work and Wages and to begin immediately the revision of the wage scales.

For the building of socialism . . .
Let's go forward with the Front!

RESOLUTIONS OF THE ASSEMBLY

The fundamental step taken by Nicaraguan workers to carry out the transformation of the political, economic, and social structures and to build a new society free of all exploitation was taken on July 19, 1979, with the conquest of political power.

The desire to build a new society inevitably leads us into antagonistic contradictions with imperialism, whose lifeblood is *exploitation.*

This has meant that step by step as we advance in reaffirming our national sovereignty, self-determination, and economic independence, imperialism increases its aggressive actions, trying to return us to a past of domination.

This means that our people had to pay and continue to pay a huge price in blood and sacrifices.

This imperialist aggression has forced us to turn our economy of reconstruction into a war economy, because all our efforts in production must be directed toward supporting military defense.

Economic production becomes the rear guard of the battle fronts, placing all the nation's resources at the disposal of the war effort. This demands of us workers a greater degree of discipline, spirit of sacrifice, and willingness to fight than we needed to overthrow the *somocista* dictatorship.

We must not forget that our productive efforts can be carried out in such a way that we achieve increases in production, raising productivity to the highest level; that our efforts can make it possible to obtain more products, which would allow us to meet the needs of the people and gradually improve our standard of living.

On the basis of this analysis, the Nicaraguan workers, meeting in the National Assembly of Unions have committed ourselves to a process of assemblies with all the workers to discuss the following resolutions:

1. To strengthen and consolidate the military defense forces, from the patriotic military service to revolutionary vigilance.

Defense of our power means our involvement in all forms of defense.

Those who have the greatest obligation to defend the power of the workers are the workers themselves, because we defend not only the right to organize ourselves, but also the right to health, to housing, to work, to life itself, as well as the right to our future and that of our children.

We workers are ready to become a firm rear guard of the battle front in order to defeat the imperialist aggression and prevail over it.

2. To struggle so that in all workplaces norms of production are worked out that permit us to achieve the highest possible productivity per worker, in line with the productive experience of each workplace.

We workers must raise the levels of production and productivity to bolster the war fronts and to maintain our people's levels of subsistence, as well as to strengthen our economy through strategic investments. This is not possible without the development of a conscious discipline to make maximum use of the working day. Through this we will gain the moral authority needed to criticize administrative shortcomings and to push forward, together with the state, policies to correct them.

3. To resolve labor problems and conflicts by means of negotiations, without halting production.

We workers must be conscious that every work stoppage means a weakening of our economy and would facilitate imperialist pretexts for an invasion.

The strike is a form of struggle utilized by the workers against their class enemy, the capitalist exploiter. This form of struggle has no place in Nicaragua, because *power* is in the hands of the workers.

4. To support distribution on a territorial basis, making sure that there is a correct distribution of stocks of goods.

We believe that territorial distribution is the fairest way to equitably share the few resources we have and thereby guarantee our subsistence.

In face of the possibility of pockets of hunger as a result of the sharpening war, we workers must push forward family and institutional gardens.

We are in favor of improving strict control over production, and we demand effective application of the Consumer Law [against hoarding and speculation].

At the same time, in the Regional Supply Commissions we will propose that in periods when trucks in our workplaces are underutilized they be used to help bring in basic products. These trucks are resources that can help the Ministry of Internal Trade to bring products from the production areas and to deliver them to local outlets.

5. To ask the revolutionary government to finalize the application of the first subsystem of the National System for the Organization of Work and Wages, dealing with categorization, and that the government immediately begin the revision of wage scales.

We workers must be conscious that the National System for the Organization of Work and Wages has yet to be applied to various sectors of workers and that it is necessary to conclude this stage in order to enter the stage of revision.

Also, we request that the revolutionary government put a stop to the incorrect practice of some administrators and directors who encourage wage anarchy by not applying the provisions of the National System for the Organization of Work and Wages.

6. To review the purchase at cost of goods produced in our work centers.

We workers must review the allotments of goods produced in our factories that are set aside for each of us. This practice is an obstacle to the rational distribution of our resources and encourages speculation; therefore we call for reducing assigned allotments.

7. To organize Sandinista *emulation* in the work centers.

We workers must promote an attitude of emulation, of

imitating the best worker or group of workers, with the goal of raising production and labor productivity, providing moral and material incentives to the best workers.

8. To recognize international solidarity.

We recognize the solidarity of the workers of the world in condemning the imperialist aggression that the Nicaraguan people suffer, and we encourage them to continue demonstrating their effective solidarity by means of material aid through shipments of inputs, medicines, spare parts, and agricultural tools in line with their abilities.

9. Absolute support for the FSLN Plan of Struggle.

With firmness and conviction we support the FSLN Plan of Struggle, which is the plan of struggle of the Nicaraguan workers and of all our people.

10. To fulfill these great challenges, the leaders participating in the National Assembly of Unions commit ourselves to maintain close ties with our rank and file, to constantly explain the main problems no matter how hard they are, and to overcome organizational failings and deficiencies in order to meet this historic challenge.

More productivity!
More discipline!
More organization!
Greater production!
Everything for the war fronts!
Everything for the fighters!
Long live the Sandinista people's revolution!

We had difficulty in grasping the ethnic character of the Miskito problem

by Tomás Borge

The following letter was originally published in the September–December 1984 inaugural issue of the magazine *Wani*. *Wani*, which describes itself as "a magazine about the Atlantic Coast," publishes articles in Spanish, English, and Miskito. The translation from Spanish for this volume is by Michael Taber.

Dear compañeros at *Wani*,

Much is said about Nicaragua's Atlantic Coast, but very little is known about it. Some believe that Miskitos are the only inhabitants of the Atlantic Coast, and many errors have arisen from this misconception. This region, in fact, covers 56 percent of Nicaragua's territory; it contains a conglomerate of ethnic groups as well as the so-called Miskito problem.

It is the Miskito population above all that has seen itself entangled in the struggle between revolution and counterrevolution. In the months following the triumph, we knew little of the particularities of each of the ethnic groups on the Atlantic Coast. Revolutionary government cadres, with much enthusiasm but with a certain lack of knowledge of these peoples' history, wanted to change everything overnight. Without giving much thought to the consequences, we wanted to develop on the Atlantic Coast structures and projects similar to those on the Pacific. Along with our good intentions we carried with us a certain amount of naïveté. For historical reasons, the Miskitos did not understand the revolutionary changes.

Along with the mutual lack of understanding between the revolution and the Miskitos, concrete actions were taken for which we cannot avoid responsibility. However, the war situation in this frontier region of the Atlantic Coast explains many of our errors and precipitous actions.

The resettlement of 10,000 Miskitos from along the edge of the Coco River to the Tasba Pri settlements in February 1982 marks the most important step in this contradictory process. Social reality and media pressure made the Miskitos newsworthy. We had to relocate them or they would have been killed, because they were in the middle of battles our forces were waging against the counterrevolution. It was a matter of survival. This explains the urgency of the resettlement.

The Miskitos were always isolated from national life. They were used by the British, the North Americans, and by Somoza. The revolution could have done the same as Somoza. We could have put off until later dealing with their backward and miserable conditions. But this would go against our revolutionary will of not abandoning this people.

It was the revolution that opened the way and gave all its support to the development of community organizations. At the end of 1979, MISURASATA arose, uniting in one organization the ethnic groups of the Atlantic Coast (Miskitos, Sumos, and Ramas), increasing the ethnic consciousness to a greater degree than ever before. Then the counterrevolution entered the picture. The leaders of this organization (principally Steadman Fagoth) converted it into a prop of the ideological radicalization that had been forged previously. They played upon the contradictions between old and new that the revolution implies.

MISURASATA, an organization created to advance the new national projections for the Atlantic Coast was converted instead into an alternative allied with the counterrevolution. The imperialist strategists at that moment grasped that the Sandinista national program did not adequately understand the Miskito problem, that it lacked experience. The imperialists therefore made it into one of their preferred points of attack, distorting the problem on the international level.

We had difficulty in grasping the ethnic character of the Miskito problem, because of our big weaknesses in confronting it correctly. Manipulating the Miskito leaders, the U.S. administration has made it appear that the Miskitos' passage over to Honduras was a people fleeing savage repression. This is what is being presented and what is known abroad. They don't take into account the powerful propaganda spread by counterrevolutionary radio, as well as the fact that the border has never existed as far as the Miskitos are concerned.

Once the Miskitos had gone to Honduras, they received military training and the contradiction between the ethnic group and the national state ceased being only a political problem, but became a military problem as well. Despite this, we have attempted to convince the Miskitos to return to their communities, to return to their land. We decreed an amnesty for the Miskitos involved in counterrevolutionary action. Many have returned; there are also many who would like to return but were instilled with terror by claims that the Sandinistas are going to kill them.

What can imperialism offer the Atlantic Coast? If we rely on experience, the only things that it can bring are hundreds of Miskito miners without lungs, the disappearance of the remaining forests, more illness for the people, and greater cultural backwardness.

Very much to the contrary, the revolution, with all the limitations imposed on us by imperialism's economic and military aggression, has tried to fulfill its historic program for the Atlantic Coast. The revolution opened the door behind which the Miskito people's dignity was hidden. With the revolution the Miskitos have recovered their dignity. They have resurged as a people.

Unlike the past, no one in Nicaragua today is afraid to speak Miskito. They have no fear of being considered inferior.

The government has supported and promoted all forms of organization within Atlantic Coast society. Currently there are radio programs in the Indian languages, various publications in Miskito and Sumo, a long-playing record ("Saumuk Raya") and other expressions of cultural identity. In addition, the government has begun a project of bilingual education through the fourth grade.

Only a few days ago MISATAN (Organization of Nicaraguan Miskitos) was created, with the participation of sixty-three Atlantic Coast communities. Its decision to organize itself and challenge the counterrevolution's threats, is a dignified act of the Miskito people. They are demonstrating that the hope for life and a peaceful development is stronger than the counterrevolution's desperation and terror.

The health centers on the Atlantic Coast have increased from twenty-six to forty-four, in addition to building the Bluefields hospital and repairing the ones at Bilwaskarma, Puerto Cabezas, Bonanza, Rosita, and Siuna. Many of these health centers have been destroyed by the counterrevolution.

The number of medical and paramedical personnel has tripled. However, the counterrevolution's robbery and destruction of medicines and medical equipment has left an irreparable toll, not only in resources but in human lives.

In spite of this, there is an important tuberculosis treatment campaign, and already 771 miners suffering from lung diseases have received pensions, the majority of them Miskitos.

Illiteracy, which before the revolution's victory reached 80 percent on the Atlantic Coast, has been significantly reduced. A total of 480 new schools have been built, incorporating 855 teachers. From 1979 to 1983 the number of students rose by 226 percent, despite the counterrevolutionary propaganda.

The agrarian reform has benefited Miskito communities with more than 2,000 manzanas of land.

But can anyone say that we've already solved the difficulties? Many things remain to be done; many things need to be improved. But these difficulties are not the problem of the people of the Atlantic Coast alone. The entire Nicaraguan people suffer from them. They are the product of our inherited backwardness and of the unjust war being waged against the Nicaraguan people by the most powerful capitalist country in the world. The economic crisis we're enduring often prevents us from satisfying all the needs of the new settlements. The shortage of basic products afflicts the whole Nicaraguan people. As a result of our lack of resources, we have deficiencies in the transportation of food, medicine, and other basic goods, and this makes the situation on the Atlantic Coast even more critical.

The revolution, that vast river of clean water, offers the people of the Atlantic Coast the possibility of happiness and land; but first we must achieve peace. Peace will enable the river to make our land fertile, so that it can run free, without a dam impeding its flow. We must first achieve peace to maintain unity and to advance, so that in the future the Miskitos and the people of the Atlantic Coast will be able to enjoy the water of the rivers and the song of the birds, so that there will be bread and work for all.

For the revolution, the fundamental demand is the right to be an independent and sovereign nation, to build and develop a just and humane social system for the entire Nicaraguan people. This necessarily signifies connecting and linking the Atlantic Coast to the Nicaraguan identity, achieving the unity of a people that speaks different languages, achieving peace for Nicaraguans to live in.

It's up to us Nicaraguans, us revolutionaries, to show the truth to the world. Therefore, the collaboration the magazine *Wani* will offer in analyzing the problems of the Atlantic Coast will play an important role. It will tell the truth to the world about our revolutionary program, of our dreams of the Atlantic and Pacific becoming brothers for all time, building a new homeland. We should study the particularities, the culture, the beliefs, and finally come to know the people of the Atlantic Coast. Only in this way will we be able to forge closer relations and look for specific solutions to the problems we confront today and those we will face in the future. Only the unity of the entire Nicaraguan people will guarantee our revolution's victory, the victory of justice and peace.

The U.S. is escalating its military and economic aggression against Nicaragua

by Daniel Ortega

The following speech was given October 2, 1984, in New York to the General Assembly of the United Nations. The translation is from the UN's provisional verbatim record.

On behalf of the Nicaragua delegation, sir [addressing Paul Lusaka of Zambia], I should like to express our satisfaction at your election as president of the thirty-ninth session of the General Assembly.

We also extend a brotherly welcome to the people and government of Brunei Darussalam on the occasion of its entry into the community of independent nations.

The United Nations came into being as a result of the cry of the peoples of the world, who, tired of wars, exploitation, and extermination, sought an organization that would help them to combat and fend off the Four Horsemen of the Apocalypse. No one can ignore the United Nations' efforts in defense of peace, justice, freedom, and the independence of peoples.

But, most unfortunately for mankind, there are policies, backed up by nuclear weapons, which blackmail, threaten, and attack the principles of the United Nations Charter. There are those that have characterized themselves by their defiance, mockery, and undermining of resolutions of this organization. There are those that have defended actions that are shocking in their irrationality and threaten the future of all mankind.

In Asia, Africa, the Middle East, Latin America, and Central America such policies are characterized by the use of force and disregard the nature of the historical problems affecting the peoples of those regions. They are aimed at solving social and economic problems by killing the hungry and ensuring the maintenance of the status quo for privileged minorities. These policies ignore the economic crisis affecting the peoples and are based on a theory of natural selection that clearly favors the most powerful and accelerates the arms race. This explains why there are those who continue to oppose the demands for immediate collective action in search of solutions to economic problems, thus really fighting for peace and development.

Nicaragua has been a victim of such a policy since the last century and throughout this century, with its legacy of backwardness, brutal exploitation, and the absence of justice and freedom—in short, the absence of democracy. Such was the Somoza dictatorship, the last monstrous offspring of this policy.

Today Nicaragua is free and for the first time in its history is building an authentic democracy, becoming an example of patriotism, nationalism, independence, and nonalignment. This is not to the liking of the United States.

When Nicaragua condemns the South African regime for its racist policies and for subjugating those who should be the rightful rulers of that land, it is not to the liking of the United States.

When Nicaragua voices its solidarity with Mozambique, Angola, Zambia, Seychelles, Lesotho, Botswana, and Swaziland, as well as with the African National Congress (ANC) and the South West Africa People's Organisation (SWAPO), the sole legitimate representative of the Namibian people, this, too, is not to the liking of the United States.

When Nicaragua demands Israel's unconditional withdrawal from the occupied territories and the right of the Palestinian people to exist as a people and nation, recognizing the Palestine Liberation Organization as their only representative, this, too, is not to the liking of the United States government.

When Nicaragua reaffirms its solidarity with the people and the government of the Sahraoui Arab Democratic Republic, when we condemn the policy of provocation against the Libyan Arab Jamahiriya, and when we express our support for the just cause of the people of East Timor, this, too, is not to the liking of the United States government.

When Nicaragua condemns the policy of aggression against Vietnam, Laos, and Kampuchea, when we support the reunification of Korea and the withdrawal of foreign troops from South Korea, and when we support an end to military maneuvers and shows of force, this, too, is not to the liking of the United States government.

Nor is it to the liking of the United States government that Nicaragua defends Puerto Rico's right to self-determination and independence, the return of Guantánamo to its legitimate owners, an end to threats to Cuba's integrity, the sovereignty of the Argentine people and nation over the Malvinas and the complete implementation of the Panama treaties, and an end to attacks launched from United States bases there against the peoples of Central America and the Caribbean.

When Nicaragua condemns the brutal coup against democracy in Chile and at the same time supports the right of the Chilean people to reestablish their basic freedoms, it is not to the liking of the United States government.

When Nicaragua condemns the heinous crime committed in the name of freedom against the people of Grenada and demands the withdrawal of foreign occupation troops so that the Grenadian people can exercise their right to free self-determination, this, too, is not to the liking of the United States government.

When Nicaragua supports a negotiated, peaceful settlement to the conflict in El Salvador which the Salvadoran people themselves must settle, this, too, is not to the liking of the United States government.

When Nicaragua supports democratic change in Latin America as a first step in solving the problems faced by our peoples, this, too, is not to the liking of the United States government.

Nicaragua rejects the dismemberment of the state of Cyprus and the proclamation of the so-called Republic of Northern Cyprus and defends the unity, sovereignty, and territorial integrity of this fellow nonaligned nation.

Nicaragua reaffirms its support for Bolivia's efforts to regain direct access to the Pacific Ocean.

Nicaragua is also saddened by the confrontation between two nonaligned nations—Iran and Iraq—and demands an end to the use of chemical weapons; we support attempts to reach a just and honorable solution to this conflict.

Because Nicaragua wants peace, justice, freedom, and democracy for the world, we shall continue to be nonaligned, even though this may not be to the liking of the United States authorities and even though this is not to the liking of the United States authorities.

Because Nicaragua wants peace, justice, freedom, and democracy for the peoples of the world, we shall continue to condemn colonialism, neocolonialism, imperialism, apartheid, and racism and we shall continue to support just causes around the world, even though this may not be to the liking of the United States authorities and even though it means more sacrifice, suffering, threats, and extermination for the heroic people of Sandino.

Forty years ago, all humanity celebrated the end of a nightmare. Five years were enough to witness all the horrors of fascism which far surpassed Dante's inferno.

But today, our country, Nicaragua, a small nation of only 3 million people, is the victim of a policy of extermination manifested over the past three years and eight months in the form of an open war of aggression which the aggressor calls covert.

That policy is manifested when the United States administration provides millions of dollars to go on murdering the peoples of Nicaragua and El Salvador; when it debates the irresponsibility of the Central Intelligence Agency (CIA) in not having informed the Senate Intelligence Committee in advance about the mining of Nicaraguan ports rather than debate the terrorist act of laying the mines; when United States Army helicopters and United States citizens—also casualties of this interventionist policy—have fallen in our country; when children, young people, women, teachers, and doctors are murdered and the people's production, schools, and food stocks are destroyed; when the decision of the International Court of Justice at The Hague and United Nations resolutions are rejected, with the United States deeming itself judge and executioner of the nations of the earth.

This entails a violation of the United States' own internal legislation and of international law.

Nicaragua wishes to reaffirm before this assembly its belief in the validity of the [UN] charter and its willingness to resolve peacefully international situations and conflicts through the means established in the charter and under international law, prominent among which is the right to petition the International Court of Justice in The Hague.

That is why we have been making countless efforts on

behalf of peace for the people of Nicaragua and the peoples of Central America. That is why Nicaragua turned to the International Court of Justice, whose decision of May 10, 1984, could not have been clearer in ordering the United States government to halt immediately military and paramilitary actions against Nicaragua, because these constitute clear and serious violations of international law and of Nicaragua's right to determine freely its own future. Its disdain and contempt of the court's ruling were condemned by the international community.

In fact everything indicates that these efforts and Nicaragua's unwavering willingness to achieve peace are not respected by the United States government, which has been escalating its military and economic aggression against Nicaragua. To each peace initiative by Nicaragua and the Contadora group, the United States government has responded with terrorist attacks, the installation of military bases, and a whole infrastructure for unleashing direct, massive military action against Nicaragua.

For almost two years the member countries of the Contadora group have been making a noble and serious effort to promote peace in Central America. This effort has enjoyed broad support from the whole world, including the Security Council and this General Assembly. As a result of that work, on September 7 the Contadora group presented to the countries of Central America the Act of Peace and Cooperation in Central America.

Now it is for the Central American governments and the United States government—whose involvement in the conflict cannot be denied by anyone—to state clearly and definitively their positions. Nicaragua has already done so. On September 21 we officially communicated to the governments of the Contadora countries our decision to sign the act of September 7 immediately, without amendments or changes of any kind, exactly as it was written by the Contadora group.

Today before this assembly, before the conscience of the world, we solemnly reaffirm Nicaragua's decision and we call on the leaders of the countries of Central America to join us in supporting the act, in the interest of the peace and tranquility of our peoples. At the same time, we applaud the support given to the act by the governments of the European Economic Community and Spain and Portugal at the recent conference held in San José [Costa Rica].

The United States authorities have said they support Contadora. Their diplomats have tirelessly traveled around our region and the world claiming they defend those negotiations and peace. The international community has the right to expect the United States government to support the Contadora act unconditionally by immediately voicing its willingness to sign the additional protocol.

The winds now blowing over Central America presage of a holocaust for our peoples. Today as we appeal for peace in this body, which itself emerged from the ruins of war in order to fight for peace, Nicaragua continues to be subjected to the genocide of the terrorist policies of the United States authorities.

Amidst all this horror, we are making truly exceptional efforts to institutionalize—by means of elections—our democratic, nationalist, nonaligned, pluralist revolution, which defends a mixed economic system.

However, despite these efforts to reconstruct our country and to institutionalize democracy, the number of victims grows. To date more than 7,000 Nicaraguans have been casualties—including children, mothers, youth and the elderly—which in relative terms is equivalent to more than three times the number of American casualties in the Vietnam war.

Moreover, there is the daily damage done to the economy by the direct impact of foreign aggression. Cooperatives, health centers, schools, machinery, construction equipment, day-care centers, food stocks, and houses are being destroyed by this daily policy of terror. Our losses during the period 1981 to 1984 total $237 million. This would represent for the United States and the European Economic Community, on a percentage basis, $102 billion and $284 billion respectively of their export earnings during the same period. To these figures should be added the credits, loans, grants, and so on that Nicaragua no longer receives as a result of United States pressure on governments and multilateral agencies.

Nicaragua is today a country besieged, attacked, and subjected to an unjust and illegal war, which is in danger of spreading. The United States has installed an impressive military infrastructure in Honduran territory bordering on Nicaragua. Its military presence has also been imposed on Costa Rican territory bordering on Nicaragua. United States warships are deployed menacingly off our coasts, and United States spy aircraft and military aircraft violate our airspace.

Dozens of mercenaries, among them United States citizens working for the Central Intelligence Agency (CIA), pilot the planes and helicopters that launch attacks against economic, civilian, and military targets and keep the aggressor forces supplied. Thousands of mercenaries function like a full-fledged army from their bases in Honduras and Costa Rica in operations coordinated and directed from military bases in Panama still occupied by the United States.

New plans are being worked out in the Pentagon and the CIA, this time to prevent the elections of November 4 in Nicaragua. Among other actions, they are contemplating renewed mining of our ports, aerial and naval attacks, and the seizing of various areas.

The military offensive is ready to begin on October 15 of this year. The mercenary forces of the CIA and the Pentagon are already concentrated in the areas bordering Nicaragua in Honduras and Costa Rica.

Also ready are the United States forces that would be used for bombings, troop landings, and direct incursions into Nicaragua.

The Central American governments are also prepared. They will go through the formality of requesting "aid" from the United States to eradicate the "Sandinista threat" from the area. And also ready is the "Paul Scoon," the puppet who would be intended to serve as the future president of the United States of Nicaragua. They have the actors in their assigned places with their roles memorized. Also prepared are the estimates of United States casualties during such an intervention. This amounts to an attempt to repeat the destructive and shameful actions against Grenada, but this time against Nicaragua.

From August 12, 1981, until September 26, 1984, Nicaragua made countless efforts on behalf of peace in bilateral talks with the United States, meeting with representatives of the United States government on sixteen occasions.

Despite the concrete proposals presented by Nicaragua, the United States has always responded evasively or with proposals which can only be described as lacking in seriousness.

In Manzanillo, Mexico, Nicaragua has been very clear, consistent, and flexible in responding to the concerns of the United States, which claims to feel its security in the region threatened by the Nicaraguan revolution.

We have been firm and reasonable in proposing specific measures which would create a framework for mutual security for the United States and Nicaragua.

The Nicaragua people, who yearn for peace, are willing to continue defending their independence, freedom, self-determination, and democracy.

We know that the United States leaders are victims of their own history of intervention and aggression. There is not a corner of the world that has not suffered in one way or another the effects of these policies. All humanity must call upon the United States leaders to be level-headed and prudent.

At this session of the General Assembly, in this month of October 1984, the people of Nicaragua want to go on record as voicing their desire for peace, while defending freedom, justice, and democracy.

If peace does not come and the war continues, and with it the likelihood of United States military intervention, we want the world to know that the Nicaraguan people—barefoot, ragged, and with empty stomachs—are going to fight to the end, until we achieve peace, by either defeating the invaders or immolating ourselves if imperialist aggression leaves us no other choice.

Such is our morale. It is the same morale that made it possible for the peoples of Europe to wage their struggle of resistance against the fascist war machine forty years ago. We are certain that our sacrifice would not be in vain and we know that all 3 million Nicaraguans could be annihilated, but our example would triumph and be multiplied among the peoples of the world—and among the people of the United States as well. This is our contribution to peace.

We wish to appeal to the leaders of the United States, in the interests of the peace and happiness of our peoples. We urge them to reflect on the enormous responsibility weighing on them at the present moment, and thus leave the road to war and join us in the search for peace. In this way, we could begin a new era in the relations between our countries, in the interest of our peoples, including the real interest of the people of the United States.

The world has a right to know if the United States is willing to live in peace with the Central American peoples or if it insists on imposing war on us.

The world has the right to demand of the current leaders of the United States a clear, definitive answer to a very concrete question: Are they for or against the Act for Peace and Cooperation in Central America presented by the Contadora Group on September 7 to all the Central American governments? Are they for, or against, peace?

Many philosophers and men of politics have been quoted from this important rostrum. I would like to quote Jesus Christ, the humble man of Nazareth, who said: "Blessed are the peacemakers." *(Matthew, 5:3)*

The producers of this country support our revolutionary government

Interview with Daniel Núñez

The following are major excerpts from an interview conducted by foreign correspondents in Managua on October 5, 1984. The October 21 assembly Núñez refers to was a National Assembly of Producers attended by 30,000 farmers and ranchers from all over Nicaragua. This translation originally appeared in the January 21, 1985, issue of *Intercontinental Press*.

To speak about the producers of Nicaragua, it is necessary to do a small historical review of the role that Nicaraguan producers, and above all the small and middle producers, have played in the history of our country.

When the Spaniards arrived in our country, we know that our indigenous people took a rebellious stance.

When the first U.S. intervention took place, represented by William Walker, our peasants, small and medium producers from the mountains of Matagalpa, closed ranks under the command of José Dolores Estrada. In the battle of San Jacinto, these ragged, barefoot peasant producers defeated the first intervention.

Small and medium producers from different regions of the country also accompanied Benjamín Zeledón, who was the son of a producer from Concordia, and resisted the aggression. And yesterday we celebrated one more anniversary of Benjamín Zeledón's rebellion when he headed a confrontation with the imperialist aggressors, thus writing one of the brilliant pages in the history of our people's rebellion.

Sandino was the son of a coffee-growing producer from Niquinohomo. And with Sandino, the small and medium producers of Las Segovias left their farms and joined the Army for the Defense of National Sovereignty. They are the ones who supported and fought with Sandino to resist the aggression and dislodged the aggressors from our homeland.

Our people, with the Sandinista front, take up those rich traditions of struggle. When the Sandinista front arose, producers of the regions of Las Segovias, of Matagalpa, of Jinotega sided with the compañeros of the Sandinista front to pick up the threads of the history of Zeledón and Sandino and thus arrived at July 19.

Within this struggle, from 1962 to 1979, more than 3,000 producers were murdered by Somoza's genocidal army. It set up concentration camps in Waslala, Río Blanco, and Cuscawás with the assistance of imperialist military personnel.

Since the triumph of the revolution, more than 400 producers—members of cooperatives and small, medium, and large producers—have been killed in the war that we Nicaraguans face from the Reagan government.

Nevertheless, against wind and tide, the Nicaraguan producers have been taking up that rich tradition of struggle of our forefathers, and in the midst of war, we are producing to guarantee food to our people.

During the forty years of the Somoza dictatorship, departments like Chontales, Boaco, Matagalpa, Jinotega, Estelí, Ocotal, and Nueva Segovia, which together had more than a million head of cattle, did not even have a single laboratory to treat cattle diseases.

This is despite the fact that our international market was the market of the United States. The organizations of the COSEP, representing ranchers, rice growers, coffee growers, and others, did not even concern themselves with establishing such a laboratory.

In our country, which has more than 13 million hectares of land, if we take all our valleys together we have more than a million hectares, the equivalent of the San Joaquin Valley in California.

Nevertheless, the backwardness of our country—its underdevelopment is such that when the revolution triumphed, we had scarcely 50,000 manzanas of irrigated land devoted to three principal crops: 20,000 for sugarcane, 20,000 for rice, and the remaining 10,000 for cotton and vegetables.

In a country of 130,000 square kilometers, with large valleys and 3 million people, the ranchers and producers of Managua could not even guarantee milk for the children of those who worked on their haciendas.

Thus, Nicaragua, a country with immense resources, which came to be the seventh largest gold-producing country in the world, is a pillaged country, where the gold and the forest resources had been completely plundered.

There were associations that claimed to represent the interests of the producers. But the small and medium producers were the victims of these associations, which bought their coffee, their cattle, their basic grains, but did not concern themselves with returning services to raise the technical level and develop this important sector of our homeland.

When the revolution triumphed, the UNAG arose like the payment on a debt—a debt that had been owed to the producers of this country for their suffering at the hands of the ruling sectors from the time of the Spaniards' arrival until July 19.

The initials of UNAG define it: the National Union of Farmers and Ranchers. It is a broad organization that has room for efficient producers, for producers who are able to maintain their Nicaraguan humility, and who have not in the past been tied to *somocismo*. Because to have been tied to *somocismo* is to have been an accomplice in murder and torture. We are making this organization the organization of those Nicaraguan producers who want to respond to the call of our homeland to produce and to defend it.

While the wounds that our people suffered were still healing, while we were still just beginning to smile at the triumph of our people, the aggression against us began anew. The proof of this are the thousands of dead we now have.

As an organization we try to make those producers who live in the mountains understand that they are the creators of the social wealth of our homeland. Nicaraguan producers, and our people in general, hate war and love peace. We want to tell you that the assembly we are going to carry out on October 21 will be to let the world know—as well as those indifferent Nicaraguans who still exist in our country—that the producers of this country, the best producers of this country, long for peace and support the policies of our revolutionary government.

We want to make our position clear, that the National Union of Farmers and Ranchers supports the policies of our government.

The producers of Nicaragua ask the producers of the world to raise their voices, because what is being committed in Nicaragua is genocide.

I could invite you to go to a cooperative in the town of Estipulas, no farther away than Matagalpa, where twenty-four heads of families were murdered, where there are twenty-four widows, twenty-four mothers who are left without sons, plus many children left without fathers.

Although producers who were affiliated to coffee-growing

cooperatives in Matagalpa were murdered and although the people denounce those crimes, there are associations of coffee growers and ranchers here that are silent before those crimes. We also want to denounce that.

We believe that to be silent before a crime against a producer is to be an accomplice in that crime.

The objective of this demonstration is to fight for peace. Because as long as there is war in Nicaragua there will be all the more difficulties for us to confront.

We struggle for the unity of all the productive sectors of our homeland. In Nicaragua there are patriotic producers, those who are with the revolution. We would like to give you some facts so that you will understand more or less what the UNAG is.

There are two major sectors of Nicaraguan agriculture, the people's property sector and the private sector. The latter comprises large producers with more than 500 manzanas, small and medium producers, Credit and Service Cooperatives, and Sandinista Agricultural Cooperatives.

The people's property sector controls 20.5 percent of the land under cultivation. It is responsible for producing 23.9 percent of the gross value of agricultural output. The large producers with more than 500 manzanas control 14 percent of the land and 25.3 percent of the gross value of production. The individual small and medium producers, together with the Credit and Service Cooperatives, have 60.7 percent of the area under cultivation and produce 44.7 percent of the total value. And the Sandinista Agricultural Cooperatives constitute 4.7 percent of the land and account for 6.1 percent of the gross value of production.

We could say that the UNAG encompasses the small and medium producers, who represent 60 percent of the production of this country. Another 20 percent is represented by the people's property sector and the other 20 percent by the private sector.

Within the private sector of large producers, there exist patriotic producers who support the revolution.

Thus we can guarantee seriously that 90 percent of the producers of this country are affiliated to the National Union of Farmers and Ranchers in one way or another. And this has been possible after three years of intense work.

We have been having assemblies throughout the country, from San Juan del Río Coco to Nueva Guinea. That is to say, we have gone to those places where the new policies for our country's agricultural sector are being developed. We have been discussing with these producers the policies, problems, and strategies of production in the midst of war in Nicaragua.

Our people have resisted thirteen interventions against our homeland, one of which lasted more than thirteen years, and faced a forty-year earthquake, the earthquake of the Somoza dictatorship. Our people—a battle-hardened, generous people, a working people, a people that is making great contributions to international society—is ready to defend itself and to produce. And it is ready above all else to struggle for peace and the happiness of our homeland.

QUESTION: A major crisis of confidence has been observed due to the war, especially in the fifth and sixth regions.* What specific measures are you taking to break down support among the peasants for the *contras* in this area?

DANIEL NÚÑEZ: If the producers of Nicaragua, if the people of Nicaragua, did not have confidence in this revolution, we would not be, for example, raising the production of coffee

---

* Nicaragua is divided into six regions and three special zones for political and administrative purposes. Region VI is the mountainous departments of Matagalpa and Jinotega in the north-central part of the country. Region V is the departments of Boaco and Chontales, to the south of Region VI. Both regions have been special targets of CIA-sponsored counterrevolutionary bands.

in the sixth region in the midst of war and even raising it to the same historic levels reached under *somocismo*. As we say, "Words move you, but deeds sweep you away."

That region is producing basic grains—corn and beans. While the cooperative, small and medium producer compañeros fight, their wives bring in the crops of corn and beans. So, I ask, what lack of confidence does this show? The counterrevolution is not creating a lack of confidence. What it is creating is the terrorism of war. More than 300 compañeros, cooperative members and small and medium producers, have been killed by these genocidal killers, who come like thieves in the night and take away the old people, women, and children to later murder them with impunity.

QUESTION: Has this terror led people to be afraid to declare themselves partisans of the Sandinista front or of the UNAG? Many people do work with the *contras*. This is a fact in the fifth and sixth regions.

NÚÑEZ: Our people are not cowardly. In Nicaragua, for historical reasons, cowardice does not exist. There is a terror, there is an armed force there, supplied by the United States, and the proofs are there—Yankee mercenaries who have fallen, planes, helicopters.

If there were fear here, in Wiwilí this past Sunday, 2,000 producers would not have come to an agricultural fair where the government, together with the UNAG and the agrarian reform, sold 600 cows and bulls. If there were fear of supporting the revolution, those peasants who are in a war zone, in the center of the war, would not have shown up there.

So, there is a policy of terror, a terrorist policy. But I will tell you one thing. In Nicaragua 50,000 producers have never before come together. And the fact is that producers from the war theater, from San Juan del Río Coco, from Wiwilí, from Pantasma, from Río Blanco, from Nueva Guinea, from Molucucú, from Siuna, and from all the national territory, will come by foot or however to this meeting [on October 21]. That will demonstrate the confidence that those producers, descendants of the best sons of our people, have in the revolution.

You have to know the history of Nicaragua, you even have to know about the indigenous chiefs of our homeland to know the valor of those peasants who are said to be afraid. Because with all the counterrevolution that exists in those mountains, if the peasantry were following it, Matagalpa and Jinotega would definitely have been taken.

We know that there are difficulties. It is true that there are some peasants who have gone with the counterrevolution, who have been fooled. There was a policy of anticommunism here. For this reason we were one of the most illiterate peoples. After Haiti we were the most backward country. Because of this, in the beginning there was confusion. But the important thing is how many are leaving the counterrevolution.

So there are difficulties, we do not say that there are none. There is a war in that region. But in a war zone like that one, if there were not support for this government the producers would already have come down to Matagalpa, and you would see thousands of peasants coming down to the cities. Nevertheless, the peasants stay to defend their piece of land, their piece of the homeland.

QUESTION: Recently *La Prensa* published a report about a supposed wave of land confiscations of large producers in Matagalpa. Would you comment on this?

NÚÑEZ: In Matagalpa the agrarian reform has been carried out more through the purchase of farms than by confiscation.

For example, only two non-*somocista* persons had their lands affected. With the other property owners, whose names I could give you, the state negotiated the sale of their farms for more than 60 million córdobas, to give the land to cooperatives. So there were negotiations there, not confiscations.

But what happens? *La Prensa* is on a campaign to defame the Nicaraguan people, and it is the Nicaraguan people that it is trying to defame because the government of this country represents the Nicaraguan people.

Jaime Cuadra is an efficient producer compañero, and we consider him an honest man. But *La Prensa* wanted to utilize him to say that his property had been confiscated, which is a lie.

La Prensa committed an insult and a slander, and, nevertheless, the revolutionary government here took no measures against it. I believe that the government should have demanded compensation. Why? Because on an international level the damage was already done. It was already announced that in Matagalpa some gentlemen had been confiscated who had not in fact been affected.

You have to understand that the problem in Nicaragua is not a land problem. There is enough land for a million people to work. The problem of Nicaragua is the problem of the war we face and the problem of underdevelopment left us by imperialism.

The Nicaraguan producers, above all our unschooled ones, small and medium producers who live in these mountains, are now pretty clear on what role *La Prensa* plays and what role is played by the revolution's mass media. We can even say with pleasure that in the mountains the peasants now read *Barricada* and *El Nuevo Diario*. This shows that the consciousness of the peasant producers of this country is advancing every day.

QUESTION: What percentage of the herds does the UNAG control and what percentage is controlled by the organizations of the COSEP? What is the annual meat production of Nicaragua, and what percentage of that is exported and what percentage is consumed in the country?

NÚÑEZ: Eighty percent of the approximately 2,200,000 head of cattle are controlled by the private sector. Of this

80 percent, the UNAG controls some 65 percent, including those large, private, patriotic producers who are supporting the revolution. The remainder of the private sector is run by those gentlemen producers who are affiliated to the COSEP through FAGANIC [the association of ranchers].

The UNAG is growing among the ranchers. Now the producers of El Sauce are turning over 7,000 cattle to the slaughterhouses. And those producers, who previously were affiliated to FAGANIC, today maintain a close relationship with us in the UNAG. That is encouraging. Yesterday we spoke with the compañeros, and they said that they are going to make efforts to increase the amount of cattle delivered next year.

QUESTION: What is the standard of living of the peasants in relation to other productive sectors?

NÚÑEZ: The Nicaraguan peasantry was the most repressed and the most exploited sector of the Nicaraguan people. Our peasantry produced the basic grains: rice, beans, and corn. Moreover, it was the sector most ravaged by the latifundists, who pressed them every day, pushing them toward the mountains.

The peasantry was repressed not only economically, but also by the dictatorship, which murdered them. We have already said that more than 3,000 peasants were murdered in the sixth region. Nevertheless, with the revolution, we have been alleviating this problem for the peasants.

For example, there was previously no electricity in Waslala, which was a concentration camp under Somoza. And the places where the peasants were tortured there still exist. Today there is electricity, there is a school, there is a hospital where the peasants come to cure their illnesses, there are stores, there is even drinking water in that town. There are offices of ENCAFE [the government agency that services coffee producers and sells their crops]. There is a branch of the National Bank. Why? Because revolutions are for transforming the peasantry, which generates the social wealth of the homeland.

In Matagalpa they have just inaugurated a regional hospital, a hospital that leaves no reason to envy hospitals in developed countries.

Thus, in five years of revolution, the peasantry has received schools, roads, health care, and financing. Moreover, the government has forgiven the peasants 500 million córdobas worth of debts they had been holding, debts that had been incurred in times of Somoza.

We can even see how the government, because of certain proposals that our organization has made, has been increasing the price paid to peasants for basic grains. Beans are now worth 800 córdobas [per 100 pounds, as opposed to 400 córdobas before September]. Sixty percent of the coffee of Nicaragua is produced by small and medium producers who are in the war zone, and those peasants are going to receive 2,500 córdobas for each load of coffee this year. So the government has adopted policies that benefit the productive sectors in the countryside.

This includes milk producers. The companies that used to operate in this country never gave them a just price for their milk. Nevertheless, today the milk producers are receiving a just price for the first time in Nicaragua.

This is why we say the happiness of the Nicaraguan people is not going to lie in the cities. It is going to be in the countryside. The development of the Nicaraguan people is there in the mountains. That is to say, the future of the country is in the countryside.

In spite of the atrocious, inhuman, and brutal war that our people are confronting and defeating, the Nicaraguan peasants, with all the difficulties, never before had the benefits that they have achieved in five years of the revolution.

QUESTION: How many producers have been murdered since the victory of the revolution?

NÚÑEZ: More than 400 producers have been murdered, including producers from cooperatives, small producers, medium producers, and even large producers.

The material damages are incalculable, because every day they are growing. For example, yesterday in the zone of Concordia the counterrevolution burned down three tobacco warehouses, and these losses reached almost 14 million córdobas.

The counterrevolution is trying to exhaust the country economically. That is what bleeds our country the most, and the damages are many. The most affected are the cooperatives, which are where the counterrevolutionaries attack the most.

But the most important thing is not the economic damage. The most important thing is that, in the face of the aggression, the Nicaraguan people are strengthening their consciousness every day. What is sadder for us than the economic damage is the loss of every child who falls, every woman who is murdered, every youth. The economic damage does bleed our people, but the saddest thing is the blood that waters the countryside of our homeland.

If the peasantry did not trust the revolution, we would be through

Interview with Daniel Núñez

The following interview was conducted by Ellen Kratka and José G. Pérez in Managua on October 9, 1984. This translation originally appeared in the February 4, 1985, issue of *Intercontinental Press*.

QUESTION: When you speak of the large producers, what type of people are you referring to?

DANIEL NÚÑEZ: Well, the large producers in Nicaragua run their farms from afar. They are people who live in the cities. They have managers on the farms, but they only go on weekends or every two weeks; they do not have a direct working participation. They are always fundamentally within the politics of the COSEP.

At the same time that they are producers, they are also merchants. There are some who own land who are also doctors or lawyers. The large producers represent 10 percent of the producers of this country.

We also have the small and medium producers—those

who do maintain a direct relationship with and live in the countryside. There they grow up, there they die. Among them are members of the cooperatives.

Among the large producers there are the patriotic producers, whose positions are different from those of other large producers. Though they are large producers, they have maintained a direct relationship with the land, and their dynamic of work in the countryside makes them rich peasants. That is to say, they have not become declassed, separated from production, by moving to the cities. This is a very important sector that exists especially in the fifth, sixth, and first regions.

QUESTION: The difference between the patriotic producer and the—how would you say . . .

NÚÑEZ: We could characterize them as the nonpatriotic producers affiliated with COSEP.

QUESTION: . . . is not just a political attitude, then, but also a connection to the countryside?

NÚÑEZ: Yes, the truth is that these COSEP producers are the ones who were outside the country, who traveled outside the country and who received a different education, while the other large producers that I am telling you about are the ones who live in the countryside. There are some patriotic producers who might have a house in the city of Matagalpa but live more on the farm than in Matagalpa. An example is Samuel Amador, a rice grower who has his house in his production center.

QUESTION: That is to say, the farms could be of the same scale of production; the connections with the countryside are what differentiate them?

NÚÑEZ: It's the attitudes, because the form of life creates the attitude. These people who live in Managua had more access to culture, to society, to the clubs, to all the comforts or deformations that that life carries with it.

It was this political sector here in Managua that always

managed and dominated the provinces. They were the ones who dictated policy, who ran and directed the producers.

But with the triumph of the revolution, with the birth of the UNAG, the UNAG began to have an impact through different policies. Those sectors completely lost the power they had in the countryside.

QUESTION: What organizations did the large producers have?

NÚÑEZ: UPANIC, CAFENIC, FAGANIC, are the organizations of rice growers, cotton growers, coffee growers, and ranchers.

QUESTION: And who dominated those organizations?

NÚÑEZ: The U.S. embassy put them together. Here the policies of the Inter-American Development Bank and the U.S. embassy shaped all those consortiums so that they would respond to a common interest. And it even joined them in a matrimonial triad—the Somoza family, the Liberals, and the Conservatives (or, to put it another way, the state), capital, and the church. And what was the purpose of this matrimonial triad? To run the social and economic policies of the country.

QUESTION: Did those organizations also dominate the medium peasants at one stage?

NÚÑEZ: Yes, they did. How did they dominate them? Through the banks. They had the Bank of America and the Nicaraguan Bank, which were among the consortiums of the Conservatives. They had control of exports. For example, in Matagalpa they had a large number of commercial houses that hoarded coffee so they could export it themselves. Then they had political, social, and economic power. They shared the power with Somoza.

QUESTION: When the revolution came, how did this change?

NÚÑEZ: The revolution nationalized their banks, taking away one of the links in the chain of their tricks and their power. The revolution now controls the exports of this country, which are coffee, beef, cotton, and sugar, the principal agricultural exports. Now with the birth of the revolutionary state, they are left without all those businesses they had.

They used to own slaughterhouses; they had everything. They used to buy coffee. They used to buy cattle. They used to buy everything to export. They themselves were the exporters of what the peasantry produced in this country.

Thus, in practice, the revolution has now taken away their power.

QUESTION: In the concrete case of the rich peasant, the patriotic large producer, one of the things we noted in the course of the period leading up to the national assembly of the UNAG was the emphasis you placed on the idea that those sectors should also be in the UNAG. They should also be included in the plans of the revolution, and not automatically identified with reaction.

NÚÑEZ: Of course, the UNAG, I would say, is a broad organization. It is what its name implies, the National Union of Farmers and Ranchers. And who should be in the UNAG? Those who were ashamed of *somocismo*. Those who were not involved in theft, or contraband, gambling, or prostitution. The noncorrupt elements, because we need to build a prestigious organization. Here we want neither opportunists nor lazy people. Nor do we want people who want us to go to them to solve their problems, but rather those who want to confront the problems together with us.

Therefore, we say: Good, the UNAG has room for those sectors. It even has room for those who are capable of saying, I was wrong and now I see that the revolution is good for everyone. But we cannot bring in those who are for the aggression, those who are for the intervention, those who support the policies of destabilization, because we cannot join God with the devil.

QUESTION: Does this campaign to involve the patriotic large

producer represent a change in the UNAG's position?

NÚÑEZ: We had already been working on these policies, because the revolution was not made to disperse, but rather to gather together those who will forge a new society. So we have to make room for all men of good will who are ready to march together in this process.

Before, these policies had not been as open as now. Nevertheless, in the National Assembly we widened what had been up to then a small opening. Why? To be able to make the revolution.

We aspire to unite all the producers of this country. We even hope that one day those in the COSEP will realize that they were wrong and that there is time to correct their errors.

QUESTION: Was there some change with respect to the rich peasants that led to this new emphasis on their role in the UNAG?

NÚÑEZ: Of course. Above all, we got rid of some confusion that had existed. For example, we used to speak only of small and medium producers. But we start from the fact that we want neither small nor medium producers; we want large producers, because the more we produce the more wealth the country will have. The revolution was not made to bring degradation, but rather social wealth, to all the sectors.

So what used to happen? If we had a policy of small and medium producers, it meant putting production in the wrong framework.

Our problem is underdevelopment of production and productivity. We have the capacity to put a million more people to work on the land in Nicaragua. We have some valleys here that, if taken together, would be the equivalent of the San Joaquin Valley in California. Yet, not even 10 percent of the best lands for agriculture are technically exploited.

What does a dictatorship give you? Backwardness. It fetters development. And that's what Somoza did here; he fettered development in order to be able to maintain his power.

QUESTION: Do the rich peasants employ labor?

NÚÑEZ: Yes, year round. There are rich peasants who employ up to 500 workers at the time of the coffee or cotton harvest. And all year round, apart from the harvest, I would say, up to some 200.

QUESTION: And people like that can be in the UNAG?

NÚÑEZ: Yes, why not? If he is a patriotic man he is in the UNAG. Just like there are priests here in the revolution, such as [Foreign Minister Miguel] D'Escoto and Ernesto and Fernando Cardenal [ministers of culture and of education]. This revolution is making contributions to the world on this. The framework should not be philosophical questions, but rather the conduct of men. No matter whether they are atheists, Marxists, or Christians, the important thing is their attitude toward life. Because the important thing is not whether one believes or does not believe, but what one does.

QUESTION: Doesn't this situation lead to frictions between the patriotic large producers who are in UNAG and the small peasants you have organized, who also may work for the large producers?

NÚÑEZ: No. In Nicaragua, the rural wage worker and the peasant who works his own land are practically two completely separate things. With the turning over of 2 million manzanas of land to the peasantry, anyone who wants land to work has it. Thus the semiproletarian peasantry—those who have land and also sell their labor power—has almost ceased to exist. Why? Because the peasant now has access to credit and services.

QUESTION: Have there been frictions with the Association of Rural Workers, the ATC?

NÚÑEZ: The ATC organizes all the rural agricultural workers who sell their labor power. We had, I would say, certain contradictions with respect to the fact that we were demanding that the workers produce more. In a country in revolution, you have to work, work, and work. Neither paternalism nor anarchy have a place because paternalism and anarchy, like the ultraright and the ultraleft, both do damage and destroy the consciousness of man by making him an opportunist.

Thus in the National Assembly of the UNAG, ATC President Edgardo García read a document supporting the demands of the UNAG. The wage norms for agricultural workers that just came out were the product of work we have been doing with the Ministry of Labor, the UNAG, and the ATC. Why? Because what interests us, what dignifies man, is work. Nothing dignifies man more than work. Nothing, absolutely nothing.

If we created a working class that did not have a spirit of sacrifice, that was not capable of understanding that in a revolution you have to work more, if we fell into paternalism, we would sink the economy of this country.

QUESTION: Didn't the agrarian reform affect the availability of labor in the countryside a great deal?

NÚÑEZ: There was incredible unemployment in this country. There was unemployment under *somocismo* because *somocismo* did not guarantee work. When the revolution triumphed there was a large number of unemployed workers. When they were given land, they came to work.

Here in Managua there is still a problem: there are more merchants than producers. We have to get rid of the *buhoneros* [small import-export merchants], the speculators, all those lazy people here. Let them go and work the land. If not, we will not go forward. If I were the government I would do away with all those things. It's madness. We have more merchants than merchandise.

QUESTION: Was it the escalation of the aggression that led to redefining the breadth of the UNAG?

NÚÑEZ: No, the UNAG was born with this breadth, the problem was that the leaders of the UNAG lacked the forcefulness to make the lines of the organization prevail.

QUESTION: So it was more a question of the work of the UNAG itself than of the development and evolution of the revolutionary process?

NÚÑEZ: The UNAG was the first organization that came into being after the revolution. The ATC already existed before the triumph, AMNLAE already existed; but the UNAG did not exist: the UNAG was born with the revolution.

And why was it born? To create an organization that would be able to respond to the interests of the producers, no matter whether they were small, medium, or large. For me, everyone, from those who produce 100 pounds to those who produce 100,000, is a producer. That is the important thing.

QUESTION: Have there been contradictions between the patriotic large producers and the small and medium producers?

NÚÑEZ: With the agricultural wage workers there have been contradictions, but with the medium and small producers there is no problem, because what holds them together is an attitude: honesty.

Here we measure producers in practice by their honesty. So there is no problem. If there were problems, the small producers would say, we do not accept the large producers.

QUESTION: At the assembly of the UNAG you proposed that the UNAG had to be more forceful in its relations with the enterprises of MIDINRA [Ministry of Agrarian Development and Reform].

NÚÑEZ: That is correct. Why? Because they are productive enterprises, independently of the fact that they are state enterprises. And as enterprises for production we have to be vigilant over how they produce. If they produce badly, we have to see why.

QUESTION: But the question of credits, fertilizers, seeds, inputs....

NÚÑEZ: You have to be forceful in everything—in credit,

in financing, in services, in technology, in everything. The problem is that the state has to be made more dynamic. Because if production stands still, it rots; if it stands still, it goes backward. Thus, if this enterprise is supposed to give me services but is blocking me, I have to move it so it will let me pass and give me services.

The policies are integral. We cannot make demands of the producers and of the COSEP if we do not make demands of the state producers.

QUESTION: And how is the problem of MIDINRA going? It seems that among the state organs, the one that receives the most criticism is MIDINRA.

NÚÑEZ: That is true. Because it is the most strategic. Therefore it has to be made to advance. And this will depend on the honesty of each functionary who works there.

QUESTION: What are the other organizations of producers, and what are your relations with them?

NÚÑEZ: We have relations with them on an individual level, because there are producers who are in UPANIC or CAFENIC, who got there for historical reasons, but who suddenly realized that these organizations are not going to solve their problems because they defend other interests. Our relations with them as organizations are relations of conflict. This is because we defend different positions. They defend reaction, we support and defend the revolution.

The counterrevolution has assassinated producers affiliated with FAGANIC and CAFENIC, and they haven't even denounced these crimes. For this reason I would say they are immoral with their own members.

QUESTION: Are there people affiliated both to UNAG and to these other organizations that are part of COSEP?

NÚÑEZ: No. Either one is in the UNAG or one is not. We cannot accept double affiliations, because we would be dishonest. However, there are producers who have been there and who are now with us.

QUESTION: The three capitalist parties that are participating in the elections have made criticisms of the agrarian reform around the question of the land titles—around whether they are titles of usufruct or of property. These parties say that they are actually rental titles that can be taken away. How does the UNAG respond to this?

NÚÑEZ: The problem of Nicaragua is not a problem of a lack of land; the problem is to work the land. The revolution is more serious than these people think. What is given is not taken away. That is a law of history. That which I give away I do not get back.

So if we give an agrarian reform title, it's because that title is for the peasant—forever. There is only one condition. He can lose it if he is dishonest with the financial system, if he does not work the land. So there is one condition, which is to work the land.

QUESTION: Can they sell the land?

NÚÑEZ: They can pass it on to their children, but not sell it, because that would be wrong. It is wrong to give a gift to someone so that they can sell it. They can give it to their children, to their wife, to their family, within the nuclear family, but not to anyone else.

QUESTION: In that sense, then, the land is inalienable in practice.

NÚÑEZ: That's right. This is a measure to protect the peasants themselves, and also their children, because there are some irresponsible fathers who sell the land and let their children die of hunger. In every way it is a correct, just, and humane measure.

QUESTION: Does this also protect the peasants from losing their lands through foreclosures?

NÚÑEZ: Yes. The government has forgiven debts, has forgiven 500 million córdobas of debts for producers of basic grains.

QUESTION: Can't the government say to the peasant, your

crop failed but you have your land; sell it and survive in that way?

NÚÑEZ: But what's involved is creating laws that protect the peasant. That example you gave is an atrocity. Because at any rate that man is producing for the country. He is producing to guarantee the food of the country.

QUESTION: Doesn't this measure make the rich patriotic peasants nervous?

NÚÑEZ: The land the revolution gave the peasant through the agrarian reform cannot be sold, but if he has his own land he can sell that. If a large private producer wants to sell his land, he sells it.

QUESTION: In other words, the only lands that are nationalized are the state lands and those of the agrarian reform.

NÚÑEZ: Yes, those that the government turns over. Because here there is private enterprise and a mixed economy.

QUESTION: Has this question of the titles and the certificates of nonaffectability now been resolved?

NÚÑEZ: A law of nonexpropriability is being studied. But neither are we going to give a title of nonaffectability to a lazy good-for-nothing or to someone who is decapitalizing or who is taking out the wealth of the country. So it depends on how they work the land.

There are producers who say, don't give me a title. If I am a good worker I don't need a title. Those who are requesting the certificates the most are the 10 percent not affiliated to UNAG. And mostly they are using it as a political question, not because they are concerned whether the small and medium producers are given titles of nonexpropriability.

QUESTION: There have been some cases reported of persons affected by the agrarian reform, in which the land was later returned to its owners. Has this been common?

NÚÑEZ: It has not been common. But the revolution has committed some errors and has recognized this.

I was director of MIDINRA in the sixth region. And

there we bought more than 60 million córdobas worth of land from landlords to divide into cooperatives.

QUESTION: Did you force the producers to sell it?

NÚÑEZ: Not forced, but negotiated. They wanted to sell it. Our problem is not one of land. Here there is land in abundance. We are a country that can do many things. Why should we start taking property away from this one or the other? What happens is that the reactionaries make a lot of propaganda around these questions. They have all these news agencies, and they have the U.S. embassy.

QUESTION: So on both questions—if there are going to be certificates of nonexpropriability and if the agrarian reform titles are going to be changed—neither of these things has made the peasant nervous?

NÚÑEZ: Absolutely not. Look, if the peasantry did not trust the revolution, we would be through.

The organized people are the backbone of the Sandinista Police
by Tomás Borge

The following are major excerpts of a speech given October 17, 1984, in Managua, at a ceremony celebrating the fifth anniversary of Nicaragua's Ministry of the Interior. At the celebration, awards were presented to outstanding members of State Security, the Sandinista Police, and the Fire Department. The speech was published in the October 18, 1984, issue of *Barricada*. The translation for this volume is by Harvey McArthur.

The U.S. government recently published a document which, like a romance novel, carries the title *Broken Promises*. In it, they continue to claim the Sandinistas broke a series of promises we made to the Organization of American States before July 19 [1979]. They denounce the "repressive apparatus" created by the revolutionary state, by which they mean the Ministry of the Interior. They say we have a secret police—they are referring to State Security—and claim it is headed by a Cuban ex-colonel who today has Nicaraguan citizenship.

And I thought Lenín Cerna [head of State Security] came from León; but now, according to the North Americans, it seems he is a Cuban ex-colonel! It's a miracle they don't claim he's Vladimir Ilyich [Lenin] himself, reincarnated!

They say the Sandinista Police is part of this enormous repressive apparatus, and that it is a body designed to reinforce totalitarianism.

They include the mass organizations as a functional part of State Security—and this, I must confess, is absolutely true. What would we do without the mass organizations? There would be no State Security. The mass organizations are the antidote to the U.S. Central Intelligence Agency; the organized people are the backbone, the irreplaceable source of strength of the Ministry of the Interior.

But just as these mass organizations make up our fundamental base of support, they are also our sharpest critics. Here I have a communication from Leticia Herrera, the national coordinator of the CDS. It says there is still a lack of coordination with and support for the CDSs on the part of the Sandinista Police and State Security. The CDSs point out that on occasion, when carrying out their assigned tasks the Sandinista Police do not give proper treatment to those arrested and to the people in general. The CDSs also believe that at times we place little importance—or do not give an adequate response to—the information and reports that come from the people's organizations. They ask, in addition, for modernization of the weapons issued to the Volunteer Police, so as to equip them more adequately for the situation of war we face.

It is likely that the analysts of the Central Intelligence Agency will never come to understand the great significance of this integration, of this relationship full of criticism and encouragement, that exists between the Ministry of the Interior and the organizations of the Nicaraguan people.

They end their cheap little novel by saying that the Ministry of the Interior, the police, and State Security are designed to perpetuate themselves within a totalitarian state.

Of course, another thing they won't understand is when I say that one day the Ministry of the Interior will disappear!

We are convinced that one day the Ministry of the Interior will disappear. Some day there will no longer be any reason for coercive organs of the state. But naturally, as long as class contradictions, both national and international, continue to exist; as long as imperialism, with all its consequences, continues to exist; as long as crime, one of the saddest scars left by the exploitation of man by man, continues to exist—the Ministry of the Interior will remain as a powerful organ of combat, control, vigilance, and coercion.

When the Ministry of the Interior no longer has any reason to exist and human society has been transformed into the reign of justice, when egotism and hatred have been driven out of man's consciousness, then some complementary tasks such as fire-fighting and traffic control will be directly assumed by organizations of the community.

The victory of the Sandinista people's revolution was our contribution to the struggle by mankind worldwide to create a better society. Each victorious revolution will mark a qualitative change in humanity's inevitable, sweeping effort to eliminate the causes of inequality—first and foremost that mountain of bones and artificial illumination, that raucous shout of arrogance that is North American imperialism.

But in the meantime the Ministry of the Interior is indispensable, and for this historical moment we are very far from proposing its extinction. On the contrary, the only possible alternative is for it to grow in quality and quantity, in organization, in operative capacity, in sharp and forceful response, in unrelenting vigilance over the happiness we have won, in technical perfection, and in full and unlimited integration with the working people.

Development of this sort means, in the long-term historical sense, negation of the ministry itself.

To the extent that we overcome crime, and above all to the extent that we negate the existence of imperialism, we will at the same time be negating the need for the Ministry of the Interior. As we increase the strategic blows we strike the enemy there will be less need for the efforts, for the very existence of the Ministry of the Interior, at least as we know it now, as a powerful, decisive body whose vitality is the very essence of the revolution.

The fighters of the Ministry of the Interior came from a great school—the school of revolution. The revolution taught us how to be police who fight crime, how to defend the security of the state by placing our lives at risk to break up operations by the counterrevolution. The revolution taught us that technique is important, but more important is consciousness of the need to commit everything to the cause of the exploited.

What use is the technique we have mastered, what good will it do us if we do not possess unbreakable morale?

What use would technique have for us if we did not fully identify with the interests of the workers and peasants?

Proof lies in the fact that in the past five years the Sandinista Police has significantly reduced criminal activity, while at the same time significantly increasing its ability to solve the crimes that are committed. In 1983, more than 6,000 of the 8,400 crimes committed were solved. This means that seventy-two out of every 100 crimes were solved by the Sandinista Police.

But the decrease in crime is also a result of the reorganization of our society, of the emergence of a new, collective morality. In 1980, a year of a high rate of crime, there was no Volunteer Police. The noticeable decrease in crime in 1983 was due in good measure to the existence of more than 8,000 Volunteer Police who, by December, will number

10,000. This participation by the people inside the structures of the Sandinista Police has also made possible an increase in the number of hours of vigilance and patrols so as to assure the safety and tranquility of our people.

The police still face a series of problems. There are delays in radio patrols responding to emergency calls. At times, when an accident happens, several hours may pass before traffic specialists report to the scene.

Although all the achievements of the Sandinista Police are a matter of pride for the revolution, we believe the principal achievement is the development of an honest and revolutionary police force. That joy, that confidence, that sparkles in our eyes when we see a member of the Sandinista Police, working beneath the sun or the rain, is the opposite of the terror once inspired by the *somocista* police and today inspired by similar police forces that defend the corrupt interests of Latin American dictators.

With the triumph of the revolution we inherited a prison system that had never sought to reeducate the prisoners. We, who were once guests in those dungeons, concluded that the concept of the revolution meant reeducating the prisoners with the aim of reintegrating them into productive labor. About 40 percent of the prison population is now involved in productive tasks, which in turn opens up for them real possibilities of being reintegrated into society. Our goal is for all prisoners to participate in productive tasks and to lead a life that is useful and less difficult.

Nonetheless, we still face serious problems of overcrowding, lack of resources to undertake reeducation on a wider scale, and a lack of adequate sites.

The compañeros of the prison system carry out perhaps one of the most difficult and self-sacrificing tasks of the Ministry of the Interior.

The lack of resources of the Ministry of the Interior has in large part been offset by a high level of consciousness and fighting spirit, a spirit and consciousness that have been reflected in exceptional acts of heroism over these last five years. Many of these acts have not received public recognition and probably will not receive it for years.

This spirit and consciousness explain how, starting with almost nothing, we developed a State Security apparatus capable not only of confronting the counterrevolution, but also of defeating the work of the CIA against Nicaragua.

It was only with the direct support of the United States and the complicity of other countries that the counterrevolution was able to establish two fronts of military struggle and two armed counterrevolutionary organizations.

The major cities of the country have been kept free of enemy activity. This left the enemy with no alternative but to attack production centers, schools, farms, and cooperatives from their foreign military bases, through aerial and marine bombardment.

Operations have been planned against our sugar mills, refineries, electric power plants and substations, textile mills, the Momotombo geothermal power plant, oil pipelines, bridges, railways, airports, radio stations, and relay stations of the Sandinista Television System. In 1983 alone, State Security uncovered more than 100 plans for assassination attempts and for other types of enemy activity.

State Security has managed to infiltrate the ranks of the counterrevolution. The courage of these silent heroes has given us advance warning of enemy attacks. They have also worked with the Sandinista People's Army and helped coordinate a number of military offensives.

The Sandinista People's Army is well supplied with troops—in both quantity and quality—as well as with technical training, especially in armored vehicles, artillery, and antiaircraft weapons.

As a whole, the EPS has attained the characteristics of a modern army. Our army, the pride of the revolution, is disciplined, conscious, and valiant.

The Ministry of the Interior has its own small bodies of troops, both in State Security and as part of the Sandinista Police. The "Pablo Ubeda" troops of the Ministry of the Interior, which have made a specialty of heroism, have been and continue to be trained for specific actions that require a high level of fighting ability. Of course, all the fighters of the Ministry of the Interior are prepared to become combat soldiers in a moment of military emergency. There is not a single official, a single officer, a single fighter of the Ministry of the Interior who is not ready and willing to take up arms for the homeland, to kill and die for our revolution.

The effort to undermine the legitimacy of the elections, postpone them, and undercut the validity of the Contadora group are not the only way [U.S. imperialism] has tried to attack us, nor are these our sole difficulties. We also face a siege on our economy, a decline in the prices paid for our products, and the heavy burden of the past, which together have created a potentially dangerous economic situation. We have to take the reins firmly and put on our spurs if we intend to ride that runaway horse—the law of value—under the present conditions of our economic system.

It is no consolation to know that the immense majority of the countries of Latin America suffer from a terrifying economic anemia, bound hand and foot by their foreign debt and the poverty of their peoples.

We are certain that the revolution is the guarantee of a future that will be far different from that dismal image of the Nicaragua of yesterday—or from the present faced by many of our sister peoples. We still have before us the objective of building a new society that will embody the paradise of the imagination, the paradise of human solidarity, where the highest form of property will be the responsibility of all of mankind to all of mankind.

To lose sight of the final objective would be like constructing a building without plans or drawings, creating a useless framework of iron and cement. We revolutionaries know that those who lose sight of the horizon lose sight of the revolution.

Building this new society means traveling a lengthy road. This road is called strategy, and each step we take along it is called tactics. The Sandinista people's revolution has to, must, survive on this long road by unraveling the strands of the web that faces us at each moment.

The greatest of errors would be to transform a tactic into a strategy, just as it would be wrong to deny coming and going, flexibility at any given moment, and intransigence when that is appropriate. Tactics and strategy are united dialectically. But—and this we must stress—tactics are the servant of strategy.

Tactics must be understood and watched over so that they contribute to, and not undermine, the revolution we are defending:

A revolution that has the stamp of approval of the majority, of the workers and peasants, of the poor.

A revolution that organizes production and distribution with an unequivocal policy of justice and democracy.

A revolution that defends the homeland we have won.

A revolution that without reservation gives land to the peasants.

A revolution that attacks economic inequality at its roots.

A revolution that ends the unequal development of the different regions, while leaving the landscape intact and seeking an understanding of the few but real national differences.

A revolution that immortalizes man's participation in his work, in his community, in the economy, in defense, and in political decision-making.

A revolution that liquidates discrimination against women,

leaving her gentleness, the miracle of her motherhood, intact.

A revolution that revives its old songs, the glory of its triumphal banners, the inevitable and beautiful existence of its origins, and that knows how to open the way to new forms of universal expression.

A revolution that seizes bits of sunlight to pass on to future generations.

A revolution that receives and extends solidarity.

A revolution that affirms and denies us as individuals, with the understanding that each one of us is a tiny particle in the great and immortal task of building a homeland that belongs equally to each of us.

Is it possible for Nicaragua to defeat the war of Yankee imperialism?
by Luis Carrión

The following speech was given in mid-November 1984 to an assembly of the Regional Committee of the FSLN in Region III, which includes Managua. Members of the leadership bodies of FSLN Base committees as well as political secretaries of the Base assemblies of the July 19 Sandinista Youth also participated in the meeting. The speech was published in the November 21 and 22, 1984, issues of *Barricada*. This translation originally appeared in the December 24, 1984, issue of *Intercontinental Press*.

We want to use this meeting, which the Regional Committee ordinarily holds with the leadership nuclei of the Base committees and which has been attended by the political secretaries of the Base Assemblies of the Sandinista Youth, to talk a little about the current situation and the tasks that it requires.

    The FSLN has always tried to act as a vanguard. In practice, since its foundation, from the early 1960s up until today, the Sandinistas have only been comfortable in the front ranks of struggle. We were born with the aim of acting as a vanguard and we will continue until the end with that aim of acting as a vanguard.

We have called you together at this critical time to remain faithful to that tradition. The graver the imperialist and mercenary aggressions against our homeland, the greater and more complex the difficulties that the Nicaraguan people face from different arenas, the greater and higher is the responsibility of each FSLN militant.

Faced with the real possibility of a direct war by U.S. imperialism against our small nation, the duty and the responsibility to be the vanguard requires, in addition to courage and will, a high level of consciousness, complete understanding of the tasks that we must fulfill, and effective organization and discipline.

Various members of the National Directorate have exposed the danger of an attack by the U.S. Army against Nicaragua. They have exposed the aggressive maneuvers that the United States is carrying out in the Pacific Ocean, in the Atlantic Ocean, and on Honduran territory. We have exposed the extremely aggressive declarations by various functionaries of imperialism, by the U.S. government threatening us with bombing or eventual massive attacks against Nicaragua. We have exposed the flights and the provocations of that vulture [the U.S. SR-71 spy plane], which in the last few days has not returned.

We have exposed the propagandistic and slanderous campaigns that the U.S. government has launched to create in the U.S. population an image of danger from Nicaragua, to create in the U.S. population a readiness to support a military adventure.

In the face of these examples that have been exposed by our leaders, it is necessary to seriously consider the risk of a direct attack by the U.S. Army. And in these circumstances the first question we put to ourselves, a question I imagine you have put to yourselves as well, is: Is it possible for Nicaragua—small, with few people, economically underdeveloped, with many material and cultural difficulties—is it possible for this little Nicaragua to defeat the attack, the war of Yankee imperialism?

In fact, compañeros, it is possible for the people of Nicaragua to defeat the imperialist war. We have not the slightest doubt about that. And this conviction arises not only from our will to win, from our desire for it to be so. This conviction arises from a scientific, revolutionary analysis of the objective conditions of the imperialist war.

It is a fact that the U.S. Army has many tanks, many planes, missiles and sophisticated weapons, and if we compare the U.S. Army with the Sandinista People's Army our disadvantages would be more than obvious.

The problem is that what is involved here is not a war between any two ordinary armies. What is involved is a war between an imperial army, fighting for a completely unjust cause, far from its country, confronting an entire people. And on the other side, on our side, it will not be just an army, but rather an entire people struggling for the most just cause of all, the cause of its independence, the cause of its sovereignty and freedom, defending the land where our people were born and lived, their own territory, our own sky. It is an entire people—made up of men, women, children, old people, youth—confronting an army, and I pity the army that has to face this Nicaraguan people.

And not only will the Yankee army confront the Nicaraguan people on its own land. In addition, the resistance and the tenacious, heroic, and determined struggle of our people will make possible the mobilization of many forces in the world and within the United States itself. We are going to struggle basically with our own forces, but we are not going to fight alone. The peoples of Latin America, of Europe, Africa, Asia, and the North American people will go into action with us against the imperialist aggression.

How many men and how much time would Yankee imperialism require to control or attempt to control three million Nicaraguans? Twenty thousand, 30,000, 40,000, 100,000 men would be insufficient.

How many men can Yankee imperialism commit in this situation of world crisis, of international tensions to try to force the Nicaraguan people into submission? And if they could send 100,000 or 200,000, how long can Yankee imperialism maintain those 200,000 men in Nicaragua, when every day they have to send back thirty, forty, fifty, or 100 coffins with U.S. soldiers? How long would the people of the United States permit the government of Mr. Reagan to do this? It is very certain that [they would stop it] sooner, much sooner, than the strategists of Yankee imperialism can be counting on.

When we say that we are going to defeat the imperialist aggression, we are not saying that the entire U.S. Army will be defeated. But we are sure that the imperialist war will be defeated because if the Yankees land they will leave sooner than they think.

Up to 500,000 soldiers went into action in Vietnam—in South Vietnam and with some air incursions over North Vietnam. During seven or eight years of an interventionist war, the United States suffered 56,000 dead in Vietnam. That's a lot of dead, but much less than Nicaragua, in relation to its population, has sustained since the triumph of the revolution.

Those 56,000 dead did not signify the breakup of the U.S. Army, not even of the part of the army that was in Vietnam, and they did not lose their ability to carry out military operations, which was more or less intact.

They did not lose their organization, but they did lose the war. They lost the war because they could not achieve their political objectives, because they could not defeat the people of Vietnam, because they could not crush their heroic resistance. And for years and years the resistance of the Vietnamese people gave rise to the resistance of the U.S. people, and Mr. Nixon had to look for excuses to leave Vietnam.

The imperialists are not invincible. The imperialists can be defeated, they have been defeated, and they will be defeated in Nicaragua. [*Applause*]

Therefore, the fundamental factor in defeating aggression is the armed and unarmed resistance, the effective, tenacious, heroic, untiring, determined resistance of the entire Nicaraguan people. That is the guarantee of victory. That is the force that is going to mobilize the whole world, and that is the force that the FSLN will have to head up in the event of an imperialist war. Each one of us must be in that front line of battle.

Now, what about this business of the war?

The imperialist aggression against Nicaragua began some years ago. We are not speaking of something new. Yankee imperialism's objective is to destroy the Sandinista people's revolution one way or another, and from the first moment of our triumph they began to work in an ever more aggressive way to destroy the revolution.

As part of that "work" to destroy us, they began the military aggression of the counterrevolutionary mercenary forces, the military provocations by the Honduran army, and the direct military provocations by the Yankee army and the CIA forces. They initiated war against the people, the most active element of which is the actions of the mercenaries against the revolution.

That war is simply the form that the imperialist war takes at this moment, because there is only a single war here. The mercenaries are the advance guard of the imperialist aggression; they are the form imperialism has been able to use thus far.

If the Yankees have not intervened here, it is not for lack

of material resources, but rather because of a political problem, because they have not been able to create the conditions within the United States and internationally to justify an aggression. When they look here they see this people ready to fight, and that greatly increases the political costs for them and makes them think twice before launching the aggression against us.

So, thus far the most aggressive form of the imperialist war has been the mercenary forces, whose maximum objective is the destruction of the revolution, since, logically, for the Yankees it would be cheapest and most ideal to destroy the revolution without having to intervene directly.

The minimum objective of the counterrevolutionary forces is to prepare or create the necessary conditions that would facilitate and justify direct imperialist intervention. That is to say, to weaken the people's capacity for resistance, to try to control territories where they could install provisional governments that would call for intervention, or some other action with the same objective.

Thus, by confronting and defeating the counterrevolution, we are confronting and defeating the imperialist war in its current form.

But up until now the counterrevolution has not lived up to Mr. Reagan's expectations and has not been able to accomplish the minimum plan, much less the maximum plan. The Yankees therefore need to create new pretexts, other justifications to launch the total attack.

So they began to speak of the MIGs, to say that Nicaragua is arming itself excessively and constitutes a danger to the security of the United States. They say that we are a threat to the security of Central America. Lastly they raise a whole outcry around that affair to try to create conditions that would justify attacking Nicaragua.

In these circumstances and in the face of the dangerous signs of aggression, we cannot remain with our arms folded, and we are not remaining with our arms folded. We are continuing to wage and even to step up the fight against the mercenary forces. At the same time, we have to raise our ability to confront a direct attack by the U.S. Army.

We are not suggesting that there is a choice, that we can decide what is more important—the struggle against the mercenaries or strengthening the defensive capacity against a direct attack by the Yankees.

These two elements simply represent two different aspects of the same war. Strengthening our defensive capacity in, let's say, the Pacific regions, to face an imminent direct attack by imperialism, also means raising our ability to deal blows to the counterrevolutionary enemy in the border regions.

When we have 40,000 or 50,000 well-organized militiamen, with their officers and their weapons, that is to say, when we have an extraordinary capacity to defend the city of Managua, we will also have the capacity to send part of those forces to carry out necessary missions in confronting the counterrevolution. And vice-versa, to the degree that we progress in the struggle against the mercenaries, that we weaken their forces, neutralize and wipe them out, we are normalizing the situation in the north and center of the country and we are creating the ability to strengthen the defense of the Pacific to confront a direct attack by imperialism. Those are two closely related tasks, two aspects of the same war, two victories that we must achieve.

The other thing that we wanted to say is that while Yankee imperialism exists, Nicaragua is going to live under a constant threat, which will have its ups and downs. Sometimes there will be more ships on our coasts and other times there will be fewer ships; there will be occasions when the president of the United States says more aggressive things and others when he says less aggressive things. But the threat, the danger of imperialist aggression will always be present, until the United States ceases to be imperialist.

Therefore, military preparedness and increased military strength cannot be viewed as conjunctural tasks; they are permanent tasks. Members of the FSLN must dedicate part of their attention to these tasks every day. And, at certain times it needs the majority of their attention.

Today we are living through a dangerous moment. A direct Yankee imperialist attack is a real possibility. Today we must put our forces in maximum readiness. This effort that we are making must come together into, must give rise to, an impenetrable and solid defensive capacity in Managua.

We have been speaking in the last few days about the capital. Why do we speak about Managua? What is the importance of Managua in case of an imperialist attack?

It has to do with the imperialists' objective. Yankee imperialism wants to destroy people's power in Nicaragua and reestablish the power of the oligarchy, the bourgeoisie, and the exploiters—the power of the *somocistas*, the proimperialists—and then they want to get out of the country as quickly as possible.

For this they have planned—and it would have to be like this—an attack that tries to gain rapid solutions. Obviously they will try not to get bogged down here, not to begin to exhaust themselves, but rather to achieve visible successes.

In order to keep the population of the United States united around an aggression against Nicaragua, they need political victories, political coups in the short term. And, obviously, that political coup is the seizure of the capital. That is the number one objective of an imperialist attack on Nicaragua.

If, three or four days after an intervention began, the U.S. Army could present an occupied capital with little damage and few losses, they would really have dealt a tremendous political and moral blow on an international and national level, because Managua is the symbol of the political power of the revolution. It is the symbol of people's power, the seat of the revolutionary power. Managua, in that sense, summarizes the homeland.

Having occupied Managua, even if the entire rest of the country were controlled by the revolution, the Yankees could present to the world the image of a victory, of an important political victory, and could continue with their plans to completely destroy the revolutionary power.

It is clear that the occupation of Managua would not signify either submission and Yankee domination or the end of the people's resistance. Indisputably, the occupation of Managua under the conditions we were mentioning would be a very hard blow; it would be an important victory for the imperialists. Therefore, for the Yankee imperialists it is very important to achieve that objective, and for the people of Nicaragua it is even more important to prevent it.

We must, then, be prepared to make the aggressors pay a very high price for every inch of terrain, every block, every house, every tree, every stone of our city. We must organize the defense of this capital in such a way that, if the Yankees succeed in penetrating to Managua, they can occupy only ruins and the blood of Managuans soaked into the soil of the homeland. [*Applause*]

Because if that is how it is, even though the Yankees might enter this territory where the capital now is, they will have gained no victory; even if they enter, they would have been defeated.

Therefore, the possibilities of resistance of the entire people, in every corner of Nicaragua are going to be seen multiplied a thousand times. The Yankees are going to have to leave Nicaragua, and this depends on us. It falls to the FSLN not only to organize a defense of this type and quality, but also to guarantee it every day in combat through our example, through action, through our very lives if necessary, in the same way that Julio Buitrago taught us with his own example that you had to kill or be killed to be able to live, and in the same way that Leonel Rugama showed us with his own life the road that must lead to victory.

Within this context, we have immediate tasks: in the shortest time possible we must have 40,000 militiamen organized in fully formed military units, with officers, with heads of squads, platoons, and companies, with battalion staffs, with general staffs of brigades. Every citizen of Managua who can be, must be registered and organized into a combat unit. Moreover, not just organized for a short while, but permanently organized, permanently assigned to his or her combat unit.

In the second place, we must make an extraordinary effort, in the shortest time possible, to raise the preparedness and combat capability of every one of the combat units in which those 40,000 militia members are organized—and 40,000 militia members is a minimum goal.

Equally, we must dedicate ourselves to preparing the defense of each area in which we are stationed as militia members. That means it is not just organizing the militia unit, it is not just personal preparation of the soldier, but also the defense of the area: trenches, engineering works, accumulating certain minimum material resources, certain minimum resources to strengthen the defense. To activate civil defense to guarantee maximum protection of our children, our old people, our invalids, all those for whose security, for whose future, we are preparing for victory.

We must raise the fighting spirit of the people and the dedication to "Free homeland or death!" We have to spiritually and politically prepare the people to be ready to sacrifice themselves if necessary.

Our cadre must be prepared for that and must know a little about the enemy, must study something of how the enemy acts and must have in mind that a war against the Yankees is much harder, much crueler, much bloodier than anything we have known. We must be spiritually and politically prepared to confront that war and defeat it.

To explain a little the concept of active resistance, we would like to say that it is something similar to the insurrection against the dictatorship. The people had a number of weapons, a few hundred weapons. Nevertheless, the war against the dictatorship was not waged by the 400 to 500 fighters of the FSLN who had military weapons. The war against the dictatorship, the insurrection against the dictatorship meant the involvement of everyone in fighting against the *somocista* [National Guards], with whatever weapons they had, with the resources that they had. There were guards who were burned to death, others who were clubbed to death or were killed in other ways.

The people's fighters, the fighters who had weapons, relied on people who made barricades, who helped them to build trenches or reload ammunition or who served as messengers or gave them coffee, or who took up the weapon when a fighter fell. Others informed when the guard was coming. Others detected the enemies of the people to execute them. Some used FAL rifles, others .22 caliber revolvers, others contact bombs. There were some who even wanted to use gas cylinders as weapons against the guards.

That is why when the *somocista* guards went out in their brand-new Becats to drive through the streets of Managua, they rode in the back part of the jeeps with their feet and their rifles pointed out. That is, their rifles were pointed at any and all Nicaraguans who passed by, because the guards understood that all the people, from the child with his basket of sweet breads, to the old woman who walked with difficulty, were their enemies.

That is how they felt and, in truth, that is how it was. And this people used every means to defeat the *somocista* guards, and among them they used the FSLN's combat organizations.

Now the number of rifles in the hands of the people is

no longer 300, 400, or 500; we have thousands of rifles and, in addition, tanks, cannons, and mortars. But the most important thing is that they are in the hands of the people to defeat the imperialist aggression with that same determination, that same will to struggle until victory. [*Applause*]

Active resistance means that we are going to begin fighting utilizing our tanks, our cannons, the weapons we have been acquiring. But if the ammunition for these weapons is used up or if the weapons are destroyed through the war itself, then we are going to keep fighting with our rifles, with our militia infantry brigades. And if the units are divided and communication is lost, each one of the groups will keep fighting, and if one of those groups gets divided into ten more pieces, each piece will keep fighting, and when one isolated fighter is left and loses contact with the rest of the compañeros, he will keep fighting. That is active resistance, when everyone ceaselessly fights to expel the invader.

We must prepare ourselves for this. The more organization we have, the more effective our resistance will be; the more damage we inflict on the imperialists, the more costly we will make their boldness.

This is why we must quickly increase Managua's defensive capability and stabilize a formidable defense of the capital.

And it is necessary to take another aspect into account. Some ask themselves if it is worth the trouble to make that whole effort, to begin running around, to prepare ourselves, etc., and perhaps the Yankees won't invade. There are some who think like that.

To put it more simply, it is better to make an extraordinary effort, to put our forces in readiness, to give of ourselves that extra bit that the Sandinistas and this Nicaraguan people have shown themselves capable of giving, because if the attack does not come, we will have taken a large step forward, since if it does not come now, it can come tomorrow, if not tomorrow, it can come the day after tomorrow, because the

Yankees want to destroy us.

What would be the alternative? With that kind of thinking we would stay so calm that if the attack does come, they will catch us with our guard down. That is something we could not forgive; that would be criminal on the part of the FSLN. To not have done everything possible to guarantee the defense of the homeland. It is from that starting point that we must make the intensive effort and then maintain that defensive capacity at a stable level, because this effort we are making today enters into the CIA's computer, and all the spies that the CIA has here report back that the people of Managua and all of Nicaragua are in fact at their battle stations, and a light goes on in Reagan's console that says, "Danger, danger, the Nicas are not such pushovers." And they are going to think about it a little more.

That is, our sweat today can save us blood tomorrow. We must not allow the Yankees to land here believing that we are weaklings; they have to know that no one here is a weakling. That is important and has a value.

The call we make today to strengthen the defense of our city in every way does not mean that we are going to stop producing, that drivers are going to stop driving, that mechanics are going to stop repairing, and that everyone will do something else.

It is precisely in these circumstances that we must be most efficient in production, that the results of our work must be the greatest, that we must conserve more resources. Because what kind of defensive preparation would it be to neglect production, to waste more, to disorganize ourselves? That is no preparation for defense; that would be preparation for nondefense, preparation for slackness and for anarchy.

For that reason, the National Directorate of the FSLN has decided that, even in these circumstances, some thousands of coffee pickers will leave the city of Managua, will go and pick coffee because when we said that we would prefer the fall of the coffee to the fall of the homeland, that did not mean that the coffee will go to hell.

It meant that we cannot harvest the coffee at the cost of unduly weakening the defense of the capital, but it did not mean that we are not going to make an effort to gather all the coffee if that is possible.

So we are mobilizing a much smaller number of people: militia members, state employees, with the perspective that they will achieve a higher average level of production than the Student Production Battalions. That means that in these circumstances of war, higher productivity is required to be able to confront the tasks of production and defense at the same time. And with a tortoise-like style, an undisciplined style, we cannot fulfill either one.

With that in mind, the compañeros who must be mobilized for the picking, should as a minimum each pick on the average between six and seven cans [per day]. [*Applause*] Only with an increase in productivity and production, an increase in discipline and in the efficiency of the working day, can we push forward the two tasks that we must fulfill.

That's why we must "charge up our batteries." We have to fulfill our tasks with regard to the coffee, with regard to production, and we have to fulfill and guarantee in the next few days and weeks the tasks directly related to the defense of the capital, the defense of the homeland.

Free homeland or death!

Today we speak naturally of Atlantic Coast autonomy

Interview with William Ramírez

The following interview was published in the December 8, 1984, issue of *Barricada*. The translation for this volume is by Michael Taber.

QUESTION: How would you define the concept of Atlantic Coast autonomy?

RAMÍREZ: Autonomy is a concept that must be viewed within the concrete reality in which we live in Nicaragua. This means that we must define the correct terms, because our interests as a revolution are not the same as those of other countries.

When we triumphed on July 19—the culmination of a long combative stage—the Nicaraguan people as a whole achieved self-determination. That is, they made the decision to take their destiny into their own hands, to have relations with whatever countries they wanted to, to have their own economic system, to have their own political system. In other words, the Nicaraguan people as a whole made the decision to be free and to maintain that freedom, independently of the fact that in some regions there may have been more fighting and in others less.

This doesn't mean that there are not some regions in our free country that are more advanced and others that are less advanced. It doesn't mean that there are not regions in our free Nicaragua with special circumstances that differentiate them from the rest of the country.

Nicaragua's reality tells us that in one part of our homeland there are regions with specific features of their own. These specific features, from the social point of view, the human point of view, the political point of view, the linguistic point of view, and the historical point of view are found in Nicaragua's Atlantic Coast, especially in the regions of Northern Zelaya and Southern Zelaya.

We have found that there are insufficient means of communication, which is different from the rest of the country. We have found that the population there does not speak Spanish only, but other languages as well, like Creole English, Miskito, and Sumo. We have found a population whose customs are different from the rest of the country.

We've been studying that reality and learning about it. Unfortunately, the U.S. aggression has prevented us from analyzing these questions in peace, and we've had to study, learn, and fight at the same time. This has also led us to commit a series of errors along with our successes. On balance, we've had more successes than errors.

That concrete reality has brought us to the point now where the administrative and the political policies that have been established in Northern and Southern Zelaya have really been appropriate to the area's characteristics that we mentioned before and relate to this reality.

QUESTION: What has this meant in practice?

RAMÍREZ: It has meant that within the revolution, within the national unity, we've had sufficient freedom to make decisions in accordance with the concrete reality of Northern and Southern Zelaya. We have been speaking in the language spoken there, we have been applying answers to the concrete realities. The revolutionary government has recognized this situation.

In fact we have achieved a high degree of participation by the people there in the fundamental decisions of the region. For example, the government ministers are from the region, both in Northern and Southern Zelaya. The bulk of the state apparatus is made up of people from the Atlantic Coast. For example, in the Indian communities, government personnel have been elected by the Indian people themselves.

Based on these advances what we feel must be done is to begin legalizing, broadening, and institutionalizing this situation. That is what we have been doing in practice, and that is the decision we have made.

QUESTION: What has led the revolution to raise these problems?

RAMÍREZ: Well, first of all, knowledge of the reality: our experience in direct work on the Atlantic Coast from the revolution's triumph up to the present. This reality led us from complete lack of knowledge at the beginning to the more or less serious knowledge we have today about the whole question of the Atlantic Coast.

Secondly, we obviously think that we have matured a bit. Our experience has helped us to reflect about and situate ourselves in the concrete reality. For example, it has helped us realize that in 1981 these things we're talking about now were taboo and we didn't touch them. We were terrified to speak of autonomy because we did not understand it. And we didn't understand it because no one understood the Atlantic Coast. Today we speak of this naturally. This signifies an advance, an advance of the revolutionary leadership which today sees things from a different perspective. Clearly, as I said at the beginning, this stems from the experience we've accumulated of successes and errors.

Thirdly, I believe that the struggle of the Indian peoples themselves has caused us to reflect, has led us to question ourselves, to ask ourselves about their attitude, which we sometimes even considered irrational. But even in this regard we've reached the conclusion that we must study these attitudes, not shut our eyes to reality. We must realize that they have interests and demands and we must learn about them.

For us, those have been the three fundamental elements.

QUESTION: What characteristics will this autonomy have in Nicaragua's case?

RAMÍREZ: In the first place, we should make clear that autonomy does not mean separation. In other words, the fact that autonomous regions can exist will not contribute to dividing the country, but rather to strengthening national unity.

There are Nicaraguan Miskitos, as there are Nicaraguan Sumos, Nicaraguan mestizos, Nicaraguan Ramas, Nicaraguan Creoles. So we have our differences, but these differences have a common denominator: Nicaraguan nationality. By respecting these differences we think that every citizen will feel better because their right to speak their own language will be respected, their right to be mobilized in their own territory—whenever and however they want—will be respected, their right to receive an education in their own language will be respected, along with access to the national language, which they must have. Autonomy would also not mean that those from the Pacific living in the Atlantic Coast would have to leave. Autonomy must guarantee the participation and the same rights for all Nicaraguan citizens who live in Northern Zelaya and Southern Zelaya.

QUESTION: This issue of autonomy has been raised as a banner by the counterrevolutionary Steadman Fagoth. In the case of Brooklyn [Rivera], how has he raised the question of autonomy?

RAMÍREZ: Well, we have not yet begun to discuss this situation with Rivera. We are discussing and have discussed for some time with the Miskitos who are here in the country because we believe that we must move forward and not wait. The dynamic of the revolution is greater and the interests of the Miskito people are greater than the special interests of whatever groups might be outside the country.

Let's remember that Rivera's is only one of the different groups that exist outside the country; the other group is Steadman's, but there are also other organizations within the country that we should see as a reality.

QUESTION: Where does this concept of autonomy come from?

RAMÍREZ: We've taken it from our own reality. There is no other revolution in Latin America similar to ours. That is why our birth has been so difficult, because there is no other experience. The closest experience to ours is the Cuban one, but it is not the same. The Cubans never had these problems, because the Spaniards exterminated the whole Indian population that existed in Cuba; therefore these problems were never presented to them. We have had to learn on our own, and that is one of the problems. Perhaps we have been a bit slow in making these decisions. This is because of the great responsibility our revolution must bear in establishing precedents for other revolutions in Latin America. Because our example, the treatment we as revolutionaries give to the national minorities, is something that will necessarily have an influence in Latin America.

QUESTION: Are the coastal peoples prepared for autonomy?

RAMÍREZ: I think that the political cadres we have in the country, that is, the Miskitos that are here in Nicaragua, are prepared. With respect to the population in its majority, you would have to carry out a deep going political effort to explain it adequately. As a result of the propaganda that has been spread, the problems of isolation we've had, and the whole history of mistreatment of the Atlantic Coast by previous governments, it's not strange that confusion exists, and that they might believe that autonomy could mean separation.

We find in some communities, in some local areas that they believe that being autonomous means being totally separate from the national government, or having absolutely nothing to do with the rest of the country. We should also take into account these problems we might have; because we must be responsible, and should foresee and warn against these problems. We must not fear this situation; it is a challenge that as revolutionaries we must admit and resolve. We must realize the transcendental importance of this step for the country, and we must assume it with the responsibility that we should exhibit in all our actions, from the smallest to the largest.

QUESTION: Five years of experience have passed. What have been the errors?

RAMÍREZ: Our first error was having had confidence in Fagoth.

The second error was not having discussed these problems with the leaders that existed at the time. In speaking with Brooklyn he agreed with this; I don't know if he will say it publicly some day. The two of us agreed that if we had sat down to discuss these problems in 1981, surely the situation would not have been the same as what happened. This doesn't mean that there might not have been contradictions. We were certainly going to have contradictions, because neither we nor he were so clear on this question. But perhaps what came about might not have occurred.

The third error we may have committed was believing that we could solve everything at the same time. We created many expectations among the Miskito people. For example, we thought—obviously with the illusion of the revolutionary triumph and of youth and of the hopes and all the affection we had toward the people—that a highway could be built in a month, and it turned out that the Waslala-Siuna highway was built in two years. We believed that a health center could be built in fifteen days and the schools could be built in eight months or a year. And what happened was that sometimes the boats didn't arrive, the planes didn't arrive, they broke down, and we had no answer.

When we told all these things to the people, they said, all right, where is the school and the highway, where is the health center? We explained to them that yes we had promised these to them, but the materials had still not arrived. All at once the enemy took advantage of this situation and Fagoth began to manipulate to turn the people against us, and not just those people over whom the enemy had direct influence.

QUESTION: What can you say about natural resources?

RAMÍREZ: We feel that a part of the wealth from the fishing, the mines, and the forests, should stay on the Atlantic Coast. I don't say all of it, but certainly a part.

QUESTION: How do you think Brooklyn could, let us say, interpret the discussions?

RAMÍREZ: I can't speak for them, but I would have to ask them why they are fighting. Are they fighting for land? We are giving them land, we are recognizing the land on which the Miskitos have always lived. Are they fighting to speak their own language? They are speaking their own language. Who has pushed bilingual education? Hasn't it been us? Previously the Miskitos were ashamed to speak in Miskito, because the *somocistas* ridiculed them. They are not fighting for land or culture, because we've developed dance and artesanry. There has never been such a wide spread of music [from the Atlantic Coast], such as the May

Pole, as there is now. And the same goes for the economic aspect, the infrastructure, roads, schools, housing, education. I haven't said that we have done everything, but we would have done more if we had been given the opportunity, because the counterrevolutionary activity has set back a whole bunch of projects.

Who left the families of Sukapín without work? Who destroyed the Prinzapolka dock? Who burned the Sumubila health center? Who burned the Simalila sawmill, the motors, the tree nurseries, the Simalila physical installations? It was not the Sandinista front, it was not us. Who—while trying to attack the fuel storage facilities at Puerto Cabezas—killed and wounded the citizens of the port? It was not the Sandinistas. Who killed people at Sumubila and Columbus? It was not the Sandinistas. Therefore that is what we have to see, that is the assessment we must make.

Appendix

Political manifesto
by Augusto César Sandino

The following political manifesto was dated July 1, 1927. Sandino's first political manifesto, it was issued from the mines of San Albino. This translation originally appeared in the July–August 1984 issue of *Tricontinental*, published in Havana.

A man who does not ask his homeland for even a handful of earth for his grave deserves to be heard, and not only heard, but believed.

I am Nicaraguan and I am proud that in my veins flows, more than any other, the blood of the American Indian, whose regeneration contains the secret of being a loyal and sincere patriot. The bonds of nationality give me the right to assume responsibility for my actions on matters of Nicaragua and, therefore, of Central America and the entire continent that speaks our language, without concerning myself over what the pessimistic and cowardly eunuchs may call me.

I am a city worker, an artisan as they say in my country, but my ideals are broadly internationalistic in nature and entail the right to be free and demand justice, although to achieve this state of perfection it may be necessary to shed my own blood and that of others.

The oligarchs, who act like geese in a quagmire, will say I am plebeian. It doesn't matter. My greatest honor is to have emerged from the bosom of the oppressed, who are the soul and nerves of the race, who have lived put off and at the mercy of the shameless assassins who helped incubate the crime of high treason: the Nicaraguan Conservatives who wounded the free heart of the homeland and who pursued us ferociously as though we were not children of the same nation.

Sixteen years ago Adolfo Díaz and Emiliano Chamorro ceased being Nicaraguans, because their greed destroyed their right to claim that nationality, as they tore from its staff the flag that flew over all Nicaraguans. Today that flag hangs idle and humiliated by the ingratitude and indifference of its sons who don't make the superhuman effort to free it from the claws of the monstrous eagle with the curved beak that feeds on the blood of this people while the flag that represents the assassination of defenseless peoples and the enmity of our race flies in Managua's Mars Field.

Who are those who tie my homeland to the post of ignominy? Díaz and Chamorro and their bootlickers who still want the right to govern this hapless land, supported by the invaders' bayonets and Springfield rifles. No! A thousand times no!

The Liberal revolution is on the march. There are those who haven't betrayed, who haven't halted, who haven't sold their rifles to satisfy Moncada's greed. It is on the march and today stronger than ever, because the only ones who remain are the brave and the selfless.

The traitor Moncada naturally failed in his duties as a soldier and a patriot. Those who followed him weren't illiterate and neither was he an emperor, to have imposed such greedy ambition upon us. I place before his contemporaries and before history this deserter Moncada, who went over to the foreign enemy with his cartridge pouch and all. An unpardonable crime that demands vindication!

The big men will say that I am very little to have undertaken such a task; but my insignificance is surmounted by the loftiness of my patriotic heart, and so I pledge before my country and history that my sword will defend the national honor and will be the redemption of the oppressed.

I accept the invitation to the struggle and I myself will provoke it, and to the challenge of the cowardly invader and the traitors to my country I answer with my battle cry. My chest and that of my soldiers will form walls that the legions of Nicaragua's enemies will crash upon. The last of my soldiers who are soldiers for Nicaragua's freedom, might die, but first, more than a battalion of you, blond invader, will have bitten the dust of my rustic mountains.

I will not be Magdalena, begging on bent knee for the pardon of my enemies—who are the enemies of Nicaragua—because I believe that nobody on earth has the right to be a demigod. I want to convince the cold-hearted Nicaraguans, the indifferent Central Americans, and the Indo-Hispanic race, that in the spur of the Andean mountains there is a group of patriots who know how to fight and die like men.

Come, you gang of morphine addicts; come murder us in our own land, I am awaiting you, standing upright before my patriotic soldiers, not caring how many you may be. But bear in mind that when this occurs, the destruction of your grandeur will shake the Capitol in Washington, reddening with your blood the white sphere that crowns your famous White House, the den where you concoct your crimes.

I want to advise the governments of Central America, especially that of Honduras, that you need not fear that, because I have more than enough troops, I will militarily invade your territory in an attempt to overthrow it. No. I am not a mercenary, but a patriot who will not permit an offense against our sovereignty.

I wish that, since nature has given our country enviable riches and has put us at the crossroads of the world, and since that natural privilege is what has led others to covet us to the point of wanting to enslave us, for that same reason I wish to break the bonds that the disgraceful policies of Chamorro have bound us with.

Our young country, that tropical brown-skinned woman, should be the one to wear on her head the Phrygian cap with the beautiful slogan that symbolizes our "red and black" emblem, and not that country raped by Yankee morphine addicts brought here by four serpents who claim to have been born here in my country.

The world will be imbalanced if the United States of North America is allowed to be the sole owner of our canal, because that would put us at the mercy of the decisions of the colossus of the North—to whom we would have to pay tribute—those practitioners of bad faith, who with no justification whatsoever seek to become its owners.

Civilization demands that a canal be opened in Nicaragua, but it should be one with capital from the whole world, and not just U.S. capital. At least half the costs of construction should be paid with capital from Latin America and the other half from the rest of the countries of the world that want to hold stock in such a company, and the United States of North America could have only the three million that they gave to the traitors Chamorro, Díaz, and Cuadra Pasos; and Nicaragua, my homeland, will receive the tariffs that by right and justice belong to it, with which we will have sufficient income to build railroads across our territory and educate our people in a real environment of effective democracy, and at the same time we will be respected and not looked upon with the bloody contempt that we suffer today.

Brothers and sisters of my people: having expressed my most ardent desires for the defense of our homeland, I welcome you in my ranks regardless of political affiliation, as long as you come with good intentions, remembering that you can fool all of the people some of the time, but you can't fool all of the people all the time.

Glossary

Agüero, Fernando – bourgeois politician from Conservative Party who ran for president in 1967 against Somoza; later made pact with dictatorship; fled Nicaragua in 1979.

Alday, Conchita – fought against U.S. Marines along with Sandino.

AMNLAE – Luisa Amanda Espinoza Association of Nicaraguan Women; the mass Sandinista women's organization.

AMPRONAC – Association of Women Confronting the National Problem; the "national problem" being Somoza; became AMNLAE after victory of revolution.

ANDEN – National Association of Nicaraguan Educators; FSLN-led teachers' union.

Aráuz, Blanca – companion and collaborator of Sandino.

Arce, Bayardo – joined FSLN in 1969; leader on northern front during 1979 insurrection; member of FSLN National Directorate and director of its political commission.

ARDE – Revolutionary Democratic Alliance; *contra* forces operating out of bases in Costa Rica; trained and armed by U.S., it began terrorist actions in April 1983.

Argüello, Patricio – FSLN member killed by Israeli forces in 1970 while participating in an airplane hijacking organized by the Popular Forces for the Liberation of Palestine.

Army for the Defense of National Sovereignty – organized by Sandino in 1927; fought a guerrilla struggle in the mountains of northern Nicaragua until U.S. Marines were withdrawn in 1933.

Astorga, Nora – Sandinista guerrilla fighter who helped bring a notorious National Guard general, torturer, and CIA informant to justice in 1978; deputy foreign minister when designated ambassador to U.S.; Washington refused to accept her credentials.

ATC – Association of Rural Workers; FSLN-led farmworkers' union.

Avilés, Olga – FSLN member who participated in 1974 takeover of the Castillo house; works in Ministry of the Interior.

Báez, Gladys – fought on western front in war against Somoza; member of regional government committee in León area and of National Assembly.

Baltodano, Mónica – Guerrilla Commander, led FSLN forces that captured city of Granada during 1979 insurrection; currently government secretary of regional affairs.

Barricada – FSLN daily newspaper founded in July 1979.

Borge, Tomás – active in student movement in 1950s; only surviving founder of FSLN; imprisoned and tortured under Somoza; member of FSLN National Directorate and Nicaraguan minister of the interior.

Buitrago, Julio – member of FSLN national leadership who headed urban underground struggle; killed July 15, 1969, in a Managua battle that pitted him and a handful of other Sandinistas against hundreds of National Guardsmen equipped with artillery, aircraft, and a Sherman tank.

Cardenal, Ernesto – minister of culture; Catholic priest.

Cardenal, Fernando – minister of education; Catholic priest.

Carrión, Luis – member of FSLN National Directorate; vice-minister of the interior; head of commission to draft Atlantic Coast autonomy statute.

CAS – Sandinista Agricultural Cooperatives, in which farmers pool their lands and jointly work them as a single enterprise.

Castro, Andrés – Nicaraguan youth prominent in struggle against William Walker in 1850s.

CCS – Credit and Service Cooperatives, in which farmers maintain their individual farms but group together to share government services.

CDS – Sandinista Defense Committees.

Chamorro, Carlos Fernando – editor of *Barricada*; son of Pedro Joaquín Chamorro.

Chamorro, Emiliano – Conservative politician; in 1914 as ambassador to Washington signed Chamorro-Bryan Treaty giving U.S. right to build inter-ocean canal through Nicaragua.

Chamorro, Pedro Joaquín – editor of *La Prensa* assassinated by Somoza in January 1978.

CONDECA – Central American Defense Council, a U.S.-sponsored military pact established in 1964.

Conservative Party – one of two traditional capitalist parties under Somoza; its major remaining faction today is the Democratic Conservative Party.

Contadora group – stated purpose is to negotiate peaceful solution to Central American conflict; composed of foreign ministers of Colombia, Mexico, Panama, and Venezuela; named after Panamanian island where it first met.

Contreras, Eduardo – a central leader of FSLN until his death in action in November 1976.

Córdoba – Nicaraguan currency; official parity of ten to U.S. dollar changed to twenty-eight to dollar in 1985.

COSEP – Supreme Council of Private Enterprise, main organization of Nicaraguan capitalist class.

Council of State – legislative body set up in 1980 with representatives from trade unions, women's and youth organizations, the FSLN and other political parties, farmers' organizations, and other groups; majority control in hands of workers and peasants; replaced in 1985 by National Assembly.

Cruz, Arturo – bourgeois economist; appointed to government junta in May 1980; ambassador to U.S. in March 1981; broke with revolution and was nominated as presidential candidate by bourgeois parties for 1984 elections but refused to run unless government opened negotiations with *contras;* supporter of *contra* forces.

CST – Sandinista Workers Federation; FSLN-led federation of trade unions.

Dario, Rubén – Nicaragua's foremost national poet; died in 1916.

D'Escoto, Miguel – foreign minister; Catholic priest.

Díaz, Adolfo – Nicaraguan president who supported U.S. intervention in 1926.

Enríquez, Magda – a founder of AMNLAE and its representative to the Council of State.

EPS – Sandinista People's Army.

Espinoza, Luisa Amanda – first woman member of FSLN to die in battle; killed by National Guard in 1970.

Estrada, José Dolores – played key role in 1856 war to oust proslavery adventurer William Walker, who had proclaimed himself president of Nicaragua.

Fagoth, Steadman – informer for Somoza regime on Atlantic Coast; a founding leader of MISURASATA, now a leader of MISURA, a counterrevolutionary group based in Honduras.

FDN – Nicaraguan Democratic Force; *contras* operating out of Honduras; organized as a result of CIA pressure in late 1981 for unity among ex-National Guard forces; trained and armed by U.S.

FMLN-FDR – Farabundo Martí National Liberation Front-Revolutionary Democratic Front; Salvadoran revolutionary forces fighting to topple proimperialist, oligarchic regime.

Fonseca, Carlos – founder of FSLN and its central leader until his death in action against the dictatorship in November 1976.

Herrera, Leticia (Vicky) – Guerrilla Commander; member of FSLN commando squad that occupied *somocista* José Castillo's house in December 1974, securing release of a number of political prisoners; currently CDS national coordinator.

Hooker, Ray – member Southern Zelaya regional government on Atlantic Coast; kidnapped by counterrevolutionary forces in 1984 and later released; elected to National Assembly on FSLN slate.

Independent Liberal Party (PLI) – bourgeois party; broke with Somoza's Liberal Party in 1944; part of original Council of State proposed in June 1979; increasingly hostile to revolution, its presidential candidate Virgilio Godoy withdrew before November elections charging they were unfair; campaigned for lifting state of emergency; criticized Sandinistas' measures to combat *contras*.

Jiménez, Lucío – general secretary, Sandinista Workers Federation.

Jirón, María Lourdes – member of FSLN general staff on western front during war against Somoza; works in FSLN Department of International Relations.

JS-19 – July 19 Sandinista Youth; FSLN-led youth organization.

Junta of the Government of National Reconstruction – top government body from 1979 until 1985; at first had five and later three members (Daniel Ortega, Rafael Córdova Rivas, and Sergio Ramírez).

Lang, Edgard – FSLN fighter killed during insurrection in April 1979.

Liberal Party – Somoza's political party; dissolved by revolution.

López Pérez, Rigoberto – young revolutionary who executed Anastasio Somoza García on September 21, 1956; he was murdered immediately afterward.

MAP-ML – People's Action Movement—Marxist-Leninist; founded in 1972 by student radicals; participated in 1979 insurrection; had representative on Council of State; leads Frente Obrero (Workers Front) trade union.

Mayorga, Silvio – one of three founders of FSLN; killed in action against the dictatorship at Pancasán in August 1967.

MISATAN – Organization of Nicaraguan Miskitos; founded as prorevolutionary group at July 1984 meeting of more than 350 representatives from 63 Miskito communities.

MISURA – Miskitos, Sumos, and Ramas United; *contra* group led by Steadman Fagoth; works with FDN.

MISURASATA – Miskitos, Sumos, Ramas and Sandinistas United; originally founded as prorevolutionary group; in February 1981, Steadman Fagoth and other leaders arrested for planning armed separatist movement; dissolved after Fagoth left for Honduras and began attacking revolution, although name still used by Brooklyn Rivera group.

Moncada, José María – led anti-U.S. Liberal forces in 1926 civil war; sold out in 1927 and signed a pact with U.S. envoy Henry Stimson.

Morales, Ana Isabel – member of FSLN general staff on western front in war against Somoza; works in Ministry of the Interior.

Morales Avilés, Ricardo – university professor and a national leader of FSLN; killed in action against the dictatorship in 1973.

Morazán, Francisco – Honduran patriot executed in 1842; advocate of Central American unity.

National Directorate – nine-member top leadership body of FSLN.

National Guard – formed by U.S. troops to combat Sandino in early 1930s; led by Anastasio Somoza García; central prop of the dictatorship until its defeat in 1979.

Nuevo Diario – prorevolution daily newspaper formed in 1980 by majority of *La Prensa* staff, who opposed latter's dishonest journalistic standards and antirevolutionary editorial policy.

Núñez, Carlos – member FSLN National Directorate; president of National Assembly.

Núñez, Daniel – member of the FSLN since 1972; freed as a result of December 1974 raid on Castillo house; elected president of UNAG in 1984.

Obando y Bravo, Miguel – archbishop of Managua and outspoken opponent of revolution.

Ortega, Camilo – FSLN leader killed in action February 26, 1978, during insurrection in Monimbó.

Ortega, Daniel – joined FSLN in early 1960s; freed as result of December 1974 raid on Castillo house after serving seven years in prison; member of FSLN National Directorate; elected president of Nicaragua, November 1984.

Ortega, Humberto – joined FSLN in 1965 and national leader since 1971; a member of FSLN National Directorate and its political commission, Nicaraguan defense minister, and commander in chief of Sandinista People's Army and Sandinista People's Militias.

Pastora, Edén – led 1978 capture of National Palace; Nicaragua's vice-minister of defense until his 1982 break with revolution; currently leads armed counterrevolutionary forces based in Costa Rica.

Pomares, Germán – a central leader of FSLN; killed in action on May 24, 1979.

Prensa, La – opposition daily newspaper during struggle against

Somoza; following 1979 increasingly became vocal opponent of FSLN and openly aligned with imperialism.

PCN – Communist Party of Nicaragua; emerged from 1967 split in PSN; characterizes FSLN as "bourgeois nationalist"; it considers agrarian reform to be "bourgeois."

PSN – Nicaraguan Socialist Party; the traditional Communist Party; leads General Confederation of Workers (Independent).

Ramírez, Sergio – prominent writer; joined FSLN in 1975; member of Junta of Government of National Reconstruction since 1979; elected vice-president in November 1984.

Ramírez, William – Guerrilla Commander; currently Nicaraguan transportation minister.

Rivera, Brooklyn – leader of MISURASATA who joined *contra* forces in 1981, although independent of Steadman Fagoth group; began holding cease-fire discussions with FSLN leaders in 1984.

Robelo, Alfonso – bourgeois opponent of Somoza; served on first Junta of National Reconstruction; resigned in April 1980 to protest course of revolution; currently a leader of armed counterrevolutionary forces based in Costa Rica.

Rocha, Brenda – fifteen-year-old militia member who was sole survivor of a counterrevolutionary attack; a photograph taken afterward of her smiling in the hospital became a symbol of resistance to the *contras*.

Rocha, Eleonora – participated in 1974 takeover of Castillo house; works in Ministry of the Interior.

Ruiz, Henry – member FSLN National Directorate; minister of foreign cooperation.

Sandino, Augusto César – Nicaragua's national hero; general on Liberal side in 1926 war; rejected Liberal betrayal in 1927 and led six-year guerrilla struggle against U.S. Marines and pro-imperialist forces; murdered February 21, 1934, on Somoza's orders; often referred to as "General of Free Men."

Schick, René – became Nicaraguan president in 1963 election engineered by Somoza; held office until 1967.

Siu, Arlen – joined FSLN as student activist; killed by National Guard in 1975.

Somoza Debayle, Anastasio – son of Anastasio Somoza García; became head of National Guard in 1956 after father's assassination; became president in 1967; fled Nicaragua on July 17, 1979; assassinated 1980 in Paraguay.

Somoza García, Anastasio – made head of National Guard in 1933 by U.S. forces; dictator of Nicaragua until his assassination in 1956; organized murder of Sandino.

Téllez, Dora María – Guerrilla Commander; a leader of 1978 Sandinista takeover of National Palace; currently political secretary of FSLN's Managua leadership committee and member of National Assembly.

Tijerino, Doris – longtime FSLN leader; imprisoned and tortured by Somoza dictatorship; currently president of AMNLAE.

Tirado, Víctor – member of FSLN National Directorate; born in Mexico, joined struggle in Nicaragua in early 1960s; currently the FSLN leader responsible for working with workers', peasants', and professional organizations.

Turcios, Oscar – FSLN member killed in action by National Guard in September 1973.

UNAG – National Union of Farmers and Ranchers; led by FSLN.

Walker, William – U.S. adventurer; led mercenary attack on Nicaragua in 1854 attempting to annex it to U.S. as slave state; made himself president of Nicaragua until driven out by Central American armies in 1856; later captured and executed.

Wheelock, Jaime – joined FSLN in 1969; member of FSLN National Directorate and its political commission; currently minister of agricultural development and agrarian reform.

Zelaya, José Santos – headed Nicaragua's first Liberal government; U.S. demanded his dismissal in 1909 when he began discussions with Germany and Japan over building interoceanic canal through Nicaragua.

Zeledón, Benjamin – led resistance to 1912 invasion of Nicaragua by U.S. Marines.

Index

African National Congress, 354, 535
Agency for International Development, 65, 131
Agrarian reform, 12, 178, 243–44, 246–49, 321–22, 418–19, 484–85, 500, 511, 514–15, 518, 550, 562, 565–66; on Atlantic Coast, 115, 489, 531
Agricultural production, 142–43, 221, 246, 250–51, 282, 321, 359, 427, 483, 484–85, 546, 549–50, 552–53, 554, 563–64
Agüero, Fernando, 77, 120–21, 185, 605
"Aims and Objectives of the New Education," 134
Air force, 38
Alday, Conchita, 109, 605
Allende, Salvador, 231, 335, 336, 357
Alliance for Progress, 178, 184, 255–56, 260
Alliances, strategy of, 208, 211, 304–5
Amnesty, 371, 372, 373–75, 376–78, 440, 441, 529
AMNLAE, 98, 101, 102, 104, 319, 605; tasks of, 400–402, 464
AMPRONAC, 104, 396–97, 605
ANDEN. *See* National Association of Nicaraguan Educators
Angola, 535
Aráuz, Blanca, 109, 605
Arce, Bayardo, 205, 605
ARDE, 605
Argentina, 28, 69–70, 141, 535
Argüello, Patricio, 188, 605

Armed struggle, 180, 182, 186
Arming the people, 279, 403, 414, 428, 437, 475
Arms race, 157, 167, 326, 353, 391
Army for the Defense of National Sovereignty, 34, 158, 209, 395, 512, 545, 605
Artisans, 255–57, 259–60, 487–88
Artists, 492–93
Association of Rural Workers (ATC), 319, 561–62, 563, 606
Astorga, Nora, 605–6
ATC. *See* Association of Rural Workers
Atheism, 226, 439
Atlantic Coast, 145–50, 151, 153–54, 446, 489–90, 591–98; and autonomy, 591–92, 593–96; FSLN errors on, 389–90, 527–29, 592–94, 596–97; Indians on, 144–45, 393–94, 593–96; problems of, 114–15, 527–32, 592–94. *See also* Miskito Indians
Avilés, Olga, 97, 606

Baéz, Gladys, 97, 396, 606
Baltodano, Mónica, 97, 606
Banks, 12, 281, 306, 419, 483, 558–59
Barricada, 15–16, 552, 606
Big Pine maneuvers, 114, 363, 462
Big Stick policy, 507, 510
Bilingual education, 155–56, 489, 597
Blockade, U.S., 326–27, 445, 447–48, 449–50
Bolívar, Simón, 293–94, 316

613

Bolivia, 233, 536
Borge, Tomás, 205, 372, 379, 606
Botswana, 535
Bourgeoisie, 56, 93–95, 128–30; Nicaraguan, 14, 56, 60, 62, 76–77, 130, 185, 195–96, 210, 211–12, 215–18, 220–21, 456. *See also* Farmers, wealthy
Bourgeois revolution, 413
Brazil, 141
Broken Promises, 568
Brunei, 533
Buitrago, Julio, 189, 227, 585, 606
Bureaucratism, 53, 66, 112, 483, 488–89

Calero Portocarrero, Adolfo, 350
Capitalism, 79, 80, 81, 83, 167, 169, 170, 176
Cardenal, Ernesto, 561, 606
Cardenal, Fernando, 561, 606
Carib Indians, 149
Carrión, Luis, 205, 606
Carter, James, 11, 36, 199, 239, 339
CAS, 606
Castillo, José María, 190, 210
Castro, Andrés, 317, 606
Cattle raising, 250, 256
CDS. *See* Sandinista Defense Committees
Censorship, 307
Central American Common Market, 178, 256, 260
Central American Defense Council (CONDECA), 194, 238, 392, 607
Central American independence, 146, 293
Central Intelligence Agency (CIA), 28, 37, 237, 272, 335, 336, 362–63, 384, 435, 436, 444, 445, 460, 461
Cerna, Lenín, 569
Chamorro, Carlos Fernando, 606
Chamorro, Emiliano, 600, 602, 607
Chamorro, Fruto, 508

Chamorro, Pedro Joaquín, 197, 228, 607
Chamorro, Violeta Barrios de, 305
Child-care centers, 100–101, 401
Chile, 117, 230–31, 335–38, 357, 435, 535
Church, Catholic, 119, 127–28, 129–30, 223, 224–26, 234, 390–91, 437–39
Civil war, 383–85
Class consciousness, 58, 129, 283
Clayton-Bulwer treaty, 146
Coffee, 81–82, 140, 141, 142, 321, 423, 553, 554, 589–90
Committees of Mothers of Heroes and Martyrs, 104
Communism, 167–68
Conservative Party, 195, 211, 507, 508–9, 558, 607
Constitution, 406
Consumer goods, 281, 425–26, 427, 428, 447–48, 451–52, 455, 483, 485–86
Contadora group, 239, 328, 332, 365, 371, 372, 461, 521, 538–39, 607
Contras, 12, 37, 38, 76, 251, 252, 268–69, 278–79, 308, 326, 384, 403, 405, 434–35, 444–53, 459, 460, 520–21, 540, 555, 598; blows against, 108–9, 363, 581–83; casualties from, 424–25, 443, 452–54, 521, 537, 539, 540, 545, 547–48, 550, 555, 564; U.S. aid to, 37, 38, 42–43, 340, 341–42, 407, 438, 453, 463–64. *See also* Central Intelligence Agency; Terrorism; United States, aggression against Nicaragua by
Contreras, Eduardo, 190, 607
Coolidge, Calvin, 34
Cooperatives, 251, 252–53, 256–57, 322, 323–24, 514–15, 518, 548, 555, 557
COSEP (Supreme Council of Private Enterprise), 196, 443, 546, 552–53,

556, 557, 560, 564
Costa Rica, 27, 142, 238, 280, 281, 460
Cotton, 65, 81–82, 176–77, 218, 219, 221–22, 321, 428–29
Council of State, 214, 229, 243, 386, 400, 420, 607
Counterrevolutionaries. *See* Contras
Court of Cassation, 409–10
Credit, 65, 162, 483. *See also* Peasants, credits to
Crime, 410–12, 480, 570, 571–72
Cruz, Arturo, 607
Cruz, Rigoberto, 186, 187
CST. *See* Sandinista Workers Federation
Cuadra, Jaime, 552
Cuadra Pasos, 602
Cuba, 39, 42, 69, 178, 179, 182, 286–87, 296, 385, 386, 506–7, 535, 595
Culture, 398, 491–93, 530, 597–98
Cyprus, 536

Darío, Rubén, 316, 472, 607
Debts: of agricultural producers, 218, 322–24, 554, 565; foreign, 141, 281, 282, 422, 426, 484, 519
Decapitalization, 65, 220, 281, 566
Defense, 39, 42, 49–51, 160, 463–71, 479, 501, 523–24; against U.S. invasion, 32, 116–17, 435, 436–37, 521–22, 578–90. *See also* Arming the people; Militia; Sandinista People's Army; Working class, and defense
Democracy, 32, 47, 118–20, 127, 135, 163, 243–45, 300–301, 401, 407, 414–15, 481–82
Dependency, on imperialism, 53, 82, 84, 433, 510–11
D'Escoto, Miguel, 272, 561, 607
Destabilization, U.S., 28, 38, 40, 45, 76, 228–29, 311, 313–14, 424–25,

436, 441, 442–43, 451–52, 460–61, 520–21
Díaz, Adolfo, 336, 600, 602, 607
Díaz, Zela, 408
Díaz Ochoa, Bernardino, 420
Disarmament, 353
Division of powers, 292, 406–8
Dollar Diplomacy, 507, 510
Domestic service, 99
Dominican Republic, 26, 233
Drought, 310
Duarte, José Napoleón, 28
Dulles, Allen, 26

Earthquake (1972), 194, 212
East Timor, 535
East-West confrontation, 31, 380–82
Economic crisis, of capitalism, 40, 41, 65, 68, 140–41, 177, 221, 251, 259, 281, 310, 328, 358–59, 423, 461
Economism, 58–59
Economy: destruction of by Somoza, 418–19, 422–23; distortion of by imperialism, 62–63, 217, 259–62, 400, 424–25, 546; mixed, 32, 117–18, 218–20, 247, 257–58, 281, 312, 482; planning of, 263–66, 312–13, 482–83
Education, 47, 71–72, 123, 125–26, 127–29, 132–39, 320, 450, 453–54, 491–92, 531
El Bluff, 153–54
Elections, 32, 230, 233–34, 241–43, 244–46, 274–75, 421; of 1984–85, 119, 309, 328, 375–76, 386–87, 475–76, 478, 539
Electrification, 249, 553
El Salvador, 27, 30–31, 39–40, 73–74, 142, 171, 233, 237, 240, 381, 462; revolution in, 37, 437, 536, 537
Employment, 68, 253–55, 452
Enders, Thomas, 28
Engels, Frederick, 167

Enríquez, Magda, 608
Environment, 79–88
Espino Negro pact, 208–9
Espinoza, Luisa Amanda, 97, 109–10, 608
Estrada, José Dolores, 347, 421, 544, 608
European Economic Community, 539, 540
Exploitation, 56, 167; elimination of in Nicaragua, 406, 476, 523
Exporting revolution, 47, 291–93, 294–95
Exports, 142, 519. See also Trade

Fagoth, Steadman, 28, 30, 77, 390, 529, 594–95, 596, 597, 608
Family Protection Office, 400
FAO (Broad Opposition Front), 212–13
Farmers, wealthy, 556–58, 559–61, 563
FETSALUD, 159, 319
Feudalism, 55–56, 127–28, 129
Fire-fighting, 570
Fishing, 147–49, 445–46, 447
Flood damage, 142, 321, 494
FMLN-FDR, 39, 42, 608
Fonseca, Carlos, 77–78, 179, 180–81, 188, 191–92, 203–4, 227, 275, 465, 470, 473, 608
Food, 152–53, 309–11, 324–26; distribution of, 430–32, 455, 485–86, 520, 522, 524–25. See also Subsidies
Foreign aid, 484
Foreign policy, 234, 512–13
Forestry resources, 146–47, 148
France, 39
Franklin, Benjamin, 292
Freedom of press, 227–29, 387–88
French revolution, 291
FSLN, 11, 14, 63–64, 98, 119, 120, 186–87, 203–5, 208–9, 243, 284, 304, 307, 577; National Directorate of, 77, 202–3, 205–8, 263, 319; in struggle for power, 175, 180–201, 209–10, 472–77; tendencies within, 193, 204–5; unity of, 193–94, 499–504; and workers and peasants, 52, 63–64, 160, 421, 512

García, Edgardo, 562
General strike, 200
Granadero I, 462
Great Britain, 69–70, 145–46
Grenada, 403, 536, 541
Gross domestic product, 142
Group of Twelve, 305
Guatemala, 26, 37, 117, 142, 233, 237–38, 279
Guerrilla warfare, 181, 182, 183, 185, 188
Guevara, Che, 318
Guido, Lea, 98

Haig, Alexander, 70
Haiti, 233
Hassan, Moisés, 305
Health care, 12, 71, 104, 150–51, 320–21, 381, 450, 451, 530–31; progress in, 73, 320, 401, 490, 494, 502
Heritage Foundation, 338
Heroes and Martyrs National Professional Confederation, 319
Herrera, Leticia (Vicky), 97, 98, 112, 569, 608
Historical materialism, 167
Honduras, 27, 28, 233, 344, 345–46, 460, 462–63, 581
Hooker, Ray, 608
Housing, 454, 493
Human rights, 388–89, 481
Hunger, 325–26, 353, 381–82

Illiteracy, 12, 398, 531. See also Literacy campaign
Imperialism, 62–63, 64, 133, 140, 196,

230–31, 244–45, 266–67; as enemy of Nicaragua, 59, 442, 506–7; and war, 169–70, 232, 236–37. *See also* United States
Imports, 82, 256, 261–62, 423, 426. *See also* Trade
Independent Liberal Party (PLI), 166, 213, 214, 608
Indians, extermination of, 144, 595
Industrialization, 255–56, 321, 518–19
Industrial revolution, 128–29
Infant mortality, 13, 270, 320, 381, 500
Inflation, 282, 430, 452. *See also* Prices
Innovators movement, 161
Institutionalization of revolution, 244, 328, 406, 501
Insurrectionalist tendency, 205
Intellectuals, 492–93
Inter-American Development Bank, 339
Interoceanic canal, 145–46, 236, 506, 511, 602
Iran, 356, 536
Iraq, 356, 536
Israel, 238, 355, 356, 435, 535

Jamaica, 145
Jefferson, Thomas, 292
Jiménez, Lucío, 608
Jirón, María Lourdes, 97, 609
Judicial system, 387, 406–11, 413–15, 488–89
July 19 Sandinista Youth, 319, 464, 609
Junta of the Government of National Reconstruction, 39, 305, 306, 318, 414, 609

Kampuchea, 535
Kennedy, John F., 184
Kirkpatrick, Jeane, 33

Kissinger, Henry, 435
Korea, 535
Kupia Kumi pact, 185

Labor shortages, 253, 254
Lake Managua, 79–88
Landowners, 195, 553
Land reform. *See* Agrarian reform
Land seizures, 112, 179, 194, 218, 322, 551–52, 565–67
Lang Edgard, 227, 609
Laos, 535
Law, 400–401, 406–15, 571–72
Law on Housing, 160
Law on Nurture, 99–100, 102, 106
Law on Political Parties, 229, 328, 387
Lawyers, 410
Lebanon, 356
Legitimate Party, 508
Lenin, V.I., 172
León, 318
Lesotho, 535
Liberal Party, 195, 214, 507–9, 558
Liberal revolution (1893), 245
Liberals, 294
Libya, 356, 535
Literacy campaign, 12, 71–72, 132, 194, 308, 320, 401, 502
Loans, foreign, 311, 313–14, 326–27, 339, 359, 423, 449
Locke, John, 407
López Pérez, Rigoberto, 177, 178–79, 473, 609
Luis Alfonso Velásquez Association of Sandinista Children, 319, 464

McKinley, William, 506
Madison, James, 292, 295
Malvinas Islands War, 69–70, 236, 344, 355, 535
Managua, defense of, 583–85, 588
Manifest Destiny, 290, 295–96
MAP-ML, 609

Martínez, Tomás, 509
Marx, Karl, 157, 166–68, 172
Marxism, 169, 172–73
May Day, 49, 50, 51, 54–55, 417–18
Mayorga, Silvio, 405, 470, 609
Mexico, 39–40, 141, 296
MIGs, 582
Militia, 51, 104, 155, 162, 334, 463–64, 465–66, 468–69, 583
Ministry of Agrarian Development and Reform, 563–64
Ministry of Internal Trade, 525
Ministry of Labor, 420
Ministry of Planning, 265
Ministry of the Interior, 29, 319, 464, 480, 568–76
MISATAN, 530, 609
Miskito Indians, 114–15, 145, 147, 388, 389–90, 527–32, 595–97; and amnesty, 372, 376–78; and *contras*, 384, 527, 528–29; relocation of, 29, 528
MISURA, 609
MISURASATA, 528–29, 609
Momotombo geothermic plant, 85
Moncada, José María, 434, 509, 609
Monimbó insurrection, 122, 197
Monroe, James, 26
Monroe Doctrine, 344, 507
Monterrey, Gladys, 98
Montesquieu, 407
Morales, Ana Isabel, 97, 609
Morales Avilés, Ricardo, 139, 186, 610
Morality, 132–33, 224
Morazán, Francisco, 294–95, 508, 610

Nación, La, 280
Namibia, 354
National Assembly, 244
National Association of Nicaraguan Educators (ANDEN), 122, 124, 132, 159, 319, 605
National Council on Agrarian Reform, 244
National Employees Union, 319
National Finance System, 323
National Guard, 11, 13, 14, 28–29, 56–57, 175, 232, 266–68, 297, 338, 347, 348–51, 381, 384, 399, 459. *See also Contras; Somocismo*
National liberation, 11, 59, 62–63, 95
National Palace, seizure of, 191, 198, 199
National Patriotic Front, 200, 213
National System for the Organization of Work and Wages, 432, 486, 522, 525
National Union of Farmers and Ranchers (UNAG), 283, 319, 323, 546–49, 550, 552–53, 558, 559–65, 566
National Union of Nicaraguan Students (UNEN), 495
Nationalizations, 12, 220, 221, 419, 514–15, 558–59
Negotiations, 42, 162; with U.S., 46, 231–32, 460, 541
Neutrality Act (U.S.), 37
Neutron bomb, 80
New York Times, 229, 338
Nicaraguan Communist Party (PCN), 611
Nicaraguan Democratic Forces (FDN), 384, 608
Nicaraguan Democratic Movement (MDN), 195–96
Nicaraguan Socialist Party (PSN), 166, 184, 213, 611
Nicaraguan Trade Union Coordinating Committee, 283
Nixon, Richard, 581
Nonaggression pacts, 30, 40–41, 42, 46
Nonaligned movement, 356, 357, 368
Nonalignment, 30, 41, 286, 314–15,

480, 513, 534, 536
Nuclear war, 157, 343, 352, 353
Nuevo Diario, El, 388, 552, 610
Núñez, Carlos, 205, 610
Núñez, Daniel, 610

Obando y Bravo, Miguel, 77, 223, 224–26, 441, 610
Obrerismo Organizado, 158
Ocotal, 503–4
October revolution (Russia), 172, 236
Oil, 65, 327
Oligarchy, 130, 218, 234
Ordóñez, Cleto, 472
Ortega, Camilo, 122, 158, 610
Ortega, Daniel, 75, 205, 610
Ortega, Humberto, 198, 205, 610

Palestinians, 239, 354, 417, 535
Panama, 357–58, 535
Pan-Americanism, 296
Pancasán front, 186–87
Paraguay, 233, 234
Pastora, Edén, 191, 198–99, 328, 341, 434, 459, 462, 610
Patriotic military service, 333, 466, 468–69, 523
Patriotic Youth, 179
Peasants, 215, 216, 398, 418–19, 420; and *contras,* 251–52, 467, 468, 549–51; cancellation of debts of, 218, 322–24, 554, 565; credit to, 484–85, 518, 563–64; and land, 47, 250, 251–52, 484–85, 518; support for revolution among, 60, 545, 546–53, 559–60, 563–64, 567
People's Civic Committees, 184, 187
People's Property Sector, 12, 222, 247–48, 251, 252, 256, 281, 548
People's Social Christian Party, 166, 213
People's war, 463, 579
Pesticides, 176

Pinochet, Augusto, 239
Pluralism, 32, 117, 118–19, 227–28, 247, 386–87
Poliomyelitis, 320
Political prisoners, 189, 210
Pollution, 82–84
Pomares, Germán, 190, 198, 470, 610
Popular Education Collectives, 320
Portillo, José López, 29, 32, 39
Prensa, La, 227–28, 341, 388, 551–52, 610–11
Prices, 68, 282, 422–23, 424, 430–31, 455, 485–86, 519–20, 554
Prisons, 572
Private sector, 312–14, 386, 548–49
Proletarian tendency, 205
Prolonged People's War tendency (GPP), 205
Prostitution, 94, 496
Providence Company, 145
Puerto Rico, 296, 354, 355, 535

Rama Indians, 149, 594
Ramírez, Sergio, 112, 611
Ramírez, William, 611
Rationing, 435–36
Raudales, Ramón, 473
Raw materials, 233, 260–62
Reagan, Ronald, 36–37, 38, 45, 162, 170–71, 228, 237, 277, 296–97, 338–39, 344, 345, 459
"Red Christmas," 28–29, 38
Religion, 76, 115, 116, 129–30, 223–27, 390–91, 438–39, 496–97
Republican Mobilization Party, 184
Resettlement, 425, 445, 454, 528
Revolutionary Patriotic Front, 119
Revolutionary Student Front (FER), 184, 187, 189
Revolutionary vigilance, 113, 480, 523, 572
Rivera, Brooklyn, 595, 596–98, 611
Robelo, Alfonso, 77, 120–21, 196, 305–6, 611

Rocha, Brenda, 104, 611
Rocha, Eleonora, 97, 611
Roosevelt, Theodore, 26, 507
Rugama, Leonel, 586
Ruiz, Henry, 205, 611
Rural Children's Services, 451

Sabotage, 461
Sahraoui Arab Democratic Republic, 535
Salazar, Jorge, 308
San Antonio sugar refinery, 219–20
Sandinista Cultural Workers Association, 319
Sandinista Defense Committees, 87, 111–13, 151, 420, 464, 569, 606
Sandinista National Liberation Front. *See* FSLN
Sandinista People's Army, 57, 456, 461, 463–64, 573
Sandinista Police, 57, 411–12, 568, 569–70, 571–72
Sandinista Workers Federation (CST), 51, 52–53, 157–58, 159, 163, 607
Sandino, Augusto César, 11, 13, 63, 117, 158, 174, 175, 180–81, 208–9, 275, 395, 421, 457, 465, 470, 473, 505–6, 513–15, 545, 599–603, 611
SCAAS, 159
Schick, René, 184, 611
Secondary Students Federation (FES), 495
Self-determination, 42, 171, 591
September 15 radio station, 30, 115
Sexism, 102–3
Seychelles, 535
Shible, Selim, 470
Shopkeepers, 485
Shortages, 422–26, 430–31, 436, 447–48, 451–52, 455, 531
Shultz, George, 460
Siu, Arlen, 97, 611
Slavery, 55, 92, 95
Social Christian Party, 211

Socialism, 49–50, 52, 171, 257; as long-term goal, 163–65; and Marx, 167–68, 172
Socialist countries, 53, 314–15
Social Security, 490
Solidarity, 44–45, 48, 69–70, 276–77, 278, 285–86, 435, 521, 526, 579–80
Somocismo, 11, 13, 147–48, 175–76, 194–97, 199–200, 211–12, 242–43, 247–48, 266–68, 301–2, 370, 389, 433, 534, 612; fight against, 324, 396–97, 398–99, 418–19, 458–59, 473–74, 499–500, 545, 587; and imperialism, 62–63, 216, 558
South Africa, 354, 417, 534
South-West Africa People's Organisation (SWAPO), 535
Sovereignty, 26–27, 31, 171, 181, 228, 508–13
Soviet Union, 286, 287, 288, 385–86
Spain, 144, 145–46, 395, 506, 544
Speculators, 68, 281, 325, 419, 442, 443, 452, 455–56, 485–86, 525
Sports, 135, 491–92
Spy flights, 38–39, 43, 342, 362, 578
Standard of living, 161, 446–47, 451–57
State of emergency, 39, 46, 49–50, 119, 171, 307
Strikes, 159, 179; after revolution, 219, 282, 431, 517–18, 522, 524
Subsidies, food, 430, 455, 483, 485–86
Sugar, 65, 81–82, 142, 311
Sumo Indians, 149, 594
Supreme Court, 214, 408–9, 414
Swaziland, 535

Taft, William Howard, 26, 507
Tardencilla, Orlando, 61
Taxes, 450, 455
Teachers, 122–26, 130–32, 133–34,

136–38, 453–54
Technicians, 488
Technology, 82, 252–54, 282
Television, 492, 493
Téllez, Dora María, 97, 98, 199, 399, 612
Terrorism, 38, 45, 76, 272, 407, 463, 464, 550, 573
Thatcher, Margaret, 344, 402
Third World, 47, 169, 281
Tijerino, Doris, 97, 186, 612
Tirado, Víctor, 188, 205, 612
Torture, 119
Trade, 258, 286–87, 385–86, 449; imbalance of, 65–66, 141–42, 359–60, 423–24, 426, 449–50, 519
Trade unions, 12, 13, 51–52, 67, 387, 420, 486–87
Transportation, 153–54, 493–94, 520
Tuberculosis, 147
Tupamaros, 285
Turcios, Oscar, 186, 470, 612

UDEL (Democratic Liberation Union), 211
UNAG. See National Union of Farmers and Ranchers
Unemployment, 13, 141, 253–54
United Nations, 46, 314, 533–34
United People's Movement (MPU), 132, 200, 213, 305
United States, 33–35, 68, 277–78, 295–97, 521; aggression against Nicaragua by, 39–40, 45–46, 75–76, 115–17, 233, 236–37, 240–41, 267–68, 276, 326–27, 328, 347–48, 361–67, 371, 379–80, 433–35, 444–53, 461–62, 502–3, 537–38, 539–41; history of aggression by, 32–33, 146, 212, 290–91, 336–37, 402–3, 422, 433–34, 458–60, 506–7, 549, 601–2; military bases of, 27, 37–38, 279–80, 402, 460; "national security" of, 26, 170, 237, 348, 382–83; policy of toward Central America, 40–41, 238–39, 240–41, 290–91, 345–46, 361–62, 402–3; relations with, 31–32, 33, 42, 75, 315
Unity, 45, 59–60, 66, 193–94, 500–501

Vietnam, 25, 33–34, 48, 356, 535, 580–81

Wages, 160, 420, 422–23, 430, 431–32, 486, 520
Walker, William, 116, 347, 361, 506, 544, 612
Walters, Vernon, 28
War, 167, 237, 278
Wheelock, Jaime, 205, 230, 612
Women, 12, 93–97, 102–3, 496; liberation of, 90, 91, 397, 399, 400–401; participation of in revolution, 62, 95, 97–99, 104, 106–8, 395–402; roots of oppression of, 91–95, 397; in work force, 99, 100, 398, 402
Workers' and peasants' government, 11, 159, 417, 419, 420–21, 524
Working class, 54–55, 58–59, 136, 160, 162–63, 164, 168; agricultural, 177, 561–62; and defense, 67, 160, 521–22, 523–26; development of, 55–56, 58, 158–59; and fight for production, 50–53, 160–62, 219, 243, 516–18, 521–26; and political power, 52, 420–21. See also Sandinista Workers Federation; Strikes; Trade unions; Workers' and peasants' government
World Bank, 339
World Court, 537–38

Zambia, 535
Zelaya, José Santos, 336, 509, 612
Zelaya, Petrona, 503
Zeledón, Benjamín, 117, 347, 421, 465, 472–73, 545, 612

THE RISE AND FALL OF THE NICARAGUAN REVOLUTION

Based on ten years of socialist journalism from inside Nicaragua, this special issue of *New International* recounts the achievements and worldwide impact of the 1979 Nicaraguan revolution. It traces the political retreat of the Sandinista National Liberation Front leadership that led to the downfall of the workers and farmers government in the closing years of the 1980s. Documents of the Socialist Workers Party by Jack Barnes, Steve Clark, and Larry Seigle. In *New International* no. 9. $16. Also in Spanish.

Women and the Nicaraguan Revolution
TOMÁS BORGE

The effort, in the early years of the Nicaraguan revolution, to lead, organize, and educate in the fight for women's rights. $6

Sandinistas Speak
TOMÁS BORGE, CARLOS FONSECA, DANIEL ORTEGA, AND OTHERS

The best selection in English of historic documents of the FSLN and speeches and interviews from the opening years of the 1979 revolution. $18

CUBA'S SOCIALIST REVOLUTION

Cuba and the Coming American Revolution
JACK BARNES

This is a book about the struggles of working people in the imperialist heartland, the youth attracted to them, and the example set by the Cuban people that revolution is not only necessary—it can be made. It is about the class struggle in the US, where the revolutionary capacities of workers and farmers are today as utterly discounted by the ruling powers as were those of the Cuban toilers. And just as wrongly. $10. Also in Spanish, French, and Farsi.

Women in Cuba: The Making of a Revolution within the Revolution
VILMA ESPÍN, ASELA DE LOS SANTOS, YOLANDA FERRER

The integration of women into the ranks and leadership of the Cuban Revolution was inseparably intertwined with the proletarian course of the revolution from the start. This is the story of that revolution and how it transformed the women and men who made it. $20. Also in Spanish and Greek.

How Far We Slaves Have Come!
South Africa and Cuba in Today's World
NELSON MANDELA, FIDEL CASTRO

Cuban internationalists "made a contribution to African independence, freedom, and justice, unparalleled for its principles and selfless character," said Nelson Mandela, speaking in Cuba in July 1991 alongside Fidel Castro. Here are their speeches on the victory by Cuban, Angolan, and Namibian combatants over the US-backed South African army that had invaded Angola. $10. Also in Spanish and Farsi.

WWW.PATHFINDERPRESS.COM

FROM PATHFINDER

Are They Rich Because They're Smart?
Class, Privilege, and Learning under Capitalism

JACK BARNES

Exposes the self-serving rationalizations by well-paid middle-class layers that their intelligence and schooling equip them to "regulate" workers' lives. Includes "Capitalism, the Working Class, and the Transformation of Learning." $10. Also in Spanish, French, and Farsi.

Is Socialist Revolution in the US Possible?
A Necessary Debate among Working People

MARY-ALICE WATERS

Fighting for a society only working people can create, it is our own capacities we will discover. And along that course we will answer the question posed here with a resounding "Yes." Possible but not inevitable. That depends on us. $10. Also in Spanish, French, and Farsi.

The Clintons' Anti-Working-Class Record
Why Washington Fears Working People

JACK BARNES

Describes the profit-driven course of Democrats and Republicans alike, and the political awakening of workers seeking to understand and resist these assaults. $10. Also in Spanish, French, Farsi, and Greek.

The Teamster series
FARRELL DOBBS

From the 1934 strikes that won union recognition to the fight by class-conscious workers to oppose Washington's objectives in World War II.

"These books are not 'manuals' or handbooks. They are the record of a concrete experience in the class struggle— one that can be studied and absorbed by class-conscious workers and farmers who find themselves in the midst of other struggles, at other times, in other conditions, speaking many different languages."
—Jack Barnes. $19 each. Also in Spanish. *Teamster Rebellion* is available in French, Farsi, and Greek.

In Defense of the US Working Class
MARY-ALICE WATERS

Hillary Clinton calls them "deplorables" who inhabit the "backward" regions between New York and San Francisco. But tens of thousands of teachers and other school employees in West Virginia set an example in 2018 with the most powerful labor action in decades. And working people across Florida mobilized and won restoration of voting rights to more than one million former prisoners. They fought for dignity and respect for themselves, their families, and for all working people. $7. Also in Spanish and Farsi.

"It's the Poor Who Face the Savagery of the US 'Justice' System"
The Cuban Five Talk about Their Lives within the US Working Class

How US cops, courts, and prisons work as "an enormous machine for grinding people up." Five Cuban revolutionaries framed up and held in US jails for 16 years explain the human devastation of capitalist "justice"—and how socialist Cuba is different. $15. Also in Spanish, Farsi, and Greek.

WWW.PATHFINDERPRESS.COM

CUBA'S INTERNATIONALIST MISSIONS WORLDWIDE

Cuba and Angola: The War for Freedom
HARRY VILLEGAS ("POMBO")

The story of Cuba's unparalleled contribution to the fight to free Africa from the scourge of apartheid. And how, in the doing, Cuba's socialist revolution was strengthened. $10. Also in Spanish.

Companion volume
Cuba and Angola
Fighting for Africa's Freedom and Our Own

FIDEL CASTRO, RAÚL CASTRO, NELSON MANDELA, OTHERS

$12. Also in Spanish.

The First and Second Declarations of Havana

Nowhere are the questions of revolutionary strategy that today confront men and women on the front lines of struggles in the Americas addressed with greater truthfulness and clarity than in these uncompromising indictments of imperialist plunder and "the exploitation of man by man." Adopted by million-strong assemblies of the Cuban people in 1960 and 1962. $10. Also in Spanish, French, Farsi, Arabic, and Greek.

Bolivian Diary of Ernesto Che Guevara

Guevara's day-by-day chronicle of the 1966–67 guerrilla campaign in Bolivia, an effort to forge a continent-wide revolutionary movement of workers and peasants and open the road to socialist revolution in South America. $25. Also in Spanish.

Voices from Prison
THE CUBAN FIVE

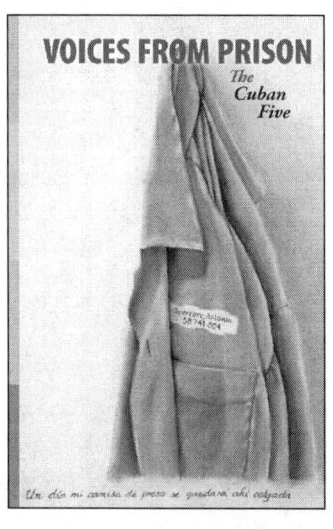

Cuban internationalists Gerardo Hernández, Ramón Labañino, Antonio Guerrero, Fernando González, and René González, known to millions worldwide as the Cuban Five, were framed up and imprisoned by Washington for up to 16 years. In the voices heard here from fellow prisoners, freedom fighters, and family members their revolutionary integrity, humanity—and humor—emerge ever more clearly. $7. Also in Spanish, French, Farsi, and Arabic.

In Defense of Socialism
Four Speeches on the 30th Anniversary of the Cuban Revolution, 1988–89
FIDEL CASTRO

Castro describes the decisive place of volunteer Cuban fighters in the final stage of the war in Angola against invading forces of South Africa's apartheid regime. Not only is economic and social progress possible without capitalism's dog-eat-dog competition, the Cuban leader says, but socialism is humanity's only way forward. $15. Also in Greek.

From the Escambray to the Congo
In the Whirlwind of the Cuban Revolution
VÍCTOR DREKE

A leading participant in Cuba's revolutionary movement for more than half a century describes his experiences as second-in-command in the 1965 internationalist mission in Congo led by Che Guevara. He describes the creative joy of working people in Cuba, at home and abroad, as they've defended their revolutionary course. $18. Also in Spanish.

WWW.PATHFINDERPRESS.COM

EXPAND YOUR REVOLUTIONARY LIBRARY

Puerto Rico: Independence Is a Necessity
RAFAEL CANCEL MIRANDA

One of the five Puerto Rican Nationalists imprisoned by Washington for more than 25 years and released in 1979 speaks out on the brutal reality of US colonial domination, the example of Cuba's socialist revolution, and the ongoing struggle for independence. $6. Also in Spanish and Farsi.

Malcolm X, Black Liberation, and the Road to Workers Power
JACK BARNES

Why the conquest of power by the working class will make possible the final battle for Black freedom—and open the way to a world based on human solidarity, not exploitation, violence, and racism. A socialist world. $20. Also in Spanish, French, Farsi, Arabic, and Greek.

Our History Is Still Being Written
The Story of Three Chinese Cuban Generals in the Cuban Revolution

ARMANDO CHOY, GUSTAVO CHUI, MOISÉS SÍO WONG, MARY-ALICE WATERS

"What was the key measure to uproot discrimination against Chinese and blacks in Cuba? It was the socialist revolution itself." New edition sheds light on Chinese Cubans' involvement in Cuba's internationalist course, including in Africa and Latin America. $17. Also in Spanish, Farsi, and Chinese.

Marianas in Combat

Teté Puebla and the Mariana Grajales Women's Platoon in Cuba's Revolutionary War, 1956–58

TETÉ PUEBLA

Brigadier General Teté Puebla, the highest ranking woman in Cuba's Revolutionary Armed Forces, joined the struggle to overthrow the US-backed dictatorship of Fulgencio Batista in 1956, when she was fifteen years old. This is her story—from clandestine action in the cities, to serving as an officer in the victorious Rebel Army's first all-women's unit. The fight to transform the social and economic status of women in Cuba remains inseparable from its socialist revolution. $14. Also in Spanish and Farsi.

The Jewish Question

A Marxist Interpretation

ABRAM LEON

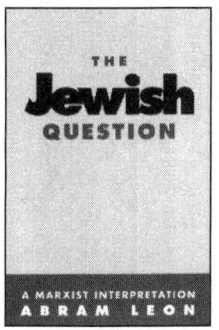

Traces the historical rationalizations of anti-Semitism to the fact that Jews became a "people-class" of merchants and moneylenders in the centuries before industrial capitalism. And how, in times of crisis, capitalists mobilize renewed Jew-hatred to incite reactionary forces and disorient working people about the true source of their impoverishment. $25. Also in Greek.

Thomas Sankara Speaks

The Burkina Faso Revolution, 1983–87

Under Sankara's guidance, Burkina Faso's revolutionary government led peasants, workers, women, and youth to expand literacy; to sink wells, plant trees, erect housing; to combat women's oppression; to carry out land reform; to join others in Africa and worldwide to free themselves from the imperialist yoke. $24. Also in French.

WWW.PATHFINDERPRESS.COM

Malcolm X Talks to Young People

"The young generation of whites, Blacks, browns, whatever else there is—you're living at a time of revolution," Malcolm said in December 1964. "And I for one will join in with anyone, I don't care what color you are, as long as you want to change this miserable condition that exists on this earth." $15. Also in Spanish, French, Farsi, and Greek.

America's Revolutionary Heritage
GEORGE NOVACK

A materialist history of the American Revolution, the Civil War and Radical Reconstruction, the genocide against Native Americans, the first wave of the fight for women's rights, and more. $25

Fascism: What It Is and How to Fight It
LEON TROTSKY

Writing in the heat of struggle against the rising fascist movement in Europe in the 1930s, Russian communist leader Leon Trotsky examines the origins and nature of fascism and advances, for the first time, a working-class strategy to combat and defeat it. $7. Also in French.

The Communist Manifesto

KARL MARX, FREDERICK ENGELS

Why communism is not a set of preconceived principles but the line of march of the working class toward power, "springing from an existing class struggle, a historical movement going on under our very eyes." The founding document of the modern revolutionary workers movement. $5. Also in Spanish, French, Farsi, and Arabic.

Che Guevara: Economics and Politics in the Transition to Socialism

CARLOS TABLADA

Quoting extensively from Guevara's writings and speeches on building socialism, this book presents the interrelationship of the market, economic planning, material incentives, and voluntary work; and why profit and other capitalist categories cannot be yardsticks for measuring progress in the transition to socialism. $21. Also in Spanish, French, and Greek.

Maurice Bishop Speaks

The Grenada Revolution and Its Overthrow, 1979–83

The triumph of the 1979 revolution in the Caribbean island of Grenada under the leadership of Maurice Bishop gave hope to millions throughout the Americas. Invaluable lessons from the workers and farmers government defeated by a Stalinist-led coup in 1983. $25

WWW.PATHFINDERPRESS.COM

RUSSIAN REVOLUTION'S WORLD EXAMPLE

Lenin's Final Fight
Speeches and Writings, 1922–23
V.I. LENIN

In 1922 and 1923, V.I. Lenin, central leader of the world's first socialist revolution, waged what was to be his last political battle—one that was lost following his death. At stake was whether that revolution, and the international communist movement it led, would remain on the proletarian course that had brought workers and peasants to power in October 1917. $20. Also in Spanish, Farsi, and Greek.

The History of the Russian Revolution
LEON TROTSKY

How, under Lenin's leadership, the Bolshevik Party led millions of workers and farmers to overthrow the state power of the landlords and capitalists in 1917 and bring to power a government that advanced their class interests at home and worldwide. Unabridged, 3 vols. in one. Written by one of the central leaders of that socialist revolution. $38. Also in French and Russian.

The Revolution Betrayed
What Is the Soviet Union and Where Is It Going?
LEON TROTSKY

In 1917 workers and peasants of Russia were the motor force for one of the deepest revolutions in history. Yet within ten years a political counterrevolution by a privileged social layer whose chief spokesperson was Joseph Stalin was being consolidated. The classic study of the Soviet workers state and its degeneration. $20. Also in Spanish, Farsi, and Greek.

BUILDING A PROLETARIAN PARTY

Tribunes of the People and the Trade Unions
KARL MARX, V.I. LENIN, LEON TROTSKY, FARRELL DOBBS, JACK BARNES

Why organizing to strengthen unions is not only crucial to workers' unity and striking power but central to building a proletarian party. The activity of a workers party neither begins nor ends with unions, however. It begins by extending the party's political reach in all directions, to cities, towns, and farms. A tribune of the people uses every example of capitalist oppression to explain why the working class and its allies can and will lay the foundations for a world based not on violence and competition but on solidarity among working people. $12. Also in Spanish.

The Changing Face of US Politics
JACK BARNES
Working-Class Politics and the Trade Unions

A handbook for working people seeking to build the kind of party needed to prepare for coming class battles through which we will revolutionize ourselves, our class organizations, and all society. $24. Also in Spanish, French, Farsi, and Greek.

What Is to Be Done?
V.I. LENIN

The stakes in creating a disciplined organization of working-class revolutionaries capable of acting as a "tribune of the people, able to react to every manifestation of tyranny and oppression, no matter where it appears, to clarify for all and everyone the world-historic significance of the struggle for the emancipation of the proletariat." Written in 1902. In *Essential Works of Lenin*. $17

WWW.PATHFINDERPRESS.COM

New International
A MAGAZINE OF MARXIST POLITICS AND THEORY

NEW INTERNATIONAL NO. 12
Capitalism's Long Hot Winter Has Begun
JACK BARNES

Published as the storm clouds of the 2008 financial crisis were forming, Barnes explains that today's global capitalist crisis is but the opening stage of decades of economic, financial, and social convulsions and class battles. Class-conscious workers, he writes, confront this historic turning point for imperialism with confidence, drawing satisfaction from being "in their face" as we chart a revolutionary course to take power. $16. Also in Spanish, French, Farsi, Arabic, and Greek.

NEW INTERNATIONAL NO. 13
Our Politics Start with the World
JACK BARNES

The huge economic and cultural inequalities between imperialist and semicolonial countries, and among classes within them, are accentuated by the workings of capitalism. To build parties able to lead a successful revolutionary struggle for power in our own countries, vanguard workers must be guided by a strategy to close this gap. $14. Also in Spanish, French, Farsi, and Greek.

NEW INTERNATIONAL NO. 7
Opening Guns of World War III: Washington's Assault on Iraq
JACK BARNES

Washington's murderous 1991 war on Iraq heralded conflicts among imperialist powers, growing capitalist crisis, and spreading wars. Working people in the region—from the Kurds, to Palestine and Israel, to Iran, Iraq, and Syria—are fighting for space to defend national rights and class interests. $14. Also in Spanish, French, and Farsi.

WOMEN'S LIBERATION AND SOCIALISM

Cosmetics, Fashions, and the Exploitation of Women
Joseph Hansen, Evelyn Reed, Mary-Alice Waters

How big business plays on women's second-class status and economic insecurities to market cosmetics and rake in profits. And how the entry of millions of women into the workforce has irreversibly changed relations between women and men—for the better. $15. Also in Spanish and Farsi.

Woman's Evolution
From Matriarchal Clan to Patriarchal Family
Evelyn Reed

Assesses women's leading and still largely unknown contributions to the development of human civilization and refutes the myth that women have always been subordinate to men. "Certain to become a classic text in women's history."
—*Publishers Weekly*. $32. Also in Farsi.

Abortion Is a Woman's Right!
Pat Grogan, Evelyn Reed

Why abortion rights are central not only to the fight for the full emancipation of women, but to forging a united and fighting labor movement. $6. Also in Spanish.

Communist Continuity and the Fight for Women's Liberation
Documents of the Socialist Workers Party, 1971–86

How did the oppression of women begin? Who benefits? What social forces have the power to end women's second-class status? 3 volumes, edited with preface by Mary-Alice Waters. $30

WWW.PATHFINDERPRESS.COM

PATHFINDER AROUND THE WORLD

Visit our website for a complete list of titles and to place orders

www.pathfinderpress.com

PATHFINDER DISTRIBUTORS

UNITED STATES
(and Caribbean, Latin America, and East Asia)
> Pathfinder Books, 306 W. 37th St., 13th Floor
> New York, NY 10018

CANADA
> Pathfinder Books, 7107 St. Denis, Suite 204
> Montreal, QC H2S 2S5

UNITED KINGDOM
(and Europe, Africa, Middle East, and South Asia)
> Pathfinder Books, 5 Norman Rd.
> Seven Sisters, London N15 4ND

AUSTRALIA
(and Southeast Asia and the Pacific)
> Pathfinder Books, Suite 22, 10 Bridge St.
> Granville, Sydney, NSW 2142

NEW ZEALAND
> Pathfinder Books, 188a Onehunga Mall Rd., Onehunga, Auckland 1061
> Postal address: P.O. Box 13857, Auckland 1643

Join the Pathfinder Readers Club
to get 15% discounts on all Pathfinder titles and bigger discounts on special offers.
Sign up at www.pathfinderpress.com or through the distributors above.
$10 a year